Henry Morse Stephens

**Revolutionary Europe, 1789-1815**

Period VII

Henry Morse Stephens

**Revolutionary Europe, 1789-1815**
*Period VII*

ISBN/EAN: 9783337231279

Printed in Europe, USA, Canada, Australia, Japan

Cover: Foto ©ninafisch / pixelio.de

More available books at **www.hansebooks.com**

# REVOLUTIONARY EUROPE

## 1789-1815

BY

### H. MORSE STEPHENS, M.A.

BALLIOL COLLEGE, OXFORD
PROFESSOR OF HISTORY AT CORNELL UNIVERSITY, ITHACA, U.S.A.
AUTHOR OF 'A HISTORY OF THE FRENCH REVOLUTION,' ETC.

*PERIOD VII*

London

RIVINGTON, PERCIVAL, & CO

1896

*Third Edition*

# AUTHOR'S PREFACE

IN this volume I have endeavoured to write a history of Europe during an important period of transition. I have reduced military details to the smallest possible limits, and have preferred to mention rather than to describe battles and campaigns, in order to have more space to devote to such questions as the Belgian revolution of 1789, the reorganisation of Prussia in 1806-12, and the Congress of Vienna. I have throughout tried to describe the French Revolution in its influence on Europe, and Napoleon's career as a great reformer rather than as a great conqueror. The inner meaning of the period and its general results I have sketched in a short introductory chapter, on which the rest of the volume is really a detailed historical commentary.

The maps which accompany the volume are intended to show the changes in the boundaries of States, and not to give the position of places mentioned in the text. Every one who reads such a volume as the present must use an atlas as his constant companion, for no book of this size could possibly contain a sufficent number of maps adequate to the illustration of the events narrated.

In conclusion, I must express my thanks to Mr. W. R. Morfill, Reader in Slavonic to the University of Oxford, for giving me a canon for the spelling of Russian proper names, and to the Editor, Mr. Arthur Hassall, for willing assistance and friendly encouragement.

H. MORSE STEPHENS.

CAMBRIDGE, 1893.

# CONTENTS

## INTRODUCTION

The Period from 1789 to 1815 an Era of Transition—The Principles propounded during the period which have modified the political conceptions of the Eighteenth Century: I. The Principle of the Sovereignty of the People; II. The Principle of Nationality; III. The Principle of Personal Liberty—The Eighteenth Century, the Era of the Benevolent Despots—The condition of the Labouring Classes in the Eighteenth Century: Serfdom—The Middle Classes —The Upper Classes—Why France led the way to modern ideas in the French Revolution—The influence of the thinkers and writers of the Eighteenth Century in bringing about the change— Contrast between the French and German thinkers—The low state of morality and general indifference to religion—Conclusion, . . 1

## CHAPTER I.

### 1789

The Treaty of 1756 between France and Austria—The Triple Alliance between England, Prussia, and Holland, 1788—The Minor Powers of Europe—Austria: Joseph II.—His Internal Policy—His Foreign Policy—Russia: Catherine—Poland—France: Louis XVI.—Spain: Charles IV.—Portugal: Maria I. — Italy — The Two Sicilies: Ferdinand IV.—Naples—Sicily—Rome: Pope Pius VI.—Tuscany: Grand Duke Leopold—Parma: Duke Ferdinand—Modena: Duke Hercules III.—Lombardy—Sardinia: Victor Amadeus III.—Lucca —Genoa—Venice—England: George III.—The Policy of Pitt— Prussia: Frederick William II.—Policy of Prussia—Holland— Denmark: Christian VII.—Sweden: Gustavus III.—The Holy Roman Empire—The Diet—The Electors—College of Princes —College of Free Cities—The Imperial Tribunal—The Aulic Council—The Circles—The Princes of Germany—Bavaria—Baden —Würtemburg—Saxony—Saxe-Weimar—The Ecclesiastical Princes —Mayence—Trèves—Cologne—The Petty Princes and Knights of the Empire—Switzerland—Geneva—Conclusion, . . . 11

## CHAPTER II

### 1789-1790

The Empress Catherine and the Emperor Joseph II.—The Turkish War—Campaign of 1789 against the Turks—Battles of Foksany and the Rymnik—Capture of Belgrade—Revolution in Sweden—Affairs in Belgium—Policy of Joseph II. in Belgium—Revolution in Liége—Elections to the States-General in France—Meeting of the States-General : struggle between the Orders—The Tiers-État declares itself the National Assembly—Oath of the Tennis Court—The Séance Royale—Mirabeau's Address to the King—Dismissal of Necker—Riot of 12th July in Paris—Capture of the Bastille—Recall of Necker—Louis XVI. visits Paris—Murder of Foullon—Session of 4th August—Declaration of the Rights of Man—Question of the Veto—March of the women of Paris to Versailles—Louis XVI. goes to reside in Paris—Effect of the Revolution in France on Europe—The Revolution in Belgium—Formation of the Belgian Republic—Death of the Emperor Joseph II.—Failure of his reign—The attitude of Louis XVI. to the French Revolution—The new French Constitution—Civil Constitution of the Clergy—Measures of the Constituent Assembly—Mirabeau—Danger threatened to the new state of affairs in France by a foreign war—Mirabeau and the French Court—Probable causes of a foreign war—Avignon and the Venaissin—Affair of Nootka Sound—The Pacte de Famille—Rights of Princes of the Empire in Alsace—The Emperor Leopold master of the situation, . . . . . . . . . 42

## CHAPTER III

### 1790-1792

The Emperor Leopold—His Internal Policy—The Policy of Prussia—Leopold's Foreign Policy—Conference of Reichenbach—Leopold and the Turks—Treaty of Sistova—Leopold crowned Emperor—Leopold and Hungary—State of Parties in Belgium—Their Internal Dissensions—Congress at the Hague—Leopold reconquers Belgium—War between Russia and Sweden—Treaty of Verela—War between Russia and the Turks—Capture of Ismail—Treaty of Jassy—Position of Leopold—The State of France—Mirabeau's advice—Death of Mirabeau—The Flight to Varennes—Its Results : in France—The Massacre of 17th July 1791—Revision of the Constitution—Its Results : in Europe—Manifesto of Padua—Declaration of Pilnitz—Completion of the French Constitution of 1791—The Polish Constitution of 1791—The Legislative Assembly in France—The Girondins—Approach of War between France and Austria—Causes of the War—Attitude of Europe—Death of the Emperor

*Contents* xi

PAGE

Leopold—Murder of Gustavus III. of Sweden—Policy of Dumouriez—War declared by France against Austria—Invasion of the Tuileries, 20th June 1792—Francis II. crowned Emperor—Invasion of France by Prussia and Austria—Insurrection of 10th August 1792—Suspension of Louis XVI.—Desertion of Lafayette—The Massacres of September in the prisons—Battle of Valmy—Meeting of the National Convention—The Girondins and the Mountain—Conquest of Savoy, Nice, and Mayence—Battle of Jemmappes—Conquest of Belgium—Execution of Louis XVI.—War declared against Spain, Holland, England and the Empire—Catherine invades Poland—Overthrow of the Polish Constitution—Second Partition of Poland—Contrast between the resistance of France and Poland, . . . . . . . . 82

## CHAPTER IV

### 1793-1795

France at War with Europe—Altered Character of the War—The Revolutionary Propaganda—First Campaign of 1793—Battle of Neerwinden—Desertion of Dumouriez—Creation of the Committee of Public Safety—Insurrection in La Vendée—Creation of the Revolutionary Tribunal—Struggle between the Girondins and the Mountain—Overthrow of the Girondins—Second Campaign of 1793—Loss of Valenciennes and Mayence—Civil War in France—Royalist and Federalist Risings—Loss of Toulon—Constitution of 1793—The work of the first Committee of Public Safety—The Great Committee of Public Safety—Growth of its Power—Position of Robespierre—The Reign of Terror—The Committee of General Security, the Deputies on Mission, the Revolutionary Tribunal, the Laws of the Suspects and the Maximum—Results of the Terror—Battles of Hondschoten, Wattignies, and the Geisberg—Relief of Maubeuge—Recovery of Lyons and Toulon—Fall of the Hébertists and the Dantonists—Campaign of 1794—Battles of Fleurus, Kaiserslautern, and 1st June 1794—Fall of Robespierre—Rule of the Thermidorians: First Phase: the Survivors of the Mountain—Conquest of Holland—The Batavian Republic—Successes on the Rhine, in Savoy, Italy, and Spain—Insurrection in Poland—The Campaign of Kosciuszko—Third and Final Partition of Poland—Contrast between the Polish and French Revolutions—Its Causes—Change in the Attitude of the Continental Powers to the French Republic—Rule of the Thermidorians; Second Phase: the Survivors of the Girondins and Deputies of the Centre—Insurrections of 12th Germinal and 1st Prairial in Paris—The Constitution of the Year III. (1795)—The Treaties of Basle—France again enters the Comity of Nations, . . . 124

## CHAPTER V

### 1795-1797

PAGE

Results of the Treaties of Basle on the Foreign Policy of France—Constitution of the Year III,—The Directory—The Legislature: Councils of Ancients and of Five Hundred—Local Administration of France—The Insurrection of Vendémiaire—The Rising of 13th Vendémiaire in Paris—The First French Directors, Councils, and Ministers—Dissolution of the Convention—England and the *Émigrés*—Treason of Pichegru—Exchange of Madame Royale—Desire for Peace in France—France and Prussia—Suggestion of Secularisations in Germany—France and the Smaller States of Europe—Attitude of Russia—Campaign of 1795 in Germany—Bonaparte's Campaigns of 1796 in Italy—Battle of Montenotte—Armistice of Cherasco—Battle of Lodi—Armistice of Foligno—Conquest of Upper Italy—Battles of Castiglione, Arcola, and Rivoli—Peace of Tolentino with the Pope—Campaign of 1796 in Germany—Battle of Altenkirchen—Retreat of Moreau—Effects of the Campaign in Germany—Treaty between Prussia and France—Internal Policy of the Directory—Pacification of La Vendée—The State of France—The Directory, Councils, and Ministers in 1796—Creation of the Ministry of Police—Alliance between France and Spain—Treaty of San Ildefonso—Battle of Cape Saint-Vincent—The Batavian Republic—Negotiations between England and the Directory—Death of the Empress Catherine of Russia—Bonaparte's Campaign of 1797 in the Tyrol—The Campaign of 1797 in Germany—Preliminaries of Leoben between France and Austria, . . . . . . . . 158

## CHAPTER VI

### 1797-1799

Elections of 1797 in France—Policy of the Clichians—Struggle between the Directors and the Clichians—Negotiations for Peace between England and the Directory—Changes in the French Ministry—Revolution of 18th Fructidor—Bonaparte in Italy—Occupation of Venice—The Ligurian and Cisalpine Republics formed—Annexation of the Ionian Islands by France —Treaty of Campo-Formio—Capture of Mayence—The Batavian Republic—Battle of Camperdown—Bonaparte's Expedition to the East—Capture of Malta—Conquest of Egypt — Battle of the Nile—Internal Policy of

*Contents* xiii

the Directory after 18th Fructidor—Foreign Policy—Attitude of England, Prussia, Austria, and Russia—The Helvetian Republic—Italian Affairs—The Roman and Parthenopean Republics formed—Occupation of Piedmont and Tuscany by France—The Law of Conscription—Outbreak of War between Austria and France—Murder of the French Plenipotentiaries at Rastadt—The Campaign of 1799—In Italy—Battles of Cassano, the Trebbia and Novi—Italy lost to France—In Switzerland—Battle of Zurich—In Holland—Battles of Bergen—Results of the Campaign of 1799—Policy and Character of the Emperor Paul of Russia—Bonaparte's Campaign of 1799 in Syria—Siege of Acre—Battle of Mount Tabor—Struggle between the Directors and the Legislature in France—Revolution of 22d Prairial—Changes in the Directory and Ministry—Bonaparte's return to France—Revolution of 18th Brumaire—End of the Government of the Directory in France, . 187

## CHAPTER VII

### 1799-1804

Constitution of the Year VIII.—The Consulate—The Council of State—The Tribunate—The Legislative Body—The Senate—Internal Policy of the Consulate—General Reconciliation—The Code Civil—Ministers of the Consulate—Foreign Policy of the Consulate—Russia—Prussia—The Pope—Campaign of Marengo—Campaign of Hohenlinden—Winter Campaign of Moreau and Macdonald—The Treaty of Lunéville—Arrangements in Italy—Policy and Murder of the Emperor Paul of Russia—The Neutral League of the North—Battle of Copenhagen—War between Spain and Portugal—Treaty of Badajoz—Campaign of 1801 in Egypt—Peace of Amiens between England and France—Reconstitution of Germany—Secularisation of the German ecclesiastical dominions—Reconstitution of Switzerland—Concordat between the Pope and Bonaparte—Internal Organisation of France under the Consulate—The new Departments—Annexation of Piedmont—The Préfectures — System of National Education — Constitutional Changes in France—Bonaparte First Consul for life—Recommencement of War between England and France—Causes—Position of Affairs on the Continent—Plot of Pichegru and Cadoudal—Execution of the Duc d'Enghien—Bonaparte becomes Emperor of the French—Francis II. resigns the title of Holy Roman Emperor for that of Emperor of Austria, . . . . . 212

## CHAPTER VIII

### 1804-1808

Napoleon, Emperor of the French—His Coronation as Emperor and as King of Italy—The Imperial Court—The Grand Dignitaries, Marshals, and Imperial Household—Institutions of the Empire —Ministers and Government—The Camp at Boulogne—Pitt's last coalition—Campaign of 1805—Capitulation of Ulm—Battles of Austerlitz and Caldiero—Battle of Trafalgar—Treaty of Pressburg —Death of Pitt—Prussia declares War—Campaign of Jena—Campaign of Eylau—Campaign of Friedland—Interview and Peace of Tilsit—The Continental Blockade—Capture of the Danish Flee by England—French Invasion and Conquest of Portugal—State of Sweden—The Rearrangement of Europe—Louis Bonaparte King of Holland—Italy—Joseph Bonaparte King of Naples—Battle of Maida—Rearrangement of Germany—Bavaria—Würtemburg—Baden—Jerome Bonaparte King of Westphalia—Murat Grand Duke of Berg—Saxony—Smaller States of Germany—Mediatisation of Petty Princes—Confederation of the Rhine—Poland—The Grand Duchy of Warsaw—Conference of Erfurt, . . . . 237

## CHAPTER IX

### 1808-1812

Napoleon's two reverses between the Treaty of Tilsit and the Congress of Erfurt—England sends an army to Portugal—Campaign of Vimeiro and Convention of Cintra—The Revolution in Spain— Joseph Bonaparte King of Spain—Victory of Medina del Rio Seco and Capitulation of Baylen—Napoleon in Spain—Sir John Moore's advance—Battle of Corunna—The Resurrection of Austria— Ministry of Stadion—Campaign of Wagram—Treaty of Vienna— Campaign of 1809 in the Peninsula—Battle of Talavera—Expedition to Walcheren—Napoleon and the Pope—Annexation of Rome— Revolution in Sweden—Revolution in Turkey—Treaty of Bucharest —Greatest Extension of Napoleon's dominions—Internal Organisation of the Empire—The new Nobility—Internal reforms—Law — Finance — Education — Extension of these reforms through Europe — Disappearance of Serfdom — Religious Toleration— Reorganisation of Prussia—Reforms of Stein and Scharnhorst— Revival of German National feeling—Marriage of Napoleon to the Archduchess Marie Louise—Birth of the King of Rome—Steady opposition of England to Napoleon—Policies of Canning and Castlereagh—Campaigns of 1810 and 1811 in the Peninsula—Signs of the decline of Napoleon's power between 1808 and 1812, . 263

## CHAPTER X

Causes of Growing Disagreement between Alexander and Napoleon— Intervention of Castlereagh and Bernadotte—The Attitude and Internal Policy of Prussia—Invasion of Russia by Napoleon—Battle of Borodino—Retreat of the French from Russia—Campaign of 1812 in the Peninsula—Battle of Salamanca—Policy of Bernadotte —Prussia declares War—First Campaign of 1813 in Saxony— Armistice of Pleswitz—Convention of Reichenbach—Congress of Prague—Austria declares War—Second Campaign of 1813 in Saxony —Battle of Dresden—Treaty of Töplitz—Battle of Leipzig—General Insurrection of Germany against Napoleon—Campaign of 1813 in the Peninsula—Battle of Vittoria—Wellington's Invasion of France —Negotiations for Peace—Proposals of Frankfort—The Allies invade France—Napoleon's first Defensive Campaign of 1814—Other Movements against Napoleon—Bernadotte—Holland—Battle of Orthez—Italy—Congress of Châtillon—Attitude of France towards Napoleon—Treaty of Chaumont—Napoleon's Second Defensive Campaign of 1814—Occupation of Paris by the Allies—The Policy of Talleyrand—The Provisional Government—Alexander's Speech to the French Senate—Napoleon declared to be no longer Emperor --Abdication of Napoleon—Provisional Treaty of Paris—Battle of Toulouse—Arrival of Louis XVIII., and his Assumption of the Throne of France—First Treaty of Paris, . . . . 299

## CHAPTER XI

### 1814-1815

The Congress of Vienna—Monarchs and Diplomatists present—History of the Congress—Treaty between France, Austria, and England— The Questions of Saxony and Poland—The German Confederation —Disposition of the provinces on the left bank of the Rhine— Mayence and Luxembourg—Reconstitution of Switzerland—Rearrangements in Italy—Questions of Murat, Genoa, and the Empress Marie Louise—Sweden—Denmark—Spain—Portugal— England's share of the spoil—The Questions of the Slave Trade and the Navigation of Rivers—Close of the Congress—Preparations against Napoleon—The first reign of Louis XVIII. in France— Napoleon's return from Elba—The Hundred Days—The Campaign of Waterloo—Occupation of Paris—Second Treaty of Paris— Napoleon sent to St. Helena—The Holy Alliance—Return of

Louis XVIII.— Government of the Second Restoration—The Chambre Introuvable—Reaction in Spain and Naples—Territorial Results of the Congress of Vienna—The Principle of Nationality—Permanent Results of the French Revolution in Europe—The Problem of harmonising the Principles of Individual and Political Liberty with that of Nationality, . . . . . . 336

## APPENDICES

APPENDIX I. The Rulers and Ministers of the Great Powers of Europe, 1789-1815, . . . . . 364

APPENDIX II. The Rulers of the Second-rate Powers of Europe, 1789-1815, . . . . . . 366

APPENDIX III. The Family of Napoleon, . . . . 368

APPENDIX IV. Napoleon's Marshals, . . . . . 370

APPENDIX V. Napoleon's Ministers during the Consulate and Empire, 1799-1814, . . . . . . 372

APPENDIX VI. Concordance of the Republican and Gregorian Calendars, 374

INDEX, . . . . . . . . . 377

## MAPS

Europe in 1789.
Europe in 1802.
Europe in 1810.
Europe in 1815.
} *At end of book.*

# INTRODUCTION

The Period from 1789 to 1815 an Era of Transition—The Principles propounded during the period which have modified the political conceptions of the Eighteenth Century: I. The Principle of the Sovereignty of the People; II. The Principle of Nationality; III. The Principle of Personal Liberty—The Eighteenth Century, the Era of the Benevolent Despots—The condition of the Labouring Classes in the Eighteenth Century: Serfdom—The Middle Classes—The Upper Classes—Why France led the way to modern ideas in the French Revolution—The influence of the thinkers and writers of the Eighteenth Century in bringing about the change—Contrast between the French and German thinkers—The low state of morality and general indifference to religion—Conclusion.

THE period from 1789 to 1815—that is, the era of the French Revolution and of the domination of Napoleon—marks one of the most important transitions in the history of Europe. Great as is the difference between the material condition of the Europe of the nineteenth century, with its railways and its electric telegraphs, and the Europe of the eighteenth century, with its bad roads and uncertain posts, it is not greater than the contrast between the political, social, and economical ideas which prevailed then and which prevail now. Modern principles, that mark a new departure in human progress and in its evidence, Civilisation, took their rise during this epoch of transition, and their development underlies the history of the period, and gives the key to its meaning.

A Period of Transition.

The conception that government exists for the promotion of the security and prosperity of the governed was fully grasped in the eighteenth century. But it was held alike by philosophers

and rulers, alike in civilised England and in Russia emerging
from barbarism that, whilst government existed for
the good of the people, it must not be administered
by the people. This fundamental principle is in
the nineteenth century entirely denied. It is now believed
that the government should be directed by the people through
their representatives, and that it is better for a nation to make
mistakes in the course of its self-government than to be ruled,
be it ever so wisely, by an irresponsible monarch. This notion
of the sovereignty of the people was energetically propounded
during the great Revolution in France. It is not yet universally accepted in all the states of modern Europe. But it has
profoundly affected the political development of the nineteenth
century. It lies at the base of one group of modern political
ideas; and, though in 1815 it seemed to have been propounded
only to be condemned, one of the most striking features of the
modern history of Europe since the Congress of Vienna, has
been its gradual acceptance and steady growth in civilised
countries.

*The Sovereignty of the People.*

The second political belief introduced during the epoch
of transition from 1789 to 1815 was the recognition of the idea of nationality in contradistinction to that of the State, which prevailed in the
last century. In the eighteenth century the State was typified
by the ruling authority. National boundaries and race limits
were regarded as of no importance. It was not felt to be an
anomaly that the Catholic Netherlands or Belgium should be
governed by the House of Austria, or that an Austrian prince
should reign in Tuscany and a Spanish prince in Naples.
The first partition of Poland was not condemned as an offence
against nature, but as an artful scheme devised for the purpose
of enlarging the neighbouring states, which had appropriated
the districts lying nearest to their own territories. But during
the wars of the Revolution and of Napoleon the idea of
nationality made itself felt. France, as a nation in arms,
proved to be more than a match for the Europe of the old

*The Principle of Nationality.*

conceptions. And it was not until her own sense of nationality was absorbed in Napoleon's creation of a new Empire of the West that France was vanquished by coming in contact with the Spanish, the Russian, and the German peoples in the place of her former foes, the sovereigns of Europe. The idea of nationality, like the idea of the sovereignty of the people, seemed to be condemned in 1815 by the Congress of Vienna. The Catholic Netherlands were united with the provinces of Holland; Norway was forcibly separated from Denmark; Italy was once more parcelled out into independent states under foreign princes. But the Congress of Vienna could not eradicate the new idea. It had taken too deep a root. And another striking feature of the European history of the nineteenth century has been the formation of new nations, resting their *raison d'être* on the feeling of nationality and the identity of race.

The third modern notion which has transformed Europe is the recognition of the principle of personal and individual liberty. Feudalism left the impress of its gradua- *The Principle* tion of rights and duties marked deeply on the *of Personal* constitutions of the European States. The sove- *Liberty.* reignty of the people implies political liberty of action; feudalism denied the propriety and advantages of social and economical freedom. Theoretically, freedom of individual thought and action was acknowledged to be a good thing by all wise philosophers and rulers. Practically, the poorer classes were kept in bondage either as agricultural serfs by their lords or as journeymen workmen by the trade-guilds. Where personal and individual liberty had been attained, political liberty became an object of ambition, and political liberty led to the idea of the sovereignty of the people. The last vestiges of feudalism were swept away during this era of transition. The doctrines of the French Revolution did more than the victories of Napoleon to destroy the political system of the eighteenth century. The Congress of Vienna in 1815 might return to the former notions of government and the State, but it did not attempt to restore the old restrictions on individual liberty. With personal freedom acknowledged, the reactionary tendency of the Congress of Vienna was left of no effect. Liberty of thought and action led to the resurrection of the conceptions of nationality and of the sovereignty of the people, which were but for the moment extinguished by the defeat of France in the person of Napoleon by the armies of united Europe.

The period which preceded the French Revolution and the era of war, from the troubles of which modern Europe was to be born, may be characterised as that of the bene- volent despots. The State was everything; the nation nothing. The ruler was supreme, but his supremacy rested on the assumption that he ruled his subjects for their good. This conception of the *Aufgeklärte Despotismus* was developed to its highest degree by Frederick the Great of Prussia. 'I am but the first servant of the nation,' he wrote, a phrase which irresistibly recalls the definition of the position of Louis XVI. by the first leaders of the French Revolution. This attitude was defended by great thinkers like Diderot, and is the keynote to the internal policy of the monarchs of the latter half of the eighteenth century towards their people. The Empress Catherine of Russia, Gustavus III. of Sweden, Charles III. of Spain, the Archduke Leopold of Tuscany, and, above all, the Emperor Joseph II. defended their absolutism on the ground that they exercised their power for the good of their subjects. Never was more earnest zeal displayed in promoting the material well-being of all classes, never did monarchs labour so hard to justify their existence, or effect such important civil reforms, as on the eve of the French Revolution, which was to herald the overthrow of the doctrine of absolute monarchy. The intrinsic weakness of the position of the benevolent despots was that they could not ensure the permanence of their reforms, or vivify the rotten fabric of the administrative edifices, which had grown up in the feudal monarchies. Great ministers, such as Tanucci and Aranda, could do much to help their masters to carry out their benevolent ideas, but they could not form or nominate their successors, or create a perfect body of unselfish administrators. When Frederick the Great's master hand was withdrawn, Prussia speedily exhibited a condition of administrative decay, and since this was the case in Prussia, which had been for more than forty years under the rule of the greatest and wisest of the benevolent despots, the falling-off was likely to be even more marked in other countries. The conception of benevolent despots ruling for their people's good was eventually superseded, as was certain to be the case, owing to the impossibility of their ensuring its permanence, by the modern idea of the people ruling themselves.

And, in truth, while doing full justice to the sentiments and the endeavours of the benevolent despots, it cannot honestly be said that their efforts had done much to improve the condition of the labouring classes by the end of the eighteenth century. The great majority of the peasants of Europe were throughout that century absolute serfs. To take once more the example of Prussia, the only attempts to improve the condition of the peasants had been made in the royal domain, and they had only been very tentative. The dwellers on the estates of the Prussian nobility in Silesia and Brandenburg were treated no better than negro slaves in America and the West Indies. They were not allowed to leave their villages, or to marry without their lords' consent; their children had to serve in the lords' families for several years at a nominal wage, and they themselves had to labour at least three days, and often six days, a week on their lords' estate. These *corvées* or forced labours occupied so much of the peasant's time that he could only cultivate his own farm by moonlight. This state of absolute serfdom was general in Central and Eastern Europe, in the greater part of Germany, in Poland and in Russia, and where it existed the artisan class was

*The Condition of the Labouring Classes. Serfdom.*

equally depressed, for no man was allowed to learn a trade without his lord's permission, and an escaped serf had no chance of admission into the trade-guilds of the cities. Towards the west a more advanced civilisation improved the condition of the labourers; the Italian peasant and the German peasant on the Rhine had obtained freedom to marry without his lord's interference; but, nevertheless, it was a leading prince on the Rhine, the Landgrave of Hesse-Cassel, who sold his subjects to England to serve as mercenaries in the American War of Independence. In France the peasant was far better off. The only serfs left, who existed on the domain of the Abbey of Saint-Claude in the Jura, on whose behalf Voltaire wielded his powerful pen, were in a far happier condition than the German serfs; they could marry whom they pleased; they might emigrate without leave; their persons were free; all they were deprived of was the power of selling their property or devising it by will. The rest of the French peasants and the agricultural classes generally were extremely independent. Feudalism had left them some annoyances but few real grievances, and the inconveniences they suffered were due solely to the inequalities of the copyhold system of tenure and its infringements of their personal liberty. The French peasants and farmers were indignant at an occasional day's *corvée*, or forced labour, which really represented the modern rent, and at the succession-duties they had to pay the descendants or representatives of their ancestors' feudal lords. The German, Polish, and Hungarian peasant, on the contrary, crushed beneath the burden of his personal servitude, did not dream of pretending to own the plot of land, which his lord kindly allowed him to cultivate in his few spare moments.

The mass of the population of Central and Eastern Europe was purely agricultural, and in its poverty expected naught but the bare necessaries of existence. Trade, commerce, and manufactures were therefore practically non-existent. This meant that the cities, and consequently the middle classes, formed but an insignificant factor in the population. In the West of Europe, on the Rhine, and more especially in France, where the agricultural classes were more independent, more wealthy, and more civilised, existence de- **The Middle** manded more comforts, and a well-to-do and intel- **Classes.** ligent commercial and manufacturing urban element quickly developed to supply the demand created. Commerce, trade, and the concentrated employment of labour produced a prosperous and enlightened middle class, accustomed for generations to education and the possession of personal freedom. With wealth always goes civilisation and education, and as there was a larger middle class in France and Western Germany than in Central and Eastern Europe, the peasants in those parts were better educated and more intelligent.

The condition of the upper classes followed the same geographical distribution. The highest aristocracy **The Upper** of all European countries was indeed, as it has **Classes.** always been, on much the same intellectual and social level. Paris was its centre, the capital of society, fashion, and luxury, where Russian, Austrian, Swedish, and English nobles met on an equality. But the bulk of the German and Eastern European aristocracy was in education and refinement inferior to the bulk of the French nobility. Yet they possessed an authority which the French nobility had lost. The Russian, Prussian, and Austrian nobleman and the Hungarian magnate was the owner of thousands of serfs, who cultivated his lands and rendered him implicit obedience. The French nobleman exacted only certain rents, either copyhold quit-rents or feudal services, from the tenants on his ancestral estates. His tenants were in no sense his serfs; they owed him no personal service, and resented the payment of the rent substituted for such service. The patriarchal feeling of loyalty to the lord had long disappeared, and the French peasant did not acknowledge any subjection to his landlord, while the Prussian and Russian serf recognised his bondage to his master.

These considerations help to show why the Revolution, which was after twenty-six years to inaugurate modern Europe, broke out in France. It was because the French peasant was more independent, more wealthy, and better educated than the German serf, that he resented the political and social privileges of his landlord and the payment of rent, more than the serf objected to his bondage. It was because France possessed an enlightened middle class that the peasants and workmen found leaders. It was because Frenchmen had been in the possession of a great measure of personal freedom that they were ready to strike a blow for political liberty, and eventually promulgated the idea of social equality. The ideas of the sovereignty of the people, of nationality and of personal liberty, did not originate in France. They are as old as civilisation. But they had been clouded in the Middle Ages by feudalism, and, after the Reformation, had been succeeded by different political conceptions, which had crystallised in the eighteenth century into the doctrines of the supremacy of the State, of the arbitrary rule of benevolent or enlightened despots. England and Holland had developed separately from the rest of the Western World. For reasons lying deep in their internal history and their geographical position, they had rid themselves alike of feudalism and absolute monarchy; they had developed a sense of their independent nationality, and had recognised the importance of personal freedom. In England especially, the abolition of the relics of feudalism in the seventeenth century had placed the English farmers and peasants in a different economical position from their fellows on the Continent. There existed in England none of the invidious distinctions between nobleman and *roturier* in the matter of bearing national burdens, which had survived in France, and, though owing to the curiosities of the franchise the larger proportion of Englishmen had but a very small share in electing the representatives of the people, the government carried on as it was by a small oligarchy of great families possessed an appearance of political liberty, and of a wisely-balanced machine for administrative purposes.

Nor must the influence of intellectual ideas, as bearing on

problems which the French Revolution was to force on the attention of the more backward and more oppressed nations of Europe, be underrated. The great movement of French writers of the eighteenth century—Voltaire, Montesquieu, Diderot, and Rousseau—had been deeply impregnated with the ideas of Locke and the English political thinkers of his school. In their different lines they insisted that government existed for the good of the governed, and investigated the origins of government and the relations of man in the social state. It was their speculations which altered the character of absolute monarchy and based its retention on its benevolent purposes; they, too, insisted upon the rights of man to preserve his personal freedom, as long as it did not clash with the maintenance and security of civil society. The great French writers of the eighteenth century exercised by their works a smaller influence on the outbreak and actual course of the French Revolution than has been generally supposed. The causes of the movement were chiefly economical and political, not philosophical or social: its rapid development was due to historical circumstances, and mainly to the attitude of the rest of Europe. But the text-books of its leaders were the works of the French thinkers of the eighteenth century, and if their doctrines had little actual influence in bringing about the Revolution, they influenced its development and the extension of its principles throughout Europe. It is curious to contrast the opinions of the great French writers of the middle of the eighteenth century, whose arguments mainly affected the general conceptions of man living in society, that is, of government, with the views advocated by the great German writers of the end of the century, who concentrated their attention upon man in his individual capacity for culture and self-improvement. Schiller, Goethe, Kant, and Herder were, further, more cosmopolitan than German. The problems of man and his intellectual and artistic development proved more attractive to the great German thinkers than the difficulties presented by the

*Intellectual movement of the eighteenth century.*

economical, social, and political diversities of different classes of society. Goethe, for instance, understood the signification of the French Revolution, and was much interested in its effects on the human race, but he cared very little about its impression on Germany.

Finally, the low state of morality in the eighteenth century had sapped the earnestness in the cause of humanity of men of all classes in all countries. Disbelief in the Christian religion was general in both the Protestant and Catholic countries of the Continent.

*Morality and Religion in the eighteenth century.*

The immorality of most of the prelates in Catholic countries was notorious, and was equalled by their avowed contempt for the doctrines of the religion they professed to teach. The Protestant pastors of Germany was quite as open in their infidelity. In the famous case of Schulz, the pastor of Gielsdorf, who openly denied Christianity, and taught simply that morality was necessary, the High Consistory of Berlin held that he was, nevertheless, still fitted to hold his office as the Lutheran pastor of his village. Christianity in both Catholic and Protestant countries was replaced by the vague sentiments of morality, which are best presented in Rousseau's *Profession de Foi du Vicaire Savoyard*. In reaction to this vague and dogmaless morality, there existed many secret societies and coteries of mystics, such as the Rosati and the Illuminati, who replaced religion by ornate and symbolical ceremonies.

Such was the political, economical, intellectual and moral state of Europe in 1789, on the eve of the French Revolution. The whole continent was to pass through twenty-six years of almost unceasing war, at the end of which it was to emerge with new conceptions and new ideals of both political and social life. The new ideas seemed indeed to be checked, if not destroyed, in 1815, but once inspired into men's minds they could not be forgotten, and their subsequent development forms the history of modern Europe in the nineteenth century.

# CHAPTER I

## 1789

The Treaty of 1756 between France and Austria—The Triple Alliance between England, Prussia, and Holland, 1788—The Minor Powers of Europe—Austria: Joseph II.—His Internal Policy—His Foreign Policy—Russia: Catherine—Poland—France: Louis XVI.—Spain: Charles IV.—Portugal: Maria I.—Italy—The Two Sicilies: Ferdinand IV.—Naples—Sicily—Rome: Pope Pius VI.—Tuscany: Grand Duke Leopold—Parma: Duke Ferdinand—Modena: Duke Hercules III.—Lombardy—Sardinia: Victor Amadeus III.—Lucca—Genoa—Venice—England: George III.—The Policy of Pitt—Prussia: Frederick-William II.—Policy of Prussia—Holland—Denmark: Christian VII.—Sweden: Gustavus III.—The Holy Roman Empire—The Diet—The Electors—College of Princes—College of Free Cities—The Imperial Tribunal—The Aulic Council—The Circles—The Princes of Germany—Bavaria—Baden—Würtemburg—Saxony—Saxe-Weimar—The Ecclesiastical Princes—Mayence—Trèves—Cologne—The Petty Princes and Knights of the Empire—Switzerland—Geneva—Conclusion.

THE states of Europe at the commencement of the year 1789 were ranked diplomatically in two important groups, the one dominated by the connection between France, Austria, Spain, and Russia; the other by the alliance between England, Prussia, and Holland. The great transformation which had been effected by the treaty between France and Austria in 1756 in the relationship between the powers of Europe was the crowning diplomatic event of the eighteenth century. The arrangements then entered into and the alliances tested in the Seven Years' War still subsisted in 1789. But the spirit which lay at the root of the Austro-French alliance was sensibly modified. The Treaty of 1756 had never been really popular in either country. In France,

*The Treaty of 1756.*

Marie Antoinette, whose marriage with Louis XVI. had set the seal on the Austrian alliance, was detested as the living symbol of the hated treaty, as *l'Autrichienne*, the Austrian woman, and the most accredited political thinkers and writers were always dwelling on the traditional policy of France, and on the system of Henri IV., Richelieu, and Louis XIV., which held the House of Hapsburg to be the hereditary and the inevitable enemy of the House of Bourbon and of the French nation. The dislike of the alliance was felt with equal intensity in Austria by the wealthy and the educated classes. The Austrian generals resented the inefficacy of the French intervention during the Seven Years' War, and the Austrian people attributed its reverses in that war to it with as much acrimony as if France had acted as an enemy instead of as an ally. The same sentiment actuated even the Imperial House. 'Our natural enemies, travestied as allies, who do more harm than if they were open enemies;'[1] such is the language in which Leopold of Tuscany, brother of Marie Antoinette, characterised the French in a letter written in December 1784 to his brother, the Emperor Joseph II. The Emperor Joseph was himself of the same opinion. He preferred his Russian ally, the Empress Catherine, to his brother-in-law, Louis XVI., King of France, and the tendency of his foreign policy was to strengthen his friendship with Russia, even at the expense of sacrificing his alliance with France. Russia, whose expansion under the great Empress had been enormous since the conclusion of the Seven Years' War, cared but little for either of the allies, and pursued independently its course of steady development. Catherine had, indeed, during most of the later years of Frederick the Great, remained in alliance with Prussia, and to some extent had been on friendly terms with England. But her natural tendency was to distrust England. In 1780 she had placed herself at the head of the 'Armed Neutrality,' which opposed the naval pretensions

[1] *Joseph II. und Leopold von Toscana.* By the Ritter von Arneth: Vienna, 1872.

of England, and in 1788 she had formally proposed a close quadruple alliance between Russia, Austria, France, and Spain.

If the relations between France, Russia, and Austria were unsettled, the Triple Alliance between Prussia, Holland, and England was hardly on a more stable footing in 1789. Prussia, since the death of Frederick the Great, had become really decrepit, while apparently remaining a first-rate military power. Though still preserving the prestige of its famous King, who died in 1786, and recognising its alliance with England, Prussia in 1789 exhibited a decaying internal administration, and a vacillating foreign policy. England had received a heavy blow by the success of the colonists in North America, and by the Treaty of Versailles, and the powers of the Continent, while envying her wealth, held her military power of but small account. This opinion prevailed even at Berlin, and the new King of Prussia gave many evidences that the alliance of England was rather distasteful to him than otherwise. The third member of the alliance, Holland, was in the weakest condition of all, and it was only by invoking the armed interference of Prussia that England had maintained the authority of the Prince of Orange, as Stadtholder, in 1787. Though this interference had led to the formation of the famous Triple Alliance of 1788, in reality the English and Prussian statesmen profoundly distrusted each other, while the forcing of the yoke of the Stadtholder upon them caused the Dutch democratic party in Holland to abhor the allies and to look for help to France.

*Prussia, England, and Holland.*

The rest of the European states were bound more or less firmly to the one or the other of the two coalitions. The smaller states of Germany, aggravated or intimidated by the measures of the Emperor Joseph II., had rallied to the side of Prussia. In the north, Denmark, whose reigning house was connected by family ties with the royal families of England and Prussia, was completely under Russian influence, while Sweden, under Gustavus III.,

*The Minor Powers of Europe.*

was actually at war with Catherine II. Poland, torn by internal dissensions, and threatened with complete destruction by its neighbours, was awaiting its final partition. The southern states of Europe were almost entirely bound to the Franco-Austrian alliance. Spain had been united to France by the offensive and defensive treaty, known as the 'Pacte de Famille,' concluded by the French minister, Choiseul, in 1761, and tested in the war of American Independence. Portugal, though connected with England, commercially by the Methuen treaty, and politically by a long course of protection against Spanish pretensions, was striving by a series of royal marriages to become the ally of Spain. In Italy, Naples was ruled by a Spanish prince married to an Austrian princess; Sardinia was closely allied with France, and the remainder of the peninsula was mainly under Austrian influence. Turkey, now travelling towards decay, was looked upon by Russia and Austria as their legitimate prey, and met with encouragement in resistance, but not with active help, from England and France.

After thus roughly sketching the general attitude of the powers of Europe to each other in 1789, it will be well to examine each state separately before entering on the history of the exciting period which followed. Great and sweeping alterations were to be effected; many diplomatic variations were to take place. The most important result of the period of the French Revolution and of Napoleon was its influence upon the minds of men, as shown in the growth of certain political conceptions, which have moulded modern Europe. But great changes were also brought about in dynasties and in the geographical boundaries of states, which can only be understood by a knowledge of the condition of Europe in 1789.

The figure of most importance in the beginning of the year
Austria: 1789 was that of the Emperor Joseph II., and his
Joseph II. dominions were those in which an observer would have prophesied a great revolution. Joseph was at that date a man of forty-seven; he had been elected Emperor in the

place of his father, Francis of Lorraine, in 1765, and succeeded to the hereditary dominions of the House of Austria on the death of his mother, Maria Theresa, in 1780. He was, perhaps, the best type of the class of benevolent despots. A singularly industrious, enlightened, and able ruler, his ideas were far in advance of those of his age,—so much in advance, indeed, that his efforts to impose them upon his subjects brought upon himself hatred instead of gratitude, and among the people turbulence and insurrection instead of peace and tranquillity. The history of the Emperor Joseph's reforms, and of the disturbances which resulted from them, belongs to an earlier volume of this series. In 1789 the whole of the hereditary dominions of the House of Hapsburg were in a state of ferment. The Emperor's scheme of welding them into an Austrian nation, by insisting on the use of the German language, by simplifying the state of the law and the administration, and assimilating the various religious and educational institutions, had roused the fire of local patriotism. In Hungary and in the Tyrol, in Bohemia, and, above all, in the Austrian Netherlands, or Belgium, there was declared rebellion, fanned by local prejudices, religious fanaticism, and the spirit of caste. The first and second of these causes were chiefly responsible in the Austrian Netherlands, the third in Hungary. The Belgians, and more especially the Brabançons, were in arms for their local rights and ancient constitutions, which had been infringed by the Emperor's decrees. The Belgian clergy, who looked upon Joseph as worse than an infidel for his treatment of the Pope and his suppression of religious houses, were inflamed at the establishment of an Imperial Seminary in Brussels as a rival to the Roman Catholic University of Louvain. But in Hungary it was the magnates of the country who had fought so gallantly for Maria Theresa and saved her throne, who were in an attitude of open disaffection. This was partly due to Joseph's infringement of their Constitution and his removal of the Iron Crown to Vienna, but still

*Joseph II.: Internal Policy.*

more to his abolition of serfdom. As has been already stated, serfdom in Europe was practically extinct in the western part of the Continent, that is, in France, in Belgium, and on the Rhine, while it increased in intensity steadily towards the east, and was as bad in Prussia Proper, Poland, and Hungary, as in Russia. 'Most merciful Emperor,' ran a petition from an Hungarian peasant to Joseph, 'four days' forced labour for the seigneur; the fifth day, fishing for him; the sixth day, hunting with him; and the seventh belongs to God. Consider, most merciful Emperor, how can I pay. dues and taxes?'[1] The iniquity of serfdom, with its practice of forced labour, was accentuated in Hungary by the constitutional custom which exempted the nobility from all taxation. The Emperor Joseph abolished serfdom in Hungary on 22nd August 1785, and inaugurated a system of removing feudal burdens, and converting forced labour, by means of a gradually diminishing tax. The condition of the hereditary dominions of the House of Hapsburg was thus, in 1789, one of seething discontent where it was not open rebellion; Belgian burghers and Hungarian magnates were alike infuriated by the Emperor's efforts at reform; and the poor serfs of Hungary and Bohemia and the working men of Belgium, whom he designed to benefit by direct legislation and financial measures, were too weak to render him any help. His hope of creating an Austrian state and an Austrian people out of his scattered dominions was fated to be thwarted; obstacles of distance, race, and language, cannot be overcome by legislation, however wise; and the Emperor's well-intentioned endeavours nearly lost his House its ancient patrimony.

The foreign policy of the Emperor Joseph II. was dictated by the same leading principle as his internal reforms—the desire to form his various territories into a compact state. His schemes to exchange the Austrian Netherlands for

---

[1] Vehse's *Memoirs of the Court, Aristocracy, and Diplomacy of Austria*, English translation. London, 1856, vol. ii. p. 305.

Bavaria in order to unite his possessions in Swabia with the nucleus of the Hapsburg territories were frustrated by the policy of Frederick the Great. His attempt to make his authority as Emperor more than nominal, and to create a real German empire based on a German patriotic feeling, proved an utter failure. Foiled in these two projects, the creation of an Austrian compact state, which he deemed practicable, and the resurrection of a mighty Germany under his headship, which he acknowledged to be but a dream, Joseph II. turned his thoughts towards Russia. The ideal of his early manhood had been his mother's foe, Frederick the Great of Prussia; the ideal of his later years was the Empress Catherine of Russia. Both were specimens of the enlightened despots of the age; both had extended the realms they ruled; both endeavoured to form their states into compact entities; both had succeeded in administration and in war; and both were cynical disciples of the eighteenth-century philosophers. They were successively his models. It is characteristic of the Emperor Joseph II. that the only picture in his private cabinet in the Hofburg at Vienna was a portrait of Frederick; the only picture in his bedroom one of Catherine. After the death of Frederick the Great, the Emperor Joseph II., despising his successor, expressed more loudly his admiration for Catherine. In 1787 he accompanied her in her famous progress to the Crimea. Fascinated by her personality and dazzled by her projects, the Emperor was persuaded to ally himself with Russia against the Turks, and hoped to partition Turkey with her, as his mother, Frederick, and Catherine had accomplished the first partition of Poland. In 1788 he accordingly declared war against the Sublime Porte. But he found that the Turks, in spite of the corruption of their government, were still no contemptible foes. His own army was demoralised by the misconduct of the aristocratic officers; disease decimated his troops; and the Emperor Joseph returned from the campaign of 1788 with the seeds of mortal illness in his system, but with his determination to pursue the war unabated.

*Joseph II. Foreign Policy.*

Russia, the chosen ally of Joseph II., was in 1789 ruled by the Empress Catherine II. This great monarch, though by birth a princess of the petty German state of Anhalt-Zerbst, ranks with Peter the Great as a founder of the Russian Empire; more Russian than the Russians, she understood the importance of the development of her adopted country geographically towards the Baltic and the Black Sea, and the capacity of her people to support her in her enterprises. She was at this time sixty years of age, in full possession of her remarkable powers, and having ruled for twenty-seven years, she had fortified her authority by experience. Peter the Great had seen the absolute necessity that the Russian Empire should have access to the sea, and had built Saint Petersburg; Catherine had moved southward and extended her dominions to the Black Sea. She hoped to make the Baltic and the Black Sea Russian lakes, and on that account was the consistent and watchful enemy of Sweden and the Turks. Upon the western frontier of Russia lay Poland. The natural policy of Russia was to maintain and even to strengthen Poland as a buffer between Russia and the military powers of Austria and Prussia. But the extraordinary Constitution of Poland, which provided for the election of a powerless king, and recognised the right of civil war and the power of any nobleman to forbid any measure proposed at the Diet by the exercise of what was called the *liberum veto*, kept the unfortunate country in a state of anarchy, unable either to defend or to oppose. It might have been possible to reform the Constitution, and make the Poles an organised nation, but the neighbouring monarchs considered it easier to share the country amongst them, and had, under the guidance of Frederick the Great, carried out in 1772 the first partition, which excluded Poland from the sea, brought the borders of the three powers, Austria, Prussia, and Russia, nearer to each other, and caused Russia to become an European instead of essentially an Eastern monarchy. Catherine grasped the fact that in her present position Russia must intervene in European politics, owing to the condition of Poland, and decided to derive what benefit she could from this circumstance. In her internal government Catherine was one of the benevolent despots. The patroness of Diderot, she expressed her admiration for the new doctrines of the Rights of Man, and even summoned a convention to draw up a Russian constitution. But she knew that the new doctrines were not applicable to the Russian people, and would be absurdly inappropriate to the nomad Tartar tribes which wandered over the southern districts of the Russian Empire. She was fully aware that their village organisation protected the peasants from many of the evils which prevailed in seemingly more enlightened countries, and gave them a right and interest in the soil to which they were attached. Russia, in fact, had experienced no Reformation, no Renaissance, no awakening of the ideas of individual and political liberty, and therefore was eminently fitted for the rule of a benevolent despot.

Next to the Austro-Russian alliance, the Austro-French alliance, sealed by the Treaty of 1756, was of the greatest significance to the peace and welfare of Europe in 1789. As has been said, in neither country was the alliance popular; France and Austria were hereditary enemies; classical policy in both courts favoured a resumption of this enmity; the friendship was rather dynastic than national, the work of Kaunitz and Maria Theresa, the Abbé de Bernis, Madame de Pompadour, and Louis XV. France still appeared a very powerful nation. Its intervention in the American War of Independence had largely contributed to England's loss of her American colonies, and the Treaty of Versailles in 1783 had involved a confession that England was beaten by her cession of the West India islands of St. Lucia and Tobago. But in spite of her seeming power, France was from political and economic causes really very weak. She had been unable in 1787 to effectually support the republican and French party in Holland, and had been forced to allow England and Prussia to reinstate the Stadtholder, the Prince of

Orange. In spite of her alliance with Austria, she had been obliged in pursuance of a peace policy, made necessary by her financial condition, to draw near to England, and had made a commercial treaty with her in 1786. The weakness of France arose from internal circumstances. The State and the Court were financially identical. The Court was extravagant, and the result was a chronic national deficit. Efforts had been made to meet this deficit, but all expedients, even partial bankruptcy, had failed. It was evident that a systematic attempt must be made to rearrange the finances by introducing a regular scheme of taxation to take the place of the feudal arrangements for filling the royal treasury, which with some modifications still survived. But a regular scheme of taxation, which should abolish feudal privileges, and make the government responsible to the nation for its expenditure, could not be established without the consent of the people, and the educated classes, who were both numerous and prosperous, claimed a voice in its establishment. The feeling of political discontent went deeper. The French people had outgrown their system of government; the peasants and farmers resented the existence of the economic, social, and political privileges dating from the Middle Ages, which had survived the duties originally accompanying them; the bourgeois argued that they should have a share in regulating the affairs of the State; the educated classes sympathised with both. The day for benevolent despotism was over in France; Louis XVI. was benevolent in disposition, but too weak to reform the system under which he ruled; and it was the system, not the person of the monarch, which the French people disliked; it was the system as a whole which they had outgrown.

Much of the strength of France rested on its intimate alliance with Spain. The two great Bourbon houses had been closely united by the 'Pacte de Famille' concluded in 1761, which bound them in an offensive and defensive alliance. Spain had loyally fulfilled her part of the bargain, and had suffered much in the War of American

*Spain: Charles IV.*

Independence against England. Spain had had the good fortune to be ruled by one of the most enlightened of the benevolent despots, Charles III., whose minister, Aranda, was one of the greatest statesmen of his century. Aranda is best known from his persecution of the Jesuits, who had spread their influence over the minds of the Spanish people so far as to be the dictators of education and opinion. Their expulsion contributed to the power of the Crown, which undertook the direction of every form of national energy. Aranda was a great administrator; he spent vast sums on the improvement of communications and on public works, and he built up a powerful Spanish navy. The two evils which had depressed the fame of Spain, the personal lethargy of the people, due to the stamping out of liberty of thought by the Inquisition, and the poverty, caused by the influx of gold from the Spanish colonies, which prevented any encouragement of national industry, were however too great for any administrator to subdue, without a national uprising and the development of a national love for liberty. Aranda was ably helped by Campomanes, who founded a national system of education to take the place of the Jesuits' schools and colleges, by Jovellanos, a great jurist and political economist, by Cabarrus, a skilful financier, who founded the bank of St. Charles, and developed a system of national credit, and by Florida Blanca, who superintended the department of foreign affairs, and succeeded Aranda in supreme power in 1774. Charles III. died on 12th December 1788, and his successor, Charles IV., whose weakness of character was manifested throughout the period from 1789 to 1815, commenced his reign by maintaining Florida Blanca at the head of Spanish affairs, with Cabarrus and other experienced ministers.

Portugal was the intimate ally of England as Spain was of France. The hereditary connection of Portugal and England dated back for many centuries, and had been strengthened by the Methuen Treaty in 1703, which had made Portugal largely dependent on England

Portugal: Maria I.

The great Portuguese minister, Pombal, who had commenced the persecution of the Jesuits and had effected internal and administrative reforms, comparable to those of Aranda in Spain, had been disgraced in 1777, but the offices of State were filled by his pupils and managed on the principle, which he had initiated, of advancing the prosperity of the people. Pombal, while holding the strongest views on the importance of maintaining the royal absolutism, believed in the modern doctrines of reform; he had abolished slavery, encouraged education, and in the received ideas of political economy had encouraged by means of protection manufactures and agriculture. The essential weakness of Portugal rested, like that of Spain, on the exhaustion and consequent lethargy of its people; the Jesuits and the Inquisition had stamped out freedom of thought. Financially, also, its condition resembled that of Spain, for the sovereign derived such wealth from Brazil as to be independent of taxes, levied on the people. Politically the aim of the House of Braganza, during the latter part of the eighteenth century, had been to endeavour to free itself from dependence on England by uniting closely through inter-marriages with the reigning family in Spain. Queen Maria I., who had succeeded Joseph, the patron of Pombal, in 1777, was a fanatical lady of weak intellect, and in 1789 the royal power was in the hands of the heir-apparent, Prince John, who was recognised as Regent some years later, and eventually succeeded to the throne in 1816, as John VI.

Italy, in the eighteenth century, was composed of a number of small states. The idea of Italian unity lived only in the minds of the great Italian writers and thinkers; it met with no support from the powers of Europe. Italy was still the home of music and the arts, which were fostered by the numerous small Courts; but politically, owing to its subdivision, it hardly counted as a power, and its diplomacy had little weight in the European State system. It was entirely under the influence of France and Austria, and showed the tendencies of the century in the good government

*Italy.*

of most of the petty rulers. The most important of the Italian states was the kingdom of the Two Sicilies, which comprised the southern part of the peninsula and the island of Sicily. The kingdom had been granted to Ferdinand IV., when his father, the celebrated Don Carlos, succeeded as Charles III. to the throne of Spain in 1759. It was in Naples that Charles III. had commenced his career as a reforming monarch, and the great Neapolitan minister, Tanucci, continued to administer the affairs of the kingdom in a most enlightened fashion during the early years of the new monarch's reign. His policy was to check the feudal instincts of the Neapolitan barons, whom he deprived of the lucrative right of administering justice, and thus to strengthen the influence of the Crown; and he also opposed the pretensions of the Pope, and concurred in the suppression of the Jesuits. The power thus acquired for the Crown was wisely used; the financial system was revised, education was encouraged, and an attempt was made to procure a general reform of the laws. The young publicist, Filangieri, whose *Science of Legislation* contained the most enlightened views on political economy and government, and who ranks next to Montesquieu as a typical political thinker of the eighteenth century, was a Neapolitan, and his speculations largely influenced the current of Italian thought. Sicily, however, remained to a great extent untouched by the influence of the great Neapolitan minister owing to its insular jealousy and the maintenance of its mediæval parliament. Ferdinand IV., in 1768, married Maria Carolina, the ablest daughter of the Empress Maria Theresa, who at once assumed the most entire sway over her ill-educated and indolent husband. She secured the dismissal of Tanucci, whom she disliked on much the same grounds that her sister, Marie Antoinette, disliked the reforming French ministers, Turgot and Necker, in 1776, and after an interval replaced him by Acton, a native of France of Irish descent, who, owing to the temper of his patroness, was not able to continue efficiently the work of Tanucci. The States of the

Church, including the Legations of Bologna and Ferrara
and the principalities of Benevento and Ponte
Corvo, were also governed in accordance with the
enlightened ideas of the eighteenth century. The Papacy
had much fallen in influence, and had been forced to comply
with the demands of Pombal, Choiseul, Aranda, and Tanucci
for the suppression of its spiritual mainstay, the order of the
Jesuits; but it nevertheless maintained its temporal sovereignty in Italy. Giovanni Angelo Braschi, who had been
elected Pope in 1775, and taken the title of Pius VI., was a
man of singular ability and courtly manners. But he had
to assent to vast reforms in Tuscany, which seriously affected
the wealth of the Church in that part of the country, and had
been unable, in spite of a personal visit to Vienna, to persuade
Joseph II. to alter his policy towards the Papacy. His most notable internal measures in the Papal States were the draining of
the Pontine marshes, and his reconstitution of the Clementine
Museum at Rome, which he placed under the charge of the
eminent antiquary, Ennius Quirinus Visconti. Tuscany
flourished under the rule of the Grand Duke
Leopold, brother and eventual successor of
Joseph II., the ablest administrator of all the
benevolent despots. His reforms extended in every direction; with the help of Scipio de Ricci, Bishop of Pistoia, he
reduced the number of bishoprics and monasteries; he
drained many of the marshes, and so benefited agriculture;
he reorganised education and encouraged the Universities
of Pisa and Siena. But his greatest reforms were legal and
economic. Tuscany having originated from a number of
mediæval republics, had been hitherto administered as a collection of semi-independent cities and districts, with their own
laws and local finances. Leopold was one of the first
monarchs to project a uniform code of laws for his state,
which he intrusted to the great jurist, Lampredi, to compile,
and he abolished all personal privileges before the law, torture, the right of asylum for malefactors, confiscation of the

property of condemned malefactors, and secret denunciations. In economics he was the pupil of the French physiocrats, and the friend of the Marquis de Mirabeau, the 'Ami des hommes,' and in consonance with their doctrines he swept away all the internal customs duties and other restrictions on industry and commerce. Lastly, Leopold, seeing that his state was not strong enough to carry on a real war, abolished the Tuscan army, to the great advantage of his finances. Next to Tuscany, the best-governed state in Italy was Parma. Fer- *Parma: Duke* dinand, Duke of Parma and Piacenza, was the *Ferdinand.* only son of Don Philip, the second son of Philip v. of Spain and Elizabeth Farnese, by Elizabeth of France, daughter of Louis xv. He was educated by the celebrated French philosopher, Condillac, and early in his reign showed the influence of the best eighteenth century ideas. He had succeeded his father in 1765, and continued his minister, a Frenchman, Du Tillot, Marquis of Felino, in office. Du Tillot, though working in a smaller sphere, was as great a reformer as Pombal and Tanucci. He brought about the suppression of the Inquisition in Parma, improved the internal administration, and encouraged education so greatly that the University of Parma, under the management of the learned scholar, Paciaudi, became one of the most famous in Europe. In 1769 Duke Ferdinand married Maria Amelia, daughter of the Empress Maria Theresa, who two years later secured the dismissal of Du Tillot from office. This dismissal was not, however, followed by a reaction, though it put a close to the progress of reform, and Parma, under the administration, first of a Spaniard, Llanos, and then of a Frenchman, Mauprat, retained its reputation as a well-governed state. It was otherwise with Modena, where the last Duke of the House of *Modena:* Este, Hercules III., reigned. This prince had suc- *Duke* ceeded to the duchies of Modena, Reggio, and *Hercules III.* Mirandola in 1780, when already a man of fifty-three, and had added to them by marriage the principalities of Massa and Carrara. His only daughter and heiress, Maria Beatrice, was married to the Austrian Archduke Ferdinand, younger brother of the Emperor Joseph, and Governor-General of Lombardy. Duke Hercules was a superstitious and avaricious ruler, whose chief care was to amass money, and, politically, he followed out the wishes of Austria. While the House of Austria, by its scions or by marriages, ruled the greater part of Italy indirectly, it possessed the direct sovereignty of Lombardy, or, more accurately, of the Milanese and Mantua. This province profited by the salutary policy of Joseph II., and was administered, under the governor-generalship of the Archduke Ferdinand, by a great statesman, Count Firmian, who understood and carried out the most important reforms. His patronage of the arts and of education was especially remarkable; he laboured ardently to restore the efficiency of the Universities of Milan and Pavia, and appointed Beccaria, the celebrated philanthropist, Professor of Political Economy at the former, and Volta, the equally celebrated man of science, Professor of Physics at the latter. The only other monarchy of Italy, that of Sardinia, was more closely related to France than to Austria. Its king, Victor Amadeus III., had married a Spanish princess, and two of his daughters were married to the two brothers of Louis XVI. of France—Monsieur, the Comte de Provence, and the Comte d'Artois. His dominions comprised the island of Sardinia, Piedmont, Savoy, and Nice, and it was a great subject of complaint to his Piedmontese subjects that he unduly favoured his French-speaking province of Savoy. He, too, was influenced by the spirit of his century; he encouraged agriculture and commerce; he patronised literature and science; he built the Observatory at Turin, and founded academies of science and fine arts; and he undertook great public works, of which the most important was the improvement of the harbour of Nice. But in one matter he pursued an opposite policy to the Grand Duke Leopold of Tuscany, for he increased and reorganised his army, and constructed fortifications of the most modern description at

Tortona and Alessandria. Lastly must be noticed three Italian republics, survivals of the Middle Ages. Of these the smallest was the Republic of Lucca, which was entirely surrounded by the Grand-Duchy of Tuscany. Its trade suffered from the encouragement given by the Grand Duke Leopold to Leghorn; but, on the whole, it was well governed and prosperous. It was otherwise with the two great aristocratic republics, in which the long continuance of oligarchical government had stamped out all vestiges of political liberty. The Republic of Genoa, of which Raphael di Ferrari was Doge in 1789, was in utter decay. Its people were poverty-stricken; its trade had gone to Leghorn and Nice; and its laws and customs were unreformed. It was so weak that it had been unable to subdue the rebels in Corsica, who had risen under Paoli for the right of self-government, and it had ended by ceding the island to France in 1768. The Republic of Venice, of which the Doge in 1789 was Paul Renier, had not fallen so low in the eyes of Europe. Its possessions on the mainland, which extended from Verona to the Tyrol and along the east coast of the Adriatic Sea, and included the Ionian Islands, were administered for the benefit of the Venetian oligarchy, and supplied it with wealth. From Dalmatia was raised a considerable army, but the administration was wholly selfish, and did not keep pace in enlightenment with that of Lombardy, Parma, Tuscany, and Naples. On the whole, where monarchy existed in Italy, it tended in the eighteenth century to benevolent despotism; and such rule was far more beneficial to the people than that of the antiquated republics. Politically, the whole country might be reckoned as a factor in the Franco-Austrian alliance.

<small>Lucca: Republic.</small>

<small>Genoa: Republic.</small>

<small>Venice.</small>

The chief power of the Triple Alliance, which balanced the loosely-defined league of Russia, France, and Austria, was England. The severe blow which had been struck by the revolt of her American colonies had made Great Britain appear weaker than she really was to the

<small>England: George III.</small>

powers of the Continent. The Treaty of Versailles, by which she had been obliged to make cessions to France, seemed to have set the seal on her humiliation. But in reality her finances were more affected than her fighting strength, and the English navy, which, from her insular position, must always constitute the principal element of her force, was as *The Policy* excellent as ever. The policy of the younger Pitt, *of Pitt.* who had come into office in 1783, was one of peace and retrenchment. The country had lasted well through the financial strain of the American War, and the chief aim of the minister was to allow its vast commercial and industrial resources to expand. As a pupil of Adam Smith, Pitt understood the great principles of political economy, and the most significant part of his foreign policy was his conclusion of the Commercial Treaty with France. A fiscal system, far in advance of that in any continental country, enabled the English Government to draw on the wealth of the nation more effectively than any other government, if the money was needed for patriotic purposes. In spite of his love of peace, Pitt was induced by his first Foreign Secretary, the Duke of Leeds, to take an active part in European politics, and was eventually led by the state of affairs in Holland to enter into the Triple Alliance. At home, England was unaffected by the intellectual movement which led to the French Revolution. She had in the previous century got rid of the relics of feudalism, which pressed so heavily on the continental farmer and peasant, and had won the boons of individual and commercial liberty, and of equality before the law; while politically, though her government was an oligarchy, supported by the class of wealthy merchants and traders, an opportunity was afforded through the existence of a free press and of the system of election, however hampered by antiquated franchises, for public opinion to make itself felt.

Prussia, the other principal member of the Triple Alliance, contrasted in every way with England. Seemingly, owing to the prestige of Frederick the Great's victories and that able monarch's careful organisation of his army, Prussia was the first military state in Europe; in reality, her repu- tation was greater than her actual power. Prussia was weak where England was strong. Prussia had no financial system worthy of the name, no industrial wealth, and no national bank; her only resources for war were a certain quantity of specie stored up in Berlin. The Prussian Government was an absolutism, in which the monarch's will was supreme; its administration was based on feudalism, of which England had entirely and France had practically got rid, with all its mediæval incidents of serfdom, privilege of the nobility, and social and commercial inequalities. The Prussian army was not national; the soldiers were treated as slaves, and the officers, who were all of noble birth, were tyrants in the maintenance of military discipline.

*Prussia: Frederick William II.*

Frederick the Great was one of the finest types of the benevolent despot of the eighteenth century, but in him the belief in the importance of his despotic power outweighed his benevolence. While wishing for the prosperity of the people, he deliberately maintained the authority of the nobility, and discouraged any desire for change on the part of the agriculturists or citizens. The former were left at the disposal of their lords, the latter trammelled by antiquated civic constitutions. The weakness of Prussia was not only inherent in its government, but was also due to geographical causes. Its component parts were scattered; its Rhenish duchies and East Friesland were separated from its main territories by many German states; its central districts, the Marks of Brandenburg, were sparsely populated, and cut off from the sea; its largest provinces, Prussia Proper, Pomerania, Silesia, and Prussian Poland were, in spite of German and French Huguenot colonies, mainly Slavonic, and as backward in civilisation as other Slavonic races in the eighteenth century. In Russia, however, the Slavonic population in its barbarism yet retained sufficient local organisation to make its lot fairly endurable; in eastern Prussia, and especially in Prussian Poland, the people had been brought into contact with the mediæval and Latin civilisation, and were consequently treated as absolute serfs without the relief afforded by local institutions. The **Policy of Prussia.** policy of Prussia, as laid down by Frederick the Great, had both Prussian and German aspirations, and in both was utterly selfish. The example set by the cynical monarch in the Silesian wars had left a deep impress on the minds of Prussian statesmen, and the maxims of justice and international law were subordinated by them to expediency. The Prussian policy of Frederick the Great culminated in the first partition of Poland, which he had suggested, by means of which Prussia united her eastern province of Prussia Proper to Brandenburg, and cut off Poland from the sea, and the aim of his successors was to pursue this path of aggrandisement, and, by further annexations, to connect Silesia directly with Prussia Proper. The German policy of Prussia was to assume the leadership of the Empire by pretending the greatest zeal for the rights of the Princes of the Empire, and posing as their protector, and it was on this ground that Frederick the Great formed the League of the Princes. The hereditary enemy of Prussia was Austria, which, though distinctly injured by the conquest of Silesia, still retained the chief influence over the Empire, and also showed a tendency to check the designs on Poland. It was Frederick the Great of Prussia who had thwarted the Emperor's scheme of exchanging the Austrian Netherlands for Bavaria, and he intrigued against Austria at the Courts both of Russia and France. It was as a counterblow to the Franco-Austro-Russian alliance that Prussia intervened in Holland, at the request of England, and formed the Triple Alliance with England and Holland in 1788. King Frederick William II. of Prussia, who succeeded his famous uncle in 1786, was a man of feeble intellect and undecided nature, but he had thoroughly imbibed the classic ideas of Prussian policy, and regarded Austria as the inevitable foe of Prussia, to be duped and taken advantage of on every possible occasion. His chief minister, Hertzberg, was a consistent enemy of Austria, but owing to the curious character of the king, the real power of the State rested not with the minister but with the royal favourites, of whom the chief at the end of 1788 were Bischofswerder and Lucchesini.

Holland was the link which bound England and Prussia together. Its military power was of no account, but the wealth of its inhabitants, derived from their vast commercial expansion in Asia and aptitude for banking, made the Republic of the United Provinces of the greatest importance. The Seven Provinces preserved the most complete autonomy; only the veriest semblance of federation held them together. Practically, the only bond of union was in the power of the Stadtholder, which had been restored in 1747. In the more wealthy provinces, such as Holland, the commercial aristocracy, which filled the ranks of the local governments, resented the position of the Stadtholder, who held the command-in-chief of the army and navy; but in the poorer and agricultural provinces, such as Friesland and Groningen, the landed aristocracy generally supported the Stadtholderate. In 1780 the United Provinces had joined in the Neutral League of the North, invented by Catherine of Russia to break the commercial supremacy of England, and in the war which followed they had suffered severe losses, and had been compelled to cede Negapatam in India to England in 1783 on the conclusion of peace. The Stadtholder, William v., Prince of Orange, in whose family the office had been declared hereditary, was vehemently accused of favouring England during this war, and when peace was declared a movement was set on foot, headed by the authorities of the Province of Holland, to oust him from his position, and to draw up a new constitution for the Dutch Netherlands on the same lines as that of the United States of America. This movement grew to its height in 1786; a French Legion, commanded by the Comte de Maillebois, was raised; the Stadtholder had to fly from the Hague, and the armed intervention of France was requested. But, as has been said, France, in spite of her seeming power, was too weak to intervene, and the Dutch patriots were abandoned to their fate. On the other side, that of the Stadtholder, England, through its able ambassador at the Hague, Sir James Harris, afterwards Lord Malmesbury, induced Prussia to act. England and Prussia had dynastic and political reasons for this conduct. The Stadtholder was, through his mother, a first cousin of George III., and had married a sister of Frederick William II., while politically, the acquisition of Holland to the Franco-Austrian alliance, through the expulsion of the Stadtholder, would bring nearly the whole of Europe into that system, and would practically enclose the Austrian Netherlands or Belgium. In September 1787, therefore, a Prussian army, under the Duke of Brunswick, had occupied Amsterdam, and placed the Stadtholder firmly in power; the Dutch patriots fled to France; the Legion of Maillebois was disbanded; and in 1788 the work was consummated by the signature of the Triple Alliance.

The two northern kingdoms, Denmark and Sweden, had adhered to the Neutral League against England in 1780, but for generations a bitter animosity had existed between them.

Denmark: Christian VII. Denmark, which in 1789 included Norway, was in an extremely prosperous condition. The philanthropic ideas of the eighteenth century had made great way, and on 20th June 1788 a royal ordinance had destroyed the last vestige of serfdom. Efforts were made to improve the condition of the people by reorganising the state of the finances, law and education, and progress was made in every direction. These reforms were not the work of the King, Christian VII., who had fallen into a state of dotage, but of the Prince Royal, afterwards Frederick VI., and of his minister, Count Andrew Bernstorff, the nephew of the greatest Danish statesman of the eighteenth century. Sweden, which in 1789 included the greater part of Finland as well as Swedish Pomerania and the island of Rügen, was under the sway of one of the most enlightened rulers of the century,

Sweden: Gustavus III.

Gustavus III. That monarch had in 1772, by a *coup d'état*, overthrown the power of the Swedish Estates, with their division into the two parties of the Caps and the Hats, subsidised respectively by Russia and France. He had made use of his absolutism to carry out some of the benevolent ideas of the time. He had abolished torture, regulated taxation, encouraged commerce and industry, and diminished, where he did not destroy, the privileges of the nobility. Had he contented himself with these internal reforms he would have won the lasting gratitude of the Swedish people, but he insisted on playing a part in continental politics, which involved the maintenance of a large army and the consequent exhaustion of the people. Though he too had joined the League of the North in 1780, he afterwards assumed a strong anti-Russian attitude, and resolved to take advantage of the Russo-Turkish war in order to regain some of his lost provinces. Accordingly he invaded Russia in the summer of 1788, while his fleet threatened St. Petersburg.

Hitherto a sketch has been given of states, which in 1789 possessed a certain unity, and were able to play a part as independent countries of more or less weight in European politics. It was otherwise with the Holy Roman Empire, which still remained in the same condition, and was ruled in the same manner, as had been arranged at the Treaty of Westphalia in 1648. True Germany, that is Germany to the west of the Oder, had been under this arrangement split up into a number of independent sovereignties, loosely bound together as the Holy Roman Empire. The number of these petty states caused the Empire to be, from a military point of view, utterly inefficient; the bond was too loose to allow of general internal reforms or of a consistent foreign policy; and the federal arrangements were too cumbrous and unwieldy to allow of Germany ranking as a great power. The Imperial Diet or Reichstag consisted of three colleges, and a majority was required in each of the upper colleges to agree to a resolution, which, when confirmed by the Emperor, became a *conclusum* of the Empire.

*The Empire.*

*The Diet.*

PERIOD VII.                                        C

The first of these colleges was that of the eight Electors, three
<small>College of</small> ecclesiastical, the Elector-Archbishops of Mayence,
<small>Electors.</small> Trèves, and Cologne, and five lay, the Electors of
Bohemia, Brandenburg, and Hanover, who were also Kings of
Hungary, Prussia, and England, the Elector of Saxony, and the
Elector Palatine, who in 1789 was also Elector of Bavaria. The
president of this college was the Elector-Archbishop of Mayence,
as Chancellor of the Empire. The second college was that of the
<small>College of</small> Princes, which consisted of one hundred voices,
<small>Princes.</small> thirty-six ecclesiastical and sixty-four lay. In this
college all the Electors had voices under different designations;
Hanover possessed six for different principalities, Prussia six
for the duchy of Guelders, the county of Mœurs, etc., Austria
three, and so on, while the Kings of Denmark and Sweden also
were represented as Dukes of Holstein and of Pomerania. Less
important princes differing in power from the Landgraves of
Hesse, the Margraves of Baden, and the Duke of Würtemburg
to the petty princes of Salm and Anhalt, possessed single voices,
and made up the number of temporal voters in the college to
sixty. The ecclesiastical princes included thirty-four of the
wealthiest bishops and abbots, many of whom ruled over considerable territories, and of whom the most important were the
Archbishop of Salzburg, the Bishops of Bamberg, Augsburg,
Würtzburg, Spires, Worms, Strasbourg, Basle, Constance, Paderborn, Hildesheim, and Münster, and the Abbots of Elwangen,
Kempten, and Stablo. The other six voices were called
collegiate, and representatives to hold them were elected by
the petty lay and ecclesiastical sovereigns who abounded in
Franconia, Swabia, and Westphalia, to the number of four lay
and two ecclesiastical representatives. The presidency of this
college was held alternately by the Archduke of Austria and
the Archbishop of Salzburg. The third or inferior college
<small>College of</small> was that of the free cities, and any opposition
<small>Free Cities.</small> on its part could prevent a decision arrived
at by the two upper or superior colleges being pre-
sented to the Emperor for his assent as a *conclusum* of the

Empire. It consisted of the representatives of fifty-two imperial free cities, divided into two 'benches,' of which the Bench of Westphalia included Frankfort-on-the-Main, Cologne, Aix-la-Chapelle, Hamburg, Bremen, and Lübeck, and the Bench of Swabia included Nuremberg, Ratisbon, Ulm, and Augsburg. The presidency of this college belonged to the city of Ratisbon, in which the Diet held its sittings. By this elaborate federative system, all sense of German unity was lost; the electors, princes, and free cities were represented only by delegates; the smaller states felt themselves swamped and were obliged to look to a great power, Austria or France, Prussia or Hanover, to preserve their political independence.

The other important institution of the Empire, the Imperial Tribunal or Reichskammergericht, which sat at Wetzlar and was intended to settle disputes between the German sovereigns, had also fallen into desuetude. Its venality and procrastination became proverbial, and it possessed no machinery to put its decrees into force. At the head of the Empire was the Emperor, who was elected and crowned with all the elaborate ceremonial of the Middle Ages. The office had been, with one exception, conferred on the head of House of Austria, since the Treaty of Westphalia, but it brought little actual authority on the holder. It was as ruler of the hereditary dominions of the House of Hapsburg that the Emperor exerted some influence, not as an Emperor. Joseph II., indeed, endeavoured to be Emperor in more than name, with the result that Frederick the Great was enabled to form the League of Princes against him. As the chief Catholic state, Austria, however, possessed a great influence in the Imperial Diet, for the ecclesiastical members of the Colleges of Electors and Princes naturally inclined to support her, and it was on their votes that she relied. She even went so far as to establish the Aulic Council at Vienna, which intervened in cases between sovereign princes, and usurped some of the prerogatives of the Imperial Tribunal of Wetzlar. The executive power of the

Empire, when it had come to a decision, was entrusted to the circles. These circles each had their own Diet, and it was their duty, for instance, to raise money and troops when the Empire decided to go to war. Of the ten circles of the Empire, originally created, one, that of Burgundy, had been extinguished or nearly so by the conquests of Louis xiv., and those situated in the eastern portion were entirely controlled by the important states of Prussia, Saxony, and Austria. It was only in Western Germany, in the circles of Westphalia, Franconia, and Swabia that the organisation was fairly tried, and the result was signal failure, whenever those circles put their contingents in the field. It could hardly be otherwise, when, owing to minute subdivision and divided authority, a single company of soldiers might be raised from half a dozen different petty sovereigns, each of whom would try to throw the burden of their maintenance on his colleagues. The Holy Roman Empire, in short, like other mediæval institutions, had fallen into decay with the mediæval systems of warfare and religion; some of its component states, such as Austria and Prussia, or in a lesser degree Bavaria, might possess a real power; but, as a whole, it was utterly inefficient to defend itself, and formed a feeble barrier between France and the kingdoms of Eastern Europe.

The impotence of the Empire for offensive and defensive purposes did not, however, greatly affect the German people; the educated classes prided themselves on being superior to patriotic impulses, and on being cosmopolitan rather than German; the poorer classes thought more of the internal administration which affected them than of the attitude of the Empire to European politics. The tendency towards benevolent despotism, which distinguished the greater powers, showed itself also in the petty states of Germany in the diminution, if not the abolition, of the ancient Estates and in the restraints placed on the authority of the nobility. The increased power of the sovereign was generally, if not universally, used to foster the prosperity of his subjects, or at least to promote literature and art. A notice of a few of the principal rulers of Germany will justify this view. Charles Theodore, the Elector Palatine, who in 1778 had Bavaria. succeeded to the Electorate of Bavaria, and united once more the territories of the House of Wittelsbach, was a most enlightened sovereign. In the Palatinate he had founded a brilliant University at Mannheim, and one of the most famous picture galleries in Europe at Düsseldorf; in Bavaria he suppressed some of the numerous convents, which stifled progress, in spite of his sincere Catholicism. He took as one of his ministers the celebrated American, Benjamin Thompson, whom he created Count Rumford, and that man of science and learning endeavoured to suppress mendicity, and made efforts to bring material comforts within reach of the very poorest. Nevertheless, in some points, the Elector Charles Theodore showed himself a bigot; he left education entirely in the hands of the Roman Catholic priesthood and ex-Jesuits, and he allowed the Protestants in his dominions to be persecuted. The Margrave Charles Frederick, who in 1771 re- Baden. united in his person the two margraviates of Baden-Baden and Baden-Durlach, was a more thoroughly enlightened prince. He was truly a benevolent despot; he was a student of political economy, on which he himself wrote a treatise, and applied its principles to his little state; he established a scheme of primary education; and on 23d July 1783 he abolished serfdom in his dominions, while maintaining the royal *corvées* and the prohibition for a subject to leave the country without obtaining his permission. The Duke Würtemburg. Charles Eugène of Würtemburg formed a contrast to his neighbours. He established, like them, his own absolutism, but he used his power to impose heavy taxes and raise an army out of all proportion to the size of his duchy. He treated his subjects like slaves, and his administration was so cruel that the Aulic Council threatened to take measures against him. Nevertheless, he was a patron of literature and the arts. He built a theatre at Stuttgart and founded the Academy of Fine

Arts there, and he defrayed the expense of the education of the poet Schiller, who, however, afterwards satirised him and fled to Weimar. Yet Charles Eugène of Würtemburg appears an enlightened monarch to such princes as Duke Charles of Deux-Ponts (Zweibrücken), whose successor, Maximilian Joseph, was to succeed the Elector Palatine, Charles Theodore, and to become the first King of Bavaria, for that prince sacrificed his people to his passion for the chase, and to William IX., Landgrave of Hesse-Cassel, who sold his subjects by the hundred to the English Government to carry on the war in America. Going further east, Saxony, which had ranked among the great states of Germany, was in a state of decline. The Electors Augustus II. and Augustus III. had been Kings of Poland, and had ruined their hereditary dominions to support their royal dignity and position. Fortunately Frederick Augustus, who was Elector in 1789, had not been elected to the Polish throne, and had been able to do something for the prosperity of his subjects. He formed a commission to draw up a code of laws, he abolished torture, encouraged industry and agriculture, and founded an Academy of Mines. But he did not go so far, for instance, as the Margrave of Baden, and made no attempt to suppress serfdom. The glory of Saxony was not, however, on the eve of the French Revolution its electoral house; its intellectual capital was not the beautiful city of Dresden. That place was taken by Weimar, where Duke Charles Augustus of Saxe-Weimar collected around him the great philosophers and men of letters who made the German name famous at the end of the eighteenth century and the beginning of the nineteenth. To his Court resorted the most illustrious Germans of the time, Goethe and Schiller, Herder, Wieland, and Musæus; and the University of his state at Jena became the most famous in Germany. It is not necessary to particularise the other states; it is enough to say that those in the north were generally very backward, especially the duchies of Mecklenburg, and that Hanover was left to the rule of an aristocratic oligarchy, which allowed no reforms, although its University at Göttingen, founded by George II., took rank with the best.

The Ecclesiastical States followed also the movement of the century. The ecclesiastical rulers were often enlightened men, but they were to a great extent the slaves of their chapters. These chapters were generally filled by younger sons of the smaller princes, who insisted on the newly-elected prelates entering into the closest bonds with them to make no changes in the feudal system in the bishoprics. The prince-bishops and abbots at the close of the eighteenth century were, therefore, generally scions of noble houses, such as, for instance, Francis Joseph, Baron of Roggenbach, Bishop of Basle, Baron Francis Louis of Erthal, Bishop of Bamberg and Würtzburg, the Baron of Rödt, Bishop of Constance, the Count of Hoensbroeck, Bishop of Liége, Count Augustus of Limburg, Bishop of Spires, Count Jerome Colloredo, Archbishop of Salzburg, and the Baron of Plettenberg, Abbot of Münster. One curious point deserves notice, that in some instances, Protestant princes had the right to present to Catholic prince-bishoprics, and in 1789 the Duke of York was Prince-Bishop of Osnabrück, and Prince Peter Frederick of Holstein-Gottorp, Prince-Bishop of Lübeck. Of higher rank and more independent of their chapters were the three archbishop-electors, who were therefore more able to rule their states in consonance with the ideas of the century. The chief of these was Baron Frederick Charles of Erthal, Archbishop-Elector of Mayence, and Prince-Bishop of Worms, the Chancellor of the Empire *ex officio*. This great prelate busied himself mostly with his pleasures, but his rank caused his countenance to be sought by all parties, and his adhesion to Frederick the Great's League of Princes was the greatest gain the King of Prussia made in his anti-Austrian policy. In 1789 he had completely abandoned the cares of internal and external politics to his coadjutor Charles, Baron de Dalberg, who was to play a leading part in the history of Germany during the period of the French Revolution and Napoleon. The Archbishop-

*Mayence.*

Elector of Trèves in 1789 was Clement Wenceslas, a Saxon prince, and an excellent ruler, who, in 1783, even issued an edict of tolerance, allowing men of any religion to settle in his state, and exercise any trade or profession there. The last Elector-Archbishop was the Archduke Maximilian, the youngest brother of the Emperor Joseph, Archbishop of Cologne, who shared his brother's liberal opinions, and patronised his predecessor's creation, the University of Bonn, which had been founded in opposition to the ultramontane University of Cologne, for the encouragement of the modern developments of science. The tendency of all these governments, lay and clerical, was to promote the prosperity of the people; Joseph II. was but the type of the German princes of his time; all wished to do good for the people, but not by them; their characters differed widely, from the enlightened Margrave of Baden to the hunting Duke of Deux-Ponts; but in their different ways and in different degrees they generally meant well. But, while the more important princes showed the tendency of the century, their poorer contemporaries were unable to do so. They were mostly in debt, owing to their efforts to rival the wealthy princes, and in order to raise money resorted to all the devices of mediæval feudalism. The few villages over which they ruled suffered from this tyranny, and it was always possible to know when a traveller crossed the frontier into one of these 'duodecimo duchies.' Beneath the petty princes were the Ritters or Knights of the Empire, who abounded in Franconia and Swabia. These knights had no representation in the Imperial Diet, and were consequently dependent directly on the Emperor. Their poverty made them take service with the wealthy princes; and to quote but two instances, Stein, the great Prussian minister, and Würmser, the celebrated Austrian general, were both Knights of the Empire. The result of this minute subdivision of Germany was to destroy the sense of national patriotism; which was not to rise again until after Germany had passed through the mould of Napoleon's domination.

The other European confederation, Switzerland, presented the same symptoms of internal decay as the Holy Roman Empire, but it was preserved from the same political degradation by the consciousness of its nationality and the persistence of its local governments.  The eighteenth century was marked in Switzerland by struggles between canton and canton, Catholics and Protestants, nobles and bourgeois. In some cantons, such as Berne, an oligarchical system was maintained in the hands of a few noble families; in others, such as Uri, a purely democratic form of government was preserved, which allowed every peasant a voice in the local administration. Where feudalism had been established, the peasants were in no better condition than in the rest of Europe, but in the mountain cantons such a *régime* was impossible, and individual and political freedom still existed. It must be remembered that the Switzerland of the eighteenth century was not identical with that of the nineteenth. The Grisons formed no part of the confederation, Neufchâtel belonged to Prussia, and Geneva was an independent republic. The part the latter had played in the intellectual movement of the century was most conspicuous. Rousseau was born in Geneva, and Voltaire retired and spent his last years in its neighbourhood. But Geneva had just before 1789 been the scene of a revolution resembling that in Holland. A struggle broke out between the bourgeois families, which monopolised the magistracy, and the mass of the people, which had ended in the victory of the former. The Genevese democrats were expelled, and many of them, notably Clavière, exercised a considerable influence on the course of the Revolution in France.

The state of Europe in 1789 showed everywhere a sense of awakening to new ideas. The bonds of feudalism were ready to break asunder; the benevolent despots had recognised the rights of individual and commercial freedom; the French Revolution was able to sow in ripe ground the two new principles of the sovereignty of the people and the sentiment of nationality.

# CHAPTER II

## 1789-1790

The Empress Catherine and the Emperor Joseph II.—The Turkish War—Campaign of 1789 against the Turks—Battles of Foksany and the Rymnik—Capture of Belgrade—Revolution in Sweden—Affairs in Belgium—Policy of Joseph II. in Belgium—Revolution in Liége—Elections to the States-General in France—Meeting of the States-General: struggle between the Orders—The Tiers État declares itself the National Assembly—Oath of the Tennis Court—The Séance Royale—Mirabeau's Address to the King—Dismissal of Necker—Riot of 12th July in Paris—Capture of the Bastille—Recall of Necker—Louis XVI. visits Paris—Murder of Foullon—Session of 4th August—Declaration of the Rights of Man—Question of the Veto—March of the women of Paris to Versailles—Louis XVI. goes to reside in Paris—Effect of the Revolution in France on Europe—The Revolution in Belgium—Formation of the Belgian Republic—Death of the Emperor Joseph II.—Failure of his reign—The attitude of Louis XVI. to the French Revolution—The new French Constitution—Civil Constitution of the Clergy—Measures of the Constituent Assembly — Mirabeau—Danger threatened to the new state of affairs in France by a foreign war—Mirabeau and the French Court—Probable causes of a foreign war—Avignon and the Venaissin—Affair of Nootka Sound—The Pacte de Famille—Rights of Princes of the Empire in Alsace—The Emperor Leopold master of the situation.

AT the commencement of the year 1789 the thoughts of European statesmen were mainly turned to the events which were passing in the east of Europe. The alliance between Catherine of Russia and the Emperor Joseph II. was regarded with anxiety not only by Pitt in England and by King Frederick William II. of Prussia, but by the French ministers and by all the smaller states of Europe. The projects of Russia and Austria for the extension of their boundaries at the expense of Turkey, Poland, and

*Catherine and Joseph II. 1789.*

## The Turkish War

Bavaria, were viewed with alarm, and the ambitious ideas of their rulers with dismay. The attention of educated people, who were not statesmen or politicians, but disciples of the philosophical teachers of the eighteenth century, was entirely concentrated on the progress of the Emperor Joseph's policy in the Austrian Netherlands or Belgium. Success seemed to have crowned the warlike measures of General d'Alton; the Belgian patriots were in prison or in exile; and the philanthropic and centralising reforms of the Emperor seemed to have ended in Belgium in the establishment of a military despotism. France was known to be in an almost desperate financial condition; and the convocation of the States-General for 1st May 1789, was generally looked upon as a means adopted by Louis XVI. to obtain financial relief. The great results, which were to follow the meeting of the States-General, were little expected by even the most acute political observers, and it was not foreseen that for more than a quarter of a century the interest of Europe was to be fixed upon France, and that a series of events in that country, unparalleled in history, were to bring about an entire modification in the political system of Europe, and to open a new era in the history of mankind.

The campaign of 1788 had, upon the whole, terminated favourably for the Austrians and Russians in their war with the Turks. Loudon, who commanded the Austrian forces, had taken Dubitza, and penetrating into Bosnia had reduced Novi on 3d October. Francis Josias, of the House of Saxe-Coburg-Saalfeld, commonly known as the Prince of Coburg, at the head of an Austrian army, had in conjunction with a Russian force under Prince Soltikov taken Choczim on 20th September. But, on the other hand, the Turks had overrun and laid waste the Banat of Temesvar and routed the Austrian army in that quarter, which was under the personal command of the Emperor. The Russians had also made some progress, and on 6th December Potemkin, with terrible loss of life, and owing mainly to the intrepidity

*The War with the Turks.*

of Suvórov and Repnin stormed Oczakoff (Ochakov). These successes, despite his own failure, greatly inspirited Joseph, who, in a letter to Prince Charles of Nassau, made the follow-

Joseph's prediction.
ing curious predictions in January 1789 :[1]—' If the Grand Vizier should come to meet me or the Russians near the Danube, he must offer a battle ; and then, after having defeated him, I shall drive him back to take refuge under the cannon of Silistria. In October 1789 I shall call a congress, at which the Osmanlis will be obliged to beg for peace from the Giaours. The treaties of Carlowitz and Passarowitz will serve as the basis for my ambassadors on which to conclude peace ; in it, however, I shall claim Choczim and part of Moldavia. Russia will keep the Crimea, Prince Charles of Sweden will be Duke of Courland, and the Grand Duke of Florence King of the Romans. Then there will be universal peace in Europe. Until then, France will have settled affairs with the notables of the nation ; and the other gentlemen think too much about themselves and too little about Austria.'

The campaign of 1789 was far from fulfilling the expectations of the Emperor Joseph. His own health had suffered too much from the privations of the previous year to enable him to take the field again in person, but he was well served by his generals. The Grand Vizier determined to adopt the

The Campaign of 1789.
offensive, and crossed the Danube at Rustchuk in March at the head of an army of 90,000 men, with the intention of invading Transylvania. But an unexpected event led to the recall of the most experienced Turkish general. The Sultan Abdul Hamid died at Constantinople on 7th April, and his nephew and successor, Selim III., at once disgraced the Grand Vizier, and replaced him in the command of the western army and the office of Grand Vizier by the Pasha of Widdin. This incompetent commander rashly advanced, and was defeated by the Prince of Coburg and

[1] *Memoirs of the Court Aristocracy and Diplomacy of Austria*, by E. Vehse, translated by Franz Demmler. London : 1856, vol. ii. p. 334.

Suvórov at Foksany on 31st July in an attempt to prevent the junction of the Austrians and Russians. The allies then took the offensive and inflicted a crushing defeat on the main Turkish army on the Rymnik, in which 18,000 Austrians and 7000 Russians routed nearly 100,000 Turks, and took all their baggage and artillery. This great victory was vigorously followed up. Loudon was appointed Commander-in-chief of the Austrian army, and he took Belgrade on 9th October, and after occupying the whole of Servia, laid siege to Orsova. For these services Joseph conferred upon him the title of generalissimo, which had only been borne before by Wallenstein, Montecuculi, and Prince Eugène. Among other results of the victory on the Rymnik, the Prince of Coburg took Bucharest and occupied Moldavia, while the Prince of Hohenlohe-Kirchberg forced his way into Wallachia. In the eastern quarter of the Turkish frontier Prince Potemkin was equally successful. He defeated the Turkish High Admiral, Hassan Pasha, in a pitched battle at Tobac, and conquered Bessarabia, capturing Bender, and laying siege to Ismail.

Doubtless Catherine and Joseph would have met with even greater successes, and perhaps they might have driven the Turks out of Europe, had not their attention been diverted directly by the affairs of Sweden and Belgium, and indirectly by the startling events which were taking place in France. The Triple Alliance looked with great disfavour on the alliance between Austria and Russia. Pitt, as has been said, prepared a great fleet, which is known in English naval history as the Russian Armament, and Frederick William II. began to negotiate an alliance with Turkey. But they limited their direct interference to inducing Denmark to make peace with Sweden. Gustavus III. of Sweden had, in 1788, forced his way at the head of 30,000 men into Russian Finland, and the sound of his guns had been heard in Saint Petersburg, which, owing to the absence of the bulk of the Russian troops, was almost defenceless. But the Swedish nobility had great influence over the army; they disliked the war with Russia;

*Revolution in Sweden.*

and took this opportunity to declare themselves. Under the secret leadership of Prince Charles, Duke of Sudermania, they refused to obey the king's orders, and hoped in the embarrassment which ensued to regain their former power. At this moment Christian VII., King of Denmark and Norway, at the instance of Catherine, invaded Sweden and prepared to besiege Gothenburg. Gustavus saw the opportunity which this invasion offered to rouse the patriotic feelings of the Swedes. He appealed to the people, and leaving the command of the army in Finland to the Duke of Sudermania, raised a fresh army of volunteers to resist the invaders. In spite of his efforts, Sweden was in great danger of falling before the combined attacks of Russia and Denmark. The Triple Alliance now intervened promptly and decisively, and by threatening to attack Denmark by land and sea, they induced Bernstorff, the Danish minister, to evacuate Sweden and to agree to an armistice. Gustavus III. returned to Stockholm with the reputation of having repulsed the invaders, and summoned the Diet to meet on 2d February 1789. Sure of the support of the Commons he proposed a new Constitution, or rather a new fundamental law for the Swedish monarchy, which is summed up in one of the articles: 'The king can administer the affairs of the State as seems good to him.' The nobility opposed a fruitless resistance; Gustavus imprisoned their leaders and completed the work of his former revolution of 1772 by this *coup d'état*. He then renewed the war with Russia, but the military operations of his campaign in 1789 were not marked by any event of importance.

While Catherine of Russia was being distracted from the vigorous prosecution of the war against Turkey by the invasion of the Swedes, her ally, the Emperor Joseph, was chiefly concerned with the state of affairs in the Austrian Netherlands or Belgium. It seemed at first as if he was to be as successful as Gustavus in changing the old constitution of the country. But there was this difference. Whereas Gustavus III. was enacting the part of a national

Affairs in Belgium, 1789.

deliverer, and had the Swedish people on his side in his overthrow of the nobility, Joseph II. was opposed not only by the Belgian nobles, but by the clergy and the people also. The country seemed quiet enough under the government of Count Trautmannsdorf and the military rule of the Captain-General d'Alton. The suppression of the risings at Brussels and Louvain, Malines and Antwerp seemed to have established the Austrian sway most firmly, and the leading opponents of the Emperor's policy were in exile. The Estates of the different provinces were convoked as usual, and all of them, except those of Hainault and Brabant, voted the customary subsidies. The Estates of Hainault were at once dissolved by a military force, and their constitution abolished on 31st January 1789. By this example the Emperor hoped to overawe the wealthy and populous province of Brabant, and when it did not have the expected effect, he directed Trautmannsdorf to summon a special meeting of the Estates of Brabant, and to require them to increase the number of deputies of the Third Estate or Commons, and to grant a permanent subsidy. He also maintained his attitude towards the Church, and tried to compel Cardinal Frankenberg, the Archbishop of Malines, to withdraw his opposition to the new Imperial Seminary at Brussels, or to resign his see. The Archbishop stoutly refused to comply, and the Estates of Brabant proved equally stubborn. Joseph then decided on a sudden blow, and by his orders Count Trautmannsdorf, on 18th June 1789, declared the 'Joyeuse Entrée,' or Constitution of Brabant abolished. The day was the anniversary of the battle of Kolin, in which, at the crisis of the Seven Years' War, the Austrians had defeated Frederick the Great. D'Alton thought he made a happy comparison in saying : 'The 18th of June is a happy epoch for the House of Austria; for on that day the glorious victory of Kolin saved the monarchy, and the Emperor became master of the Netherlands.' But the victory was not to be won so easily. The two parties of opposition, the Van der Nootists, or partisans of Van der Noot, the supporter of the ancient constitutional rights, and the Vonckists, or followers of Vonck, the advocate of popular or democratic ideas, united. The Triple Alliance was as glad to hamper Joseph's activity in the East by encouraging these Belgian patriots, as it had been to leave Gustavus free to harass Catherine, by stopping the interference of Denmark in the north, and the ministers of England, Holland, and Prussia all entered into relations with Van der Noot. That partisan, encouraged by hopes of active assistance, formed a patriotic committee at Breda, on the Dutch frontier, and raised an army of exiles, which was placed under the command of Colonel Van der Mersch. Joseph was not to be intimidated. D'Alton put down popular riots, which broke out in various towns, notably at Tirlemont, Louvain, Namur, and Brussels, with unrelenting severity. A sweeping decree was issued on 19th October against the exiles or *émigrés*, declaring that ordinary emigration would be punished by banishment and confiscation of property, and that joining an armed force on the frontier for the purpose of invasion would be punished by death, and that informers against *émigrés* would receive a reward of 10,000 livres and absolute-impunity.[1] But all the Emperor's measures and decrees were of no effect. The meeting of the States-General in France had been followed by the capture of the Bastille and the bringing of the King of France from Versailles to Paris by a Parisian mob; and the effects of the French Revolution on affairs in Belgium was soon to be perceived.

In the bishopric of Liége, which, from its situation, always reflected and repeated any political troubles that took place in Belgium, the influence of the French Revolution was immediately felt. The inhabitants of the bishopric had long resented the rule of the prince-bishops, and felt the anomaly of being subject to an ecclesiastical sovereign. Many exiles from the democratic party in Belgium assembled in the bishopric, and on the news of the capture of the

*Revolution in Liége.*

[1] *L'Europe et la Révolution Française*, by Albert Sorel, vol. ii. p. 50.

Bastille, the people of Liége needed little persuasion to renew their former insurrection. The revolution was carried out without the shedding of blood. On 16th and 17th August 1789 the people of the city of Liége rose in rebellion; on the 18th MM. Chestret and Fabry were chosen burgomasters by popular acclamation, the garrison was disarmed, and the citadel occupied by bourgeois national guards. On the same day the Prince-Bishop, Count Cæsar Constantine Francis de Hoensbroeck, was brought into the city, and he signed a proclamation acknowledging the revolution and abrogating the despotic settlement of 1684. The other towns in the bishopric followed the example of the capital, and in each of them free municipalities were elected and national guards raised and armed. The Prince-Bishop, after accepting the loss of his political power, fled to Trèves, and considered himself fortunate to be allowed to escape.

It is now time to examine the course of the events in France, which led to such important developments upon its north-east frontier, and which distracted the attention of all the monarchs and ministers of Europe, except Catherine of Russia, from the wars in the North and East. It was owing to the increasing difficulty of raising money for carrying on the administration of the State and paying the interest on the national debt, and the consequent necessity for revising the system of taxation and reorganising the financial resources of France that Louis XVI., on the advice of his minister, Loménie de Brienne, had vaguely promised in November 1787 to summon the States-General for July 1792, and had definitely convoked the ancient assembly of France on 8th August 1788 to meet at Versailles on 1st May 1789. But the arrangements for the elections were not made by Loménie de Brienne, who retired from office in the same month as the States-General was convoked, but by his successor Necker, who was recalled to office as an expert financier, in view of the fact that the summons of the States-General was looked on as a purely financial expedient. The

*The Elections to the States-General.*

procedure to be adopted in electing deputies gave rise to much anxious deliberation and heated controversy in the public press, and the Notables of 1787 were again assembled to give their advice. The burning question was as to the representation of the Tiers État, Third Estate or Commons. The ancient representative assembly of France was known to consist of the three orders of the Nobility, the Clergy, and the Tiers État, and the disputed question was as to the proportion of the number of deputies of the Tiers État to that of the two other orders. This and the other electoral questions were finally settled by the Résultat du Conseil published on 27th December 1788. It was decreed that the royal bailliages and royal sénéchaussées, feudal circumscriptions which had long fallen into disuse, should be treated as electoral units, and that they should elect, according to the extent of their population, one or more deputations, each consisting of four members, one chosen by the Nobility, one by the Clergy, and two by the Tiers État. The elections were to be made in two and sometimes in three degrees, and at each stage *cahiers* or statements of grievances and projects for reform were to be drawn up by the electoral assemblies.[1] In provinces, where there were no royal bailliages or sénéchaussées, and consequently no Grand Baillis or Grand Sénéchals to preside, corresponding circumscriptions were adopted or invented. During the early months of 1789 the French people were fully occupied in the election of the deputies to the States-General. Whatever might be the opinion of the French Court or the French Ministry, the people,—and more especially the educated bourgeois of the towns and the country lawyers,—looked upon the future assembly as something more than a financial expedient; they trusted to it to draw up a new political system for the State, which should admit the representative principle and allow the taxpayer a voice not only in the granting, but in the spending of the national revenue. The working classes,

[1] *A History of the French Revolution*, by H. Morse Stephens. Vol. i., chapter i. gives a detailed account of the method of election.

whether in the towns or the rural districts, did not take much active interest in the elections, and their representatives in the secondary electoral assemblies were generally educated bourgeois, but they vaguely built high hopes on the meeting of the States-General, and expected it to give them land or higher wages. Considering the novelty of choosing representatives in France; it is extraordinary that the electoral operations were carried out as peacefully and as efficiently as they were. This was mainly due to the success of a little revolutionary movement in Dauphiné, where an unauthorised and irregular assembly had met in July 1788 to protest against the abolition of the provincial Parlements by Loménie de Brienne. That minister had left office, when he was not permitted to put down the assembly in Dauphiné by force, and Necker hoped to save the prestige of the monarchy by summoning a new assembly of the province in its place. But the ruse was quickly perceived; the men who had sat in the illegal assembly were elected to its successor, and in the eyes of France the representatives of the Dauphiné had won a signal victory over the Court. The new assembly in Dauphiné became the court of appeal in every electoral difficulty, and its secretary, Mounier, the leader of the Tiers État of France. Owing to his energy and ability local jealousies of town against town, province against province, class jealousies and personal rivalry, were set at rest, and it was more owing to Mounier than to any one else that the deputies to the States-General were legally and quietly elected, and that the acts of the future assembly could not be stigmatised as the work of a factious or unrepresentative minority of the French nation.

On 5th May 1789 the first States-General held in France since the year 1614 met at Versailles. Barentin, the Keeper of the Seals, and Necker harangued the collected deputies, and the latter explained the desperate financial situation of the State and the necessity for immediate action to relieve the national treasury. The representatives of the nobility and clergy then retired to separate chambers, leaving their colleagues of the Tiers État in the great hall. No word was spoken about the relation of the three orders to each other. It was assumed that each order was to deliberate separately. The representatives of the Tiers État were placed in a most difficult position. There was no advantage in their being as numerous as the two other orders put together, if the three orders were to be independent of each other, for in that case the majorities of the privileged orders could outweigh the opinion of the majority among themselves. The question of *vote par ordre*, which would give each order equal authority, or *vote par tête*, which would allow the numerical preponderance of the Tiers État to take effect, had been long recognised as crucial. It had been assumed from the grant of double representation to the Tiers État that the Government intended to sanction the *vote par tête*, and the tacit acknowledgment of the separation of the orders and consequent recognition of the *vote par ordre* on 5th May disconcerted for the moment the popular leaders.

But the deputies of the Tiers État, under the guidance of Le Chapelier, a Breton lawyer from Rennes, and of Rabaut de Saint-Étienne, a Protestant pastor from Nîmes, proceeded to take up a most skilful attitude. They resolved on a policy of masterly inactivity. They refused to form themselves into the assembly of the Order of the Tiers État; they refused to open letters addressed to them under that title; they refused to elect a president or secretaries; and stated that they were a body of citizens, representatives of the French nation, waiting in that hall to be joined by the other deputies. This attitude received the unanimous approval of the people of Paris, and threw upon the Government the onus of declaring that the double representation of the Tiers État was merely a sterile gift. The representatives of the two privileged orders treated the situation very differently. The nobility accepted the separation ·of the orders to distinct chambers, and resolved to constitute their chamber by 188 votes to 47, while the clergy only decided in the same sense by 133 votes to 114. Even this majority was not really significant. For, owing to a tendency which had developed during the course of the elections, the greater part of the deputies of the clergy were poor country curés, who sympathised with the Tiers État, from which they sprung, and not with the prelates and dignitaries of the Church, who belonged to the nobility. This tendency of the true majority of the clergy was well known to the leaders of the Tiers État and encouraged them in their passive attitude. In vain the King and Necker attempted to terminate the deadlock; the deputies of the Tiers État persisted that they did not form an order, and they were reinforced by the representatives of Paris, where the elections were not concluded until the end of May. At last, on 10th June, on the proposition of the Abbé Sieyès, deputy for Paris, a final invitation was sent to the deputies of the nobility and the clergy to join the deputies of the Tiers État, and it was resolved that whether the request was granted or refused the Tiers État would constitute itself into a regular deliberative body. The invitation was rejected by the nobility, and only a few curés, including the Abbé Grégoire, belonging to the Order of the Clergy, complied with it. The deputies then verified their powers, and elected Bailly, a famous astronomer and deputy for Paris, to be their president. But what sort of assembly were they? They denied that they were representatives of an Order, and they were certainly not the States-General of France. The question was hotly debated, and on 16th June they declared themselves the National Assembly. They then declared all the taxes, hitherto levied, to be illegal, and ordered that they should only be paid provisionally. This defiant conduct disconcerted the King and his ministers, and it was announced that a Séance Royale, or Royal Session, would be held by the King in person to settle all disputed questions.

*The Tiers État declare themselves the National Assembly.*

On 20th June the deputies of the Tiers État, or of the

National Assembly, as they now termed themselves, were excluded from their usual meeting-place. They therefore met in the Jeu de Paume or Tennis Court at Versailles, and, amidst a scene of wild excitement, swore that they would not separate until they had drawn up a new Constitution for France. By this act they practically became rebels, and the French Revolution really commenced. On 22d June they met in the Church of Saint Louis at Versailles, where they were joined by 149 deputies of the clergy, who thus recognised the act of rebellion. On 23d June the Séance Royale was held. In the speech from the throne it was announced that the King, 'of his own goodness and generosity,' would levy no taxes in future without the assent of the representatives of the people, but it was also declared that the financial privileges of the nobility and clergy were unassailable, and that the States-General was to vote *par ordre*. This was the most critical moment in the first stage of the Revolution. If the deputies of the Tiers État had given way, the oath of the Tennis Court would have seemed only an idle threat. But they found a leader in the Comte de Mirabeau, deputy for the Tiers État of Aix, a man of extraordinary ability, who in the course of a tempestuous career had travelled much and learned much. He courageously faced the situation, and after making a reply to the Grand Master of the Ceremonies that the deputies of France would only be expelled by force, he induced the National Assembly to declare the persons of its members inviolable. Sieyès summed up the situation by telling the deputies: 'Gentlemen, you are to-day what you were yesterday.' Before this daring opposition the King gave way: on 25th June the minority of the Order of the Nobility, consisting of forty-seven deputies, headed by the Marquis de Lafayette, the friend of Washington, joined the National Assembly, and two days later the majority of that Order reluctantly followed their example at the command of the King.

The rapid transformation of the deputies of the Tiers État

into a National Assembly, which defied the royal authority and spoke of drawing up a new Constitution for France, exasperated the courtiers, who looked with disgust at all attempts to modify the *ancien régime*. The King did not share their feelings; he was honestly desirous of doing his duty by his people, and preferred the diminution of his royal prerogative to coming into open conflict with his subjects and to initiating a civil war. He had hitherto trusted to Necker and followed Necker's advice. But the result had not been encouraging. His minister had repeatedly put him in a false position. He had been made to speak in a haughty tone to the deputies of the Tiers État at the Séance Royale on 23d June, and then to eat his words by directing the deputies of the Nobility to join the self-created National Assembly. This great concession seemed to have been wrung from him; the deputies of the Tiers État appeared to have won a great victory in the face of the royal opposition, when in reality the King had yielded from the goodness of his heart. Since he found that following the advice of Necker had only resulted in a loss of authority, combined with profound unpopularity, without improving the financial prospect, Louis XVI. not unnaturally turned his attention to the enemies of the minister. These enemies were headed by the Queen, Marie Antoinette, who resented Necker's endeavours to restrain the extravagance of the Court and his admission of the need to make concessions to the will of the people, and by the King's younger brother, the Comte d'Artois, a staunch supporter of the absolute prerogative of the Crown and of the system of the *ancien régime*. Yielding unwillingly to the arguments of the enemies of Necker and of the National Assembly, the King determined to use force, and he began to concentrate troops in the neighbourhood of Paris and Versailles. The National Assembly did not know what to do; Mounier and other leaders had formed a committee to draw up the bases of a new constitution; but they had no force on which they could depend to resist the royal troops, and felt that they would probably be arrested and the Assembly dissolved long before the foundation of the Constitution was laid. At this crisis Mirabeau again came to the front. With the most daring audacity he attacked and revealed the policy of the Court on 8th July, and on 9th July carried an address to the King on the part of the Assembly, requesting the immediate removal of the troops collected in the neighbourhood, but protesting the loyalty of the Assembly to the person of the King. But the King was now under the influence of the opponents of the Assembly. His answer to Mirabeau's address was the dismissal of Necker and his colleagues on 12th July, the banishment of Necker, and the appointment of the Maréchal de Broglie, an experienced general, who detested the idea of change, to be Minister for War and Marshal-General of the troops in the neighbourhood of Paris.

*Mirabeau's Address to the King. 9th July.*

*Dismissal of Necker. 12th July.*

Hitherto the struggle had been between the Court and the deputies of the Tiers État; the popular element was now to intervene; and the people of Paris was for the first time to make its influence felt. The news of Necker's dismissal was received in Paris with wrath and dismay. A young lawyer without practice, named Camille Desmoulins, announced the event to the crowd collected in the Palais Royal and incited his hearers to resistance. His words were eagerly applauded. The population of Paris, both bourgeois and proletariat, had watched the course of events at Versailles with unflagging interest, and the formation of a camp of soldiers in the neighbourhood with terror. The working classes, who lived near the margin of starvation, expected that the National Assembly would cause in some way a rise in wages and a decrease in the price of necessaries, and were exasperated at the prospect of the non-fulfilment of their hopes. They had already sacked the house of a manufacturer, named Réveillon, who was reported to have spoken scornful words of their poverty, on 28th April, and were ready for any mischief. From the Palais Royal, excited by the news and the words of Camille Desmoulins, started a tumultuous procession bearing busts of Necker and of the Duke of Orleans, a prince of the royal house, who had been exiled by the King for previous opposition to him, and who was regarded as a supporter of the popular claims. The procession was charged by a German cavalry regiment in the French service, commanded by the Prince de Lambesc, a near relative of the Queen, and the mob dispersed to riot and to pillage. The more patriotic rioters broke into the gunsmiths' shops to seize weapons, the rest pillaged the butchers' and bakers' shops, and burned the barriers where octroi duties were collected. This scene of riot brought about its own remedy. The bourgeois, terrified for the safety of their shops, took up arms, and on the following day formed themselves into companies of national guards for the preservation of the peace. The guidance of this movement was taken by the electors of Paris, who, after completing their work of electing deputies for Paris, continued to meet at the Hôtel de Ville. *Formation of National Guards.*

The 14th of July found the capital of France organised for resistance. The Gardes Françaises, the force maintained for the security of Paris, were devoted to the cause of the National Assembly, and were resolved to fight with the people, not against them. And it was ascertained that the soldiers in the camp were very lukewarm in their attachment to their officers, and were likely to refuse to attack the citizens. Under these circumstances an idea arose that an armed demonstration of the Parisians at Versailles would strengthen the King, whose sentiments were well known, to resist the Court party and to recall Necker. With this notion, large crowds approached the Hôtel des Invalides and the Bastille, the two principal storehouses of arms in Paris. The crowd, which went to the Hôtel des Invalides, had no difficulty in seizing the arms there, in spite of the opposition of the Governor. But it was otherwise at the Bastille. The mob, which collected in the Governor's Court in that fortress and shouted for arms, was isolated by the raising of the outer drawbridge and fired upon by the weak garrison in *Capture of the Bastille. 14th July.*

the Bastille itself. The sound of this firing brought a number of armed men from other parts of the city; the outer drawbridge was cut down, and preparations were being made to force a way into the fortress itself, when the garrison surrendered. The result of the firing upon the mob in the Governor's Court had been to kill eighty-three persons and wound many others. The sight of the corpses and the cries of the wounded excited the anger of the successful conquerors of the fortress. A panic arose, and three officers and four soldiers of the garrison were murdered. Then the more disciplined of the conquerors started to take the rest of the defenders of the Bastille to the Hôtel de Ville. On the way the Governor and the Major of the fortress were murdered by the mob, and M. de Flesselles, the Provost of the merchants of Paris, who was accused of encouraging the Governor to resist, was also slain. By these events the people of Paris felt that they had commenced a war against the Crown; entrenchments were thrown up and barricades were erected in the streets; all shops were shut up; the barriers were closed; no one was allowed to leave the city, and preparations were made to stand a siege.

But if the people of Paris were ready to fight, the King was not. As has been said, he loathed the idea of civil war, and when he heard of the capture of the Bastille and of the martial attitude of Paris, he at once gave up the idea of opposing the revolutionary movement by force. He dismissed his reactionary ministers and recalled Necker, and he declared himself ready to co-operate with the National Assembly in restoring order. The first victories of the Assembly had been won by its statesmanlike inaction in the month of May and its courage on 23d June; the victory over the party of force had been won by Paris on 14th July. The Assembly prepared to take advantage of this fresh success. On 16th July it legalised the establishment of National Guards and elective municipalities all over France, and recognising that the only way to convince the Parisians that the King had accepted the new situation and had abandoned the idea of

*Recall of Necker. 15th July.*

employing force, was to induce the King to visit Paris in person, it proposed that he should do so at once. Louis XVI. was not devoid of personal courage, and consented. On 17th July, accordingly, he entered Paris accompanied by 100 deputies, and amidst wild acclamation put on the tricolour cockade, which the Parisians had assumed as their badge, and consented to the nomination of Bailly, the President of the National Assembly, to be Mayor of Paris, and of Lafayette to be Commander-in-chief of the Paris National Guard. These concessions, and the victory of the National Assembly and of Paris threw consternation among the court party of reaction: the Comte d'Artois and those of his adherents, who were most hated as conspicuous reactionaries or who had advocated the employment of force, fled from the country. *The King's visit to Paris. 17th July.*

The immediate results of the capture of the Bastille were no less important in the provinces of France. In every city, even in small country towns, mayors and municipalities were elected and National Guards formed; in many the local citadels were seized by the people; in all the troops fraternised with the people; and in some there was bloodshed. This movement was essentially bourgeois; where blood was shed and pillage took place at the hands of the working classes, the new National Guards soon restored order. The general excitement was so great that it is surprising that there was not more bloodshed and that peace was so quickly and efficiently established. Among these outbreaks the most noteworthy took place in Paris itself, where on 21st July Foullon de Doué, who had been nominated to succeed Necker on 12th July, and his son-in-law Berthier de Sauvigny were murdered almost before the eyes of Bailly, the new Mayor of Paris. But these occasional town riots were speedily quelled by the armed bourgeois. Far more widespread and important was the upheaval in the rural districts of France. *Murder of Foullon. 21st July.*

The peasants believed that the time had come, when they

were to own their land free from copyhold rights or the relics of feudal servitudes. Even the better-educated farmers for their own interests favoured this idea. The result was a regular jacquerie in many parts of France. The châteaux of the lords were burnt, or in some instances only the charters stored in them, and the lords' dovecotes and rabbit-warrens were generally destroyed. In certain provinces the National Guards of the neighbouring towns put down these rural outbreaks, occasionally with great severity, but as a rule they ran their course unchecked.

On 4th August a deputy named Salomon read a report on these occurrences to the National Assembly, or as it is generally called from the Constitution it framed, the Constituent Assembly. His report was followed by a curious scene, which marked the transition from feudal to modern France. The scene was opened by the sacrifice by some of the young liberal noblemen of their feudal rights. Privileges of all sorts, privileges of class, of town and of province were solemnly abandoned. Feudal customs and all relics of feudalism were condemned and declared to be abolished. Even tithes were swept away, in spite of a protest from Sieyès, and the 'orgie,' as Mirabeau termed it, closed with a decree that a monument should be erected to Louis XVI., 'the restorer of French liberty.'

*The Session of 4th August.*

But it was not possible to restore peace and prosperity to France by the abolition of the relics of feudalism. Destruction of former anomalies and of a crumbling system of government would inevitably lead to anarchy, unless accompanied by the construction of a new scheme of central and local administration. It was here that the Constituent Assembly failed. The deputies were quick to destroy but slow to construct. For two months they wasted time instead of hastening to draw up a new constitution for France. They first wrangled over the wording of a Declaration of the Rights of Man, which they resolved to compile in imitation of the founders of the American Republic. They then

*The Declaration of the Rights of Man.*

debated lengthily whether the future representative assembly of France should consist of one or two chambers, and whether the King should have power to veto its acts. The first question was decided in favour of a single chamber, more because the English Constitution sanctioned two chambers, and the deputies feared to be thought imitators, than for any logical reason. And the debate on the second question terminated in the grant to the King of a suspensive veto for six months, in spite of the eloquence of Mirabeau, who saw that a monarchical constitution, which gave the King no more power than the President of the United States of America, would prove unworkable, because it would divorce responsibility from real authority, leaving the former to the King and the latter to the Legislature. The Suspensive Veto.

During the two months occupied by these debates the situation had again become critical. Necker's only idea to relieve the financial situation was to propose loans, which the Assembly granted, but which he could not succeed in raising. The King was again being acted upon by the Court party, which advocated the use of force and the dissolution of the Assembly, and this party was encouraged by the Queen and by the King's sister, Madame Elizabeth. He was also urged to leave the neighbourhood of Paris and to establish himself in some provincial town, where the populace could be more easily restrained by the regular troops. He would not heartily agree to either of these courses, but weakly consented once more to concentrate troops round his person. Everything advised at Versailles was soon known in Paris. The journalists, who had since the capture of the Bastille sprung up in the capital to advocate the views of the popular party, and of whom the ablest were Loustalot, editor of the *Révolutions de Paris*, and Marat, editor of the *Ami du Peuple*, kept warning the people of Paris against treason on the part of the King, and prophesying dire consequences if he were allowed to leave the neighbourhood or to concentrate troops. Their words did not fall on unheeding ears. The working classes feared a siege of Paris again as they had done in July, and looked on the King's presence in Paris as the only means to keep down the price of necessaries. The thinking bourgeois, whether liberal deputies in the Assembly or national guards in Paris, feared a sudden forced dissolution of the Assembly, and not only the loss of the advantages they had gained but punishment for the part they had played. Both these elements were perceptible in the movement which followed. The description given in the popular journals of a banquet at Versailles, honoured by the presence of the royal family, at which the national cockade had been trampled underfoot, on 1st October, roused the people of Paris to a frenzy of wrath and fear. On 5th October a crowd of women collected in Paris, declaring that they were starving, and were led to Versailles by Maillard, one of the conquerors of the Bastille, followed by a mob. The representatives of the women interviewed the King, and the mob prepared to spend the night outside the palace walls. Late at night they were followed by a powerful detachment of the National Guard of Paris, under the command of Lafayette, who protested that he came to save the King. Nevertheless, owing to bad management, some of the mob broke into the palace before daybreak on the morning of 6th October and murdered two of the royal bodyguards. Lafayette came to the rescue and demanded that the King and royal family should come to Paris and take up their residence at the Tuileries. The King, horrified by the events of the morning, and obliged to obey Lafayette, consented, and the royal family, accompanied by the mob, and escorted by the National Guard, at once proceeded to the capital. This second victory of the Parisians was not less important than the first: on 14th July the people of Paris had terrified the King into abandoning the idea of dissolving the National Assembly by force; on 6th October they brought him amongst them, so that if he again conceived the idea, he would be unable to execute it.

The capture of the Bastille caused the most profound

astonishment in Europe. Where the people possessed some amount of political liberty, as in the United States of America and in England, it appealed to the imagination, and the French were regarded as the conquerors of their freedom. In the neighbourhood of France, in the Rhenish principalities, in Belgium, and above all in Liége, it caused a general sense of discontent and even riots. The despotic monarchs of Europe and their principal ministers did not pay so much attention to the capture of the Bastille as did the inhabitants of free countries; they did not for one moment believe that the National Assembly would be allowed to alter the old constitution of France, and looked upon the whole of the popular movement with a favourable eye as likely to weaken France and prevent her from interfering in the affairs of the Continent. They took care, however, to suppress all similar risings in their own states. The King of Sardinia and the Elector of Mayence were especially severe; the Emperor's General d'Alton was more than severe in Belgium; and the King of Prussia sent General Schlieffen with a strong force to restore the authority of the Bishop of Liége. This attitude of the continental monarchs was encouraged by the first French *émigrés*, who loudly declared that the success of the Assembly was due to the culpable weakness of Louis XVI.  *Effect in Europe.*

The tidings of the events of 5th and 6th October showed both the French *émigrés* and the continental monarchs that they were wrong in their estimate of the Revolution. That the French royal family should be triumphantly brought to Paris and be practically imprisoned in the Tuileries under the eyes of the Parisian populace was a startling proof of the power of the people. It proportionately encouraged the supporters of all the popular movements on the French borders. Of these, the most important was that which had already made so much progress two years before in Belgium. The first result of the removal of the King of France to Paris was the Belgian Revolution of 1789, which filled almost as large a place in the eyes of contemporaries  *The Belgian Revolution. Oct. 1789— Jan. 1790.*

as the French Revolution itself. Encouraged by the Triple Alliance, and more especially by Frederick William II. of Prussia, the Belgian exiles of both wings, the supporters of Van der Noot, the advocate of the ancient Constitution, and of Vonck, the radical, had formed a patriotic army at Breda. The news of the events of 5th and 6th October determined them to act. On 23d October the army under Van der Mersch crossed the border, and on 24th October Van der Noot issued a manifesto declaring the Emperor Joseph deprived of his sovereignty over the Duchy of Brabant for having violated its fundamental charter.

The march of the patriotic army was both rapid and successful. Bruges and Ostend opened their gates to the exiles; the fort of St. Pierre at Ghent was stormed; and the Estates of Flanders at once assembled, published a declaration of independence, and called on the other provinces to join in the movement. In Brabant the excitement was at its height. Trautmannsdorf in vain promised to restore the 'Joyeuse Entrée,' to abolish the Imperial Seminary at Brussels, and to declare a general amnesty. The patriots would not trust him, and Van der Mersch advanced into the Duchy and occupied Tirlemont. The people of Brussels then rose in insurrection. From 7th to 12th December was a period of long-continued riot and street fighting. Many of the Austrian soldiers deserted to the popular side, and those who remained true to their colours were shot at from windows and refused to charge. The advance of Van der Mersch set the seal upon d'Alton's discomfiture. He made a capitulation on 12th December, and marched out of Brussels, leaving his guns, military stores, and military chest containing 3,000,000 florins behind. He retreated to Luxembourg, the only province which remained faithful to the House of Austria, and his example was followed by the imperial garrisons of Malines, Antwerp, and Louvain, which were abandoned to the patriots. D'Alton himself died at Trèves, it is said by taking poison, on being summoned to Vienna to be tried by a court-martial, and was succeeded in command of the Austrian troops in Luxembourg by General Bender.' On 18th December the patriot committee entered Brussels, headed by Van der Noot, who was hailed by the people as the Belgian Franklin. On 7th January 1790 representatives from all the provinces of the former Austrian Netherlands met at Brussels under the presidency of Cardinal Frankenberg, Archbishop of Malines, and on 10th January they passed a federal constitution for the 'United Belgian States,' resembling that of Holland, under which each province was to preserve its internal independence, and only foreign affairs and national defence were left to the central government. Van der Noot was chosen Minister of State, and he at once asked for the official recognition of the new Belgian Constitution by the Triple Alliance, whose ministers at the Hague, Lord Auckland, Count Keller, and Van der Spiegel had, he asserted, promised to guarantee the independence of the new United States of Belgium. Frederick William II. of Prussia endeavoured to carry out this promise. He authorised one of his officers, General Schönfeld, to organise the Belgian army, and ordered General Schlieffen at Liége to enter into communication with the new government. But England and Holland, though approving the insurrection of Belgium as affording a powerful counterpoise to the Emperor's policy in the East, were in no hurry to guarantee the new Republic, and Van der Noot then determined, under the influence of the radicals or Vonckists, to solicit the help of France, and announced the new Belgian Constitution in a significant manner both to Louis XVI. and to the President of the National Assembly.

 The news of the declaration of the independence of the Belgian provinces, and of the revolution which had led to it, proved to be the death-blow of the Emperor Joseph. To the Prince de Ligne, a native of Belgium, he said, just before his death, 'Your country has killed me; the taking of Ghent is my agony; the evacuation of Brussels is my death. What a disgrace this is

PERIOD VII.   E

for me! I die; I must be made of wood, if I did not. Go to the Netherlands; make them return to their allegiance. If you do not succeed in the attempt, remain there. Do not sacrifice your fortune for me; you have children.' The dying Emperor in his despair made concessions in every direction. He humbled his pride to entreat the Pope to use his influence with the Belgian clergy. He gave in to the Hungarian magnates, who demanded the repeal of his great reforms with threats of insurrection; and on 28th January 1790 he issued his 'Revocatio Ordinationum quæ sensu communi legibus adversari videbantur,' by which he revoked all his reforms in Hungary, except the edict of toleration and the decrees against serfdom; and on 18th February he ordered the Crown of St. Stephen to be sent back to Pesth. He assented to the suspension of his reforming edicts in Bohemia, and even in the Tyrol, where an insurrection was on the point of breaking out. Then, feeling his life a failure, he prepared for death. He confessed and received the ordinances of the Church; the last words he was heard to say were: 'I believe I have done my duty as a man and a prince,' and on the morning of 20th February he died. The words he wished to be written on his grave were: 'Here rests a prince, whose intentions were pure; but who had the misfortune to see all his plans miscarry;' but the people of Vienna, with a deeper sense of the merits of the great ruler who had lived in their midst, placed on his statue the inscription, 'Josepho secundo, arduis nato, magnis perfuncto, majoribus præcepto, qui saluti publicæ vixit non diu, sed totus.' The failure of the career of Joseph, the noblest sovereign of the eighteenth century,—one of the noblest sovereigns of any century,—was a proof of the fallacy of the eighteenth century conception of benevolent despotism. He had tried to accomplish in his dominions the very measures of reform which the Constituent Assembly had undertaken in France. The abolition of the relics of feudalism, the creation of a spirit of nationality, based upon the existence of uniform laws, the nationalisation of the

Church and of education, the removal of all caste privileges, whether in the payment of taxes or in eligibility for public employment, and the maintenance of good internal administration, the primary aims and the great achievements of the Revolution in France, were also the objects of Joseph's reforms. But everything was to be done for the people, nothing by the people, and it is doubtful whether, if Joseph had been in the place of Louis XVI., the French people would have relished the advantages he might have conferred. The spirit of locality was perhaps not so strong in France as in the hereditary dominions of the House of Austria. Dauphiné and Burgundy did not differ from Brittany and Normandy as much as Bohemia and Hungary, Belgium and the Milanese differed from each other. Yet the abolition of local distinctions might have been resented in France, as it was in the dominions of Joseph, if it had been accomplished by the monarch, instead of being the work of elected representatives. It is indeed remarkable that, allowing for the want of exactness in the parallel, owing to the difference of local conditions, the very reforms, which rallied all France to the side of the Revolution, should have led to the disastrous termination of the Emperor Joseph's reign, and it is difficult to avoid coming to the conclusion that the whole subject illustrates the grand distinction between the eighteenth and the nineteenth centuries, the distinction between alterations in the political, social, or economical conditions of a state made by a monarch for his people, and by a people for itself.

Louis XVI., indeed, showed himself a very different type of monarch from Joseph. He wished for the good of his people as ardently as his brother-in-law, but he had during the early years of his reign been satisfied with wishing for reforms, instead of energetically initiating them. When the success of the Revolution was assured by the policy of the deputies of the Tiers État, by the capture of the Bastille and by his own establishment at Paris, he never thought of setting himself at the head of the party of reform. He did not openly ally himself with the Tiers État, to vanquish the opposition of the nobles, as Gustavus III. of Sweden had done; he did not dream of outbidding the National Assembly for popularity by lavish promises, as other monarchs before and since have done; and he did not even try to share the credit of the representatives of the people by exhibiting an ardent zeal for reform. The horror he felt for civil war was not recognised; his partial yielding to the Court party of reaction in July and October, though at so late a date and so half-heartedly as to nullify any chance of its success, was imputed to him as a crime; and the difficulty presented by the fact that his dearest relatives, his Queen, Marie Antoinette, and his sister, Madame Elizabeth, were against all reform, was never fully appreciated. In consequence, the King's real wishes to please his people and avoid bloodshed were looked on as simulated by the members of the National Assembly, and not only Louis himself, but the very principle of the French monarchy, were regarded as hostile to representative institutions. Louis XVI. was as weak as Joseph II. was energetic, but he was equally well-intentioned; and it was a distinct misfortune, both for himself and for France, that the value of the passive inertness, which he generally opposed to the reactionary schemes of his family and of the partisans of the *ancien régime*, was not adequately recognised.

This attitude towards the King had an important effect upon the constitution which the Constituent Assembly was engaged in framing during the year 1790. Only the main points in the growth of this Constitution, which occupied the greater part of the time of the Assembly from 1789 to 1791, can here be touched upon. But one striking feature must first be observed, that it was drawn up and applied piecemeal, not as an organic whole, like the later French constitutions of the revolutionary period. The first important principle was decreed upon 12th November 1789, when it was resolved that all the old local divisions of France, which perpetuated the memory of the gradual growth

*The New French Constitution. 1789-1791.*

of the French provinces into France, should be abolished, and that the country should be divided into eighty departments of nearly equal size. It was naturally some months before the new division was effected, and still longer before the further division of each department into districts, and each district into cantons was finished. No wiser step for converting France from a congeries of provinces into a nation could have been devised. On the basis of the new divisions a new local government was established. Each department and district was to be administered by elected authorities, elaborately chosen by a system of double election. Next to the local government, the judicial system was reorganised. The Parlements were all abolished, and local courts, consisting of elected judges of departmental and district tribunals, and elected justices of the peace, were substituted. A uniform system of law was projected, and juries were sanctioned in criminal but not in civil cases. In these sweeping reforms one natural blemish is perceptible: from having no elected officials the other extreme was adopted of having all officials elected.

The mania for election affected the reform of the ecclesiastical arrangements of France, and directly brought about the schism, which so largely contributed to the misfortunes of France during the revolutionary period. On 2d November 1789 it had been resolved, in the face of the financial distress, that the property of the Church in France should be confiscated or resumed, as it was represented by opposite parties, while acknowledging the duty of providing and paying curés and bishops. This implied the formation of a State Church, a measure which needed the most delicate handling. On 13th February 1790 all monasteries and religious houses were suppressed; but as there had already been a partial suppression a few years previously, this would not by itself have caused a schism. It was otherwise with regard to the Civil Constitution of the Clergy. It was resolved to reduce the number of bishoprics to one for each department, and that all the beneficed clergy, from

*The Civil Constitution of the Clergy*

curés to bishops, should be elected. This violation of a fundamental principle of the Catholic Church could not be allowed to pass unchallenged, and when the Constituent Assembly found that opposition was raised, it drove matters to a crisis by ordering that every beneficed ecclesiastic should take an oath to observe the new Civil Constitution of the Clergy. This oath was generally refused by the bishops and dignitaries, and largely by the parochial clergy, and it was resolved by the Assembly, on 27th November 1790, that all who refused the oath within one week should be held to be dismissed from their offices. The King sanctioned this decree on 26th December 1790, and the great schism in France began. It was doubtful at first whether apostolical succession could be preserved in the new Church of France. Only four beneficed bishops, including Loménie de Brienne, Cardinal Archbishop of Sens, and Talleyrand, Bishop of Autun, out of one hundred and thirty-five, and three coadjutor bishops, or bishops *in partibus*, including Gobel, Bishop of Lydda, consented to take the oath, but by them the first of the elected bishops of departmental sees were consecrated.

The measures of the Constituent Assembly in abolishing the old provincial divisions and law courts, and substituting new and more modern arrangements for administration, were in the nature of great reforms, though marred by the mania for election; the attempt to establish a Gallican Church, though obviously opposed to the discipline of the Catholic Church, and seriously discounted by the same mania, was patriotic, if not very wise; but the arrangements for the central administration were utterly absurd. In their dislike of the system of the *ancien régime*, and their fear of a strong executive, the Constituent Assembly thought it could not do enough to hamper the authority of the throne and of the central administration. The King, under the new Constitution, was left powerless. He was to be the first functionary of the State, nothing more. His veto on the measures of the Legislature was to have effect for only six months; his guards were suppressed, and his position made untenable for a strong monarch, and unbearable for a weak one. The ministers were invested with supreme executive authority, but more regulations were made to ensure their responsibility and limit their actual power, than to define their functions. They were to be answerable to the Legislature, in which they were not allowed to sit; and their measures were to be criticised by an irresponsible representative assembly. Under such regulations the King and his ministers, that is, the executive, were put in a position of inferiority, which no vigorous man could be expected to accept, to the inevitable derangement of the whole administrative machine. In addition to the Constitution, the Constituent Assembly carried several measures of the greatest importance to a free state. All citizens, of whatever religion or class, were declared eligible for employment by the State; and on 13th April 1790 a noble decree, declaring the most absolute and entire toleration of every form of religion, was carried. The Constitution of 1791 was, on the whole, a praiseworthy effort of untried legislators to give their country a representative constitution. It was marred only by the fatal jealousy of giving due authority to the executive, and the mania for election. But it was in no way democratic. For the election to all offices was to be by at least two degrees, and no man was to have a vote unless he was an 'active citizen.' To be an active citizen, a man had to contribute to the direct taxation of the country an amount equivalent in value to three days' wages in his locality. Further, to be eligible for office, a candidate had to pay taxes of the value of a 'silver mark,' which inevitably restricted all offices to the bourgeois, or very prosperous working men.

Though the main occupation of the Constituent Assembly was the building up of the Constitution of 1791, it interfered only too much in matters of current administration. It was soon obvious that its power exceeded that of the King, and it has been observed that Van der Noot announced the new Belgian Constitution alike to the

Other acts of the Constituent Assembly.

King and the President of the Assembly, as to authorities of equal importance. The mischief produced by this constant interference was perceptible in every department of government. Mirabeau, who was a profound master of state-craft, saw through the fallacies of endeavouring to separate the legislative and executive powers in the State, and, what was implied in the preponderance of a legislature in which the ministers had no seat, to divorce authority from responsibility. He understood and approved of the English system, and as soon as the Constituent Assembly had removed to Paris in October 1789, after the establishment of the King at the Tuileries, and he had got the ear of the Court through his friend, La Marck, Mirabeau proposed the formation of a constitutional ministry, after the English fashion, from among the leading members of the Assembly. His scheme got noised abroad: the Assembly in its fear of the executive, which was afterwards consecrated in the Constitution of 1791, and stimulated by Lafayette, who dreaded the influence of a strong ministry, passed a motion on 7th November, that no member of the Assembly could take office as a minister while he remained a deputy, or for three years after his resignation.

The spirit, which lay at the root of this decree, showed itself in other ways. The fear of the influence of the Crown extended itself to the army and navy, as the natural instruments of the Crown for re-establishing its former authority. The army, already disorganised by the emigration of many of its officers, was practically destroyed in its efficiency as a fighting machine by the relaxation of discipline among the soldiers, caused not only by the actual decrees of the Assembly, but by the impunity allowed to desertion and mutiny. The Marquis de Bouillé, the general commanding at Metz, did indeed put down a military mutiny at Nancy on 31st August 1790, but his action, though applauded by the Assembly, which could not openly encourage mutiny, was isolated and not imitated. In the navy matters were even more desperate, for a larger proportion of officers deserted, resigned, or emigrated than in the army, and loss of discipline is even more disastrous in a naval than in a military force. The weakness of the army was intended to be compensated by the enrolment of national guards. But these citizen soldiers could not be treated with the strictness of regular troops. They were chiefly of the bourgeois class, and had the prejudices of that class, caring more for the protection of their property than for military efficiency. In Paris they were of the most importance, owing to their numbers, and their commander-in-chief, Lafayette, probably the most powerful man in France in 1790. The framing of the Constitution, and the disorganisation of the central authority and its instruments were the chief results of the labours of the Constituent Assembly in 1790; but among its minor acts should be noted the abolition of titles of nobility, liveries and other relics of social pre-eminence on 13th July 1790, as an evidence of its desire to extirpate even the outward signs of the *ancien régime*.

Only one man seems to have understood the dangers to which France was drifting owing to the policy of the Constituent Assembly, and that man was Mirabeau. He had done more than any man to assure the victory of the Tiers État in June 1789; he was the greatest orator and greatest statesman the revolutionary crisis had produced. Mirabeau, however, hated anarchy as much as he did despotism. He saw the absolute necessity of establishing a strong executive, if the crisis of 1789, the dissolution of the old authorities, the unpunished riots in towns, and the jacquerie in the rural districts were not to lead to anarchy. Foiled in his prudent scheme of selecting a strong ministry from the Constituent Assembly[1] by the vote of 7th November 1789, Mirabeau saw that it was impossible to overcome the distrust of the Assembly for the executive. He therefore turned to the Court, and in May 1790 he became the secret adviser of the King through the mediation of his friend La Marck. In a series of memoirs

[1] On Mirabeau's proposed Ministries, see *A History of the French Revolution*, by H. Morse Stephens, vol. i., pp. 246 and 247.

or notes for the Court of surpassing political wisdom, Mirabeau analysed the situation of affairs and proposed remedies. The two main dangers were the state of the finances and the fear of foreign intervention. Mirabeau's horror of national bankruptcy was as great as his personal extravagance in expenditure. In September 1789 he advocated Necker's scheme of a general contribution, though it was accompanied by stipulations which were certain to make it almost entirely unproductive, and he personally disapproved of it; in December 1789 he grudgingly acquiesced in the first issue of 'assignats' or promises to pay, based on the value of the property of the Church, resumed or confiscated by the Assembly, and to be extinguished as this property was sold. In August 1790 he went yet further. Comprehending that men are mainly influenced by their pecuniary interests, he advocated a wide extension of the system of assignats, down to small sums, on the grounds that they would then be able to reach the hands of the poorer classes and give them an interest in their maintaining their value, and would also frustrate the machinations of speculators, who began to make money by depreciating the exchange of specie against the new paper currency. But he also wisely proposed and successfully carried severe regulations for the extinction of assignats as the national property was realised, regulations which, unfortunately, were not strictly observed. His decree was followed in September 1790 by the retirement of Necker from office, and it is a significant proof of the change in popular opinion that the final retirement of the minister, whose dismissal in July 1789 had brought about the capture of the Bastille, was received without excitement.

The other great danger which France incurred, by the disorganising policy of the Constituent Assembly, was the possibility of the armed intervention of foreign powers. Mirabeau thought that if national bankruptcy and the interference of foreigners could be avoided, the anarchy, which was making itself felt, might soon be quelled. He did not fear civil war; indeed, he argued that it might be a positive advantage, and that as long as the King did not retract his concession of a representative constitution, a large portion of his subjects would support him in winning back the legitimate authority of the executive. But foreign war was to him an evil to be feared as much as national bankruptcy. He knew the spirit of his countrymen well, and that they would in case of national disaster submit to any despotism rather than submit to the dictation or the interference of a foreign power in their internal affairs. Success in a foreign war owing to the state of the army was not to be expected, but if it did come, it would with almost equal certainty lead to the despotism of the conquering government, whether it were the reigning monarch, his successor, or a victorious general. To avoid a foreign war it was necessary as far as possible to leave the conduct of foreign affairs in the hands of the King. This was Mirabeau's intention in the great debate on the right of declaring peace and war in May 1790, and he succeeded in getting the Assembly to sanction the initiation of peace or war as part of the duties of the King. But at this period Louis XVI. was too weak or too unwilling to understand the paramount necessity of maintaining peace. Mirabeau, therefore, got himself elected to a special Diplomatic Committee of the Constituent Assembly, and as its reporter endeavoured throughout the year 1790 to keep France clear of international complications.

Unfortunately neither Louis XVI. nor his ministers, and still less Marie Antoinette, grasped the truth of Mirabeau's memoirs for the Court. On the contrary, the one idea of the Queen was to get her brother, the Emperor Leopold, to interfere, and, if necessary, by force of arms to restore the power of the French monarch. The King, too, was startled at Mirabeau's ideas; he felt no horror at the notion of a foreign war, but would suffer anything rather than engage in a civil war. The wise advice of the great statesman went unheeded; both King and Queen regarded their connection with him as the clever muzzling of a dangerous revolutionary leader. They could not comprehend

*Mirabeau and the Court.*

his desire to establish a strong executive for the sake of France, and looked on it as a bit of personal ambition. The King was not sufficiently far-seeing, nor the Queen sufficiently patriotic to understand his views. If the Constituent Assembly distrusted the Court, the King and Queen no less strongly distrusted Mirabeau.

As reporter of the Diplomatic Committee, Mirabeau had three different problems to solve, in which the policy of the Assembly came in contact with foreign powers, the affairs of Avignon, the maintenance of the Pacte de Famille with Spain, and the interference caused by the legislation of the Assembly with the Princes of the Empire who owned fiefs of the Empire in Alsace.

The city of Avignon and the county of the Venaissin, though inhabited by Frenchmen and surrounded by French territory, were under the sovereignty of the Pope. As early as the 'orgie' of 4th August 1789 the Constituent Assembly had pronounced on the expediency of uniting both the city and the county with France. A French party was formed in Avignon; and a free municipal constitution after the model of those just established in France was framed and assented to by the Cardinal Vice-Legate in April 1790. The Pope, however, annulled his deputy's assent, with the result that fierce street fighting took place in the city, which was only stopped by the intervention of the National Guard of the neighbouring French city of Orange. The result of these events was that the city of Avignon, or at least the French party there, declared Avignon united to France on 12th June 1790. The inhabitants of the Venaissin, on the other hand, declared their attachment for the Pope, and their wish to remain subject to him. When these circumstances became known in Paris a strong party showed itself in the Assembly in favour of accepting the union of Avignon with or without the Pope's assent. Mirabeau skilfully averted the danger of a flagrant breach of international law by securing the appointment of an

Avignon Committee, and when it became necessary to send regular troops to maintain order in the city, he secured their despatch thither without the assumption of any rights of sovereignty.

Far more serious was the question which arose in May 1790, and which gave rise to the debate in the Constituent Assembly on the right of declaring peace and war, for it brought into prominence a doubt whether the Assembly should recognise the treaties made by the French monarchy. Of these treaties, the most popular in France, and the first to be brought into evidence, was the Pacte de Famille, which had been concluded in 1761 by Choiseul between France and Spain. Charles IV. had succeeded his able and accomplished father, Charles III., on 12th December 1788. The new monarch was completely under the influence of his wife, Marie Louise, a princess of Parma, who in her turn was governed by a young guardsman, her lover, Godoy. Charles IV. made a friend of Godoy, a fact which of itself shows the essential weakness of his character. He, as well as his Queen, was, outwardly at least, deeply religious, and it was pretty certain that before long a reaction would take place at the Spanish Court against the liberal *régime*, which, in the previous reign, under the administration of Aranda and Florida Blanca, Campomanes and Jovellanos, had done so much for Spain. But for the first three years of his reign, Charles IV. maintained his father's experienced ministers, with the assent of the Queen, who did not dare at once to introduce her lover into the ministry, or invest him openly with power. Florida Blanca, the Spanish minister, with Spanish pride, refused to recognise the actual weakness of Spain, and was particularly active in maintaining her supremacy in America. When, therefore, Vancouver Island was demonstrated to be an island and not a peninsula, he claimed its possession for Spain, and also alleged pre-colonisation. But he went further. Spanish officers had seized an English ship in Nootka Sound, now St. George's

*The Affair of Nootka Sound. May 1790.*

Sound, in Vancouver Island, had destroyed an English settlement there, and had even insulted an English naval captain. When Pitt demanded reparation, Florida Blanca replied haughtily, and claimed the possession of the island on the grounds stated. Pitt at once sent one of the ablest English diplomatists, Alleyne Fitzherbert, afterwards Lord St. Helens, to threaten to declare war, and prepared a great fleet, known in English naval history as the Spanish Armament.

Both Pitt and Florida Blanca knew that a war between England and Spain would only be seriously undertaken if France decided to intervene. Florida Blanca claimed the assistance of France under the terms of the Pacte de Famille, and Pitt, who understood that power had passed from Louis XVI. to the Constituent Assembly, sent two secret emissaries to Paris to see if the Assembly was inclined to maintain the policy of the *ancien régime*. One of these emissaries was Hugh Elliot, brother of Sir Gilbert Elliot, afterwards Lord Minto, an old schoolfellow of Mirabeau, who was expected to influence the orator, and the other, William Augustus Miles, who was to ally himself with the leading democratic deputies. The question came before the Constituent Assembly on a letter from the Comte de Montmorin, Minister for Foreign Affairs. The enthusiasm in the Assembly for the maintenance of the Spanish Alliance was extreme, defiance was hurled at England, Spain's faithful adherence to the Pacte de Famille in the Seven Years' War and the War of American Independence was remembered, and a fleet for active service was ordered to be got ready at Brest, and sixteen new ships of war built. But the first burst of enthusiasm soon cooled. Some deputies feared war would strengthen the monarchy, others did not like to be bound by the treaties, especially the dynastic treaties of the *ancien régime*, and others again, headed by Robespierre and Pétion, inveighed against the idea of any offensive war. The whole question was referred to the Diplomatic Committee. Mirabeau, who knew perfectly well that Spain would not fight without the aid of France, read an able report, recommending that the Pacte de Famille should be changed to a simple defensive treaty, which was adopted. The Court of Spain, seeing that no help was to be got from France under these circumstances, resigned its pretensions to Vancouver Island, and consented to pay the compensation demanded by England. This diplomatic victory of England exasperated the Spaniards; Charles IV. was surprised and disgusted at the concessions made by Louis XVI., and declared them a breach of the Pacte de Famille; and by her conduct France lost the friendship of her closest ally of the eighteenth century.

The third question in which the new state of things in France touched the diplomatic system of old Europe and threatened to cause international complications, *The Rights of which might lead to a foreign war, was concerned the Princes of the Empire in* with the fiefs of the Empire in Alsace. By the *Alsace.* Treaty of Westphalia that province had been ceded to France in full and entire sovereignty, but reserving the rights of the Empire. The complications caused by this ambiguous arrangement had raised perpetual difficulties throughout the reigns of Louis XIV. and Louis XV., and many separate treaties had been concluded with individual princes, by which they recognised the sovereignty of France in Alsace, in return for the acknowledgment of all their ancient rights. A further problem was added by the fact that the more important princely landowners in Alsace were also ruling and independent sovereigns across the French border. They were thus supreme, save for the loose over-lordship of the Emperor in Germany, and subject to the French monarchy for their domains in Alsace. Among the principal of these rulers were the three ecclesiastical electors, the Archbishops of Mayence, Trèves, and Cologne, the Bishops of Strasbourg, Spires, Worms, and Basle, the Abbot of Murbach, the Dukes of Würtemburg and of Deux-Ponts or Zweibrücken, the Elector Palatine, the Margrave of Baden, the Landgrave of Hesse-Darmstadt, and the Princes of Nassau, Leiningen, Salm-Salm, and Hohenlohe-Bartenstein. These princes were naturally profoundly affected by the abolition of feudalism decreed by the Constituent Assembly, which further complicated their position. They felt as German princes, and appealed against the measures of the Assembly as contrary to international law, and violating the Treaty of Westphalia and the many separate treaties. The protests of certain of these princes were laid before the Assembly on 11th February 1790, and referred by it to the Feudal Committee on 28th April. The reporter of the Committee on this matter was Merlin of Douai, one of the greatest French jurists and statesmen of the whole revolutionary period. On 28th October he read his report, in which he insisted on the new principle of the sovereignty of the people. He asserted that the unity of Alsace with France rested not on ancient treaties, but on the unanimous resolution of the Alsatian people to be Frenchmen But at the same time he argued that in practice old rights ought to be maintained. Mirabeau, with his usual sagacity, saw that international complications might, on this ground, be adjourned, if not altogether avoided; and it was on his motion that the Constituent Assembly resolved to uphold the sovereignty of France in Alsace, and the application of all its decrees to that province, but at the same time requested the King to arrange the amount of indemnity to be paid to the Princes of the Empire as compensation for the rights of which they were thus deprived. These princes, however, with but very few exceptions, refused absolutely to accept any monetary compensation, and appealed to the Diet of the Empire. It was on this question, therefore, that foreign intervention most seriously threatened France at the end of 1790, in spite of the diplomatic knowledge and skill of two of her leading statesmen, Mirabeau and Merlin of Douai.

While Mirabeau was doing his best to keep France from the disturbance, and even disasters, which a foreign war would cause in the midst of her new development, the Queen cast all her hopes for the restoration of the power of the French monarchy on the armed help of foreign states. Louis XVI. in

## The Position of Leopold

a half-hearted fashion was opposed to foreign interference, but his younger brother, the Comte d'Artois, and the French *émigrés*, who had established themselves on the borders of France, declared that the King was not in his right senses, and that he was forced to yield to the measures of the Constituent Assembly against his will. They felt no patriotic misgivings, and loudly invoked the assistance of all monarchs in the cause of monarchy and the feudal system. The ruler on whom the Queen chiefly relied, and to whom she appealed most fervently, the monarch to whom the *émigrés* looked with most confidence, was Leopold, the brother and successor of Joseph II. He held the key of the position; he was the sovereign especially feared by the leaders of the Constituent Assembly, and as Emperor and as brother of Marie Antoinette he was expected by the royalists to intervene in the affairs of France.

# CHAPTER III

## 1790-1792

The Emperor Leopold—His Internal Policy—The Policy of Prussia—Leopold's Foreign Policy—Conference of Reichenbach—Leopold and the Turks—Treaty of Sistova—Leopold crowned Emperor—Leopold and Hungary—State of Parties in Belgium—Their Internal Dissensions—Congress at the Hague—Leopold reconquers Belgium—War between Russia and Sweden—Treaty of Verela—War between Russia and the Turks—Capture of Ismail—Treaty of Jassy—Position of Leopold—The State of France—Mirabeau's advice—Death of Mirabeau—The Flight to Varennes—Its Results: in France—The Massacre of 17th July 1791—Revision of the Constitution—Its Results: in Europe—Manifesto of Padua—Declaration of Pilnitz—Completion of the French Constitution of 1791—The Polish Constitution of 1791—The Legislative Assembly in France—The Girondins—Approach of War between France and Austria—Causes of the War—Attitude of Europe—Death of the Emperor Leopold—Murder of Gustavus III. of Sweden—Policy of Dumouriez—War declared by France against Austria—Invasion of the Tuileries, 20th June 1792—Francis II. crowned Emperor—Invasion of France by Prussia and Austria—Insurrection of 10th August 1792—Suspension of Louis XVI.—Desertion of Lafayette—The Massacres of September in the prisons—Battle of Valmy—Meeting of the National Convention—The Girondins and the Mountain—Conquest of Savoy, Nice, and Mayence—Battle of Jemmappes—Conquest of Belgium—Execution of Louis XVI.—War declared against Spain, Holland, England and the Empire—Catherine invades Poland—Overthrow of the Polish Constitution—Second Partition of Poland—Contrast between the resistance of France and Poland.

THE successor of Joseph II., the Emperor Leopold, was, except perhaps Catherine of Russia, the ablest monarch of his time. He had had a long experience in the art of government, for he had succeeded to the sovereignty of the Grand Duchy of Tuscany in 1765, on the death of his father, the Emperor Francis of Lorraine. While his brother Joseph

*The Emperor Leopold.*

was kept until 1780 by Maria Theresa in leading-strings as far as the actual administration of the Hapsburg dominions was concerned, and was only able to exert his authority as Emperor, Leopold had from his boyhood been an absolute and irresponsible sovereign, and had imbibed from his education an Italian knowledge of statecraft. During his long reign in Tuscany he showed the finest qualities of a benevolent despot in his measures for increasing the material comforts of his people, combined with tact and diplomatic subtlety. His reforms were as sweeping as those of Joseph, but were so managed as not to set his dominions in a flame. With the help of Scipio de Ricci, Bishop of Pistoia, he freed the people of Tuscany from the heavy burden of an excessive number of ecclesiastics; he reorganised the internal administration, and especially the judicial system; and he showed such intelligence in grasping and partially applying the new principles of political economy as to be called 'the physiocratic prince.' He had been Grand Duke of Tuscany for twenty-five years, and when he succeeded his elder brother Joseph as King of Hungary and Bohemia in February 1790, he had earned the reputation of a singularly wise and prudent statesman, and of one who, if it could be done, might be expected to restore the power of the House of Austria. He abandoned the Grand Duchy of Tuscany to his second son Ferdinand, and at once applied himself to the difficult task bequeathed to him by Joseph II.

Leopold found the power of Austria seriously affected by dangers from within and dangers from without. He at once undid much of Joseph's work. He recognised the difference between consolidating and unifying a nation, which was essentially one, and a congeries of nations speaking different languages, belonging to different races, and geographically widely separated. In Tuscany he had accomplished a great work in abolishing the local franchises of the cities and building up a Tuscan state, but he understood that such a work was impossible in the divided hereditary dominions

*Policy of Leopold.*

of the House of Hapsburg, and that the Emperor Joseph had been attempting a hopeless task. Leopold's first step was, therefore, to restore the former state of things in such parts of his dominions as were not in open insurrection. In Austria proper, in Bohemia, in the Milanese, and in the Tyrol, the concessions of Leopold were received with demonstrations of popular gratitude. He abolished the new system of taxation and the unpopular seminaries; he recognised the separate administrations of provinces which were essentially diverse; he gave up futile attempts at unification. But, at the same time, he maintained the edict of religious toleration, the most noble of Joseph's reforms, and introduced many slight but appreciable improvements in the local institutions which he restored. Having thus assured the fidelity of an important body of his subjects, he prepared to deal with the declared rebels in Belgium and the unconcealed opposition in Hungary. It was here that Leopold suffered most from the foreign policy of Maria Theresa and Joseph, for it was indisputable that the prevalent discontent and insurrection in Belgium and Hungary was fostered by the Triple Alliance, and especially by Prussia. He had a serious war with the Turks on his hands; his ally, Catherine of Russia, was too much occupied with her wars with the Swedes and Turks and with the affairs of Poland, to come to his help; France, excited by her internal dissensions, and with the Assembly indisposed to the maintenance of the Treaty of 1756, might almost be reckoned an enemy; the Empire had been roused to distrust by the policy of Joseph, and the Triple Alliance was openly hostile. Under these circumstances Prussia appeared at once the chief power on the Continent and the principal enemy of Austria, and it was with Prussia that Leopold first resolved to deal.

The events of the year 1789 had greatly improved the position of Prussia on the Continent. The pretensions of Joseph to Bavaria had made Frederick William II., as it had made Frederick the Great, the real leader of the Princes of the Empire, and the Triple Alliance had done more to improve and strengthen his position in Europe. The classic policy of Prussia was consistent opposition to Austria, and Hertzberg, the Prussian minister, in pursuance of this policy, had made use of all Joseph's mistakes to lower the power of the House of Hapsburg. He felt it necessary, indeed, to disavow a treaty with the Turks, which the too zealous Prussian envoy had signed in January 1790, but he was eager to make use of the difficulties of Russia and Austria caused by the Turkish war to forward Prussia's designs on Poland. His main aim was to obtain the cession of the important Polish cities of Thorn and Dantzic, which would give Prussia complete control of the great river Vistula. The ablest Prussian diplomatist, Lucchesini, was sent to Warsaw, and on 29th March 1790 he signed a treaty of friendship and union with the Poles, by which Poland was to cede Thorn and Dantzic to Prussia in return for the retrocession of part of Austrian Galicia, which had fallen to Austria at the first partition, while Prussia promised to guarantee the territory and constitution of Poland, and to send an army of 18,000 men to the help of the Poles if they were attacked.

*The Policy of Prussia.*

This treaty, shameless even in its epoch for its desertion of allies, breach of former engagements and absence of good faith, was highly approved by Frederick William II. and Hertzberg. They would not have dared to conclude it but for the seeming weakness of Russia and Austria, the partners in the former partition. Russia was hampered by the Swedish and Turkish wars, and the discontent of the ceded provinces of Poland. Austria was in a still more desperate condition. With the Turkish war still unconcluded, with open insurrection in Belgium, and disaffection in Hungary, unpopular in the Empire, and deprived of the alliance of France by the unconcealed dislike of the Assembly to the Treaty of 1756, it seemed as if the House of Hapsburg must now give way entirely to the House of Hohenzollern. Of the active encouragement given to the Turks, the Belgians, the Hungarians, and the Princes of the Empire against Austria by Prussia, mention has been made.

Not less skilful was the conduct of the Prussian ambassador at Paris, Goltz, who intrigued with the more extreme leaders in the Assembly, and especially Pétion,[1] against Austria, and in particular did all in his power to increase the growing unpopularity of Marie Antoinette and to insist that she was a traitor to France.

Had a less able statesman than Leopold been the successor of Joseph, the schemes of Prussia might have been crowned with success. But he had not ruled in the native city of Machiavelli for a quarter of a century for nothing; and he set to work to checkmate the designs of Hertzberg and Frederick William II. His wise measures of conciliation speedily rallied the heart of the hereditary dominions to him; and he determined to use diplomacy to establish his position in Europe before he dealt with Belgium and Hungary. He quickly perceived that Prussia's real strength lay in the support of the Triple Alliance; her financial situation was such that she dared not undertake a serious war without the active countenance of England and Holland. He knew that it was worse than hopeless to rely upon France, and therefore at once applied to England. He protested that he did not share his brother's attachment for Russia, or his schemes for the division of the Ottoman provinces; and he further hinted that he would abandon all attempt to reconquer Belgium and surrender it to France unless he received some assistance. Pitt felt the weight of these considerations; he did not care much about what happened to Poland, but he cared a great deal that the French should not occupy Belgium. When, therefore, the King of Prussia mobilised a powerful army in Silesia, and demanded through Hertzberg that Austria should on the one hand make an armistice with the Turks, and on the other restore Galicia to Poland, Leopold, trusting that he had broken the harmony of the Triple Alliance, made no elaborate warlike preparations, but demanded a conference.

*The Policy of Leopold.*

[1] Sorel, *L'Europe et la Révolution Française*, vol. ii. p. 69.

The King of Hungary and Bohemia thoroughly understood the character of the Prussian king and the intrigues of his courtiers and ministers; he knew that Hertzberg was the real enemy of Austria, and that Frederick William was unstable and easily persuaded. He felt that his own strength lay in diplomacy, not war. On 26th June the two Austrian envoys, Reuss and Spielmann, arrived at the headquarters of the Prussian army in Silesia at Reichenbach, and demanded a conference. Rather to the disgust of the Prussians, their allies of the Triple Alliance insisted on being present, and a regular congress was held, at which Hertzberg and Lucchesini represented Prussia, Reuss and Spielmann, Austria, Ewart, England, Reden, Holland, and Jablonowski, the Poles. Even the Hungarian malcontents and the Belgian rebels, relying on the promises of Frederick William, ventured to send envoys. The conclusions of the congress justified Leopold's diplomatic skill. When Hertzberg laid the Prussian demands in full before the assembled envoys, to his surprise Jablonowski declared that the Poles would never cede Thorn and Dantzic, while the representatives of England and Holland not only advocated the maintenance of the *status quo*, but refused the co-operation of their governments in Prussia's schemes for aggrandisement. The policy of Hertzberg and Kaunitz, of perpetuating the rivalry of Prussia and Austria, had failed. Leopold was far too acute to leave these matters to ministers. He placed himself in direct communication with the King of Prussia and his personal favourites, Lucchesini and Bischofswerder; he argued that the interests of the two great German states both with regard to Poland and France were identical, and on 27th July 1790 the Convention of Reichenbach was signed, by which Austria promised at once to make an armistice with the Turks, and eventually to conclude peace with them under the mediation of the Triple Alliance, while, on the other hand, the powers of the Triple Alliance guaranteed the restoration of the Austrian authority in Belgium. It was more privately arranged that Prussia should withdraw from encouraging discontent in Hungary and Belgium, and support Leopold's candidature for the Imperial throne. This great diplomatic victory did more than merely check the active enmity of Prussia; it established the ascendency of Leopold over the weak mind of Frederick William; and it eventually, in May 1791, brought about, not indeed his actual dismissal from office, but the removal of Hertzberg, the sworn foe of Austria, from the charge of the foreign policy of Prussia.

The first actual consequence of the Convention of Reichenbach was the conclusion of an armistice between Austria and the Turks. The war had never been looked on with favour by Leopold, who regarded Joseph's infatuation for the grandiose schemes of Catherine of Russia as absurd, and the dismemberment of Turkey as impracticable, and at the present time undesirable. He had not attempted to press matters against the Turks, and had withdrawn many of his best troops under Loudon from the seat of war to Bohemia to strengthen his position at Reichenbach. The Prince of Coburg, who succeeded Loudon, aided by an earthquake, took Orsova, and laid siege to Giurgevo, but he was defeated in his camp after a severe battle on 8th July 1790. This defeat was only partially compensated by a victory won by Clerfayt, and by the capture of Zettin by General de Vins on 20th July. Under these circumstances Leopold was not sorry to conclude an armistice for nine months at Giurgevo on 19th September. Shortly afterwards a congress of plenipotentiaries from Austria, Turkey, and the mediating powers met, as had been arranged at Reichenbach, at Sistova. The negotiations lasted for many months; Leopold insisted on the cession by Turkey of Old Orsova and a district in Croatia, which would make the Danube and the Unna the boundary between Austria and Turkey; Prussia at first strongly protested against any cession to Austria; the congress even for a time

*Leopold and the Turks.*

*The Treaty of Sistova. 4th Aug. 1791.*

broke up; and it was not until Leopold adroitly got Lucchesini, the Prussian envoy, on his side, that the important Treaty of Sistova upon the terms desired by Leopold was concluded on 4th August 1791.

By this treaty the hereditary dominions of the House of Hapsburg were relieved from the danger of foreign war; the next result which Leopold drew from the Convention of Reichenbach was the re-establishment of the Austrian ascendency in Germany. Assured of the support of Prussia, Leopold travelled to the Rhine. On 30th September 1790 he was unanimously elected King of the Romans; on 4th October he solemnly entered Frankfort, and on 9th October he was crowned Emperor. But it was not enough for him to be crowned Emperor; he had to destroy the bad effect of his brother Joseph's attitude towards the Empire; he had to become the real as well as the nominal head and leader of the German princes, and to win back the advantages which Prussia had secured by forming the League of Princes. The opportunity was afforded to him by the disinclination of the German princes, who owned territories in Alsace, Lorraine, and Franche Comté, to accept the compensation offered to them by the French Constituent Assembly. Their protests took the shape of a clause in the 'capitulation' laid before him and accepted by him on his election as Emperor by which he promised to intervene on behalf of the Empire for the preservation of the rights, sanctioned by the Treaty of Westphalia, of the princes, whose interests were affected. Leopold thus seized this opportunity to pose as the head of the German Empire, and on 14th December 1790 he wrote a very strong letter to Louis XVI., in which he said: 'The territories in question have not been transferred to the kingdom of France; they are subject to the supremacy of the Emperor and the Empire: no member of the Empire has the right to transfer that supremacy to a foreign nation. It follows, therefore, that the decrees of the Assembly are null and void so far as concerns the Empire and its members,

*Leopold crowned Emperor. 9th Oct. 1790.*

and that everything ought to be replaced on the ancient footing.'[1]

Leopold and Hungary.
After being crowned Emperor at Frankfort, Leopold returned to Vienna and proceeded to establish his power firmly in Hungary. The discontent aroused in the most backward part of his dominions by the Emperor Joseph's measures had not been appeased by that monarch's wholesale retractation, nor even by the return of the Crown of St. Stephen. The Hungarian nobles regarded Joseph's retractation as a sign of weakness, and, encouraged by the intrigues of Prussia and the difficulties in which Leopold was involved by the war with the Turks, resolved to obtain more sweeping concessions. The example of France exerted an influence even in Hungary, and the following sentences from a memorial,[2] presented to Leopold by the people of Pesth, might have been written by a Parisian popular society: 'From the rights of nations and of man, and from that social compact whence States arose, it is incontestable that sovereignty originates from the people. This axiom our parent Nature has impressed on the hearts of all; it is one of those which a just prince (and such we trust Your Majesty will ever be) cannot dispute; it is one of those inalienable, imprescriptible rights which the people cannot forfeit by neglect or disuse. Our constitution places the sovereignty jointly in the king and people, in such a manner that the remedies necessary to be applied according to the ends of social life for the security of persons and property, are in the power of the people. We are sure, therefore, that at the meeting of the ensuing Diet, Your Majesty will not confine yourself to the objects mentioned in your rescript; but will also restore our freedom to us, in like manner as to the Belgians, who have conquered theirs with the sword. It would be an example big with danger to teach the world that a people can only protect or regain their liberties by the sword, and not by

[1] Sorel, *L'Europe et la Révolution Française*, vol. ii. p. 194, footnote.
[2] Coxe's *Hist. of House of Austria*, ed. 1847, vol. iii. p. 552, footnote.

obedience.' The Hungarian Diet, which Leopold had summoned for the ceremony of his coronation, and to which the people of Pesth alluded in this remarkable address, was largely attended. The Hungarian nobility regarded its convocation as a further sign of weakness, for none had been held since the accession of Maria Theresa, and prepared an inaugural act or compact, which would have reduced the kings of Hungary to a similar position to that occupied by the kings of Poland. Full of confidence in themselves they even went so far as to send envoys, as has been mentioned, to the Congress of Reichenbach. Leopold, however, had no intention of yielding to these demands; his only desire was to gain time until he had secured his position by diplomacy. Meanwhile he tried to stir up opposition in Hungary itself, by encouraging the other nationalities in the kingdom, such as the inhabitants of Croatia and the Banat. But when the Congress of Reichenbach was over, the armistice of Giurgevo concluded, and his coronation as Emperor performed, Leopold proceeded to deal with the Hungarians. He first ordered the army of 60,000 men, which he had concentrated in Bohemia to support his attitude against the Prussians, to Pesth, and then directed the Diet to remove to Presburg for his coronation as King of Hungary. He then declared that nothing would induce him to accept the proposed new constitution, or to consent to an infringement of the Edict of Toleration, and that he would only consent to the terms of the inaugural acts of his grandfather, Charles VI., and his mother, Maria Theresa. The Hungarian nobles, overcome by his firmness and the presence of his troops, yielded; the Emperor appointed his fourth son, the Archduke Leopold, to be Palatine of Hungary in the place of the late Prince Esterhazy; and it was from him that he received the Crown of St. Stephen on 15th November, on the terms he had stipulated. *(Leopold crowned King of Hungary. 15th Nov. 1790.)*

Having gained this victory by his firmness, Leopold proceeded to win popularity by a timely concession, and proposed a law, obliging every future king to be crowned within six months of his accession. This concession was received with the wildest enthusiasm, as it obviated the possibility of conduct resembling that of Joseph II. ; the Diet granted the Emperor a gift of 225,000 florins instead of the usual 100,000 florins; and the disaffected attitude of the nobility was changed for one of hearty admiration and gratitude. The bourgeois of Pesth and their declarations were disavowed; the echo of the French Revolution, which had been heard there, was quickly stifled; and the Hungarian nobility, well contented with Leopold, declined to encourage the popular aspirations.

The difficulties which the Emperor Leopold encountered in Hungary were trifling to those which faced him in Belgium. But in this quarter time had worked for the House of Hapsburg, and when the Congress of Plenipotentiaries, arranged at the Congress of Reichenbach, met at the Hague in October 1790, the situation had entirely changed. The victory of the Belgian rebels in 1789 had been followed by internal dissen-

Parties in Belgium.

sions, which appeared directly the new Constitution was proclaimed. The first difference was between the Van der Nootists, or Statists, as they termed themselves, and the Vonckists. The latter, inspired by the success of the French Revolution, advocated a thoroughly democratic constitution, and the organisation of a new elective system of local administration, to the great disgust of the Statists, who desired simply the restoration of the old order of things, but with the central government controlled by elected assembly instead of being in the hands of the House of Hapsburg. Curiously enough popular feeling ran in a direction very different from that followed in France. Influenced by the priests, the Belgian people, and more especially the mob of Brussels, were convinced that the Vonckists were atheists; the democrats were attacked in the streets, maltreated and imprisoned; the bourgeois National Guards refused to protect them; they were proscribed by Van der Noot and the party in power; and after many riots and disturbances Vonck fled to France in April 1790. These events greatly weakened the Belgian Republic, for the democratic party, which had been energetic in the revolution, numbered in its ranks many of the ablest and most enlightened men in the country. But even more serious was the result abroad, for the National Assembly of France and Lafayette were surprised and disgusted at the persecution of the democrats, and the sympathy of the French people was entirely alienated from the Belgian leaders. Still more striking in its effect was the conduct of the Van der Nootists towards the gallant officer, Van der Mersch, who had commanded the patriot troops in the invasion of October 1789. Not satisfied with superseding him by the Prussian general, Schönfeld, the Van der Nootists had him arrested on a charge of disorganising the Belgian army and imprisoned at Antwerp, to the great wrath of the people of Flanders, of which province Van der Mersch was a native. The conquering party was further divided. The nobility and clergy, headed by the Duc d'Aremberg, were jealous of the ascendency assumed by Van der Noot, and of the continued omnipotence of the Assembly at Brussels. Under these circumstances it was a significant fact that the Austrian troops in Luxembourg under the command of Marshal Bender were able with the help of the people themselves to occupy the province of Limburg.

In October 1790 the Congress, which had been resolved on at Reichenbach, met at the Hague. The Austrian plenipotentiary was the Comte de Mercy-Argenteau, the most accomplished Austrian diplomatist and ambassador at Paris, and the representatives of England, Prussia, and Holland were Lord Auckland, Count Keller, and the Grand Pensionary Van der Spiegel. Leopold now reaped the advantages of his skilful diplomacy at Reichenbach. England and Holland understood that the new Emperor was a very different man from his predecessor, and Prussia dared not act without them. As he had promised, Leopold solemnly announced his intention to restore all

*Congress at the Hague. Oct. 1790.*

the charters, laws, and arrangements, which had existed in Belgium in the time of his mother, Maria Theresa, under the guarantee of the three powers, and further promised a general amnesty if his authority was recognised by 21st November. The Belgian States-General made no reply to Leopold, and the Emperor proceeded to concentrate 45,000 men under Bender in Luxembourg. Then the Belgian leaders applied to the Congress at the Hague for a prolongation of the armistice and the restoration of the state of government existing in the time of Charles VI. and not in that of Maria Theresa. These demands were supported by the representatives of the Triple Alliance, but rejected by the Austrian ambassador. On 21st November the Belgian States-General elected the Archduke Charles, the third son of the Emperor, to be hereditary Grand Duke, but the time had gone by for com-

*Leopold reconquers Belgium.* promises, and on the following day Bender entered Belgium. The experiences of a year of revolution made the Belgian people not unwilling to return under the sway of Austria; the cities surrendered without a blow, and on 2d December 1790 Brussels capitulated. Van der Noot fled with his chief friends, and Belgium was won back by Leopold as easily as it had been lost by Joseph. On 8th December the Comte de Mercy-Argenteau assented to the restoration of the liberties recognised in the inaugural act of Charles VI., but Leopold disavowed his ambassador and insisted on the authority possessed by Maria Theresa at the close of her reign. Under these circumstances the mediating powers refused their guarantee, a refusal which rather gratified the Emperor than otherwise, as it freed him from the fear of foreign interference. Not only in Belgium itself, but in the neighbouring bishopric of Liége also, Leopold established Austrian ascendency. The princes of the Circle of the Empire, which adjoined, were dissatisfied with the conduct of *The Austrians* Prussia and General Schlieffen, and appealed to *at Liege.* the Emperor. He was only too glad to assert his authority; Schlieffen evacuated the territory; and on 13th

January 1791 it was occupied by an Austrian force, which re-established the Prince-bishop in all his former authority.

The entire reversal of Joseph's policy by Leopold, the arrangements made at Reichenbach, and the friendly attitude of the new Emperor towards the powers forming the Triple Alliance, deprived Russia of her only ally at a time when the Empress had on her hands two exhausting wars with Sweden and Turkey. *Russia and Sweden.* The former was the most serious. Gustavus III., freed from the dangers of a Danish invasion, and by his *coup d'état* from the formidable plots of his nobility, rejoined his army in Finland and prepared to carry on the war vigorously by land and sea. His army was too small to effect much in spite of his near approach to St. Petersburg, and his chief confidence was in his fleet. This fleet was soon blockaded in the Gulf of Vyborg by the Russian admiral, the Prince of Nassau-Siegen, one of the most famous soldiers of fortune of the century; an attempt it made to break out on 24th June 1790 was repulsed, and the Russians even hoped to force it to capitulate. But, to their surprise, the Swedes broke the blockade on the 3d July, though with a loss of 5000 men, and on 9th July won a great naval victory in Svenska Sound,' in which the Russians lost 30 ships, 600 guns and 6000 men. But this victory led to no corresponding diplomatic result. Catherine, defeated though she was, made overtures in no humiliated spirit to the King of Sweden, and proposed to him that, instead of quarrelling with his neighbours, he should turn his attention to the state of affairs in France. The chivalrous and romantic king was not unwilling to listen to her suggestions; he had, during a visit to Paris, been much impressed by Marie Antoinette, and was full of pity at the situation of the royal family of France and of disgust at the progress of the Revolution. He felt, too, that the war with Russia was not popular among his people, and on 14th August 1790 he signed a treaty of peace at Verela, by which the *status quo ante bellum* between Russia and Sweden was restored without *Treaty of Verela. Aug. 14th 1790.*

any compensation in money or territory being obtained by the victorious Swedes.

While resisting the Swedes, Catherine made her chief effort against the Turks. In this quarter the defection of Leopold and the Armistice of Giurgevo seriously compromised her position. The war had resolved itself into the siege of the strong city of Ismail, where the Turks defended themselves with the utmost tenacity. The Russian attacks were foiled again and again, and Potemkin resigned the conduct of the siege in despair. His place was taken by Suvórov, whose brilliant victory on the Rymnik in 1789 had marked him as the greatest Russian general of his time. His valour and constancy equalled those qualities in the Turks; and Ismail was stormed on 20th December 1790, after a scene of carnage which cost the lives of 10,000 Russians and 30,000 Turks. In the following year the Russians pressed onwards towards Constantinople, and on 9th July 1791 the Russian General Repnin, under whom served Suvórov and Kutuzov, defeated the Grand Vizier at Matchin. But the Empress Catherine was not inclined to follow up these military advantages. The policy of Leopold had isolated her; the Treaty of Sistova had deprived her of an auxiliary army against the Turks; the state of affairs in Poland demanded her most serious attention; and she had to observe the action of Europe on the French Revolution and of the French Revolution on Europe, in the hope of deriving some advantage for Russia from the complications. She, therefore, signed a treaty of peace with the Turks at Jassy on 9th January 1792, by which Russia retained only Oczakoff and the coast line between the mouths of the Bug and the Dniester. By making this peace, Catherine only deferred the prosecution of the schemes of Russia against the Ottoman Empire, and certain clauses with regard to the Danubian Principalities, affording a pretext for future wars, were skilfully included in the Treaty of Jassy.

The success of the policy of the Emperor Leopold entirely altered the situation of the European states and their attitude towards each other. He was in 1791 not only master in his own dominions, but the recognised representative of the Empire, in fact as well as in name. He had broken down the combination against Austria and the solidarity of the Triple Alliance. England was far more favourably inclined to him than she had ever been to Joseph II.; Frederick William II. of Prussia was his ally not his enemy. He was, therefore, able in 1791 to turn his thoughts to the situation of France, and to see what advantages could be drawn from the position of affairs there for the benefit of Austria. The political effacement of France in foreign affairs was due to the assumption of all real authority by the Constituent Assembly, while leaving the responsibility to the King's ministers, and Leopold did not doubt that the result of an entire victory of the popular party would be a recurrence to the classical policy of opposition to Austria and the rupture of the Treaty of 1756. It was to his interest to prevent this, and he had therefore political, as well as personal, ends to secure in endeavouring to restore the authority of the King of France. The capture of the Bastille and the transference of the royal family to Paris were great events in the history of France, but they only affected Leopold as weakening the authority of Louis XVI. and Marie Antoinette, the faithful allies of Austria. The behaviour of the Constituent Assembly gave him pretexts for interfering in France, in spite of the diplomatic ability of Mirabeau, and he was earnestly besought by the French *émigrés*, or opponents of the new state of things in France, who had gone into voluntary exile with the King's younger brother, the Comte d'Artois, at their head, to intervene on behalf of the French monarchy.

The conduct of the Constituent Assembly in disorganising every branch of the executive in France had its natural effect by the commencement of 1791. The army, in spite of the effort of General Bouillé to restore discipline by making an example of some Swiss mutineers at Nancy in 1790, was rendered inefficient by the disaffection of the soldiers and the exaggerated royalism of most of the officers; the navy was in a still worse condition; the Civil Constitution of the Clergy had caused a schism, which disturbed the minds of men in all parts of France, and created an army of opponents to the work of the Assembly, who had peculiar influence over the rural communities; the issue of assignats on the security of the confiscated domains of the Church had in-flated the currency, and, while giving an appearance of fictitious prosperity, had really given a feeling of insecurity to all trade and commerce; the old internal administrations of the provinces had been replaced by the new administrations of the departments, which were filled by inexperienced men, utterly unable to cope with the difficulties of a time of unrest and revolution. The practical disorganisation of the executive was meanwhile being consecrated by the measures of the Constituent Assembly, which, in the Constitution it was drawing up, in its fear of the power of the monarchy, so hampered the authority of the executive as to destroy the necessary foundations of good government.

*The state of France, 1791.*

In its ardour for the Rights of Man and the principle of election, the Constituent Assembly forgot the need for enforcing the authority of the law, and the necessity for providing a strong arm to carry it into effect. Mirabeau had clearly perceived that France was drifting into a state of anarchy. In his secret notes for the Court he insisted on the importance of restoring its proper power to the executive, and he advised the King to leave Paris and call the partisans of order to his side. Civil war, he contended, was preferable to anarchy, cloaked by fine words; it would openly divide France into the adherents of order and of disorder, and result in the maintenance of the popular rights sanctioned by the royal power. The King was to acknowledge the right of the people to legislate, and tax themselves through their representatives, but was to point out the importance of maintaining a strong government to secure the happiness of the governed. Against foreign war, however, Mirabeau strongly protested; foreign interference would rouse the spirit of national patriotism, and if the King was suspected of favouring the foreigners, it would result in the overthrow of the monarchy, and in a long struggle before the country could agree on a new form of government. However, on 2d April 1791, Mirabeau died, and France was deprived of its most sagacious, if not its only, statesman. In truth, Louis XVI. and Marie Antoinette had no wish to take Mirabeau's advice; the King regarded civil war as a horrible calamity, and to be shunned in every way and at any sacrifice; the Queen longed for the interference of her brother, the Emperor, and begged him to intervene to restore the royal authority. The King's religious convictions were wounded by the Civil Constitution of the Clergy; the Queen was roused to wrath by the feeling that she was a prisoner, by daily insults in the press, and by the degradation of the power of the monarchy. On 18th April 1791 the royal prisoners were prevented by the Parisians from going to Saint-Cloud for Easter, and on 18th May the Emperor Leopold issued a circular to all crowned heads calling attention to the position of the King of France in his capital. On 20th May he had an interview with the Comte de Durfort, a secret emissary from the Tuileries, at Mantua, and charged him to tell the King and Queen of France that 'he was going to concern himself with their affairs, not in words, but in acts.'

*Death of Mirabeau.*

The action of the Parisian mob on 18th April caused Louis XVI. and Marie Antoinette to resolve to escape secretly from Paris, since they were obviously prisoners and could not leave openly. They determined, contrary to the advice so often given by Mirabeau, and contrary also to the wishes of the Emperor and of his able representative at the Hague, the Comte de Mercy-Argenteau, who knew France better than any living diplomatist, to fly towards the frontier. Leopold, under the pretext of supporting his authority in Belgium and Luxembourg, and that

*The Flight to Varennes. 21st June 1791.*

of his allies, the Elector-Archbishop of Trèves and the Bishop of Liége, massed his troops upon the frontier in readiness to succour or assist, and Bouillé, who commanded at Metz, made preparations to have the part of his forces on which he could rely ready to receive the fugitive monarch. On 20th June 1791 the royal family left Paris by night, after the King had drawn up a declaration protesting against the whole of the measures of the Constituent Assembly, and disavowing them. The flight, from a combination of circumstances, ended in the royal family being stopped at Varennes, and being brought back to Paris in custody. It had the most momentous results upon the history of the French Revolution, which are sometimes disregarded in the recollection of the romantic circumstances attending it.

The primary result of the flight to Varennes was the sudden comprehension by France that Louis XVI. was an unwilling collaborator in the work of reconstituting the French government on a new basis. Hitherto the people, and even the leaders of the Constituent Assembly, had believed in his acquiescence, if not in his hearty assistance. But the declaration, left behind on the occasion of his flight, proved the contrary. The statesmen of the Constituent Assembly, including the makers of the new Constitution, such as Le Chapelier and Thouret, and the triumvirate of Duport, Barnave, and Lameth, who, after Mirabeau's death, were the undisputed leaders of the majority, saw they had gone too far, and that in their desire to weaken the royal authority, they had seriously weakened the executive, and had made the King's position intolerable. They therefore threw the blame of the flight to Varennes on the subordinates in the scheme, ignored the King's declaration, and acted on the supposition that he was misled by bad advisers. This attitude not being wholly approved by the Jacobin Club, which, through its affiliated clubs in the provinces, exercised the most powerful sway in the formation of public opinion, the believers in the royal authority seceded and formed the

*Results of the Flight to Varennes.*

Constitutional Club, or Club of 1789, which temporarily weakened the power of the Jacobins in Paris. But this secession was entirely sanctioned by the bourgeois classes both in Paris and throughout France, who had the strongest interest in the maintenance of order, and who sent in numerous declarations of their adhesion to the cause of monarchy. Moreover, their chief representatives in arms, the National Guard of Paris, under the command of Lafayette, had soon an opportunity of giving practical proof of this loyal disposition. The Cordeliers Club, which was chiefly influenced by Danton, a lawyer of Paris, who had Mirabeau's gift of seeing things as they really were, felt it impossible to hush things up. They understood the King's declaration to mean a declaration of war against the new Constitution; his flight to Varennes they rightly interpreted to show that he was trusting to the intervention of foreign powers to re-establish him in his former position; and they resolved to draw up a petition for his dethronement. This petition was largely the work of Danton and of Brissot, a pamphleteer and journalist, who had been imprisoned in the Bastille, and had imbibed republican notions in America, and a large crowd assembled to sign it on the Champ de Mars. Lafayette determined to disperse this crowd, and the National Guard, under his command, fired on the people, killing several persons. This vigorous measure, which was intended to show the power of the party of order, was followed by vigorous steps against the party for dethronement.

*The Massacre of 17th July in Paris.*

The leaders of the Cordeliers were proscribed. Danton and Marat fled to England, and the party of order seemed triumphant. A revision of the Constitution was undertaken, and various reactionary clauses, specially directed against the press, the popular clubs or societies, and the rights of assembly and of petition, were inserted. But this new attitude of the Constituent Assembly had but a slight effect upon France, for the king's flight had caused the people in general to believe that he was the enemy of their new-born

*Revision of the Constitution.*

liberties, and a traitor in league with foreign powers to overthrow them.

The flight to Varennes proved to the people of France, as well as to the monarchs and statesmen of Europe, that Louis XVI. was a prisoner in Paris, and an enemy to the new settlement of the government, as laid down by the Constitution in course of preparation. The Emperor Leopold, as brother of Marie Antoinette, as Holy Roman Emperor and supporter of dynastic legitimacy, as the leading monarch of Europe, decided to intervene. On 6th July 1791 he issued the Manifesto of Padua, in which he invited the sovereigns of Europe to join him in declaring the cause of the King of France to be their own, in exacting that he should be freed from all popular restraint, and in refusing to recognise any constitutional laws as legitimately established in France, except such as might be sanctioned by the King acting in perfect freedom. The English Government paid little or no attention to these requests of Leopold, but the Empress Catherine, and the Kings of Prussia, Spain, and Sweden, for different reasons and in different degrees, heartily accepted Leopold's views, and armed intervention to carry them into effect was suggested. But Leopold had no desire for war. His policy since his accession had been distinctly in favour of peace. He was a diplomatist, not a soldier, and he desired to frighten France by threats, rather than to fight France for the liberty of Louis XVI. and his family.

*Effects of the Flight to Varennes.*

*Manifesto of Padua. 6th July 1791.*

The sequel to the Manifesto of Padua was a conference at Pilnitz between the Emperor Leopold and King Frederick William II. of Prussia, accompanied by their ministers, in August 1791. At this conference the King's brothers, Monsieur, the Comte de Provence, afterwards Louis XVIII., who had escaped from France at the time of the flight to Varennes, and the Comte d'Artois, afterwards Charles X., who had fled in July 1789, at the epoch of the capture of the Bastille, were present. They had their

*Declaration of Pilnitz, 27th Aug. 1791.*

own aims to serve. They were disgusted at the weak conduct, as they termed it, of Louis XVI. in yielding so far as he had done to the popular wishes; they desired to undo the whole effect of the Revolution and to restore the Bourbon monarchy in its ancient authority by the arms of the monarchs of Europe. But Leopold did not care about the French princes or the Bourbon monarchy. He cared rather for the safety of his sister, Marie Antoinette, and the maintenance through her of the Franco-Austrian alliance. In the Declaration of Pilnitz, which was signed by the Emperor and the King of Prussia on 27th August 1791, the two sovereigns declared that the situation of the King of France was an object of interest common to all European monarchs, and that they hoped other monarchs would use with them the most efficacious means to put the King of France in a position to lay in perfect liberty the bases of a monarchical government, suited alike to the rights of sovereigns and the happiness of the French nation. Provided that other powers would co-operate with them they were willing to act promptly, and had therefore placed their armies on foot. These threats exasperated but did not terrify the French people. Leopold had no intention of entering upon hostilities, and found a loophole by which to escape from declaring war in the acceptance by Louis XVI. of the completed Constitution on 21st September 1791. He then solemnly withdrew his pretensions to interfere in the internal affairs of France. *Completion of the Constitution.*

While the first Constitution of France, sanctioning the representative principle and the rights of the people, was being slowly built up in the midst of troubles and intrigues in Paris, a not less remarkable constitution was promulgated in Poland, manifesting the same ideas. The partition of Poland in 1773 had proved to all patriotic Poles that their independence as a nation was in the utmost peril. A serious effort was therefore made to organise the country, and to place the government on a settled and logical basis. The army was made national instead of feudal; *The Polish Constitution. 3d May 1791.*

an attempt was made to establish a national system of finance, and a scheme of national education was propounded and partly carried into effect. But these measures were but steps in the work of making Poland a nation, instead of a loose confederation of nobles; the final decision was taken in 1788, when the Polish Diet elected a Committee to draw up a new Constitution, raised the national army to 60,000 men, and decreed regular taxes in order to replenish the national treasury. This consciousness of nationality enabled Stanislas Poniatowski, King of Poland, to negotiate as an independent and powerful sovereign with Prussia in 1789, and to send his envoys to Reichenbach in 1790 to act with the envoys of the other powers. The leading member of the Polish Constitutional Committee was Kollontai, a most remarkable man, and a Catholic priest, who had done good service as Rector of the University of Cracow, which he reorganised, and who had been made Vice-Grand-Chancellor of the kingdom. He was the principal author of the Polish Constitution, which was accepted by the Diet of Warsaw on 3d May 1791. This Constitution was noteworthy in what it abolished and what it created. It abolished the elective monarchy, the source of so many evils and intrigues, and declared the throne of Poland hereditary in the House of Saxony in succession to Stanislas Poniatowski, and it also abolished the *liberum veto*, which had enabled one member of the Diet to thwart the wishes of the majority. It created a regular government, conferring the legislative power on the King, the Senate, and an elected Chamber, and the executive power on the King, aided by six ministers responsible to the Legislature. The cities were permitted to elect their judges and deputies to the Diet; but the plague-spot of serfdom was too delicate to touch, and the Diet only declared its willingness to sanction all arrangements made between a lord and his serfs for the benefit of the latter. In some respects this Constitution compares favourably with that of France drawn up at the same time; if it does not proclaim so firmly the liberty of man, it at any rate is free from the lamentable fear of the power of the executive, which vitiated the work of the French reformers. France feared its executive after a long course of despotic monarchy; Poland felt the need of a strong executive after a long history of anarchy. Both countries, trying to be free, were affected in different ways, and with very different results, by the intervention of foreign powers.

The acceptance of the completed French Constitution was the signal for the dissolution of the Constituent Assembly. It was at once succeeded by the Legislative Assembly, elected under the provisions of the new Constitution. The new Assembly consisted, owing to a self-denying ordinance passed in May 1791, on the proposition of Robespierre, forbidding the election of deputies sitting in the Constituent Assembly to its successor, of none but untried men, who had no experience of politics. They were mostly young men who had learned to talk in their local popular societies, and who at once joined the mother of such societies, the Jacobin Club at Paris. They were forbidden by a clause in the Constitution of 1791 to interfere with constitutional questions, which could only be touched by a Convention summoned for the purpose, and so could only interfere in current politics and matters of administration. In such interference they were justified by the position of powerlessness into which the executive authority, the King and his ministers, were reduced by the Constitution. The two burning questions which first came before them were, the treatment of the clergy who had not taken the oath to observe the Civil Constitution of the Clergy, and of the *émigrés*. Both questions gave plenty of opportunity for the display of fervid revolutionary and patriotic eloquence, for the priests, who had not taken the oath, were undisguisedly stirring up opposition to the Revolution in the provinces, and the *émigrés* were forming an army on the French frontier. And the Legislative Assembly was in a greater degree than either its predecessor, the Constituent, or its successor, the Convention, liable to

*The Legislative Assembly.*

be swayed by oratory. The deputies liked to listen to glowing words and patriotic sentiments, and were largely influenced by the speeches of three great orators, Vergniaud, Gensonné, and Guadet, who all came from Bordeaux, the capital of the department of the Gironde, and to whose supporters posterity has given the name of Girondins. But these orators were in their turn influenced by a Norman deputy, Brissot. This veteran pamphleteer was a sincere republican; he also, having long been a journalist, believed himself a master of foreign politics. He desired to bring about a war between France and Austria. He believed that such a war would either cause the King to throw in his lot heartily with the Revolution, or, what was more likely, would make him declare himself openly against it, and would thus enable the advanced democratic party to call him a traitor, and by rousing all France against him, pave the way for his overthrow and the establishment of a republic. The first step was taken to make Louis XVI. appear the opponent of the Revolution by passing a decree against the priests, who had not taken the oath, which his conscience would not permit him to sign; the second by passing a decree against the *émigrés*, who were led by his own brothers, and an instruction that he should ask the Emperor and the German princes on the Rhine to prevent the *émigrés* from forming an army, and to expel them if they did so.

The question of the expediency of war with Austria was soon taken up in France, and not only the Legislative Assembly but the popular clubs busied themselves in discussing it. The Declaration of Pilnitz exasperated the whole nation, which resented dictation or interference in the internal affairs of France, and the warlike and menacing attitude of the army of *émigrés*, which had been formed by the Prince de Condé on the French frontier at Worms, increased the universal wrath. Louis XVI., whose ministers had been but feeble figure-heads during the Constituent Assembly, at this juncture appointed the Comte de Narbonne, a young man of distinguished ability, to be Minister for War. Narbonne

*Approach of War between France and the Emperor.*

grasped the situation. He saw the people wished for war, and he therefore declared that the King was as patriotic as his subjects, and was also ready for war if satisfaction were not given to France. Three large armies were formed and placed upon the frontiers under the command of Generals Rochambeau, Lückner, and Lafayette, of whom the two former were created Marshals of France. By this policy Narbonne took the wind out of the sails of Brissot and the Girondins; he hoped that if the Austrian war was successful the King would be sufficiently strengthened in popularity to regain his authority as head of the executive; while, if it failed, the nation in its extremity would turn to its legitimate sovereign and invest him with dictatorial power. The leaders of the democratic party in Paris, which had been scattered by Lafayette in July 1791, saw this equally clearly with Narbonne, and therefore opposed the war with all their might. The Jacobin Club had become their headquarters; most of the deputies who came up from the provinces joined the mother society in Paris, and it soon became more powerful than ever in creating public opinion. The effect of the secession and consequent formation of the Club of 1789 only made the Jacobins more frankly democratic, while the presence of many of its members in the Legislative Assembly strengthened the influence of the Jacobin Club. It was in the Jacobin Club during the debates on the war that the difference between what were to be the Girondin and the Mountain parties in the Convention first appeared. Brissot and the Girondin orators argued in favour of war; while Marat, Danton, and still more Robespierre, whose career in the Constituent Assembly had made him exceedingly popular, opposed it. The last-mentioned orator was indeed the chief opponent of the war; he saw through Narbonne's schemes, and hinted that the projected war was merely a court intrigue to promote the power of the King. The political strife became personal, and Robespierre, Marat, and Danton became the sworn foes of Brissot and the Girondins.

The main causes of the war were the questions of the rights of the Princes of the Empire in Alsace and of the *émigrés*. The defence of the former rights as rights of the Empire had been pressed upon Leopold at the time of his election as Emperor, and on 26th April 1791 the Prince of Thurn and Taxis, as Imperial Commissary, summoned the Diet to meet. It assembled, and after a long discussion a *conclusum* was arrived at, that the Empire maintained the Treaties of Westphalia and of the eighteenth century now violated by France, and requested the Emperor to take severe measures against the revolutionary propaganda. The Emperor Leopold, as sovereign of Austria, had withdrawn from the position he had taken up at Pilnitz, but as Emperor he was obliged to submit this *conclusum* of the Diet to the King of France, which he did in a strongly-worded despatch drawn up by the Chancellor Kaunitz, which was laid before the Legislative Assembly on 3d December 1791. It was as Emperor also that Leopold defended the conduct of the border princes of the Empire, notably the Elector-Archbishops of Trèves, Cologne, and Mayence, and the Bishops of Spires and Worms, in sheltering French *émigrés*. On 29th November 1791 the Assembly had desired the King to write to the Emperor and to these border princes protesting against the enlistment of troops by the *émigrés*, and the Emperor's answer defending the conduct of the princes concerned was read to the Assembly on 14th December. The replies of Leopold were referred to the Diplomatic Committee, and on its report, the Assembly resolved on 25th January 1792 that the Emperor should be requested to explain his attitude towards France and to promise to undertake nothing against her independence in forming her own constitution and settling her own mode of government before 1st March 1792, and that an evasive or unsatisfactory reply should be considered as annulling the Treaty of 1756 and as an act of hostility. The answer to this demand, which was drafted by Kaunitz, was read to the Assembly on 1st March; it censured the course which was being taken by

France, stigmatised the Revolution and accused the Jacobins of fomenting anarchy, and its first results were the dismissal of Narbonne, the impeachment of De Lessart, the Foreign Minister, and the formation of a Girondin ministry.

In the position he had taken up the Emperor Leopold was generally supported. The Princes of the Empire, as was represented in their *conclusum* passed at the Diet, not only resented the interference of France with historic rights in Alsace and her dictation as to whom they should shelter, but were beginning to fear the contagion of the revolutionary conceptions of the rights of man and political liberty. Throughout the Rhine provinces the peasants had risen in partial rebellion against their lords; in all the great cities of western Germany the more enlightened bourgeois protested against their exclusion from political influence. This contagion, however, did not spread far in these early days. The Empress Catherine, the King of Prussia, and the King of Sweden, who chiefly urged Leopold to make a brave stand against the Legislative Assembly, were urged by other motives. Catherine wished to see Austria and Prussia embroiled with France so as to have her hands free to deal with the Poles, who seemed likely with their new Constitution to ward off destruction. Frederick William II. was disgusted by the disrespect shown to the principle of monarchy by the Parisians' treatment of Louis XVI. Gustavus III. had imbibed a knightly admiration for Marie Antoinette, and felt a personal desire to relieve her from her position of humiliation. Each monarch showed his inclination characteristically. Catherine received some French *émigrés*, who found their way to her distant court, with kindness, and dismissed the French ambassador; Gustavus hurried to Spa to consult with the French *émigrés*, and proposed an immediate expedition to carry off the French court; Frederick William signed an offensive and defensive alliance with the Emperor on 2d February 1792, which saved him the trouble of personal decision, and left to the Emperor the harassing business of arranging the details of the war and of so carrying out the necessary diplomatic negotiations which preceded an open rupture, that the interference of the powers should seem justified. In the midst of his preparations the Emperor Leopold died suddenly on 1st March 1792, the very day on which his last manifesto was read to the Legislative Assembly. His death was an irreparable blow for Austria, for Germany, for France, and for Europe. In his short reign he had shown himself to be a monarch of extraordinary ability, possessing alike singular tact and great force of character. He was succeeded in the hereditary dominions of the House of Hapsburg by his eldest son Francis II., an inexperienced youth, quite unfitted to continue Leopold's policy in the troublous times approaching.

*Death of Leopold, 1st March 1792.*

Europe had hardly recovered from the shock of the Emperor's sudden death, when it was startled by the news of the murder of Gustavus III. of Sweden, who was shot on his way from a masked ball at Stockholm by an officer named Ankarström, on 16th March 1792. He lingered till 29th March, when he died, and was succeeded on the throne of Sweden by his infant son, Gustavus IV. Duke Charles of Sudermania was appointed Regent. He at once reversed the policy of the late king; he felt none of the sympathy so warmly expressed by Gustavus III. for Marie Antoinette, and he distrusted the close alliance which had been entered into with Russia after the Treaty of Verela. His first measure was to place Sweden in a position of absolute neutrality, from which she never swerved during his tenure of power.

*Murder of Gustavus III. 29th March 1792.*

Of the ministers who came into office in France in March 1792 through the influence of the Girondins in the Legislative Assembly, the most notable were Roland and Dumouriez. The former was a sincere republican, who was induced by his wife to take up an offensive attitude to the King, the latter an experienced soldier and diplomatist, who was well fitted for the ministry of foreign affairs. Dumouriez at once accepted war with Austria as inevitable, and

*Policy of Dumouriez.*

directed all his efforts to isolate her. He was a sworn enemy of the Austrian alliance, entered into by the Treaty of 1756, and cemented by the marriage of Marie Antoinette, and his first step was to endeavour to detach Prussia. He was sanguine enough to believe in the possibility of doing this, but he did not understand the character of Frederick William II. It was difficult to induce that monarch to make up his mind, but when he did make it up he was obstinate. The French party at his Court, headed by his uncle Prince Henry, and in his ministry, represented by Haugwitz, was very strong; but, on the other hand, he had been convinced by Leopold that the cause of Louis XVI. was the cause of monarchy, and the German party at Berlin hinted that if he allowed Austria to pose as the defender of the rights of the Empire by herself, the policy of Frederick the Great to make Prussia the leader of Germany would be undone. Frederick William II., therefore, listened coldly to the overtures of Dumouriez, and made preparations to support his ally in the field. On 20th April 1792 the Legislative Assembly assented almost unanimously to the King's proposition, as read by Dumouriez, to declare war against the King of Hungary and Bohemia, as Francis II. was at this time styled, and the great war, which was to rage with but slight intermissions for twenty-three years, began.

War declared by France against Austria. 20th April 1792.

The commencement of the first campaign of 1792 proved how thoroughly the French army had been disorganised and demoralised by the policy of the Constituent Assembly and the general course of the Revolution. An attempt was made to invade the Austrian Netherlands or Belgium on four lines; but one column was seized with panic and rushed back to Lille, murdering its general, Theobald Dillon. The other commanders found their soldiers filled with a spirit of distrust for their officers and hardly amenable to discipline, and it soon became obvious that France would have to stand on the defensive. This news profoundly moved the people of France and especially of Paris. The word treachery was freely used in connection with the Court, and it was asserted that the plan of campaign had been revealed to the Austrians by the Queen. This was true; Marie Antoinette had always looked to Austrian help to rescue her from her position, and Louis XVI. had now entirely come round to her view. At this juncture he dismissed his Girondin ministers on their insisting upon his signing a decree, which had been passed by the Assembly ordering the deportation of priests who had not taken the oath, and even accepted the resignation of the ablest of them, Dumouriez, who had offered to form a new ministry. The populace of Paris was intensely excited by the failure of the attack on Belgium, the concentration of the Prussian army on the frontier, and the dismissal of the popular ministers, and a body of petitioners, after filing through the hall of the Assembly, burst into the Tuileries and for some hours filled the palace, insulting the King and Queen and forcing the former to put on a red cap of liberty. The invasion of the Tuileries marked the final breach between the King and the people. Louis XVI. longed more ardently than ever for the arrival of the allied monarchs; and the Jacobin leaders, who perceived the impossibility that France should be successful in war with an unwilling king at her head, began to plot for his overthrow. His last chance was lost, when he rejected the proffered assistance of Lafayette, who returned from his army without leave and offered to bring the National Guard of Paris to his help.

*Invasion of the Tuileries. 20th June 1792.*

The news of the invasion of the Tuileries by the mob on the 20th June further decided the allied monarchs to take immediate action. Francis II., who was crowned Emperor at Frankfort on 14th July 1792, was eager to come to his aunt's help. The position of the allies was now reversed. Instead of Austria in the person of the experienced Emperor Leopold guiding Prussia, it was now Frederick William II. of Prussia who directed the policy of the young Emperor Francis. It was arranged that the Prussians should invade Champagne,

*Francis II. Emperor. 14th July 1792.*

## Capture of the Tuileries

supported by a *corps* of Austrians and *émigrés* on their left, and joined midway by a *corps* of Austrians from their right, while an Austrian army under Duke Albert of Saxe-Teschen was to march from the Netherlands and invest Lille. The central Prussian army was placed under the command of the Duke of Brunswick, who issued a proclamation, drafted by an *émigré*, M. de Limon, and filled with violent language by Count Fersen, threatening to hold Paris liable for the safety of the King, and vowing vengeance on the French people as rebels.

Brunswick's proclamation was the very thing to complete the exasperation of the French people. National patriotism rose to its height; the country had been declared in danger, and thousands of volunteers were arming and preparing to go to the front; the threats of the Prussians only increased the national spirit of resistance; and the universal feeling was one of defiance. But there was obviously no chance of success while the executive remained in its present hands. *Insurrection of 10th Aug. 1792.* The King's power of interfering with the preparations for resistance had to be stopped. This was clearly understood by the democratic leaders, who, ever since 20th June 1792, had been organising an armed rising. They waited till some volunteers from Marseilles entered the capital, singing the song that bears their name, and then they struck. The royal plans for the defence of the Tuileries were thwarted; a number of the most energetic democrats ousted the Council-General of the Commune of Paris, and formed an Insurrectionary Commune; and the men of the poorer districts of Paris, the Faubourgs Saint-Antoine and Saint-Marceau, headed by the Marseillais, advanced to attack the royal palace. Before the assault commenced, Louis XVI., accompanied by his family and his ministers, took refuge in the hall of the Legislative Assembly. The attack was gallantly resisted by the Swiss Guards, who garrisoned the palace, but the people were eventually successful and the Tuileries was taken. The Legislative Assembly at once declared the King suspended from his office, *Suspension of Louis XVI. 10th Aug. 1792.*

PERIOD VII. H

and ordered him to be confined with his family in the Temple. It then elected a new ministry, consisting of three of the former Girondin ministers, Roland, Clavière, and Servan for the Interior, Finance, and War, and three new men, Danton, Monge, and Lebrun for Justice, the Marine, and Foreign Affairs. This ministry, with the help of an extraordinary Commission of Twenty-one, elected by the Legislative, and of the Commune of Paris, displayed the greatest energy. By means of domiciliary visits, those suspected of opposition to the insurrection of 10th August were seized and imprisoned; a camp was formed for the defence of Paris; men were everywhere raised and equipped and sent to the front; and commissioners were sent throughout France, and especially to the armies, to tell the tale of the insurrection and to secure the adhesion of the people. Danton was the heart and soul of the defence movement and of the ministry, and inspired confidence and patriotism into those who hesitated; the Commission of Twenty-one, whose mouthpiece was the great orator Vergniaud, aided him to the best of their power; the Legislative directed the convocation of the primary assemblies, without distinction of active and passive citizens, for the election of a National Convention; and the Commune of Paris took measures to prevent any attempt at a counter-revolution.

But no amount of energy and patriotism could in a moment make trained armies and enable France to repulse the most famous troops in Europe. Fortunately for France, in this crisis, her untrained soldiers behaved admirably. Lafayette, on the news of the insurrection of 10th August, arrested the commissioners sent to him by the Legislative Assembly, and endeavoured to induce his army to march to the aid of the King. But his men refused; the former commander of the National Guard of Paris deserted, and Dumouriez took command of his army. Lille made a gallant resistance to the Austrians, who had formed the siege, but the Prussians met with no such obstinate opposition. Longwy surrendered to them on 27th August, and Verdun on 2nd

September, and they continued their march directly on Paris. Dumouriez fell back with his main army to defend the uplands, —they can hardly be called the mountains,—of the Argonne. He summoned to him the *corps d'armée* on the Belgian frontier under Arther Dillon, and a detachment from the Army of the Rhine under Kellermann, while he was also reinforced by some thousands of undisciplined, and therefore useless, volunteers, and by a fine division of old soldiers collected from the garrisons in the interior. In Paris the news of the Prussian advance caused a panic; it seemed impossible that Dumouriez' hastily concentrated army could oppose an effective resistance; and even Danton and Vergniaud could hardly keep up the enthusiasm they had at first aroused. At this juncture the Parisian volunteers were half afraid to go to the front for fear that the numerous prisoners, arrested during the domiciliary visits, would break out and revenge themselves on the families of the volunteers. This feeling induced the horrible series of murders, known as the Massacres of September, in the prisons. The massacres began fortuitously, and there were not more than 200 murderers at work; but the crowd, including national guards, stood by and saw them committed without raising a hand to help the victims. All Paris was responsible for the murders; they could have been easily stopped; but no one wanted to check them: the feeling which allowed them was the popular feeling; neither Danton, nor Roland, nor the Commune of Paris, nor the Legislative Assembly cared to interfere; the massacres were the answer to the Prussian advance and the capture of Longwy, as the insurrection of 10th August was the reply to Brunswick's manifesto. *The Massacres of September 1792.*

On 20th September 1792 the main Prussian army, which had reached the Argonne, attacked the position occupied by Kellermann at Valmy, and was repulsed. The victory was not a great one; the battle was not very hotly contested; the losses on both sides were insignificant; but its results both military and political were *Battle of Valmy. 20th Sept. 1792.*

immense. The King of Prussia, who complained that the Austrians had not fulfilled their engagements, and that the whole burden was thrown on him, was easily persuaded by the Duke of Brunswick to order a retreat. The Duke of Brunswick was induced to give that advice from military considerations, in that his army was wasted by disease and harassed by the inclement weather, and from policy, because, like many Prussian officers, he considered it unnatural for Prussians and Austrians to fight side by side. The retiring army was not hotly pressed; Dumouriez still hoped to induce Prussia to quit the coalition against France, and pursued with more courtesy than vigour until the army of Brunswick was beyond the limits of French territory.

On the day of the battle, or as it is with more correctness termed the cannonade, of Valmy, the National Convention met in Paris and assumed the direction of affairs. It contained all the most distinguished men who had sat in the two former assemblies on the Left, or democratic side, and its first act was to declare France a Republic. After this had been unanimously carried, dissensions at once arose, and a fundamental difference between two groups of deputies appeared, which threatened to end in the proscription of the one or the other. On the one side were the distinguished orators of the Gironde, who have given their name to the whole party, reinforced by the presence of several old members of the Constituent Assembly and of a few young and inexperienced men. This group was roughly divided into Buzotins and Brissotins, or followers of Buzot, a leading ex-Constituant, and of Brissot, the author of the war; but some of the greatest of them, like Vergniaud, refused to ally themselves with either leader. The chief meeting-place of the Buzotins, who included most of the younger men, was Madame Roland's salon. On the other side, taking their name from the high benches on which they sat, were the deputies of the Mountain, including almost the whole of the representatives of Paris, and all the energetic republicans, who had brought about the insurrection

*Meeting of the Convention. 20th Sep. 1792.*

*Parties in the Convention.*

of 10th August. This group comprised Robespierre, Danton and Marat, Collot-d'Herbois and Billaud-Varenne, all deputies for Paris, and none of whom, except Robespierre, had ever sat in either of the former assemblies, with some leaders of the extreme party in the Legislative, Merlin of Thionville, Chabot and Basire. It was not long before open quarrels arose between the two groups. The Girondins accused the leaders of the Mountain of having in the Insurrectionary Commune fomented the massacres of September in the prisons, and abused them as sanguinary and ambitious anarchists. This accusation was formally indeed brought against Robespierre by Louvet, a Rolandist Girondin, in an elaborate attack delivered on 29th October; while at the same time the Mountain accused the Girondins of being federalists and desiring to destroy the essential unity of the Republic, an accusation which was used with deadly effect at a later date. Both groups,—they cannot be called parties, for they had no party ties and recognised no party obligations,—appealed to the great majority of the Convention, the deputies of the Centre, who sat in the Plain or Marsh. The representative of this vast majority was Barère, an ex-Constituant, who trimmed judiciously between the two opposing groups.

The Convention, which had been elected in days of deepest dejection, if not despair, when the Prussians were moving on Paris and the Austrians were besieging Lille, was soon raised by a succession of conquests to a state of patriotic exaltation, bordering on delirium. In the month of September, just after the battle of Valmy, General Montesquiou occupied Savoy, and General Anselme the county and city of Nice, territories belonging to the King of Sardinia, without striking a blow. This was followed by a more important series of successes. Though not as a body engaged in war with France, many princes of the Empire had sent contingents to the aid of the Prussians and Austrians. In reply, still without declaring war on the Empire, the French attacked the Rhenish princes. On 1st October General

Custine, commanding a corps of the Army of the Rhine, took Spires, on October 4 Worms, and on October 21 Mayence, one of the bulwarks of the Empire and the capital of the Elector-Archbishop. From Mayence Custine detached divisions in other directions, and held the wealthy city of Frankfort-on-the-Main to ransom. Not less startlingly rapid were the conquests of Dumouriez on the north-east frontier. After the retreat of the Prussians he turned north against the Austrians; he raised the siege of Lille, which had been heroically defended, and on 6th November he defeated the Austrians in a pitched battle at Jemmappes, near Mons. This victory laid Belgium open to him. He occupied the whole country, entered Brussels as a conqueror, and established his headquarters at Liége. The conquest of Belgium intoxicated the Convention; they believed their armies to be invincible; they regarded themselves as having a mission to carry the doctrines of the French Revolution as embodied in the Rights of Man and the Sovereignty of the People into all countries; they declared themselves on 19th November ready to wage war for all peoples upon all kings; and in disregard of all international obligations, they declared the Scheldt, which by treaty had been closed to commerce for years, a free river, because it had its source in a free country.

*Capture of Mayence. 21st October 1792.*

*Battle of Jemmappes. 6th Nov. 1792.*

The intoxication which followed this series of unparalleled successes blinded the Convention to the need of improving and disciplining their troops. The French republicans did not comprehend that the chief cause of the facile conquests of their armies was that they met with the sympathy of the conquered. Belgium, the Rhine provinces, Savoy, and Nice were all filled with revolutionary enthusiasm, and welcomed the French as liberators; they requested to be united to France, when primary assemblies were summoned by the French commissioners, and on 9th November Savoy and Nice, and on 13th December the Austrian Netherlands or Belgium, were declared a part of France. In spite of these military successes, the republican army could not be organised in a day; the seeds of anarchy sown by the Constituent had gone too deep to enable discipline to be restored except by sharp measures; the administration of the army, that is, the commissariat, the war office, etc., was in a state of chaos; the soldiers, both officers and men, of all the armies, kept their eyes too closely fixed on the course of politics in Paris to do their duty efficiently at the front.

The burning question which divided the Convention at the end of 1792 was the treatment to be meted out to Louis XVI. Robespierre urged that, as a political measure, he should be put to death; but the Girondins, filled with an idea of imitating the English republicans of the seventeenth century, decided on a royal trial. When the trial, which was but a defence of Louis XVI. by his counsel, was over, the Girondins, in their desire to avoid responsibility, or perhaps from a genuine belief that it might save the King's life, proposed that the sentence on him should be submitted to the primary assemblies of the people. The deputies of the Mountain feared no responsibility, and taunted the Girondins with being concealed royalists. The motion for an appeal to the people was rejected; the King was sentenced to death by a small majority; and on 21st January 1793 Louis XVI. was guillotined at Paris. *Execution of Louis XVI. 21st Jan. 1793.*

The result of the execution of Louis XVI. was to give a pretext to the countries of Europe which had not yet declared war against the French Republic to do so. Charles IV. of Spain, in the hope of saving the chief of the Bourbon family, maintained his minister at Paris until the last possible moment, and it was with reluctance that he placed his army in the field on the news of the King's execution. The French Republic accepted the challenge, and early in March declared war against Spain. The war with Holland stood on a different basis. Dumouriez, after his conquest of Belgium, looked on Holland as an easy and particularly wealthy prey. He believed that by conquering *War with Spain, Holland, England, and the Empire.*

Holland, France would have in her hands a means of forcing England to keep the peace. His views were supported by Danton, who was sent on mission to Dumouriez' headquarters. The contrary was the result. Pitt sincerely wished for peace, and was essentially a peace minister, but he had no idea of allowing the faithful ally of England, Holland, to be overrun and held to ransom by the French. The opening of the Scheldt had crowned the long series of French breaches of international law, and Pitt resented the assumption of the Convention that the law of nature, as interpreted by themselves, was to take the place of the law of nations. Pitt's hand was also forced in two directions; the philippics of Burke had roused the fears of English property-holders against the spread of French principles; and George III. was as anxious as any Continental monarch to preserve the dignity of kings. Pitt and his foreign minister, Grenville, gradually became convinced that the French meant to fight England, and that war was inevitable, and Chauvelin, the French ambassador, was ordered to leave London. The French leaders were under a misconception with regard to the spread of their ideas in England; they knew that a large body of educated men sympathised with them, and expected a national democratic rising which should overthrow not only Pitt, but the English monarchy. They did not understand that an English parliamentary opposition, in spite of its words, is as staunchly loyal as the ministry, and that it would never foment or encourage insurrection. Under these circumstances and deluded by these misconceptions France declared war against England and Holland on 1st February 1793. Many smaller nations entered on the fray. Sweden under the prudent government of the Regent Duke of Sudermania, Denmark under Christian VII. and Bernstorff, and Switzerland declared their neutrality. But Portugal, where the heir-apparent, afterwards King John VI., had become regent for his mother, Maria Francisca, who was insane; Tuscany, whose Grand Duke, Ferdinand, was a brother of the Emperor; Naples, or rather the Two Sicilies, whose king was a Bourbon, and whose queen was a sister of Marie Antoinette, all declared war on the French Republic. Catherine of Russia wore mourning for Louis XVI. inveighed against the wickedness of the French republicans, and proceeded to take advantage of the occupation of the rest of Europe in the affairs of France to prosecute her schemes on Poland. Last of all, the Holy Roman Empire, which had decreed the armament of the contingents of the circles, on 23d November 1792, after the news of the capture of Mayence, solemnly, and with all the circumlocution inseparable from the movement of the unwieldy machine, declared war against France on 22d March 1793.

While regenerated France was at bay with nearly the whole of Europe, regenerated Poland was being conquered by a single power. While Europe pretended to fight France on behalf of the principle of monarchy, Catherine invaded Poland, because by the Constitution of 3d May 1791 it had strengthened its monarchy. France was attacked because it was asserted to be in a state of anarchy, Poland because it had by wise reforms tried to put an end to an historic system of constitutional anarchy. As soon as Catherine had made peace with the Turks at Jassy, and Austria and Prussia were engaged in war with France, she intervened to overthrow the new Polish Constitution. It was not difficult to find Polish nobles who resented the abrogation of the old system, and, under Catherine's encouragement, Branicki, Felix Potocki, and some others formed the Confederation of Targovitsa, and protested against the abolition of the *liberum veto* and the reforms of 3d May 1791. They then asked Catherine to send a Russian army to their assistance. She willingly complied, and on 18th May 1792 published a manifesto, stating that she was the guarantor of the ancient Polish Constitution, and stigmatising the reformers of 1791 as Jacobins. Suvórov at once entered Poland at the head of 80,000 Russians and 20,000 Cossacks, and by force of numbers defeated the Polish army under Joseph

Poniatowski at Zielencé on 18th June 1792, and under Kosciuszko at Dubienka on 17th July. These defeats caused the reformers of 1791, including Kollontai and Kosciuszko, to go into exile; their place at the Diet was taken by the leaders of the Confederation of Targovitsa, and the Constitution of 3d May 1791 was abrogated. The conquest of the Polish patriots by Russia greatly excited the King of Prussia and the Emperor, and was one of the causes which induced Frederick William to order Brunswick to retreat after his trifling check at Valmy. The Polish patriots appealed to Prussia for help under the terms of the alliance of 1790, but the King only answered that he had not recognised the Constitution of 3d May 1791, and that the Polish leaders were Jacobins and imitators and allies of the French revolutionary leaders. A Prussian army, therefore, entered Poland to co-operate with the Russians and to share the spoil. A treaty of partition was signed by Catherine and Frederick William on 4th January 1793, by which Russia was to annex eastern Poland, including the whole of Minsk, Podolia, Volhynia, and Little Russia, and Prussia was to have Posen, Gnezen, Kalisch, and the cities of Dantzic and Thorn. Austria was too hotly engaged in the war with France to be able to claim a share, but the conduct of Prussia at this time in excluding her from the partition of Poland was never forgotten nor forgiven, and increased the hereditary feeling of distrust between the two powers. The Emperor Francis regarded himself as duped, and Prussia by acting alone broke the solemn engagements entered into with Leopold, and commenced the policy which was to end in the conclusion of the Treaty of Basle with the French Republic. Though the second partition of Poland was agreed upon in 1792, it was not consummated until the following year. A Diet was called at Grodno, and there, in the presence of the Russian soldiers, Stanislas Poniatowski and the Diet consented in silence, on 24th September 1793, to the arrangements made between Russia and Prussia. On 16th October Catherine signed a

*Second partition of Poland. 24th Sept. 1793.*

treaty, guaranteeing the liberty of Poland, that is, the abuses of the old Constitution, which were certain to give Russia the opportunity of finishing the work of blotting out the Poles as an independent nationality from the map of Europe.

The close of the year 1792 thus witnessed at the same time the overthrow of Poland and France in arms against foreign aggression. Each country was to make a violent effort for independence. The French were to be successful, because under the influence of personal and political freedom every Frenchman felt it his duty to resist foreign interference; Poland was to fail, because it was not the Polish people, but only the enlightened Polish nobles and bourgeois, who appreciated the situation.

# CHAPTER IV

## 1793-1795

France at War with Europe—Altered Character of the War—The Revolutionary Propaganda—First Campaign of 1793—Battle of Neerwinden—Desertion of Dumouriez—Creation of the Committee of Public Safety—Insurrection in La Vendée—Creation of the Revolutionary Tribunal—Struggle between the Girondins and the Mountain—Overthrow of the Girondins—Second Campaign of 1793—Loss of Valenciennes and Mayence—Civil War in France—Royalist and Federalist Risings—Loss of Toulon—Constitution of 1793—The work of the first Committee of Public Safety—The Great Committee of Public Safety—Growth of its Power—Position of Robespierre—The Reign of Terror—The Committee of General Security, the Deputies on Mission, the Revolutionary Tribunal, the Laws of the Suspects and the Maximum—Results of the Terror—Battles of Hondschoten, Wattignies, and the Geisberg—Relief of Maubeuge—Recovery of Lyons and Toulon—Fall of the Hébertists and the Dantonists—Campaign of 1794—Battles of Fleurus, Kaiserslautern, and 1st June 1794—Fall of Robespierre—Rule of the Thermidorians: First Phase: the Survivors of the Mountain—Conquest of Holland—The Batavian Republic—Successes on the Rhine, in Savoy, Italy, and Spain—Insurrection in Poland—The Campaign of Kosciuszko—Third and Final Partition of Poland—Contrast between the Polish and French Revolutions—Its Causes—Change in the Attitude of the Continental Powers to the French Republic—Rule of the Thermidorians: Second Phase: the Survivors of the Girondins and Deputies of the Centre—Insurrections of 12th Germinal and 1st Prairial in Paris—The Constitution of the Year III. (1795)—The Treaties of Basle—France again enters the Comity of Nations.

**France at War with Europe.** THE first months of 1793 found France at war with Europe. Though such minor states as Denmark and Sweden and Venice declared their neutrality, they manifested no desire to assist the French Republic, and their neutrality was but of slight service. It was otherwise with the neutrality of Switzerland. The Swiss cantons had nearly been drawn into the general war by the support given to the revolutionary party in the Republic of Geneva by the French ministry, which included among its members Clavière, a Genevese exile. The canton of Berne went so far as to occupy the city of Geneva, and it was only by the exercise of much diplomatic skill that open war was avoided. The neutrality of Switzerland made the land blockade of the French Republic of no avail. Through secret agents in Switzerland, arms, provisions, and necessaries were obtained from Southern Germany, and diplomatic relations were maintained with the democrats residing in the states of the belligerent powers. The declaration of war by the Holy Roman Empire completed the armed opposition of the greater countries of Europe against France. Of these countries Russia alone sent no army or fleet against the Republic, and Catherine satisfied herself with stating that she was engaged in conquering Jacobins in Poland.

The character of the war in 1793 differed from that waged in 1792. In 1792 France was invaded on behalf of Louis XVI., and the fighting was carried on according to the principles which had existed in the eighteenth century. But in 1793 the powers were at war with France for a different and more far-reaching reason. The revolutionary propaganda, that is, the idea consecrated in the decree of the Convention on the 19th of November 1792, that France was to spread among all countries the new doctrines of liberty, equality, and fraternity, vitally affected every government in Europe. England in particular, which had studiously kept aloof while the Revolution was pursuing its course at home, only felt obliged to interfere when the new rulers of France announced their intention of disregarding all principles of international law, and of converting other nations to their doctrines. It was this common opposition to the revolutionary propaganda which united the powers of Europe against France in 1793. England made herself the paymaster

<small>Altered character of the War.</small>

of the coalition. She lavished money freely, not only in subsidies to Prussia and Austria, but to less important countries, such as Spain and Sardinia. With this community of aim necessarily came a community of action. The war against France became a matter of principle and not of intrigue. This new attitude was marked by changes of ministry both in Prussia and in Austria. The failure of the invasion of 1792 disgusted Frederick William II. with his advisers. The Duke of Brunswick fell into open disgrace, and Schulemburg, the foreign minister, made way for Haugwitz. At Vienna, Count Philip Cobenzl, the Vice-Chancellor of State, who had managed foreign affairs owing to the old age of Kaunitz, was dismissed, and his place was taken by Thugut, a man of low origin, whose sole political object was the humiliation of France, and his guiding principle a horror of French principles. Even in the secondary states similar ministerial changes took place, of which the most remarkable was the dismissal of Aranda in Spain, who was succeeded in power by Godoy, the Queen's lover.

The first result of the formation of the coalition was a determined attack upon Dumouriez' position in Belgium. That general had hitherto not despaired of detaching Prussia from Austria, but the execution of Louis XVI. destroyed his last hope. Both Prussia and England declined to listen to his lavish promises; his army had wasted away while in winter quarters; the first volunteers returned to their homes in thousands when France was freed from the invaders; the troops he retained were deprived of all necessaries by the disorganisation of the French War Office; and the people of Belgium, finding that their country was annexed to the French Republic, in spite of their patriotic desire for independence, showed their hostility in every way, and harassed instead of aiding the French troops. Under these circumstances, Dumouriez' invasion of Holland failed, as it was certain to fail. His right wing, which was besieging Maestricht under the command of General Miranda, was defeated by the

*First Campaign of 1793.*

Austrians under the command of the Prince of Coburg, and he had to withdraw his advanced divisions, for fear of being cut off from France. He was rapidly pursued. An English army, under the Duke of York, joined the Austrians, under the Prince of Coburg, and Dumouriez was utterly defeated by the allies at Neerwinden on the 21st March 1793. The defeat became a rout, and the French were driven from Belgium as speedily as they had conquered it. Dumouriez then made a fruitless effort to lead his army against the Convention. He arrested four deputies and the Minister for War who had been sent to suspend him from his command, but, finding that his army would not follow him, he deserted to the Austrians on the 5th April. *Battle of Neerwinden. 21st March 1793.*

The effect of Dumouriez' reverses, and, finally, of his desertion, on the temper of the Convention was most striking. The enthusiasts who believed in the inauguration of a new era, who boasted that free Frenchmen, even without arms and discipline, would be able to defeat all foreign armies, and who considered that the career of the Republic was certain to be one of victory, were rudely awakened. The need of the creation of a strong government was forced upon the attention of the Convention. Danton, recurring to the views of Mirabeau, proposed that a new ministry should be chosen from among the members of the Legislature. But the republicans had the same horror of the power of the executive as the constitutionalists, and Danton's motion was rejected. Nevertheless, it was quite impossible that an unwieldy assembly and a discredited ministry could defend France with any degree of success. As early as January 1793, a Committee of General Defence had been elected by the principal committees of the Convention; this was replaced, on the news of the defeat at Neerwinden, by a Committee of General Defence of twenty-five members chosen directly by the Convention; this was still too unwieldy, and on the news of the desertion of Dumouriez, the first Committee of Public Safety of nine members, *Effect on the Convention.*

exercising supreme executive authority, was appointed. But
the question was, how was the Committee to be
enabled to rule. Its first duty was to raise soldiers
to meet the enemies upon every frontier. For
this purpose eighty-two deputies of the Convention were sent
through France, two and two, to raise by volunteering where
possible, but by conscription if other measures failed, 300,000
men. This call for recruits caused disturbances in many parts
of France; in La Vendée it started civil war. It was to protest
against the conscription, and not to defend the Church or the
nobility, that the people of La Vendée rose in insurrection. But the leadership of the movement,
which had at first been taken by gamekeepers and
postillions, was speedily assumed by members of the ancient
French clergy and nobility. Cohesion was thus given to the
insurgents, and a large and important district in the west of
France maintained for a time a successful opposition to the
decrees of the Convention. But the reverses and desertion
of Dumouriez not only caused, for the first time in the history
of the Revolution, the creation of a real executive, it caused
also the forging of the weapons by which that executive was in
the future to establish the Reign of Terror. On 9th March
the Revolutionary Tribunal of Paris was established. Its
special object was the summary punishment of all enemies of
the Revolution. On the 4th of April the Convention decreed
that a maximum price of food should be fixed. Extended
powers were granted to deputies sent on mission to the
armies or to the departments; and an army, consisting of the
very poor, or *sans culottes*, was proposed.

While these measures, which did not take full effect for
some months, were being debated, the Convention was torn
by the opposition between the Girondins and the deputies of
the Mountain. The details of the struggle are not important.
The arguments used by the Girondins were that their enemies
were responsible for the massacres of September in the
prisons, that they were under the influence of the Commune

*The Committee of Public Safety.*

*Insurrection in La Vendée, 1793.*

of Paris, and that they encouraged anarchy. The Mountain, on their side, alleged that the Girondins were concealed royalists, because they had voted against the execution of Louis XVI., that they were federalists, who desired to destroy the unity of the Republic, and that they preferred a weak to a strong government. The struggle was mainly carried on in the tribune of the Convention; Robespierre attacked Brissot, Vergniaud, and Guadet, and these orators replied by attacking Robespierre and Danton. The latter for a time endeavoured to avoid breaking with the Girondins, but he was so violently impeached for his conduct while on mission in Belgium, and accused of being an accomplice of Dumouriez, that in self-defence he was forced to take up the gauntlet. He had been elected to the first Committee of Public Safety, and though his constitutional indolence prevented him from becoming its most important member, he shared with Cambon, the financier, the chief responsibility of the new method of government. Meanwhile, worse news kept coming from every frontier. It was felt to be both injudicious and unpatriotic for the Convention to be occupied in personal squabbles when the fate of France was in the balance. The Commune of Paris decided to intervene. The deputies who sat in the Plain, or Centre of the Convention, were more influenced by the eloquence of the Girondins than by the energy of the Mountain, and it was with regret that they felt obliged to yield to the Commune of Paris. On the 31st May 1793, regular troops and national guards, under the direction of Hanriot, the commander of the National Guard of Paris, surrounded the Tuileries, to which the Convention had removed on the 10th May, and the Commune demanded that the leading Girondins should be expelled from the Convention, and sent for trial before the Revolutionary Tribunal. The *coup d'état* was completed on the 2d June, when these demands were complied with, and from that date the Girondins as a political party in the Convention ceased to exist.

PERIOD VII.

The desertion of Dumouriez left the way clear for the
Second Cam- Austrians and English to invade France. They
paign of 1793. advanced slowly and did not attempt, like the
Duke of Brunswick in the previous year, to mask the frontier
fortresses and move straight upon Paris. On 24th May the
French camp at Famars was stormed; on 12th July Condé,
on 28th July Valenciennes, were taken after making an
obstinate resistance, and the allies were thus firmly established
in France. Then, fortunately for the Convention, the allied
commanders-in-chief quarrelled. The Duke of York, acting
under the orders of the English ministry, besieged Dunkirk,
which port he desired to hold for the disembarkation of
supplies. The Prince of Coburg, with the Austrians, refused
to assist in the siege of Dunkirk, and invested Le Quesnoy.
Further south the Prussians captured Mayence on the 22d of
July, and a mixed army of Austrians and troops of the Empire
under Würmser forced their way into Alsace. At both ends
of the Pyrenees Spanish armies invaded the French Republic.
In the eastern Pyrenees nearly the whole of Roussillon was
conquered, and in the western Pyrenees the passage of the
Bidassoa was forced. These repeated reverses in so many
quarters did not destroy the courage of the Convention or of
the French people, but they proved that hastily raised undisciplined masses can never be a match for trained soldiers.
The successes of Dumouriez and Custine had been as much
the result of accident and of the hearty reception given to
them by the natives of the districts they invaded as of talent
and bravery, but the first defeats showed how thoroughly the
policy of the Constituent Assembly had sapped the discipline
of the French army.

To add to the dangers which threatened France during the
Civil war in summer of 1793, civil war in many quarters re-
France. doubled the perils caused by the foreign invasion.
The war in La Vendée increased in magnitude almost daily,
and the soldiers of the Republic were frequently defeated by
the hardy peasants who fought in guerilla fashion among their

woods and marshes. Throughout Brittany and in the mountains of Auvergne similar movements took place, generally guided by priests and country gentlemen; but except in La Vendée there was no serious royalist manifestation. But the expulsion of the Girondins from the Convention had given rise to another movement of even greater importance. The insurrections in La Vendée and similar risings in country or mountain districts were the work of ignorant peasants; the movement in favour of the Girondins was headed by wealthy and intelligent cities. The news of the *coup d'état* of the 2d of June was received with consternation in most of the chief cities of France. Girondin journals had long preached the wickedness of the Commune of Paris, and that the leaders of the Mountain were either anarchists or ambitious men aiming at power. These words now had their effect. Several of the deputies proscribed on the 2d of June escaped into the provinces, and a group of them, collected at Caen in Normandy, endeavoured to organise an army against the Convention. Other cities followed the example. Marseilles arrested the representatives on mission; Bordeaux refused to receive the deputies sent to it; Lyons started a counter-revolution and executed Chalier, the leader of the local democratic party; and several cities agreed to send detachments of local troops to form a central army against the Convention at Bourges. For a few days matters looked most threatening for the victorious members of the Mountain, but they were well served by the deputies on mission. The Norman army was easily defeated at Pacy on the 13th of July; Bordeaux and Marseilles quickly submitted, and Lyons was invested. But the success of the Mountain was due to something more than the vigour of its representatives in the provinces. The general sentiment in France was that the conduct of the Girondins in causing civil war showed the very excess of want of patriotism; even if the Commune of Paris had done wrong in interfering with the Convention, the Girondins had behaved worse in attempting to rouse the provinces, and owing to this sentiment many departments and many cities speedily repented of the encouragement they had given to the Girondin designs, and withdrew their support to the proposed concentration of local troops at Bourges.

The deputies of the Mountain met the unparalleled dangers of foreign and civil war with undaunted courage. Their first measure was to draw up with extreme rapidity a republican constitution, which is known as the Constitution of 1793. As it never came into effect, the details of this proposed system of government need not be described. But the fact that it was drawn up, promulgated, and sent before the primary assemblies of the people, deprived the Girondin insurgents of one of their chief weapons. They had asserted that the Mountain admired anarchy and wished to retain power for the Convention and themselves. To these allegations the issue of the Constitution of 1793 was an adequate reply. But it was quite impossible, according to the leaders of the Mountain, for the Convention to abandon the reins of power. A general election at such a time would but increase the difficulty of the situation. So, while declaring the existence of the new Constitution, it deferred putting it into effect, and strengthened the authority of its new executive, the Committee of Public Safety. The advantages to be derived from the concentration of authority in a few hands became quite clear to the Convention after the expulsion of the Girondins. It may be doubted whether the distinguished orators who directed Girondin opinion, from their constant apprehension of the dangers of a strong executive to individual liberty, would ever have perceived them. The existence of the Committee made it possible for representatives on mission and other agents of government to have a central authority on which to rely. It was the Committee which directed the short campaign in Normandy which overthrew the most promising movement of the escaped Girondin deputies; it was the prudence of a member of the Committee, Robert Lindet, which pacified Normandy, after the victory had been won, by ruthlessly tracking down the ringleaders and generously sparing those who had been led away; it was the Committee which first attempted to re-establish discipline in the armies and to supply them with provisions and munitions of war; and it was on the motion of the most important member of the first Committee, Danton, that the fatal decree of the 19th of November, which consecrated the revolutionary propaganda, and gave good reason for the continued opposition of foreign powers, was repealed. This good work in all directions showed the members of the Convention that they were acting in the right direction.

On 10th July 1793 the first Committee was dissolved on the motion of Camille Desmoulins, but a new Committee with similar powers was at once elected. This Committee, which may be called the Great Committee of Public Safety, remained in power for more than a year. Danton was not a member of it, partly because he believed he could do better work outside, partly because of his dislike of continued labour; Cambon also was not re-elected, preferring to confine himself to the charge of the finances of the Republic as the principal member of the Financial Committee. The nine members originally elected in July were Barère, who acted as reporter throughout its tenure of office, and was therefore in some respects the most important of them all; Jean Bon Saint-André, who took charge of naval matters; Prieur of the Marne and Robert Lindet, whose main duties were to provide for the feeding of the armies; Hérault de Séchelles, the chief author of the Constitution of 1793, who busied himself with foreign affairs; Couthon, Saint-Just, Gasparin, and Thuriot. Robespierre entered the Committee in the place of Gasparin on the 27th of July; Carnot and Prieur of the Côte-d'Or were added on the 14th of August to superintend the military operations on the frontiers; Billaud-Varenne and Collot-d'Herbois were added on September the 6th to establish the Reign of Terror; and on the 20th of September Thuriot retired. The steps in the growth of the supremacy of this second Committee of Public Safety are significant. On the 1st of August 1793 Barère read his first report to the Convention. In it he proposed the most energetic, not to say sanguinary, measures. The war was to be carried on with the utmost energy; La Vendée was to be destroyed; and Marie Antoinette was to be sent for trial before the Revolutionary Tribunal. On the same day Danton proposed that the Committee should be formally recognised as a provisional government, and that the ministers should be directed to act as its subordinates. This motion was not carried, but the entire control over the resources of France, and the lives of Frenchmen, which Danton contemplated, was secured without the passing of a formal decree. The Convention seems to have been very glad to rid itself of the work of government. It accepted without a murmur every measure proposed by the Committee of Public Safety; it re-elected the members month after month; it threw all responsibility upon them and registered all the decrees they proposed. As has been said, it definitely gave them the charge of the military operations by the election of Carnot and Prieur of the Côte-d'Or, and it established the unity of their internal administration by the election of Billaud-Varenne and Collot-d'Herbois.

The rule of the second or Great Committee of Public Safety is generally known as the Reign of Terror. The Committee itself divided the chief functions of government among its members. The special functions of all, except those of Robespierre, Couthon, and Saint-Just, have been already noticed. Robespierre was the only one amongst them who had any reputation outside, or indeed within, the walls of the Convention. His conduct during the session of the Constituent Assembly, his clear-sighted opposition to the war with Austria, his sagacious views on the subject of the treatment of the King, his war against the Girondin federalists, his oratorical talent, and above all his reputation for being absolutely incorruptible and sincerely patriotic, made him the man of mark among the Committee. He was well aware of the importance of his position. His

*The Position of Robespierre.*

colleagues on the Committee used him as their figure-head to represent them on great occasions, and he made it his business to lay down the general principles which underlay the system of revolutionary government—that is, of the Reign of Terror. But though to the Convention and to France at large Robespierre was the most conspicuous member of the Committee of Public Safety, he really exercised but very slight influence on the actual work of government. He had no department of the State given into his charge; he had not the necessary fluency or facility to take Barère's place as ordinary reporter; he was not on terms of friendship with the majority of his fellow-workers; he was made use of, but was neither trusted nor liked by the real governors of France. It was to their benefit that the system of the solidarity of the Committee was established, which gave to all their measures the sanction of Robespierre's great reputation for incorruptibility and patriotism. The majority of the Committee had no positive views on government; they tried to do the work which lay to their hands in the best way they could; Robespierre alone hoped to evolve out of the Reign of Terror a new system of republican government. His only real friends in the Committee were the two men least suited to give him effectual help, for Couthon was a cripple, and unable to attend with the necessary assiduity, and Saint-Just was but five-and-twenty, the youngest of the Committee, and was generally absent from Paris on special missions.

The system by which the Great Committee of Public Safety regulated the Reign of Terror was based upon two important institutions. The first of these was the Committee of General Security which sat in Paris, and was elected from the members of the Convention, and which exercised general police control over all France. On great occasions its members sat with the Committee of Public Safety as a Committee of Government, but its special functions were to deal with men, while the Committee of Public Safety dealt with

*The Reign of Terror.*

*Committee of General Security.*

measures. Danton, who was the principal creator of the supremacy of the Great Committee of Public Safety—though he himself refused to join it—saw the importance of subordinating in fact, if not in name, the Committee of General Security to the Committee of Public Safety. On 11th September 1793 a Committee of General Security had been elected, containing certain deputies of independent character, and Danton, fearing a rivalry would arise between the two Committees, at once obtained its dissolution, and secured, on September the 14th, the election of a Committee of General Security which would act in harmony with the great Committee. The members elected at this time were with but few exceptions re-elected every month.

The second instrument by which the Great Committee ruled were the deputies on mission. The practice of sending deputies on special missions originated in August 1792. It had grown in importance, and the deputies proved their value in their vigorous suppression of the Girondin movement in the provinces in the summer of 1793. The power of deputies on mission was more than once specifically declared to be unlimited. On grounds of public safety they were not only permitted, but were ordered, to alter the composition of local authorities, whether municipal or departmental. They had full powers to arrest and to make requisitions. They were consistently supported by the Committee of Public Safety sitting in Paris, and the greatest latitude was given to them in administering the local government. As long as they preserved the peace and sent up plenty of supplies of money, and, when demanded, of recruits to Paris, their methods of government were not minutely inquired into. Besides the deputies on mission employed in the internal administration, another important body of similar representatives were kept at the headquarters of the different armies. These deputies likewise had unlimited authority. They could arrest even generals-in-chief at their absolute will; they could degrade officers of any rank; they could interfere with

*Deputies on Mission.*

military operations ; and could overrule the orders of a general in the field. The Committee of General Security and the deputies on mission ruled by means of inspiring terror. This terror was based on the existence of the Revolutionary Tribunal in Paris, and of its imitations termed revolutionary or military commissions in the provinces, and the armies.

The Revolutionary Tribunal took cognisance of all political offences, and its sentence was almost invariably death. Nearly every Frenchman or Frenchwoman could be brought within the net of the Revolutionary Tribunal by the Law of the Suspects. By this law, which was most carefully drafted by Merlin of Douai, any one who for any reason could be suspected of disliking the new state of affairs could be arrested. All relatives of *émigrés* or of noblemen came into this category as well as all former functionaries and officials of whatever sort. But since the Law of the Suspects was not sufficiently wide to impress the ordinary bourgeois, more especially the petty bourgeois, with terror, a new weapon was forged in the Law of the Maximum. This law was put into operation in September 1793. The laws of political economy could not be seriously affected by such a measure as the Law of the Maximum, which fixed maximum prices at which all articles of prime necessity were to be sold. Such a law was certain to be evaded ; but its existence, and the fact that evasions of the Law of the Maximum brought the offender under the Revolutionary Tribunal, was enough to establish the Reign of Terror over the petty bourgeois. There were other means for extending the system which need not here be particularised, such as the necessity of every person carrying a card with him giving a full history of his conduct during the Revolution, the encouragement of denunciations by the bestowal of rewards, and similar precautions. The Revolutionary Tribunal was provided with victims under these measures by the Committee of General Security, and by the numerous little Revolutionary Committees sitting in every section of Paris, and in every city, district, and village

*Law of the Suspects.*

*Law of the Maximum.*

throughout France. The Revolutionary Committees consisted of tried Jacobins, and were in the provinces appointed by the deputies on mission. They were frequently purified by the expulsion of any member who gave evidence of moderate opinions. The Revolutionary Committees filled the prisons— it was the business of the Revolutionary Tribunal to empty them. This it did with much expedition. The death sentences of the Revolutionary Tribunal of Paris, which only averaged three a week from April to September 1793, averaged thirty-two a week from September 1793 to June 1794, and 196 a week in June and July 1794. This increase was very gradual; it became an established system to send batches of victims to the guillotine every day; and the numbers in these batches increased steadily. The Committee of Public Safety, through its agent, the Committee of General Security, did not much care who were executed as long as a considerable number went to the scaffold every day. Exceptions to this rule are, however, to be noted in the executions of Marie Antoinette on 16th October 1793, of twenty-one Girondins on 31st October, of certain generals, such as Custine, Houchard, and Biron, and of the Duke of Orleans and Bailly, which intimidated courtiers, deputies, generals, and ex-Constituants.

This system of terror was not suddenly evolved—it was the result of gradual growth. The two men mainly responsible for systematising it and carrying it into effect were Billaud-Varenne and Collot-d'Herbois, who were specially added to the Committee of Public Safety to superintend the internal administration of France. On 10th October 1793, on the motion of Saint-Just, the Constitution of 1793 was declared suspended, and revolutionary government, that is, the Reign of Terror, was ordered to continue until a general peace. On 10th December Billaud-Varenne read a report which defined the system, of which the most important clause was the substitution of national agents nominated by the government, —that is, by the deputies on mission,—to take the place of the

## Capture of Toulon

elected procureurs-syndics of the districts. The Reign of Terror in the provinces varied greatly. Some proconsuls, such as Carrier at Nantes and Le Bon at Arras, carried out their government in the most bloodthirsty fashion, but the 'Noyades,' or drowning of prisoners wholesale at Nantes, must not be regarded as typical of the terror in the provinces. Many proconsuls, such as André Dumont, contented themselves with threats, and while filling their prisons with suspects declined to empty them by means of the guillotine. Other proconsuls, such as Bernard of Saintes, preferred to send an occasional batch of prisoners to Paris to having a revolutionary tribunal of their own; but in every case except those of Carrier and Javogues, which were too atrocious to be passed over, the Committee of Public Safety gave its agents in the provinces a free hand to rule as they would so long as they maintained internal tranquillity and passive obedience to the decrees of the revolutionary government.

While the government of the Committee of Public Safety was being organised in Paris and in the provinces, disasters succeeded each other with rapidity both on the frontiers and in the interior of France. The Prussians, after the capture of Mayence, only advanced a short distance into France; but the Austrians made steady progress in the north-east in conjunction with the English, and, under Würmser, penetrated Alsace and stormed the lines of Wissembourg. The Comte d'Artois declared his intention to place himself at the head of the insurgents in La Vendée, at Lyons, and in the mountains of Auvergne. The English also promised to send armed assistance in every direction. But the younger brother of Louis XVI. thought it enough to make promises—he did absolutely nothing to fulfil them. The English on their part confined themselves to one important operation. They had on the outbreak of war despatched a fleet to the Mediterranean under the command of Lord Hood, and on the 4th of August 1793 the insurgents at Toulon, in the course of their opposition to the Convention, surrendered their city to the allied English and Spanish

*Results of the Terror.*

fleets. In Lyons the same progress of opposition was to be observed. The original insurgents had professed federalist opinions, but when the Convention sent an army against them open royalists took the place of the federalists. The vigorous action of the new government soon freed the French Republic from its foreign and internal foes. Carnot, on taking charge of military measures, saw that the only means of defeating the invaders was to take advantage of the numbers of his soldiers and to act in masses. Acting on this policy General Houchard Battles of Hondschoten and Wattignies. 1793. raised the siege of Dunkirk and defeated the English and Hanoverians in the battle of Hondschoten (8th September). In spite of his victory Houchard was disgraced for not following it up with vigour. Jourdan, his successor, carrying out the same policy, concentrated his army against the Austrians, raised the siege of Maubeuge, and defeated the Austrians at Wattignies (16th October). These victories did not drive the Anglo-Austrian army out of France, but they stopped the progress of the allies and caused them to stand upon the defensive. Farther south the same vigour was displayed. Saint-Just restored discipline in the armies of the Rhine and the Moselle. Hoche, at the head of the latter, won the victory of the Geisberg (25th September) over the Austrians and Prussians, while Pichegru, at the head of the Army of the Rhine, relieved Landau and drove Würmser across the Rhine. Almost at the same time a powerful army, of which the best regiments were the former garrison of Valenciennes, captured Lyons on the 9th of October, and on the 18th of December Toulon was retaken by an army under the command of General Dugommier. It was at the siege of Toulon that Napoleon Bonaparte first made himself conspicuous and won the rank of general of brigade. The republican armies were equally successful against the Spaniards. The Army of the Eastern Pyrenees, under D'Aoust, recovered Roussillon, while that of the Western Pyrenees, under Müller, drove the Spaniards across the Bidassoa. In La Vendée equal success was achieved. The former garrison of Mayence, which was composed of excellent soldiers who had gained experience and discipline from their long resistance to the Prussians, destroyed the Vendéan armies, and the insurrection of the province was severely punished by Carrier at Nantes and by the infernal columns which, under General Turreau, were directed to devastate the country. These repeated successes in every quarter reconciled the French people to the hideous *régime* of the Reign of Terror. Its despotism was excused because of its success, and its absolute authority reluctantly submitted to as a necessary evil.

In Paris the supremacy of the Committee of Public Safety and the Reign of Terror met with opposition in two distinct quarters. On the one hand the Commune of Paris, which was principally influenced by the Procureur-Syndic, Chaumette, and his substitute, Hébert, soon began to resent the loss of its former authority. The Commune had actually carried out the *coup d'état* which overthrew the Girondins, and had expected to reap the chief advantage for itself. In order to form a party it demanded that the revolutionary government should cease and that the Constitution of 1793 should be put into force. But this cry did not raise a sufficiently powerful support. The leaders of the Commune, therefore, allied themselves with the most extreme democratic party, which met generally at the Cordeliers Club. This extreme party professed absolutely atheistic principles. It proclaimed the Worship of Reason; it celebrated that worship with orgies in the cathedral of Notre Dame; it induced Gobel, Bishop of Paris, to resign his see; it carried its opposition to Christianity to an extreme; and started a system of persecution against the Christian religion. In home politics it did not defend the socialistic notions which had found some currency in Paris, but it nevertheless declared itself the party of the *sans culottes*, and denounced all rich men and bourgeois as selfish egotists and enemies of the people. In foreign policy it adopted the doctrines of the revolutionary propaganda and declared it the

*Fall of the Hébertists and Dantonists.*

destiny of France to destroy all tyrants. The Committee of Public Safety, as soon as its power was firmly organised, resolved to overthrow this party of opposition by striking at its leaders. Robespierre attacked them in the Jacobin Club, and caused them to be excluded as atheists and enemies of all government; Danton denounced the Worship of Reason as a disgraceful masquerade; Camille Desmoulins exhausted his resources of eloquence and sarcasm to hold them and their doctrines up to reprobation in the *Vieux Cordelier*. As soon as the extreme party, which is commonly called the Hébertist party, after its most conspicuous leader Hébert, the editor of the *Père Duchesne*, was thoroughly discredited, the Committee of Public Safety struck. On 24th Ventôse (14th March 1794) Hébert and his principal supporters were arrested on the report of Saint-Just. They were at once sent for trial before the Revolutionary Tribunal, and on 4th Germinal (24th March) they were guillotined.

The Hébertists fell because they opposed the despotism of the new government. The Dantonists, who followed them to the guillotine, fell because they believed the Reign of Terror to be carried too far. Danton had done more than any man to bring about the supremacy of the Great Committee of Public Safety. Convinced as he was that only a strong executive could possibly disentangle France from the dangers which beset her on every side, he had consistently advocated the creation of a strong government. Though not himself a member of the Great Committee, he had believed it to be his duty to support its power on every possible occasion. He had not only been the chief author of its supremacy, but the principal creator of the system by which it ruled. But he began to believe, in the beginning of the year 1794, that the Reign of Terror was being too stringently exercised. He was quite in accord with Billaud-Varenne and Collot-d'Herbois in considering it necessary to frighten the people of France into acquiescence with the new order of things, but he did not consider that it was necessary to shed so much blood to accomplish the work of fright. His friend Camille Desmoulins had in the *Vieux Cordelier* not only exposed the Hébertists, but had hinted at the need for mercy and the advantages of appointing a Committee of Mercy. The Great Committee of Public Safety was not only determined to maintain its autocratic power, but to defend its system of government. Danton's influence in the Convention was still sufficiently great to give the members of the Committee a cause for uneasiness. It therefore resolved, in order to stop all murmuring against the Reign of Terror, and to establish a reign of terror over the Convention itself, to make an example of the most vigorous patriot in France. On 10th Germinal (30th March 1794) Danton, Camille Desmoulins, and their chief adherents were arrested, and on 16th Germinal (5th April 1794) the Dantonists followed the Hébertists to the guillotine. These two blows ensured the supremacy of the Committee of Public Safety and the continuance of the Reign of Terror.

The Great Committee of Public Safety knew that its tenure of power rested on its successful conduct of the foreign war. Throughout the interior tranquillity prevailed except in La Vendée, where the sanguinary measures adopted perpetuated a guerilla warfare. *Campaign of 1794.* The French troops were, in 1794, in a very different condition from that in which they had been left at the commencement of 1793. The measures of terror which pacified France had been in the army the cause of the restoration of discipline. Constant fighting had converted the men into efficient soldiers. Excellent officers had come to the front during the campaign, and, owing to the rapidity of promotion, most of the generals were young and energetic men. All that was best in France had gone to the front. There, and there alone, men who might have fallen under the terrible Law of the Suspects at home, were not only safe themselves, but by their presence in the ranks of the Republic protected their relatives. All the resources of France were laid at the disposal of her armies. The country became one vast arsenal. The soldiers were well fed, clothed, and armed, and the ablest administrators were employed in rendering them efficient. The result of this concentration of France upon the foreign war was success in every quarter. In the spring of 1794 the various armies took the offensive, the Army of the North, under Pichegru, marched by the northern line into Belgium, while a new army, afterwards called the Army of the Sambre-and-Meuse, which was formed out of the Army of the Ardennes, and a wing of the Army of the Moselle penetrated Belgium from the south. Before these two armies the English and Austrians fell back. They were rapidly pursued, and on the 26th of June 1794 Jourdan won the battle of Fleurus. This victory, like the victory of Jemmappes the year before, laid Belgium open to the French armies. Brussels was reoccupied; the English and Dutch retired into Holland; the Austrians fell back behind the Meuse. Meanwhile, the Army of the Moselle, under René Moreaux, stormed the Prussian position at Kaiserslautern, and with the Army of the Rhine drove the Austrians across that river. The Army of Italy, which had taken Toulon, also took the offensive, and defeated the Piedmontese at Saorgio. Dugommier, with the Army of the Eastern Pyrenees, turned the tables on the Spaniards, and crossing the mountains penetrated into Catalonia, while the Army of the Western Pyrenees invaded Spain in that quarter, and threatened San Sebastian.

*Battle of Fleurus. June 26, 1794.*

The only checks which the Great Committee received were at sea. Whether it was because it is more difficult to improvise a navy than an army, or because sufficient attention was not paid to the republican navy, it is impossible to decide, but it is quite certain that the sailors of the Republic did not rival the soldiers in success, though they did in valour. One reason for this was that all the best sailors preferred the lucrative work of preying upon the commerce of the world in frigates and privateers to serving in the regular fleets, where no prizes were to be made. The two principal French fleets were those stationed at Toulon and at Brest. An ineffectual effort had been made by Sir Sidney Smith to burn the Toulon fleet when the English and Spaniards evacuated that port. Nevertheless, a new fleet was soon prepared, but its action against the English and the Spaniards who blockaded the coast were ineffectual. The English on leaving Toulon had proceeded to Corsica. That island had been raised against the Convention by the native patriot, Paoli, who invited the English to come and take possession in the name of George III. In Corsica, owing to the weakness of the French Mediterranean fleet, the English remained unmolested for nearly a year. The Brest fleet, however, came to blows with the English Channel fleet, under the command of Lord Howe. The United States of America had agreed to pay part of the debt which they owed France for money lent during the War of American Independence in grain, and a convoy was sent to protect the grain-ships. Lord Howe was directed to cut off this convoy, and the French fleet left Brest to ensure its safe arrival. From one point of view, the action of the French fleet was crowned with success, for the convoy arrived safely, but the fleet itself was utterly defeated by Lord Howe on the 1st of June 1794. Since the object had been attained, the Committee of Public Safety claimed credit for the action in which the fleet had been engaged, and the reports which Barère read daily from the tribune of the Convention were invariably of battles won and of feats of valour. *Battle of the 1st of June.*

The brilliant successes which followed the establishment of the power of the Great Committee of Public Safety justified its despotism in the eyes of France, but as soon as those successes had freed France from the invaders, it was generally felt that the weight of the Reign of Terror was intolerable, and that it had become unnecessary. It was at this period of most brilliant military triumphs that the Terror grew to its greatest height in Paris. On 22d Prairial (10th of June 1794) a law was passed to accelerate the procedure of the Revolutionary Tribunal, *Fall of Robespierre, 9th Thermidor (27th July) 1794.*

and the number of deaths upon the guillotine increased to an average of 196 a week. Robespierre, who, as has been said, was more of a statesman than his colleagues upon the Committee of Public Safety, who were simply administrators, understood the tenor of feeling in France. He believed that the time was coming when the Reign of Terror should cease, and a new Reign of Virtue, carrying into effect the maxims of Rousseau, could be established. The working members of the Committee allowed Robespierre to theorise to his heart's content; as long as he did not interfere with them, he might advocate what principles he pleased. The first evidence of Robespierre's new tendency appeared in his establishment of the Worship of the Supreme Being. He was a profoundly religious and virtuous man, and the chief cause of his hatred of Hébert and Danton was his belief that they were immoral atheists. On 18th Floréal (7th May 1794) Robespierre made his most famous speech in the Convention, by which he induced the Convention to officially acknowledge the existence of a Supreme Being and the immortality of the soul. The speech was followed on 20th Prairial by a great festival in honour of the Supreme Being, at which Robespierre presided. This was the day when his power seemed greatest, but many of his colleagues laughed at his assumption of virtue and at his posing as a high priest. He perceived clearly that he could not establish his chimerical Reign of Virtue without destroying the scoffers who refused to believe in him and his doctrines. He absented himself for six weeks from the meetings of the Committee, and prepared a speech by which he hoped to induce the Convention to proscribe his opponents.

On 8th Thermidor (26th July 1794) he read this speech to the Convention, and attacked covertly, and without mentioning many names, not only certain of his colleagues in the Committee of Public Safety, but also the majority of the Committee of General Security and of the Financial Committee. These men, who had been governing France while Robespierre was theorising, would not tamely submit to be ejected from power and guillotined. On the evening of the same day Robespierre read his speech to the Jacobin Club, which was the headquarters of the puritans who believed in the possibility of a Reign of Virtue. But on 9th Thermidor the accused deputies determined to act. It was not only the working members of the Committees, but also the friends of Danton, the independent deputies of the Mountain, and the members of the Centre, who felt threatened, and their attitude was speedily declared. Saint-Just began to read a report accusing Billaud-Varenne and Collot-d'Herbois by name, but he was interrupted, and Robespierre himself, with Couthon, Saint-Just, and two other deputies were, after a stormy scene, ordered under arrest. But the puritan party were not only strong in the Jacobin Club; they dominated the Commune of Paris ever since the overthrow of the Hébertists. Hanriot, the commandant of the National Guard of Paris, rescued Robespierre and the other imprisoned deputies, and took them to the Hôtel-de-Ville, where a scheme of government was discussed.

The Convention did not wait to be attacked. It declared Robespierre and all his adherents to be outlaws, and Barras, Fréron, and Léonard Bourdon collected columns of regular troops and national guards to attack the Hôtel-de-Ville. The Convention was completely successful. The people of Paris, like the people of all France, persisted in considering Robespierre as the author of the Reign of Terror, while not only his enemies but his colleagues threw upon him the responsibility for all the atrocities included under the name of the Terror. Though personally he had very little influence in the Committee, he was represented and regarded as its master. Consequently no hand was raised to protect Robespierre and the puritans; the Hôtel-de-Ville was easily occupied by Barras; Robespierre was wounded in the mouth by a gendarme, and on 10th Thermidor (28th July) he was guillotined, and was accompanied or followed to the scaffold by the small group of colleagues who had been impeached with him, and by the majority of the Commune of Paris.

The death of Robespierre did not lead to a change of government, but it led to an alteration in the system by which the government was administered. The deputies who had been most instrumental in the revolution of Thermidor belonged to the Mountain, and expected to retain power in their hands; but they saw the necessity of preventing such a permanence of power as had existed during the previous year. It was, therefore, resolved that the Committees of Government—that is, the Committees of Public Safety and of General Security—should be renewed by a quarter every month, and that the retiring members should not be eligible for re-election until a month had passed. The survivors of the Great Committee still believed in the system of government by terror, but their new colleagues understood that now that France was victorious the country would no longer submit to such rigorous measures of repression. The victory of Fleurus had done away with the necessity of continually employing the guillotine. The system of terror was therefore tacitly abandoned; the supremacy of the Committees continued; the Law of the Suspects was unrepealed; the Revolutionary Tribunal continued to exist; representatives were still sent on mission with unlimited powers; but the succession of executions ceased, and the method of government, though arbitrary, was no longer sanguinary. The men who ruled France from Thermidor (July) 1794 to Ventôse (March) 1795 were all deputies of the Mountain, men of the type of Carnot and Robert Lindet, the most sagacious of the members of the Great Committee of Public Safety. The most conspicuous of the new men of this period were Merlin of Douai and Treilhard, who took charge of the foreign policy. These statesmen, while Carnot superintended the carrying on of the war with his accustomed vigour and success, finally broke with the propagandist doctrines which had made the war of unparalleled magnitude and bitterness, and Merlin of Douai, on 14th Frimaire (4th December) 1794 read a report in the name of the Committee of Public Safety, declaring that the Republic did not wish to be at war with Europe for ever, and laying down the bases on which treaties of peace honourable to France could be made. While the Thermidorians were administering the government strongly and honourably, they were beset with cries of vengeance against the Terrorists of the previous year. They felt it necessary to yield to the general outcry, and on 21st Brumaire, Year III. (11th November 1794), Carrier, the most ferocious of the proconsuls of the Terror, was sent before the Revolutionary Tribunal. He was tried and eventually executed for his crimes. The agitation was stronger against the organisers of the Terror, Billaud-Varenne, and Collot-d'Herbois, with whom were associated in the popular hatred Barère, the reporter, and Vadier, who had been the most conspicuous member of the Committee of General Security. Both the doctrines and the men of the Terror had still plenty of supporters in Paris, who now dominated the Jacobin Club, which was therefore closed by the Thermidorians in December 1794. Almost at the same date the Law of the Maximum was repealed. In the same month the survivors of the seventy-three deputies who had protested against the proscription of the Girondins, and consequently been imprisoned, were recalled to their seats in the Convention.

Meanwhile the series of victories which had commenced during the rule of the Great Committee of Public Safety continued. Pichegru at the head of the Army of the North pursued the English and their Dutch and Hanoverian allies. On the 9th of October he took Nimeguen, and forcing his way across the frozen rivers drove the English through Holland. He occupied Amsterdam, and then with his hussars took the Dutch fleet, which was unable to leave its moorings in the Texel owing to the ice. By the end of January 1795 the whole of Holland was in the possession of the French. The Stadtholder, the Prince of Orange, fled to England, and the English troops were soon after withdrawn. The conquest of Holland was

*Conquest of Holland. 1794-5.*

*The Batavian Republic.*

of the greatest service to the Thermidorians, for it enabled them, by drawing upon the wealth of that country, to relieve the financial distress of the French Republic. With regard to Belgium there was no difficulty in coming to a decision as to its future, for the Decree of Reunion passed in the days of Dumouriez' success remained unrepealed, and the Austrian Netherlands were therefore organised as part of the French Republic. It was otherwise with regard to Holland. The Thermidorians did not desire to further aggravate the fears of Europe by annexing that country, but at the same time they were quite resolved that it should not again fall under the power of the English. Reubell and Sieyès, two ex-Constituants who had remained in obscurity during the Reign of Terror, were despatched to Holland to see what could be done. They found many Dutch admirers of the doctrines of the French Revolution, and speedily conciliated the burghers of the Dutch cities, who had always resented the power of the Stadtholder. With the help of these parties and of the Dutch patriots who had been exiled in 1787, and who now returned from France full of enthusiasm for democracy, they organised a Batavian Republic on the model of the French Republic, and in March 1795 a Treaty of Peace and Alliance was signed between the French and Batavian Republics. In other quarters the French Republic was likewise triumphant. Maestricht was taken by Kléber on the 4th of November 1794. Jourdan with the Army of the Sambre-and-Meuse, defeated the Austrians under Clerfayt at Aldenhoven on the 2d of October, and marching south occupied Aix-la-Chapelle, Bonn, Cologne, and Coblentz. Meanwhile the Army of the Moselle, under René Moreaux, finally drove the Prussians out of France and occupied the Palatinate and the whole of the Electorate of Trèves. On the southern frontier there were similar successes. The Army of the Eastern Pyrenees, which had invaded Catalonia, stormed the Spanish camp at Figueras on the 20th of November 1794, and took Rosas on the 3rd

*Successes in other quarters.*

of February 1795. In the first of these actions the French General Dugommier was killed in action. Moncey, with the Army of the Western Pyrenees, took Bilbao, Vittoria, and San Sebastian. The Army of Italy won the victory of Loano on the 24th of November, which opened communication with Genoa. The Army of the Alps finally reached the summits of Mont Cenis and the Little St. Bernard, and drove the Piedmontese before it.

While the French nation had thus after much suffering and long submission to the Reign of Terror secured its independence and made itself feared by Europe, a Polish insurrection had taken place which was not crowned with the same success. The second partition of Poland, which was consummated in 1793, has been described. But the Polish nation was not inclined to acknowledge its extinction without another blow. Many Polish exiles came to France, and the leader of the Polish patriots, Kosciuszko, received a flattering reception, though no promise of active help. On the 23d of March 1794 Kosciuszko entered Cracow and raised the standard of national independence. This news caused a general rising in Prussian Poland, where the new administrators of Prussia had behaved with extreme cruelty. Stanislas Poniatowski, King of Poland, acting under the influence of the Russian general commanding at Warsaw, Igelstrom, disavowed Kosciuszko and declared him a rebel. But the Polish people welcomed Kosciuszko as a liberator. He defeated the Russians at Raclawice on the 4th of April 1794, and after a further victory occupied Warsaw on the 19th. Both Russians and Prussians prepared to defend the provinces they had annexed in 1793, and laid siege to Warsaw in July 1794. By the beginning of September all Prussian Poland was in a flame of insurrection; Frederick William II., who was conducting the siege in person, rapidly retreated and summoned to his assistance a large proportion of the troops hitherto employed against France. But though the Prussians had temporarily retired, Catherine of Russia determined, at all

*Poland. 1794-5*

hazards, to conquer the Poles. She gathered a great army from all parts of her empire, and placed it under the command of the most famous of the Russian generals, Suvórov. Caught between the army of Suvórov and the army of Fersen, who had succeeded Igelstrom in command of the Russians already in Poland, the Polish patriots were utterly defeated at Maciejowice on the 12th of October 1794, when Kosciuszko was wounded and taken prisoner. On the 4th of November, Praga, the suburb of Warsaw on the right bank of the Vistula, was stormed by Suvórov, and on the 9th of November the capital surrendered. Catherine determined to complete the work of the destruction of Poland. Stanislas Poniatowski was removed from Poland on the 7th of January 1795, and on the 25th of November 1795 he abdicated the throne.

The division of the spoils caused much trouble to the allies. The Austrians, who had been left in the lurch at the second partition, claimed a share, and, like the Prussians, weakened their armies on the frontier of France in order to de-

Extinction of Poland. 1795. fend their claims on Poland. By the final partition, which was arranged between the powers in 1795, Prussia received Warsaw and the surrounding palatinates; Austria received Cracow and the rest of Galicia, and the Russians were content with rectifying their frontier from Grodno to Minsk. It is interesting to contrast the simultaneous failure of the Poles and success of the French. The cause lay in the fact that the great bulk of the Polish people were serfs, to whom it mattered little what master they served, whereas the French people had long thrown off the bonds of personal serfdom, and had just succeeded in getting rid of the last shackles of the privileged classes. The Polish Constitution of 1791 was the work of a few enlightened noblemen and priests, and was gladly accepted by the educated bourgeois of the cities, but the peasants were in too degraded a condition to understand what personal liberty meant. In France every peasant, every farmer had profited by the Revolution, and was wedded to its cause not only for political reasons, but because of the purchases of ecclesiastical property which he had made. The national feeling in France embraced the whole people, and made France successful against her foreign foes; the national feeling in Poland only existed among a minority of the population, and the result was that Kosciuszko was unable to attain the triumph which he so well merited.

The successes of the French Republic and the failure of the Polish national movement affected the attitude of the coalition both towards France and towards its own members. The Prussians, ever since the defeat of Brunswick in 1792, had openly expressed their belief that the Austrians were betraying them and using them as catspaws. Frederick William II. for a long time battled against these views, which were held by the chief Prussian statesmen, such as Haugwitz and Alvensleben, by the most respected Prussian generals such as Kalkreuth and Möllendorf, and by his own personal clique of favourites, headed by Lucchesini. In the year 1793 he had confined his operations against France to the siege of Mayence, while his best troops were directed on Poland, and in 1794 he had still further reduced the number of his soldiers upon the Rhine. England, which had paid large subsidies to the Prussian government, resented this conduct, and declared its intention of withdrawing all subsidies unless Prussia would do as she was directed. Frederick William II. declared that he would not receive the English subsidies on these terms; but the truth was, that his attention was far more occupied by the gains he hoped to get in Poland than with the prosecution of the war against France. Austria, also, where Thugut had in 1794 become the nominal as well as the real director of the foreign policy of the Emperor Francis, was getting tired of the war with France. Prussia's conduct in making the second partition of Poland in 1793, and leaving the Emperor out, had sown the seeds of discontent. Thugut was determined that the same thing should not occur again, and, therefore, when the Polish insurrection broke out

*Change in the attitude of Continental Powers.*

in 1794, Austria also denuded her armies upon the French frontier. This attitude of Prussia and Austria does not entirely account for the victories of the French republican armies, but it explains to some extent the ease with which those victories were obtained. Spain also was weary of the war. Godoy felt that his tenure of office was imperilled by the existence of two French armies in Spain which might easily march upon Madrid, and the Queen, and therefore the King, was entirely under the influence of Godoy. Many of the princes of the Holy Roman Empire likewise wished to see the war at an end, for it was their states upon the left bank of the Rhine which were occupied by the French armies; it was their states upon the right bank of the Rhine which would be invaded by the passage of that river, whereas the home dominions of Austria and Prussia were far to the east, and not likely to be reached by an invading army. England was the only power which seriously desired to prosecute the war, for in England a national feeling of repulsion against the French had arisen. The English government, however, was unable to strike any effective blow; Hoche destroyed a body of *émigrés* landed from English ships at Quiberon Bay in July 1794; the continental powers who received subsidies were not very earnest in doing the work for which they were paid; the French occupation of Holland had deprived England of the only base from which an army could act in Europe; and the English government had therefore to be contented with blockading the French ports and occupying the French West Indian Colonies.

The recall of those sympathisers with the Girondin party, who had been imprisoned, in December 1794 was followed in March 1795 by the recall to their seats in the Convention of the outlawed Girondin leaders, of whom the most conspicuous were Lanjuinais and Louvet. The return of these victims increased the clamour against the surviving Terrorist leaders and proconsuls who had ruled France in 1793-94 in Paris, or on mission in the provinces. Hot debates took place on the necessity of punishing what

*The Rule of the Thermidorians. Second Phase.*

was now termed 'Robespierre's tail.' In Paris a powerful section of the populace—namely, the young bourgeois, who were commonly called the Jeunesse Dorée, or after their leader Fréron the Jeunesse Fréronienne—never ceased to demand the punishment of the Terrorists. Popular sympathy was generally with the Jeunesse Dorée; conspicuous Jacobins of the Terror were beaten in the streets; the heart of Marat was taken from the Pantheon and thrown down a sewer; and the busts of Marat, who was regarded as the apostle of Terrorism, were everywhere broken. The former rulers of Paris, the old members of the Jacobin Club and the Revolutionary Committees, were not inclined to submit to popular vengeance without striking a blow. On 12th Germinal, Year III. (1st April 1795) they raised an insurrection in the turbulent Faubourg Saint-Antoine, and the insurgents broke into the Convention shouting 'Bread and the Constitution of 1793.' The only result of this riot was that Billaud-Varenne, Collot-d'Herbois, Barère, and Vadier were ordered to be deported to French Guiana without trial. The persecution of the Terrorists continued. A commission was appointed to inquire into the acts of the former proconsuls; power passed into the hands of the returned Girondins and the members of the Plain or Centre. Certain of the remaining deputies of the Mountain, supported by the Jacobins of Paris, then resolved on a second insurrection. On 1st Prairial, Year III. (20th May 1795) the Convention was again invaded by a Saint-Antoine mob, headed by women who had gained the unenviable name of the 'Furies of the Guillotine.' A deputy named Féraud was taken for Fréron and murdered on the spot, and throughout the day the hall of the Convention was occupied by a howling mob, which vainly endeavoured to compel the President, Boissy-d'Anglas, to pass the decrees they desired. Meanwhile the Committees of Government prepared to act with vigour. With the help of some regular troops quartered in Paris, of the national guards of the bourgeois sections, and of the

Jeunesse Dorée, they expelled the mob, and on the following days a force composed of these elements under the command of General Menou, an ex-Constituant, disarmed the revolutionary sections. The victory of the Committees was the victory of the enemies of the Reign of Terror. Some of the former Terrorist deputies were condemned to death and committed suicide, others were impeached and placed under arrest, and the Mountain as a party ceased to exist. The expulsion of the deputies of the Mountain caused the Committees of Government to be filled by the members of the Centre, the men who during the Reign of Terror had been peacefully occupied in the legislative and educational reforms, which were the most lasting works of the Convention. Of these new members the most typical is Cambacérès, the great jurist and principal law reformer of the period, on whose labours Napoleon compiled the Code Civil. While the Committees were engaged in the work of government, a commission of eleven deputies was appointed to draw up a new Constitution which should avoid the errors of its predecessors. The chief authors of this Constitution, which is known as the Constitution of the Year III., were Boissy-d'Anglas and Daunou.

The direction of foreign policy was still mainly conducted by Merlin of Douai, who was now aided in this department by Cambacérès, Sieyès, and Reubell. Their great work—indeed the great work of the Thermidorians —was the conclusion of the Treaties of Basle. The causes of these treaties have been shown in the examination just made of the changed attitude of the powers of Europe towards the French Republic. The agent of the French Republic in Switzerland, Barthélemy, was the diplomatist who negotiated the series of treaties. Switzerland had throughout the Reign of Terror been the centre of diplomatic action, for in Switzerland alone France could meet the representatives of foreign powers. The first and the most important of the Treaties of Basle was that between France and Prussia, which was signed upon the 5th of April 1795. By it not only was peace concluded between the contracting powers, but a line of demarcation was agreed to be drawn by which Prussia might secure safety from French invasion for the states of Northern Germany. One point only was left in abeyance by Barthélemy and Hardenberg, the negotiators of this treaty. The French Government insisted that France, in reward for her exertions, and in compensation for the long war, should receive her natural limits of the Rhine. Prussia's territory upon the left bank of the Rhine was very small in amount, and it was agreed that the amount of compensation she should receive for ceding it to France should be left unsettled for the present. Frederick William II., who posed as a guardian of the Holy Roman Empire, refused openly to assent to the doctrine that France should reach the Rhine and thus consecrate the infringement of the limits of the Empire. He had no desire to appear ready to consent to any such arrangement, for he felt that such a policy would leave to Austria the position of protector of the Empire. The Treaty of Basle with Prussia was succeeded at the same place by a treaty with Spain on the 22d of July, and finally by a treaty with the most energetic of the petty princes of the Empire, the Landgrave of Hesse-Cassel, on the 29th of August. Peace had already on February 9th been made with Tuscany, which had most unwillingly declared war on France under pressure from England. Of these treaties, the most important was that with Spain, which was excessively popular at Madrid, and won for Godoy the high-sounding title of 'Prince of the Peace.' Thus, after three years of war, France re-entered the comity of nations and broke up the coalition formed against her independence.

# CHAPTER V

## 1795-1797

Results of the Treaties of Basle on the Foreign Policy of France—Constitution of the Year III—The Directory—The Legislature: Councils of Ancients and of Five Hundred—Local Administration of France—The Insurrection of Vendémiaire—The Rising of 13th Vendémiaire in Paris—The First French Directors, Councils, and Ministers—Dissolution of the Convention—England and the *Emigrés*—Treason of Pichegru—Exchange of Madame Royale—Desire for Peace in France—France and Prussia—Suggestion of Secularisations in Germany—France and the Smaller States of Europe—Attitude of Russia—Campaign of 1795 in Germany—Bonaparte's Campaigns of 1796 in Italy—Battle of Montenotte—Armistice of Cherasco—Battle of Lodi—Armistice of Foligno—Conquest of Upper Italy—Battles of Castiglione, Arcola, and Rivoli—Peace of Tolentino with the Pope—Campaign of 1796 in Germany—Battle of Altenkirchen—Retreat of Moreau—Effects of the Campaign in Germany—Treaty between Prussia and France—Internal Policy of the Directory—Pacification of La Vendée—The State of France—The Directory, Councils, and Ministers in 1796—Creation of the Ministry of Police—Alliance between France and Spain—Treaty of San Ildefonso—Battle of Cape Saint-Vincent—The Batavian Republic—Negotiations between England and the Directory—Death of the Empress Catherine of Russia—Bonaparte's Campaign of 1797 in the Tyrol—The Campaign of 1797 in Germany—Preliminaries of Leoben between France and Austria.

THE conclusion of the Treaties of Basle in the spring and summer of 1795 brought France once more into a recognised position among the nations of Europe. The idea of a revolutionary propaganda had been entirely abandoned by the leading Thermidorians, who looked upon it as the first duty of the French Government to secure peace for France. All the great statesmen of the revolutionary period, from Mirabeau to Danton

*Result of the Treaties of Basle.*

and Robespierre, had protested against the absurd notion that it was the mission of France to secure the pre-eminence of democratic ideas throughout the whole of Europe. Events had shown that it was a task of quite sufficient difficulty to secure the prevalence of such ideas in France. The abandonment of the revolutionary propaganda broke up the league of old Europe against new France. When the Prussian state, and still more the ancient monarchy of Spain, had consented to make peace with France, the rest of the powers of the Continent felt that they could no longer affect to treat the French republicans as beyond the pale of humanity, or the French Republic as having destroyed the title of France to be reckoned as a nation.

The Thermidorians, not satisfied with their diplomatic success, constructed a new government for France. The authors of the policy, which resulted in the Treaties of Basle, were also the sponsors of the 'Constitution of the Year III.' The task of drawing up the bases of a new Constitution was referred upon 14th Germinal, Year III. (3d April 1795) to a committee of seven deputies, but the details were worked out by a subsequent commission of eleven. Among the seven the most important were Sieyès, Cambacérès, and Merlin of Douai, who were also at this period the three principal members of the Committee of Public Safety. Just as in making the Treaties of Basle, they and their colleagues had recurred to the fundamental ideas and policy of the old French Monarchy, so in the new Constitution they exhibited the influence of bygone ideas. The experience of the Constituent and Legislative Assemblies, and of the Convention until the formation of the Committee of Public Safety, had shown the utter inadequacy of intrusting supreme executive and administrative authority to an unwieldy deliberative assembly. The power of the monarchy in all modern states has rested upon the conviction of the importance of consolidating, as far as possible, the executive authority; the founders of the United States of America understood this truth, and invested their President

*Constitution of the Year III.*

with power resembling that exercised by kings; and the Convention, when it yielded to the voice of Danton, and conferred supreme authority upon the Committee of Public Safety, had reaped the advantage in its victories upon all the frontiers. Even the most obtuse of the deputies who sat in the Convention had learnt this lesson. And the founders of the Constitution of the Year III. had no difficulty in carrying the most important point in their programme. This was the entire separation of the executive and legislative powers. The Constitution of 1791, in its jealousy of the monarchy, had practically deprived the king and his ministers of all real authority, while leaving him the entire responsibility. The Constitution of 1793 had placed all executive authority in the hands of the Legislature. The Constitution of the Year III. endeavoured to separate the executive and legislative authorities.

Under the new arrangement the executive was placed in the hands of five Directors. One was to retire every year and was not eligible for re-election; his successor was to be chosen by the Legislature. In order to secure an entire separation between the members of the Directory and of the Legislature, no member of the latter could be elected a Director until twelve months had elapsed after the resignation of his seat. The Directors were to appoint the Ministers, who were to have no connection whatever with the Legislature, and who were to act as the agents of the Directors. The individual Directors were to exercise no authority in their own names. They were to live under the same roof in the Palace of the Luxembourg at Paris. They were to meet daily, and the will of the majority was to be taken as the will of the whole. They were to elect a President every month, who was to act as their mouthpiece at the reception of foreign ambassadors and on all occasions of ceremony. The control of the internal administration, the management of the armies and fleets, and all questions of foreign policy were entirely left to the Directors. But treaties, declarations

*The Directory.*

## The Constitution of the Year III

of war and similar acts had to be ratified by the Legislature. The Directors had nothing whatever to do with the work of legislation, and their assent was not needed to new laws. With regard to the revenue, the administration of the finances and of the treasury rested with the Directors, but they could not impose fresh taxes without the assent of the Legislature.

The Legislature, under the Constitution of the Year III. consisted of two chambers—the Council of Ancients and the Council of Five Hundred. It is a curious commentary upon the debates which took place in the Constituent Assembly in August 1789, when the establishment of two chambers was rejected with scorn as being an obvious imitation of the English Parliament, that in 1795 this very principle was almost unanimously adopted. The experience of the three great revolutionary assemblies had convinced Sieyès and his colleagues of the inexpediency of leaving important measures to be decided in a single chamber. The delay necessitated by a law being obliged to pass before two distinct deliberative bodies now appeared most advantageous, when compared with the headlong precipitation which had marked all the earlier stages of the Revolution. The Council of Ancients was to consist of men forty-five years old and upwards, and, therefore, presumably not liable to be carried away by sudden bursts of enthusiasm. For the Council of Five Hundred there was no limitation of age, and elderly men were not precluded from being returned to it. The Council of Five Hundred consisted, as its name implies, of five hundred deputies; the Council of Ancients of two hundred and fifty. Dictated by experience, also, were the measures taken for the election of deputies. In order to avoid the inconvenience which had resulted from the election of an entirely new body of representatives at one and the same moment, as had happened in 1791, it was resolved that one-third of the two Councils should retire yearly. Deputies were to be chosen by an elaborate system of primary and secondary assemblies

*The Legislature.*

held in each department of France, and a property qualification was demanded both for the electors and the deputies. With these safeguards Sieyès and his colleagues believed they had secured a practical means of obviating all the errors of the past. The Council of Five Hundred had allotted to it as its special function the initiation of all fresh taxation and the revision of all money bills. The Council of Ancients was the court of appeal in diplomatic questions, such as the declaration of war. In actual legislation the consent of the majority of both chambers was needed for a new law. For their most important function—the yearly election of a new Director—the two chambers were to form one united assembly.

By this Constitution, the conspicuous drawbacks of the two former Constitutions, namely, the enforced weakness of the executive and the undefined powers of the Legislature were avoided. But the local administration established by the Constitution of 1791 had proved so excellent that it was only slightly modified and not radically altered. The great achievement of the Constituent Assembly—the abolition of old provincial jealousies by the division of France into departments—was maintained. The wise step which had been taken by the Great Committee of Public Safety in abolishing the directories of the departments and of the districts was sanctioned, and the council-generals were left to act alone. The main distinction between the administrative systems of 1791 and 1795 was that the elected *procureurs-syndics* and *procureurs-généraux-syndics*, established by the former, were replaced by officials nominated by the supreme executive at Paris. These officials went under the name of agents during the Directory, but possessed the same authority and carried out the same functions as the *sous-préfets* and *préfets* afterwards appointed by Napoleon. The courts of justice, whether local, appellant, or supreme, established by the Constitution of 1791, were left untouched by the Constitution of the Year III.

*Local Administration of France.*

In spite of the glories of the conquest of Holland, the passage of the Rhine, the victory of Quiberon, and the invasion of Spain,—in spite of the even greater credit justly earned by the Treaties of Basle,—in spite of the new Constitution, which, if faulty in places, was superior to those which had preceded it—the Thermidorians were intensely unpopular in France. The recollection of the Reign of Terror weighed upon the imaginations of the people even after the death of Robespierre, the deportation of Billaud-Varenne, and the closing of the Jacobin Club. The Convention was still in the minds of men shrouded by the remembrance of the innocent blood that had been shed. The inauguration of the new constitutional system was looked upon as an opportunity for driving the members of the Convention from power, and threats of vengeance were everywhere heard against them. Intriguers, some of them possibly royalists, who desired the return of the Bourbons, but most of them bourgeois or aristocrats who had personal reasons for desiring revenge, hoped to take advantage of this general feeling to overthrow the Republic. But the mass of Frenchmen were sincerely republican, and were clear-sighted enough to perceive that the return of the Bourbons would be followed by the loss of the material advantages that had been gained by the sale of the lands of the Church and the nobility. The members of the Convention understood the intentions of the intriguers, and understood also that the French people sincerely loved the Republic. They proceeded to frustrate the designs of their enemies by decreeing that two-thirds of the new Legislature must be elected from among the deputies of the Convention. The intriguers in Paris, thus foiled in their expectations of a certain majority in the new Legislature, tried to rouse the people of Paris into active insurrection. There can be no doubt that not only in Paris, but throughout France, the action of the Convention in ordering the election of so large a proportion of the old deputies was profoundly unpopular, but it was one thing to dislike a measure and another

*The Insurrection of Vendémiaire.*

thing to involve France in a fresh revolution. In the provincial towns there was universal grumbling but no active opposition. In Paris, however, where the intriguers abounded, it was hoped that the *jeunesse dorée*, who had played so great a part in the previous winter, assisted by the bourgeois Sections, would be able by making an imposing display of force to compel the Convention to revoke the obnoxious decree.

This project of the agitators in Paris was soon known in the Convention, and had the result of causing the divided forces of the Thermidorians to close up their ranks. The three chief groups in this party were the returned Girondins, the leaders of the Plain, and the former adherents of the Terror. The leaders of all these groups united in the presence of a common danger, for they felt that the dissolution of the Convention without some such measure of security as the re-election of the two-thirds to the forthcoming Legislature would lead to their own proscription. They therefore appointed Barras, who had commanded in the attack upon the Hôtel-de-Ville upon the 9th Thermidor of the previous year, and overthrown the supporters of Robespierre assembled there, to watch over their safety. Barras summoned to his assistance Napoleon Bonaparte, who was then in Paris engaged in protesting against his recall from the Army of Italy. The antecedents of this young general, his well-known Jacobin principles and his former friendship for Augustin Robespierre, had led to his recall and to his being placed upon the unemployed list. Barras had under his command the garrison of regular troops quartered in Paris and the armed guards of the Convention. The Royalist agitators counted on the *jeunesse dorée* and the bourgeois Sections. Bonaparte perceived that in numbers each party was evenly matched, and he at once sent for the artillery quartered at Meudon. The Convention declared itself *en permanence*, the troops were stationed round the Tuileries, Bonaparte's guns were mounted in the gardens and the Place du Carrousel. The attack on the Convention was made on

*Fighting in Paris, 13th Vendémiaire (5th October 1795).*

the 13th Vendémiaire (5th October) in a very slovenly manner. No effort had been made to concentrate the force of the assailants at a given moment, and as the first column marched carelessly down without recognised leaders, it was fired upon and almost entirely cut to pieces by Bonaparte's artillery. Nevertheless column after column of devoted national guards approached the Tuileries with the utmost gallantry to meet the same fate. The insurrection of 13th Vendémiaire cannot be compared with the other famous insurrections of the 14th July 1789 and 10th August 1792, for not one of the defenders of the Convention was wounded. It was a butchery, not a battle.

The Convention, conscious of its unpopularity, and not desiring to increase it, made but slight efforts to discover and punish the leaders of the insurrection of 13th Vendémiaire. Only a few military executions, after trial by court-martial, of a few prisoners taken with arms in their hands were permitted, and no vigour was shown in hunting down even the most conspicuous agitators. It was resolved at once to proceed to the election of the first Directors under the new system. Sieyès refused to be one of them. It was generally agreed, though not formally declared, that the first Directors should all be deputies of the Convention who had voted for the death of Louis XVI., and who might therefore be presumed to be faithful to republican institutions, if not from inclination at least from fear. The five deputies actually elected were—Barras, whose conduct on the 9th Thermidor, and on the 13th Vendémiaire, had obtained for him the gratitude of the majority of the deputies; Reubell, an ex-Constituant and an Alsatian, who was believed to have a special knowledge of foreign affairs; Revellière-Lépeaux, another ex-Constituant, a member of the Committee of Public Safety, a good lawyer, and the future inventor of a new religion; Carnot, the famous military member of the Great Committee of Public Safety, who was selected for his strategic ability; and Letourneur, an ex-officer of Engineers, like Carnot, who was

*The First Directors.*

expected to act as Carnot's assistant. To the Council of Ancients and the Council of Five Hundred were elected among the two-thirds chosen from the Convention the more conspicuous Thermidorians, including Sieyès, Cambacérès, Tallien, and Treilhard. The six first ministers were appointed by the Directors on 14th Brumaire (5th November). They were Merlin of Douai and Charles Delacroix, two ex-deputies of the Convention who had not been elected to the new Legislature, appointed to the Ministries of Justice and of Foreign Affairs, Aubert-Dubayet, a distinguished general, to the Ministry of War, and Faypoult, Benezech and Admiral Truguet to the Ministries of Finance, the Interior, and the Marine.

The first Directors elected and the new Legislature constituted, the Convention had to decree its own dissolution. The three years during which it had sat are perhaps the most important and most critical in the whole history of France. The Convention had not merely witnessed the rise and fall of many cliques and many parties; it had allowed the Reign of Terror to be established, and had punished its inventors with death or deportation. It had passed through nearly every variety of government, and had seen France in her greatest degradation and at the height of her success. Its last act, passed on the very day on which it dissolved itself, 4th Brumaire (26th October), was worthy of its best and greatest days, for it was an act declaring a complete amnesty for all political offences, or supposed offences, since the declaration of the Republic.

<small>Dissolution of the Convention.</small>

The successful establishment of the Directory and the victory won over the royalist agitators on 13th Vendémiaire had a profound effect upon the policy of England. Hitherto Pitt and Grenville, inspired by their agent in Switzerland, William Wickham, had believed in the vain promises of the royalist *émigrés*, and had hoped by their means to restore the Bourbon monarchy in France. The headquarters of the royalist agitators were, as they had always been, in Switzerland. Neither the Comte de Provence, who,

<small>England and the Emigrés.</small>

since his nephew's death, called himself Louis XVIII., nor the Comte d'Artois were really deceived by the hopes held out by their royalist friends. But the English ministers, deluded by the extravagant promises of the *émigrés* and by the reports of Wickham, considered the prospects of an overthrow of the Republic to be excellent. They had shown their confidence in the *émigrés* by the active assistance they had given to the expedition to Quiberon Bay, and still more by the large sums of secret-service money which had been expended in Switzerland. The efforts of the royalist *émigrés* took two directions; on the one hand, they had fomented the feeling of discontent in Paris which had culminated in the insurrection of 13th Vendémiaire, and, on the other, they had attempted to affect the loyalty of the generals of the Republic. The general on whom they counted most was Pichegru, the con- queror of Holland. This general, like Dumouriez in 1793, was more ambitious to attain wealth and power for himself than success for the Republic. During his sojourn in Paris in the spring of 1795 he had formed a close alliance with the royalist agitators in the capital, and on proceeding to take up the command of the Army of the Rhine-and-Moselle he entered into direct communications with the Prince de Condé, the general commanding the *émigré* army in Germany. Condé promised Pichegru the government of Alsace, the Château of Chambord, a million livres in cash, an income of two hundred thousand livres a year, and the rank of Marshal of France, if he would undertake to restore the Bourbons. Great hopes were built upon these negotiations, and the Comte de Provence left Verona to take part in them. But the success of these intrigues was nullified by the victory of 13th Vendémiaire; the Margrave of Baden-Baden refused to allow the Pretender to enter his territory; Wickham was unwillingly convinced that the purchase of the general did not include the purchase of his army; and the Directory, as soon as it had firmly seized the reins of power, recalled Pichegru, whose transactions with Condé had been more than suspected, and replaced him by a thorough republican, Moreau. These failures convinced Pitt and Grenville that there was no advantage to be gained in trusting to the promises of the émigrés.

The Directory, on assuming power, resolved to continue the policy of the Thermidorians, and not to recur to the notions of the revolutionary propaganda. It desired to show Europe that France was ready to enter into the comity of nations, and did not presume for the future to interfere with the internal arrangements of other countries. It, therefore, on grounds of humanity, took up again the negotiations which had been commenced in July 1793 for the release of the children of Louis XVI., and, using Spain as an intermediary, entered into communications on this subject with the bitterest enemy of France—Austria. The death of the Dauphin, commonly called Louis XVII., had left only one of the children of Louis XVI. and Marie Antoinette in the hands of the Republic. The Thermidorians had, at the instigation of one of their leaders, Boissy-d'Anglas, seen the expediency of proving to Europe that the French republicans were not barbarians, by offering to surrender the person of Madame Royale to her Austrian relatives. This project was carried out by the Directory. On 20th December 1795 Madame Royale was exchanged in Switzerland for the four deputies and the Minister of War whom Dumouriez had handed over to the Austrians, and for another deputy, Drouet, the former postmaster at Sainte-Menehould, who had been taken prisoner by the Austrians in 1793.

*Exchange of Madame Royale.*

The exchange of Madame Royale was a manifest evidence of the desire of the Directors to conclude peace. The Prussian ambassador at Paris reported to his government on 28th December 1795, 'The general cry in Paris is, "Make peace and you will have money and bread."'[1] Peace, indeed,

---

[1] *Preussen und Frankreich von 1795 bis 1807 : Diplomatische Correspondenzen.* Ed. by P. Bailleu, vol. i. p. 41.

was the desire not only of the people of Paris, but of the
people of all France, of the majority in the new  Desire for
Legislature, and of the Directory. It was hoped  Peace in
that the Treaties of Basle were but the prelimin-  France.
aries of a general peace throughout Europe. But the two
remaining enemies of the French Republic, England and
Austria, did not see their way to meeting the Directory half-
way. Pitt and Grenville argued that a peace made with the
Directory would be only of the nature of a truce. They were
ready enough to make peace, but considered it inadvisable to
negotiate with a government which seemed to them in its
essence unstable. Owing either to the intrigues of the *émigrés*,
or to their own knowledge of politics, they grasped the fact that
the new government of France was constructed on a faulty
basis, and that a peace concluded with it would not be lasting.
The attitude of Austria was somewhat different. Thugut, the
Austrian minister, believed that France was exhausted, and
that by a continuance of war substantial concessions could
be wrung from her. Reubell, the Director who took charge of
the conduct of Foreign Affairs, expressed himself as follows to
the Prussian ambassador at Paris: 'The war with Austria
troubles us less than the war with England. Our means for
supporting the former are ready, but not without having exhausted all the resources of the Republic. It will be probably
the last effort of the two belligerent powers. . . . Our plan of
campaign is almost settled; the war will be defensive in
Germany and offensive in Italy. It is important to us to
detach Austria from England and Sardinia from Austria.'[1]
Contrary to their wish, therefore, the Directors found themselves obliged to continue the war with England and Austria.

While continuing the war with these two powers, the French
Directory, like the Thermidorians, hoped to obtain  France and
not only the neutrality of Prussia and Spain, which  Prussia.
had been secured by the Treaties of Basle, but their active
co-operation. One of its first diplomatic endeavours was to

[1] Bailleu, *op. cit.* vol. i. p. 48.

enter into close relations with Prussia. Some of the ministers of Frederick William II., notably Alvensleben, were in favour of an alliance with France; but the King himself, though he had been forced by the emptiness of his treasury, and his projects on Poland to make peace with the French republicans, looked on the idea of making an alliance with them with horror. In this attitude he was supported by his two ablest ministers, Haugwitz and Hardenberg. By the terms of the Treaty of Basle Hardenberg had secured the preponderance of Prussia in northern Germany. A line of demarcation or neutrality was drawn across Germany, and the northern states, which were thus freed from the fear of a French invasion, looked to Prussia as their leader and saviour. An excuse for not forming an offensive and defensive alliance with France was found in the occupation by the French troops of the Prussian territories on the left bank of the Rhine. Prussia would only negotiate on the basis of the restoration of the *status quo ante bellum*, and the French Directory, like its predecessors, the Thermidorian Committee of Public Safety and the Great Committee of Public Safety, insisted on the cession to France of all territory up to the Rhine. The Directors, had they wished, could not have opposed the universal feeling in France in favour of making the Rhine the frontier, and proposed that Prussia should take compensation for its cessions on the left bank of the Rhine, by secularising the bishoprics and abbeys of northern Germany and annexing their territories. This proposal, which would bring in its train the overthrow of the Constitution of the Holy Roman Empire, could not be sponsored by Prussia. The policy of Frederick the Great had been to assume that Prussia, not Austria, was the true defender of the rights of the Empire, and his nephew, in spite of Alvensleben's representations, feared to break with the hereditary policy. The arrangement with regard to the line of demarcation had placed Prussia in the position of the guardian of the Empire; the acceptance of the French propositions would have made her seem its destroyer. The attempts of the

Directory, and afterwards of the Consulate, to secure an alliance with Prussia, were therefore foredoomed to failure.

The victories of the French Republic were received with more than toleration in the smaller states of Europe, which feared the aggressions of Austria, Prussia, and Russia far more than any invasion by the French. Switzerland had profited greatly by the strict neutrality it had maintained. The wealth of France had poured freely into the cantons for the purchase of provisions and other necessaries; the residence of the diplomatists of Europe at Berne, the headquarters of Wickham, and at Basle, the headquarters of the French minister Barthélemy, had also been profitable to the country, while the Swiss, ready as ever to accept money from all sides, were enabled to make very considerable gains. Of the Princes of Italy, Ferdinand, Grand Duke of Tuscany, and brother of the Emperor, had, to the disgust of the Court of Vienna, made a separate peace with the French Republic in February 1795; Ferdinand of Naples had followed his example, and the King of Sardinia alone remained in armed opposition to France. With Portugal the Directory and the Committee of Public Safety, refused to treat, for, like the French statesmen throughout the eighteenth century, the Directors regarded Portugal as merely a province of England. With the smaller northern powers the Directory established the most friendly relations. Christian VII. of Denmark had always maintained his neutrality, and through the French minister, resident at his Court, many important secret negotiations had passed with Prussia. In Sweden, Charles, Duke of Sudermania, the guardian of the young King Gustavus IV., abandoned the policy of Gustavus III., and now made a treaty of friendship and a commercial treaty with the French Republic. The only other state to be mentioned is Turkey. The Turks looked upon the events which were passing in the West of Europe with unconcern; still they were inclined to be friendly with the French Republic, because it was engaged in fighting with Austria, and thus distracted the attention of one of the hereditary enemies of the Sublime Porte.

Catherine of Russia, now at the close of her long reign, still regarded the French Revolution as affording a happy opportunity for her to pursue her schemes on Poland without active interference from Prussia or Austria. Her one desire was that France should continue the war, and for this reason she cordially received at her court the Comte d'Artois, and encouraged the presence of French *émigrés*. The Treaties of Basle had greatly offended her, for Prussia was thus left free to interfere in Poland, but Catherine was too wise to attempt to do more than intrigue with the affairs of Western Europe. She had no idea of intervening actively.

*Russia.*

The campaign of 1795 on the Rhine frontier is chiefly important in regard to the treason of Pichegru. The Elector of Bavaria, who was at the same time the Elector Palatine, had, as has already been said, been uniformly friendly to the French. It was by his connivance that two of the most important fortresses upon the Rhine, Mannheim and Düsseldorf, were surrendered to Pichegru and Jourdan respectively. Meanwhile Marceau besieged the fortress of Ehrenbreitstein, and Kléber the city of Mayence. There can be little doubt, though it is not absolutely proved by documents, that it was because of the negotiations he had commenced with the Prince de Condé that Pichegru did not advance into Germany. Jourdan, who did advance with the Army of the Sambre-and-Meuse, therefore found himself unprotected on his right, and was forced to retire with considerable loss. Marceau succeeded in taking Ehrenbreitstein, but the same treacherous inaction of Pichegru allowed the Austrian General Clerfayt to force Kléber to raise the siege of Mayence. It was on 20th October 1795 that Jourdan recrossed the Rhine; on the 29th Kléber was driven from before Mayence; and on the 30th Pichegru was defeated and driven behind the Queich. The first operations of the French armies under the Directory were, thus, owing to Pichegru's treachery, unsuccessful, and on the 21st December an armistice was made between the French and the Austrians on the Rhine.

*Campaign of 1795.*

In the north, owing to the Treaties of Basle, there were no military operations of importance during the autumn of 1795, and the French army maintained its position on the frontier of Holland. In the south considerable alterations were made. The treaty of peace with Spain enabled the experienced and warlike soldiers of the two armies of the Pyrenees to be despatched to reinforce the Army of Italy, which was also joined by the bulk of the troops of the Army of the Alps. General Schérer, who commanded the Army of Italy, pushed forward, and by a victory at Loano on the 24th November 1795, opened up a direct communication with Genoa and cut off the Sardinians from the sea. In the four armies of the Directory which had thus taken the place of the thirteen armies of the Republic, there were under arms at the close of 1795 about 300,000 men under experienced generals, excluding what was known as the Army of the Interior, which guarded Paris and garrisoned the chief cities of France.

Reubell, in his conversation with the Prussian ambassador at Paris, openly declared that the chief military effort of France in 1796 was to be made in Italy. Hitherto the Army of Italy had been overshadowed by the operations of the armies engaged upon the Rhine; but the Directory now desired to attack Austria in a vital place. Upon the Rhine they were in reality waging war with the Empire and not with Austria. Mayence, for instance, was the capital of an Elector, not an Austrian city, and blows struck in that quarter affected the Empire and the petty princes of the Empire far more than they did Austria. But in Italy the House of Austria owned an important possession in the Milanese. Between the Milanese and the French Army of Italy was Piedmont, the principal state of the King of Sardinia. Victor Amadeus III. of Sardinia was the only petty monarch in Europe who had not attempted to make peace with the French Republic. In his resentment at the loss of Savoy and Nice he had thrown himself into the arms of Austria, and had borrowed an Austrian general, Colli, to command his small

*Campaign in Italy, 1796. First Stage.*

but well equipped army. This was the situation when Napoleon Bonaparte, who had been nominated to the command of the Army of Italy by the Directory, on the proposition of Barras, to whom he had rendered such signal service on 13th Vendémiaire, arrived to take up his new command on the 27th of March 1796. He understood the policy of the Directory, and determined to crush the King of Sardinia first, in order to be free to attack the Austrians in the Milanese. He therefore turned the Maritime Alps and separated the Austrian from the Sardinian army. The rapidity of his success was such as to surprise the Directors. After turning the Alps Bonaparte struck north and defeated the Sardinians at Montenotte, Millesimo, and Dego on the 12th, 13th, and 15th April, stormed their camp at Ceva on 16th April, and finally defeated them at Mondovi on 22d April. He then threatened Turin, and the King of Sardinia signed an armistice with him at Cherasco on 28th April, abandoning to the French army his most important frontier fortresses. As the first result of these military operations the King of Sardinia sued for peace, which he was only granted on recognising the cession to France of Savoy and Nice, and as a second result General Bonaparte was enabled to attack the Austrians in Lombardy without leaving a hostile power behind him.

*Armistice of Cherasco. April 28, 1796.*

The operations of the second stage of the famous campaign of 1796 were as rapid and as completely successful. On the 8th May Bonaparte crossed the river Po by skilfully misleading the Austrians as to his intentions, and on 10th May he forced the passage of the Adda at Lodi, where he won one of his most famous victories. The Austrian General Beaulieu felt himself incapable of holding the lines of the other rivers, and fled into the Tyrol. Bonaparte first occupied Milan, and then forced the Dukes of Parma and of Modena to submit to his demands, and to send ambassadors to treat for peace at Paris. To these petty princelets Bonaparte behaved with the utmost arrogance; not satisfied with making large requisitions of money and

*The Campaign in Italy. Second Stage.*

## Battle of Castiglione

provisions, he selected their finest pictures and works of art, and directed them to be sent to Paris. Far more important, from his spiritual position, though not of greater military strength, was the Pope. The French armies occupied the Legations of Ferrara and Bologna, and Bonaparte then threatened to march on Rome. In terror Pope Pius VI. concluded, on the 24th June 1796, an armistice at Foligno, by which he abandoned Ancona, and promised to send to Paris the large sum of 20,000,000 livres, with many manuscripts and works of art. The conquest of Italy revealed to Europe the French Republic in a new light. It showed the monarchs, and especially the rulers of little states, that the revolutionary propaganda which they had hated and dreaded so much had given way to an even more dangerous military policy, directed by a victorious and ambitious general.

But Austria was not going to be driven out of Italy by a single campaign. The beaten army of Beaulieu was reorganised by General Melas, and reinforced by 30,000 picked men from the Rhine. This army, amounting in all to 70,000 men, was placed under the command of Marshal Würmser, who, at the end of July, debouched from the Tyrol and invaded Italy by the two sides of Lake Garda. Bonaparte, whose army did not exceed 40,000 men, broke up the siege of Mantua which he had formed, and utterly defeated the Austrians in the great battle of Castiglione on 5th August 1796. Würmser fell back, but in September, the following month, he invaded Italy by the valley of the Brenta, and threw himself into Mantua. Bonaparte, now considering himself for a time freed from the danger of another Austrian attack, made an effort to reconstitute Northern Italy. Several of the cities, notably Modena, Bologna, and Ferrara, had declared themselves republics, but Bonaparte could see no advantage in little republics, and summoned a general assembly of deputies from the whole of Lombardy to meet at Milan. This assembly was disposed to form a Lombard Republic, but before it

*The Campaign in Italy. Third Stage.*

could complete its deliberations Bonaparte had to fight another Austrian army.

The Austrians, disgusted and surprised by these successive defeats, prepared to make a great effort. For the first time, the Emperor appealed directly to the patriotism of the people, and more especially of the nobility. A new army was equipped, which, if not so numerous, was more enthusiastic than the former armies, and was placed under the command of General Alvinzi. Bonaparte had received few or no reinforcements, and felt himself unable to face an army of 60,000 men. He waited, therefore, patiently in his headquarters at Verona while Alvinzi advanced slowly down the Brenta. Having learnt experience from their former defeats, the Austrians were in no hurry to come to blows, even with the small French army in front of them. Alvinzi entrenched himself in a formidable position on the heights of Caldiero, and repulsed a French attack upon the 12th of November. Another such check meant the ruin of the French army. Bonaparte decided to turn the position. Advancing along the causeway through the marshes upon Alvinzi's left, he fought the celebrated battle of Arcola on the 16th of November, and Alvinzi, finding his position untenable, retreated into the Tyrol.

*The Campaign in Italy. Fourth Stage.*

Even yet the Austrians were not finally discouraged. Würmser held out in Mantua; the Pope, incited by the Court of Vienna, did not observe the Armistice of Foligno, and determined to raise the Italian populace against the French; and it was resolved to make a final effort. In the depth of winter Alvinzi advanced down the eastern shore of Lake Garda, but was stopped and utterly defeated at Rivoli on the 14th January 1797. Provera, who had endeavoured to relieve Würmser by the Brenta, while Alvinzi occupied the main French army at Rivoli, was also defeated, and on 2d February 1797 Mantua surrendered. These successive blows destroyed the military power of Austria in Italy, and Bonaparte began to make

*The Campaign in Italy. Fifth Stage.*

## Campaign of 1796 in Germany

plans for invading Austria itself. But before he started it was necessary to establish peace behind him. The behaviour of the Pope showed the general that His Holiness could not be trusted, and it was only under the pressure of a French advance upon Rome that Pius VI. signed a treaty of peace with the French at Tolentino on 19th February 1797. By this treaty Bonaparte's lines of communication were secured; the people of Lombardy were his enthusiastic admirers, and everything promised a speedy and successful advance upon Vienna. *Treaty of Tolentino. Feb. 19, 1797.*

As Reubell had stated to the Prussian ambassador, the chief effort of the French armies was directed in the year 1796 against the Austrians in Italy. But the operations in Germany were nevertheless of extreme importance; not on account of what was achieved, but because of their effect on the policy of the Princes of the Empire. Carnot, who was left in entire charge of military affairs by the Directory, combined a skilful plan of campaign. He directed the Army of the Rhine-and-Moselle, now under the command of Moreau, and the Army of the Sambre-and-Meuse, still under the command of Jourdan, to make a simultaneous advance into the heart of Germany, and to unite their forces upon the Danube. The generals were sufficiently able, and the troops sufficiently experienced in war, to carry out this movement; but at the head of the Austrians, for the first time since the outbreak of the war, there appeared a general of real military genius. The Archduke Charles, the third son of the Emperor Leopold, and the brother of the reigning Emperor, Francis II., was only a young man, but he proved himself to be a profound strategist. On the 1st June 1796 he announced to the French generals that the armistice, which had lasted six months, was at an end. Jourdan at once advanced from Düsseldorf, and after taking Frankfort and Würtzburg invaded Franconia. The Archduke Charles immediately opposed him with his whole army, and Jourdan had to fall back after a three weeks' campaign. *Campaign in Germany, 1796.*

PERIOD VII.   M

Moreau was not able to cross the Rhine until 24-25 June 1796. The operation was one of extreme difficulty, which was chiefly overcome by the skill and gallantry of Desaix. Moreau then proceeded to carry out Carnot's orders; he advanced with great rapidity; he defeated the Prince de Condé and his army of *émigrés* at Ettlingen; he occupied Stuttgart, and forced his way into Bavaria, reaching the Danube in the month of August. To oppose him the Archduke Charles marched rapidly to the south, and Jourdan once more left Düsseldorf and invaded Franconia. The Archduke Charles soon understood the intentions of Carnot, and took up a central position between the two French armies at Ingolstadt. He waited until the French generals had penetrated far from their base of operations, and then, leaving but a weak division in front of Moreau, he attacked Jourdan in force. The French Army of the Sambre-and-Meuse was overcome by the weight of numbers; on the 3d of September it was driven from Würtzburg, and on the 20th of September defeated at Altenkirchen, where Marceau, one of the most renowned of the young generals of the republican period, was killed. Having driven back Jourdan, the Archduke Charles turned upon Moreau. That general had imprudently continued to advance into Bavaria, and did not perceive until late in September the critical position in which he had been left by the retreat of Jourdan. When he did perceive it, he extricated himself by one of the most famous retreats known in military history. For forty days he fell back through a hostile country, with bad roads, and offering almost innumerable difficulties from its lofty mountains and dense forests, and harassed by the presence of a victorious Austrian army attempting to cut off his retreat, and eventually he recrossed the Rhine on the 24th of October.

From a military point of view, apart from the intrinsic interest presented by the operations of the armies, the chief importance of the campaign of 1796 in Germany lay in the fact that it occupied a considerable force of Austrian troops, which were thus prevented from being sent as reinforcements to the Austrian army in Italy. From the diplomatic point of view, the campaign had results almost rivalling those achieved by Bonaparte in Italy. The advance of the French threw the states of Southern Germany into the hands of Prussia. They felt a natural sentiment of jealousy at perceiving the states of Northern Germany escaping the horrors of war, owing to the line of demarcation established by the Treaty of Basle. Many of the smaller states, and at least one of the larger states, Saxony, implored the intervention of Prussia. Frederick William II., only too glad to pose as the guardian of the Empire, made use of all his influence to induce the French Directory to consent to the further extension of the line of demarcation. Reubell, the Director who took charge of foreign policy, was possessed by the idea that Prussia and France were natural allies, and induced the Directory to meet the views of Frederick William II.; but in return he demanded that Prussia should enter into an offensive and defensive alliance with the French Republic. The King of Prussia, in his hatred of Jacobin principles, was inclined to reject this proposal, but his ministers, notably Haugwitz and Alvensleben, persuaded him that it was impossible to refuse entirely. A compromise was arranged, and on 5th August 1796 a secret supplement to the Treaty of Basle was signed between France and Prussia. By this secret convention Prussia definitely promised to recognise the limits of the Rhine for the French Republic, and in return France guaranteed that at a general peace not only the King of Prussia should receive compensation for the territories he surrendered, by the cession of some ecclesiastical states, but also that his brother-in-law, the Prince of Orange, should receive a sovereignty in Germany, to make up for the loss of the Stadtholderate in Holland. It proved impossible to extend the line of demarcation to the southern states of Germany as long as the Austrian army of the Archduke Charles remained there. And therefore the petty rulers endeavoured to make peace with France on their own account. The Duke of Würtemburg and the Margrave of Baden both opened negotiations, and since the Elector of Bavaria had fled into Saxony on the advance of Moreau, the Estates of Bavaria signed a treaty of peace with the French general at Pfaffenhofen on the 7th September 1796. But the successes of the Archduke Charles and the retreat of Moreau put an end to these peaceful dispositions. The Elector of Bavaria refused to ratify the treaty his Estates had made; the Duke of Würtemburg dismissed the minister who had conducted his negotiations; and in spite of all the efforts of Prussia, the predominance of Austria continued in Southern Germany.

The successes of Bonaparte in Italy, and the operations of the French armies in Germany which, though they had ended in retreat, had not been discreditable to the generals or soldiers, reacted very favourably upon the position of the Directory. The French, as a nation, have always been dazzled by military glory, and since the armies of the Directory were victorious, they were inclined to look upon the government of the Directory as excellent. But military successes did not merely add to the reputation of the Directors; by means of them their financial difficulties were relieved. The doctrine that invading armies should live upon the resources of the invaded countries was a most convenient one. Not only did the armies in Italy and Germany maintain themselves free of cost to the Directory, but the generals sent large sums of money to Paris. It was therefore unnecessary to impose fresh taxes or issue more paper money. But the relief of financial distress was not the only result of the government of the Directory in 1796; it restored internal peace. Hoche, after his defeat of the *émigrés* at Quiberon Bay in 1795, devoted himself to the pacification of Brittany and La Vendée. The chief credit due to the Directors is that they gave the young general a free hand. While putting down armed insurrection, and defeating the Vendéan chiefs whenever they appeared, Hoche used the most conciliatory measures towards individuals. His policy, as he himself declared in one of his proclamations, was to make the Republic loved. While punishing brigandage severely, he conveniently forgot all past offences as long as the offenders occupied themselves peacefully; and on the 15th of July 1796 the Directory was able to announce to the Legislature that the whole of France was at peace. In truth, all political disturbances were at an end. The majority of the French people frankly accepted the Republic, and seemed to care very little what was the actual form of the republican government. But though political disturbances were over, the troubled times through which France had passed had left only too much scope for private animosity. In the south armed bands, resembling the Companies of Jehu of 1795, pretended to be acting for the defence of religion, when they were really moved by desire of plunder and booty. In the centre the pretext of religion was not alleged, but armed bands of brigands collected in the forests and the mountains, and, like the banditti in Italy, pillaged travellers on the high roads, and held whole villages to ransom. These evils steadily diminished with the consistent enforcement of the law, but it was some years before France became absolutely safe for travellers. Of less importance were the insurrections fomented by the extreme democratic party. Democracy was discredited by the recollection of the Reign of Terror, and the plot of Babeuf in May, and an attack on the camp at Grenelle in November 1796, were easily suppressed.

By the terms of the Constitution of the Year III. no change in the Directory or the Legislature was to be made until February 1797. By this arrangement a period of consistent government was secured. The Directors, on the whole, acted harmoniously together. The pre-eminence of Reubell and Carnot was generally recognised; Barras occupied himself chiefly with his pleasures; Revellière-Lépeaux was engaged in establishing his new religion of Theo-philanthropy, which made some converts

*First changes in the Directory and the Legislature, 1797.*

in the towns, but found no followers in the villages; and
Letourneur simply acted as Carnot's lieutenant. In the Legislature the chief leaders, such as Sieyès, Cambacérès, and Boissy-d'Anglas, showed occasionally their jealousy of their former colleagues in the Convention; but, on the whole, they did not try to interfere with their measures. The only heated debates which took place in the Council of Five Hundred were on the nature of the disturbances in the south of France. These were roundly asserted by the opposing parties to be caused by intrigues of priests, or by intrigues of Jacobins. Fréron, who had been sent by the Directory to settle these troubles, was very violently attacked, and with difficulty exculpated himself from the charge of political partisanship. But, on the whole, the debates in both branches of the Legislature were very tame. Nevertheless there appeared, during 1796, the germ of what in 1797 was known as the Clichian party, so called from its meeting at the Club de Clichy. This party was not openly royalist, but the chiefs of the French *émigrés*, supported by the funds supplied by Wickham, believed they could use it to serve their own purposes, as they had made use of the agitators in the Paris Sections in 1795. In the ministry no changes of great importance were made in 1796; Ramel, the former colleague of Cambon in the Financial Committee of the Convention, replaced Faypoult as Minister of the Finances; and Pétiet, a former commissary-general, was appointed Minister of War in succession to Aubert-Dubayet. Of more importance was the creation of a seventh ministry, of General Police, in January 1796, for it was an evidence of a new spirit, and the first symptom of the elaborate scheme for muzzling public opinion, which was developed to its height by Fouché at a later date. Merlin of Douai left the Ministry of the Interior for three months to organise the new department, and was succeeded in April 1796 by Cochon de Lapparent, a former member of the Convention.

Changes in the Ministry.

It has been said that the Directors endeavoured in vain to form an offensive and defensive alliance with Prussia. They were more successful with regard to Spain. The power of Godoy, who for the negotiations at Basle had been created Prince of the Peace, rose to its height. General Pérignon, who had been sent as ambassador to Madrid by the Directory, skilfully flattered the vanity of the new prince, and, to the astonishment of all Europe, an offensive and defensive alliance was signed between the French Republic and the ancient Bourbon monarchy of Spain at San Ildefonso, on the 19th of August 1796, by which Spain agreed to declare war against England, and the French promised to assist in the conquest of Portugal, which was to be divided between the two allies. From a military point of view the alliance with Spain did not yield any advantage to France, but from a naval standpoint it proved of incalculable value. The English were obliged to abandon Corsica, their only foothold in the Mediterranean, and to concentrate their fleet at Gibraltar. The Spanish navy, to which much attention had been paid throughout the eighteenth century, had certainly improved, and, united with a few French men-of-war, far outnumbered the English Mediterranean Fleet. This was the year of the great English naval mutiny at the Nore, and the profound discontent which possessed the English sailors was equally perceptible at Gibraltar. But fortunately the English admiral, Sir John Jervis, was a man of singular ability, who understood the English sailor perfectly. He showed no mercy to ringleaders, but maintained discipline, and even made it popular by looking after the men's food, and appealing to their patriotic feelings. He understood that, on the eve of a battle, the sailors would cease their disaffection. Accordingly he kept at sea for several months after the junction of the French and Spanish fleets, announcing his intention to offer battle ; and when discipline was restored he utterly defeated the French and Spaniards off Cape St. Vincent, on the 14th of February 1797. By this victory, in which Nelson greatly distinguished himself, the Spanish fleet was practically destroyed for offensive purposes, and the high hopes that the Directory had built on the naval assistance of Spain were frustrated. England had promptly, as in former days, come to the help of Portugal, and sent an army under the Hon. Sir Charles Stuart to defend the country, and a general, the Prince of Waldeck, to reorganise the Portuguese army.

While the Directory made an alliance with Spain, and hoped **The Directory and England.** to make one with Prussia, its sentiments of hostility towards England remained undiminished. It had been expected in France that the conquest of Holland and the formation of the Batavian Republic, in close alliance with the French Republic, would have struck a more serious blow at the prosperity of England than it had really done. As a matter of fact, the loss of Holland proved but a slight commercial disaster; the commerce of the North of Europe, which passed through English hands, merely moved from Amsterdam to Hamburg, and the English merchants suffered little. From a naval point of view, the French possession of Holland made it necessary for England to set on foot a powerful fleet to watch the Dutch navy in the Texel, while she also had to maintain a fleet blockading the French port of Brest in addition to her Mediterranean fleet. The English government was more profoundly affected by Bonaparte's victories in Italy than by the loss of Holland. In November 1796 Lord Malmesbury was sent to Paris to discuss the bases of a peace. He began to negotiate for the restoration of the *status quo ante bellum*, and demanded the surrender of Belgium to the Emperor. Such terms were ridiculous; the French Directors, even had they wished, would not have dared to withdraw from their policy of making the Rhine the frontier of France. The diplomatic habitudes of Lord Malmesbury were regarded by the Directors as proofs of his double-dealing, and he was abruptly ordered to leave Paris on the 20th December 1796. There was little real expectation of peace on either side. At the very time Lord Malmesbury was in Paris the Directory was preparing a naval expedition in Brest harbour.

It was announced that the expedition was intended for the West Indies, and it was placed under the command of Hoche. On the 16th of December it set sail for Bantry Bay, for the Directory had really recurred to the old French idea of attacking England through Ireland. But a terrible storm scattered the French Fleet, and only two or three ships reached Bantry Bay, and they returned to France without effecting a landing.

Though the history of Europe during the year 1796 is chiefly bound up in the policy and military achievements of France, the close of the year witnessed the disappearance of the greatest monarch of Eastern Europe. On the 17th November 1796, Catherine of Russia died. The importance of her reign belongs to the period prior to the French Revolution, and her attitude towards the series of events grouped under that title, was chiefly dictated by the course of events in Poland. She was succeeded on the throne of Russia by her son, the Emperor Paul. The new monarch soon gave evidence of the aberration of intellect which led him into the strange excesses that brought about his assassination. His first step in foreign politics was to decline to assist Austria with his armies, and he even withdrew a Russian fleet which his mother had recently sent to the assistance of England. In conversation he expressed his detestation of the French as Jacobins, but none the less he opened negotiations with the Directory by means of his ambassador at Berlin, Kolichev, who communicated freely with the French ambassador Caillard.

*Death of Catherine of Russia. Nov. 17, 1796.*

In the commencement of the year 1797 the interest of Europe was concentrated upon Bonaparte and his army. Being master of Italy he now determined to invade the home domains of the House of Austria. He begged the Directory to act with energy in Germany in order to prevent reinforcements being sent against him. The Emperor recalled his brother, the Archduke Charles, from the Rhine, and placed in him command of the Austrian army in the Tyrol. On the 16th of March 1797 Bonaparte

*Bonaparte's Campaign of 1797.*

forced the passage of Tagliamento. Joubert, who was acting independently in the district of Friuli, made his way by that route into the Tyrol, and joined his general-in-chief at Klagenfurt on the 13th of March. With the combined army Bonaparte pursued the Austrians. He defeated the Archduke Charles at Neumarkt and Unzmarkt, and on 7th April he entered Leoben. The Archduke Charles felt it impossible to oppose the French longer, and on the 17th of April 1797 preliminaries of peace were signed at Leoben.

Simultaneously with Bonaparte's advance the Armies of the Rhine-and-Moselle under Moreau, and of the Sambre-and-Meuse under Hoche, were set in motion. The latter advanced from Düsseldorf, defeated the Austrians in five engagements, took Wetzlar, and was already marching on Giessen in Hanover when his progress was stopped by the news of the signature of the Preliminaries of Leoben. Moreau, on his side, had not been able to cross the Rhine until 20th April, and had made no further offensive movement, when he was ordered to cease operations.

*Campaign of 1797 in Germany.*

By the Preliminaries of Leoben the war between France and Austria, which had lasted without intermission for five years, came to a termination. By the Convention signed at that place, Austria agreed that the Rhine should be recognised as the frontier of France, which involved the cession of Belgium. In Italy the Emperor promised to give up the Milanese, and to receive Venice in compensation. These were the territorial bases agreed to, and General Bonaparte was intrusted by the Directory with the task of concluding a definitive peace with Austria. But this Convention only bound Francis II. as head of the House of Hapsburg, not as Emperor. It was therefore agreed that a congress should be held at Rastadt, at which terms of peace should be arranged between the French Republic and the Empire. The Preliminaries of Leoben crowned Bonaparte's great victories, and the monarchs of Europe quickly recognised that they had no longer to deal with the French Republic, but with the young Corsican general.

*Preliminaries of Leoben. April 17, 1797.*

# CHAPTER VI

## 1797-1799

Elections of 1797 in France—Policy of the Clichians—Struggle between the Directors and the Clichians—Negotiations for Peace between England and the Directory—Changes in the French Ministry—Revolution of 18th Fructidor—Bonaparte in Italy—Occupation of Venice—The Ligurian and Cisalpine Republics formed—Annexation of the Ionian Islands by France—Treaty of Campo-Formio—Capture of Mayence—The Batavian Republic—Battle of Camperdown—Bonaparte's Expedition to the East—Capture of Malta—Conquest of Egypt—Battle of the Nile—Internal Policy of the Directory after 18th Fructidor—Foreign Policy—Attitude of England, Prussia, Austria, and Russia—The Helvetian Republic—Italian Affairs—The Roman and Parthenopean Republics formed—Occupation of Piedmont and Tuscany by France—The Law of Conscription—Outbreak of War between Austria and France—Murder of the French Plenipotentiaries at Rastadt—The Campaign of 1799—In Italy—Battles of Cassano, the Trebbia and Novi—Italy lost to France—In Switzerland—Battle of Zurich—In Holland—Battles of Bergen—Results of the Campaign of 1799—Policy and Character of the Emperor Paul of Russia—Bonaparte's Campaign of 1799 in Syria—Siege of Acre—Battle of Mount Tabor—Struggle between the Directors and the Legislature in France—Revolution of 22d Prairial—Changes in the Directory and Ministry—Bonaparte's return to France—Revolution of 18th Brumaire—End of the Government of the Directory in France.

IN the month of May 1797 a new Director and a new third of the Legislature were, in accordance with the Constitution of the Year III., elected in France. These elections were entirely favourable to the Clichian party. This party, which had gradually grown up since the dissolution of the Convention, and took its name from the Club de Clichy, was led by men of very considerable ability. The sentiment which united them was a loathing of

*The Elections of 1797 in France.*

the memory of the Reign of Terror and a desire to expel from power those who had taken part in it. This sentiment was very general in France, and the new legislators returned to the Council of Ancients and the Council of Five Hundred were, with but few exceptions, men who had not sat in the Convention. Many of them were former members of the Constituent and Legislative Assemblies, and had a considerable knowledge of parliamentary tactics. Foremost among this group was Barbé-Marbois, who had, under the Bourbon monarchy, been intendant of San Domingo, but the deputy belonging to it who attracted most attention was General Pichegru. The first success of the Clichian party was won in the election of the new Director. The retiring Director on whom the lot had fallen was Letourneur, and to fill his place was chosen Barthélemy, a former marquis, and the diplomatist who had negotiated the Treaties of Basle. This election was very significant. It seemed to presage a consistent peace policy. It afforded a guarantee that the proscription of the nobles of the *ancien régime* was to be ended.

In foreign policy it was indeed the aim of the Clichians to bring about a universal peace. Their home policy was Policy of the neither so definite nor so logical. In their hatred Clichians. of the Terrorists there can be no doubt that the wiser heads among the Clichians desired a return to a monarchical government. Pichegru and the more self-seeking among them thought that they could obtain money and power by a new revolution. Never were the prospects of a counter-revolution more promising. The Clichians, recognising the impossibility of restoring the Bourbon Monarchy in its former authority, were in favour of a constitutional, limited monarchy after the English pattern. But Louis XVIII., and the Comte d'Artois, buoyed up by the hopes of the *émigrés* refused to make the slightest concession; they would not acknowledge the Constitution of 1791; they would not even promise to consent to the slightest limitation of the old monarchical power. Under these circumstances the Clichians had to look for a king elsewhere. A few, among whom may possibly be counted Pichegru, were ready to accept Louis XVIII. on his own terms. A larger party were in favour of the Duke of Orleans, son of Philippe Égalité, and, in the future, King of the French as Louis Philippe. Others favoured the accession of a Prussian prince, and negotiations were opened at Berlin to see whether Prince Francis, the nephew of Frederick William II., would accept the throne. With such divisions of opinion, there was no doubt that the internal policy of the Clichians, even though backed by large subsidies from England, which passed to them through Switzerland, was certain to bring about no result. Nor was their peace policy more likely to succeed. The wars of the French Republic had organised a body of valiant and experienced soldiers whose trade was war, and to whom the idea of peace was repugnant. Both Bonaparte and Hoche, the two greatest generals of the Directory, naturally looked with suspicion and dislike upon the policy of the Clichians.

It need hardly be said that the attitude of the Clichians was one of open hostility to the four original Directors. Their one adherent in the Directory, Barthélemy, proved to be a very weak support, and his brother Directors soon saw that it was unnecessary to trouble themselves about him. The four remaining original Directors were united in their dislike of the new theories, and also as regicides had reason to fear their success. A severe struggle was therefore imminent between the majority of the Legislature and of the Executive. A crisis had arisen which tested the political theories which had found their expression in the Constitution of the Year III. The Legislature endeavoured to encroach upon the authority of the Directory; the Directors refused to yield one jot of their power. The first active measure of hostility in the Councils was an attack upon the Foreign Minister, Charles Delacroix. Pitt had decided to make a second attempt to bring about peace between England and France, though without much expectation

*Struggle between the Directory and the Clichians.*

of its success, and a conference was opened at Lille on the 4th July 1797, at which Lord Malmesbury was presented as the English plenipotentiary. He presented, on behalf of England, almost the same demands as had been rejected in the previous December, and the negotiations were speedily broken off. Using this as a pretext, the hostile majority in the Council of Ancients and Council of Five Hundred accused the Directors of not sincerely wishing for peace, and threw the chief blame for the rupture of the conference on their minister, Delacroix. The Directory yielded. Charles Delacroix was sent as ambassador to Holland, and was succeeded as Foreign Minister by Talleyrand. This skilful and subtle diplomatist saw that the rivalry between the two powers in the State must lead to an open rupture. He sided strongly with the Directors; he communicated with Hoche and Bonaparte, and there can be little doubt that he was one of the principal, if not the principal, author of the *coup-d'état* or revolution which followed. The dismissal of Delacroix was perhaps the most important episode; but the other ministers were likewise violently attacked by the Councils, and in addition to the Foreign Office every department of State, except the ministries of Finance and Justice, changed hands in July 1797. François de Neufchâteau became Minister of the Interior, General Schérer Minister for War, Pleville de Peley Minister of the Marine, and Lenoir-Laroche, who was succeeded in a few days by Sotin de la Coindière, Minister of Police.

[Sidenote: Negotiations for Peace between England and the Directory.]

The revolution of the 18th Fructidor was one which created but little interest among the people of France. It was the result of an intrinsic weakness in the Constitution, not of a popular movement. Two co-equal powers can never exist in the government of a State: when a collision takes place one must be overthrown. In their measures for overthrowing or muzzling the leaders of the opposition in the Legislature, the four senior Directors could not agree. Carnot, the greatest of them all, disliked

[Sidenote: The Revolution of 18th Fructidor. (4th September 1797.)]

any interference with the Constitution, and looked upon the employment of force as likely to lead to great disasters. The other original Directors, Barras, Reubell, and Revellière-Lépeaux, were, however, perfectly agreed. They were determined to use the regular troops that formed the garrison of Paris; Hoche, from Holland, sent them a sum of money; and Bonaparte instructed one of his best generals, Augereau, to act according to their orders. Accordingly, on the morning of the 18th Fructidor (4th September 1797) fifty-five of the leaders of the Clichian party in the Legislature, including both Barbé-Marbois and Pichegru, were arrested, and were at once deported, with the ex-minister of Police, Cochon de Lapparent, and several other individuals, without trial, to Cayenne and Sinnamari. The same harsh measures were not taken with regard to the two dissentient Directors, Carnot and Barthélemy, who were given every facility for escaping from France. This revolution was carried out without the shedding of a single drop of blood, and the success of the Directors was acquiesced in by the people of France.

Merlin of Douai, the great jurist and statesman, and François de Neufchâteau, a dramatist and former member of the Legislative Assembly, were elected as the new Directors in the place of Carnot and Barthélemy, and were succeeded in the ministries of Justice and the Interior by Lambrechts and Letourneur.

After the conclusion of the Preliminaries of Leoben Bonaparte returned to Italy and established himself at Montebello, near Milan. He was appointed plenipotentiary of the French Republic to conclude a final treaty with Austria, but the negotiations lasted for many months. During this time the young general was chiefly engaged in settling Italy. He first made a terrible example of the city of Verona, where the people had risen in revolt during his campaign in the Tyrol, and had murdered the wounded French soldiers left in their city. He next occupied Venice, and exacted from it

*Bonaparte in Italy.*

*Occupation of Venice.*

a heavy contribution in money. Having thus established his power throughout northern Italy, Bonaparte began to set up new governments. On the 15th of June 1797 he insisted on the dissolution of the ancient government of Genoa, and **The Ligurian** formed that city and the surrounding districts into **Republic.** a new Ligurian Republic. Piedmont, by the terms of the Treaty of Cherasco, was left to the King of Sardinia, but Bonaparte at once formed Lombardy, Modena, Reggio, Bologna, Ferrara, the Romagna, Brescia, and Mantua into one **The Cisalpine** State, which he named the Cisalpine Republic. **Republic.** The Constitution of this new Republic, which was modelled on the Constitution of the Year III., was promulgated on the 9th of July 1797. In these measures Bonaparte had carefully avoided any annexations by France. It was otherwise with regard to the Ionian Islands, which were ceded to the French Republic by Venice. Corfu was occupied on the 28th of June 1797, and Bonaparte believed that by this cession the French fleet in the Mediterranean would be able to close the Adriatic Sea.

During the months in which Italy was being thus reconstructed, the Austrian plenipotentiary, Cobenzl, was skilfully delaying the signature of a definitive treaty between France and **Treaty of** Austria. In truth, the Austrians, like the English, **Campo-** Thugut, like Pitt, hoped that the Clichian party **Formio.** **17th October** would win the day. The successful *coup d'état* of **1797.** 18th of Fructidor destroyed his hopes, and on 17th of October 1797 the Treaty of Campo-Formio was signed. The bases laid down by the Preliminaries of Leoben were generally followed. The frontier of the Rhine for France was solemnly recognised. The new arrangements in Italy were also agreed to, and to Austria was ceded Venice and all the territories of Venice in Istria and Dalmatia and up to the Adige, in compensation for the loss of the Milanese. The Emperor also engaged to use his influence at the Congress of Rastadt to secure peace between France and the Holy Roman Empire. The Treaty of Campo-Formio really struck a more severe blow at the Empire than at the House of Austria. The cession of the Rhine frontier to France implied the loss to the Empire of the electorates of Trèves, Mayence, and the Palatinate, while it only deprived Austria of her mutinous and rebellious subjects in Belgium. A secret clause was also added to the Treaty, by which the French Republic promised to guarantee the whole of Bavaria to the House of Austria, in return for the immediate evacuation of all the fortresses which the Austrians occupied upon the Rhine. Immediately upon receiving the news of the Treaty of Campio-Formio the Directory equipped a special army under the command of General Hatry for the capture of Mayence, the only place on the left bank of the Rhine not in the possession of France. Deprived of the assistance of Austria, the troops of the Empire and of the Elector of Mayence could make but little resistance, and on 29th of December 1797 Mayence was once more surrendered to the French Republic. *Capture of Mayence. 29th December 1797.*

The Batavian Republic, which had been established in 1795 in Holland, was also considerably affected by the revolution of 18th Fructidor. The Dutch Legislature had been influenced by every current of feeling in France, and during the predominance of the Clichians had made no real effort to support their French allies. After the conclusion of the Convention of Leoben, and the consequent cessation of hostilities in Germany, the Directory despatched Hoche to Holland. He there busied himself with another effort for his favourite scheme for the invasion of England. For this purpose he relied upon the powerful Dutch fleet, which was being blockaded by an English squadron under Admiral Duncan in the Texel. During the mutiny at the Nore in the summer of 1797 the position of the blockading English fleet had been very critical, and on one occasion it is stated that two English ships were left to watch fifteen Dutch. Directly after the revolution of Fructidor, the Directors, who did not feel certain of the support of Moreau, removed Hoche from *Holland. The Batavian Republic.*

Holland and placed him in command of the united Armies of the Rhine-and-Moselle and the Sambre-and-Meuse under the title of the Army of Germany. Hardly had he taken up his command when the most distinguished rival of Bonaparte died on the 18th of September 1797. Though deprived of the active superintendence of Hoche, the government of the Batavian Republic, under the influence of the vigorous war policy of the new Directory, ordered the Dutch fleet to leave the Texel. It was met at sea by Admiral Duncan off the dunes or downs of Kampe (Camperdown), and entirely defeated after the most hotly contested naval battle of the war. The naval policy of the Directory had thus resulted in the destruction of the Spanish fleet in the battle of Cape St. Vincent and of the Dutch fleet in the battle of Camperdown.

<small>Battle of Camperdown. 11th October 1797.</small>

On the 5th of December 1797 General Bonaparte arrived in Paris. The death of Hoche had left him without a rival, and the revolution of the 18th of Fructidor had been so entirely the result of the assistance of the army that its greatest general was practically the master of the political situation. The Directors received him with transports of enthusiasm and gave him a public reception, but, nevertheless, they were overawed by the extent of his reputation and afraid that he might attempt to take an active part in politics. He was appointed to the command of the Army of the Interior, which was intended for the invasion of England. Bonaparte, like Hoche, sincerely wished that such an invasion should be effected, but he understood the extraordinary difficulty inherent in any attempt to transport an army across the Channel in the presence of a powerful fleet. He therefore advised the Directory that it would be wiser not to attack England directly, but to make an effort to overthrow her power in Asia. It seemed to him more practicable to invade India than to invade England. His imagination was stirred by the conception of an expedition to the East, and the Directory was only too glad to remove from France for a time its most able and ambitious general.

<small>Bonaparte in Paris.</small>

*Bonaparte in Egypt*

On the 9th of May 1798 Bonaparte left Toulon at the head of a picked force of his veterans of Italy, and accompanied not only by his favourite generals, but also by some of the leading savants and men of letters of France. On the 9th of June the fleet reached Malta, and on the 12th the Knights of St. John of the Hospital, who had held the island ever since the Middle Ages, surrendered it to the French general. Leaving a garrison in Malta, Bonaparte then proceeded to Egypt. He disembarked in front of Alexandria on the 1st of July, and upon the 4th he occupied that city. He then advanced on Cairo, and on the 21st of July he defeated the Mamelukes at the Battle of the Pyramids, and on the 24th he occupied Cairo. The English fleet in the Mediterranean, under the command of Nelson, had been intended to stop the expedition to Egypt, but it had been misdirected, and was unable to prevent the disembarkation of the French forces. On the 1st of August, however, Nelson appeared before Alexandria, and in the battle of Aboukir Bay, generally known as the Battle of the Nile, he destroyed the French fleet. This victory entirely cut off Bonaparte and his army from France. The English held the Mediterranean, and for many months prevented the despatch of either news or reinforcements. In November they strengthened their position in the great south European sea by the occupation of Minorca by an army under the Hon. Sir Charles Stuart, and in 1800 the French garrison in Malta surrendered to General Pigot and Captain Sir Alexander Ball.

Before Bonaparte left Paris the time had come round for the election of a new Director. The lot fell upon François de Neufchâteau to retire, and his place was filled by Treilhard, a former member of the Constituent Assembly and of the Convention. Treilhard had been himself one of the leading Thermidorians, and since the close of the Convention he had been employed first as Minister in Holland and then as one of the French plenipotentiaries at the Congress of Rastadt. There is little doubt that Sieyès might have entered the Directory had he so wished, but he preferred to act in a different capacity. François de Neufchâteau at once returned to his former office of Minister of the Interior, and the only other alteration in the ministry was the appointment of Admiral Bruix to be Minister of Marine. The Directory, inspired by its victory on the 18th of Fructidor, did not hesitate to infringe the terms of the Constitution of the Year III. The Royalists or Clichians had not dared to appear at the elections to the Councils in 1798, and the democrats had been able to elect whom they wished. But the Directors did not intend to be subject to the democrats any more than to the Clichians, and without the slightest show of legality they quashed many of the elections to the Councils and gave the vacant seats to their own nominees. This disregard of the law was also shown in other branches of the internal policy of the Directory. The Directors, in spite of the Constitution, interfered with the finances, and, by the advice of Ramel, followed Cambon's example of declaring a partial bankruptcy. This, however, had but little effect in France, for, owing to the depreciation in the value of the government paper money, very little interest was expected by the creditors of the State. In purely internal administration the weariness of the French people of political disturbances enabled the agents of the Directory to maintain the public peace without difficulty. The lack of capital in the country was compensated by the fact that the government was the only great employer of labour, and the spoils of the conquered countries enabled it to pay the workmen sufficiently. It seems surprising that this bankrupt government should have been acknowledged without opposition throughout France, but the cause is to be found in the universal attention paid to the course of foreign affairs.

The Peace of Campo-Formio had, as has been shown, left France face to face with England, and it was to strike a blow at the power of England that Bonaparte proceeded to Egypt. For the same reason the Directory carried out the favourite scheme of Hoche, and despatched a force to Ireland under General Humbert in August 1798, which was forced to surrender to Lord Cornwallis in September. But though the powers of the Continent had been compelled to acknowledge the military superiority of France, they were only seeking a loophole by which to enter once more upon a general war. The departure of Bonaparte seemed to offer them a good opportunity, and pretexts were not wanting for the formation of a new coalition against France. The English ministry understood this attitude of the Continental powers, and their emissaries were busy in all the Courts of Europe. The Directors knew of these efforts of Pitt and did their best to counteract them. The keynote of the French policy was, as it had always been, to make an ally of Prussia. For this purpose Sieyès, who, though not in office, was probably the most influential man in France, obtained his nomination to a special embassy to Berlin. He hoped by mixed measures of conciliation and of menace to induce Frederick William III. of Prussia, who had succeeded his father in November 1797, to enter into an offensive and defensive alliance. But that monarch, in spite of the weakness of his personal character, had absolutely determined to maintain his father's policy of strict neutrality, and neither the arguments of Sieyès nor those of Mr. Thomas Grenville, the brother of the English Foreign Minister, could induce him to swerve from it in either direction. The efforts of England were crowned with more success at Vienna and St. Petersburg. The Emperor Francis, and still more the Austrian people, were profoundly disgusted by the triumphs of the French, and flattered themselves that their defeats had been due to the genius of Bonaparte more than to the valour of the French soldiers. On the conclusion of the Treaty of Campo-Formio, Bonaparte had, without consulting the Directory, nominated General Bernadotte to be the French Ambassador at Vienna. The Austrian people took this appointment as an insult; Bernadotte, though well received by the Emperor

*The Foreign Policy of the Directory.*

and his ministers, soon found that he was most unpopular in Vienna, and on the 13th of April 1798 the Viennese mob collected in front of the French Embassy, insulted the ambassador, and tore down the insignia of the French Republic. In spite of this insult the Directors did not at once declare war against Austria, but it afforded a pretext for dwelling on the inborn hatred of the Austrians for the French in their proclamations to the French people. Since such was the disposition of the Austrian people, it need hardly be said that the English envoy was heartily welcomed at Vienna. At St. Petersburg the application of Pitt for armed help was favourably received. The Emperor Paul, though already showing signs of the brutal insanity which was to lead to his assassination, still preserved the prestige of being the heir of the great Catherine. His ministers were those of Catherine; his policy was based on hers. But whereas Catherine had steadfastly refused to go to war with France, Paul showed a decided inclination, which was fostered by his generals, to see whether the Russian army would not be more successful than the Prussian or the Austrian against the seemingly invincible French republicans.

The French Directory, though recognising that it might have soon to contend again with the power of Austria, and for the first time with that of Russia, nevertheless roused without any reason fresh enemies upon the French frontiers. Its greatest mistake at this period was its interference with the affairs of Switzerland. For this interference there was no real cause, but the Directors could not resist the temptation of inflicting their special form of republic upon the Swiss. The organisation of most of the cantons of Switzerland was essentially feudal and oligarchical. The government of each canton and of each city was in the hands of a very few families, and the people were in much the same condition politically, socially, and economically as the people of France before the Revolution. The Swiss peasants had caught the contagion of revolution from France, and in the

*The Helvetian Republic. April 1798.*

## The Helvetian Republic

beginning of 1798 the people of the Pays de Vaud rose in insurrection against the authority of the Canton of Berne. This rising was followed by popular tumults in other cantons, and the peasants everywhere destroyed the signs of the feudal system and declared themselves in favour of 'Liberty—Equality—Fraternity.' The popular leaders appealed to France for help, and a powerful army under the command of General Brune invaded Switzerland. The militia of the cantons was speedily routed; Brune occupied Berne and sent the national treasury to Paris, and a freely-elected Constituent Assembly was summoned. This assembly proclaimed an Helvetian Republic, one and indivisible, with a Directory, two Councils, and Ministers, in imitation of the French, the Cisalpine, and the Batavian Republics, to take the place of the old Swiss federal constitution. Great reforms were speedily accomplished; on the 8th of May 1798 internal customs-houses were abolished, and on the 13th of May torture was forbidden in judicial processes; on the 3d of August marriages between persons of different religions were declared legal; and eventually all feudal rights were suppressed. Great as were these reforms, they were not entirely acceptable to the Swiss people. The mountaineers of Uri, Schweitz and Unterwalden, the descendants of the founders of the ancient Swiss liberties, objected to be freed under the influence of French bayonets, and the cry of national patriotism soon raised an army against the French liberators of the peasants. The French troops had to remain perpetually under arms, and the Helvetian Republic, in spite of the popular freedom which it secured, was hated even by the peasants whom it had relieved. The hatred for the French name was increased by the arbitrary conduct, and it was asserted by the corrupt behaviour, of Rapinat, the French commissioner, who was a near relative of Reubell, the Director. The intervention of the Directory had, therefore, in Switzerland, roused a people in arms, even though it had been dictated by the best of motives.

When Bonaparte left Italy he had been succeeded in the command of the French troops which occupied the frontiers of the Cisalpine Republic by General Berthier. This general, desirous of emulating the successes of Bonaparte, took the opportunity of the murder of the French ambassador at Rome, General Duphot, to occupy the Eternal City. The Pope, Pius VI., fled from Rome to the Carthusian monastery at Pisa, and the Roman people declared themselves to be once more the Roman Republic. Consuls and Tribunes, as in ancient days, were elected; the Directory, full of classical recollections, recognised the Roman Republic with transports of enthusiasm; and General Berthier took the opportunity to send large sums of money to Paris. The King of Naples, or to speak more accurately, the King of the Two Sicilies, regarded the new republic with anything but favour. Encouraged by English and Austrian envoys, and still more by the news of Nelson's victory at the Battle of the Nile, he determined to attack Rome. He placed one of the most distinguished of the Austrian generals, Mack, at the head of his army, and, without declaring war, occupied Rome on the 29th of November 1798. The French troops for the moment had to retire. But Championnet, who had succeeded Berthier, quickly concentrated his army, and on the 15th of December he reoccupied Rome in force. Championnet then took the offensive; he invaded the Neapolitan territory, and he quickly conquered all Ferdinand's dominions in Italy. The King fled to Sicily, and in January 1799 the Parthenopean Republic was solemnly installed at Naples. The two remaining independent states of Italy were also occupied by the French armies. The one of these, Piedmont, was conquered without any declaration of war or any pretext by General Joubert in November 1798, and King Charles Emmanuel IV. fled to Sardinia. The other, Tuscany, in spite of the desire of the Grand Duke to remain at peace with France, was the next victim, and on the 25th of March 1799 the French troops occupied Florence.

The occupation of the whole of Italy and of Switzerland did not increase the military strength of France; on the contrary, the proceedings of the Directory only aroused the most profound disgust and fear in Austria, Russia, and England. The Directors felt that a far more terrible war than they had yet been engaged in was about to break forth, and it may be assumed that, on the eve of hostilities, they even regretted the absence of Bonaparte. Enormous numbers of soldiers would be necessary in a new war. Trained and experienced officers and non-commissioned officers existed, but the difficulty was how to fill the ranks. It was no longer possible to have recourse to the measures of the Convention, to the *levée en masse*, and to the appeal for volunteers with the cry that the country was in danger. The Republic had now become a military power, and the question was how to recruit its armies, not how to rouse the whole population. On the 19th of Fructidor, Year VI. (5th September 1798), the Councils of the Ancients and of Five Hundred, on the application of the Directory, passed the first Law of Conscription. By this law all Frenchmen between the ages of twenty and twenty-five with certain exceptions were declared to be subject to military service. They were divided into five classes, and one or more classes could be called out by the executive authority after receiving the consent of the Legislature. This law is the starting-point of the military levies which formed the army of Napoleon, and the principle of conscription was thus laid down many months before Bonaparte became First Consul.
[Sidenote: The Law of Conscription. 5th Sept. 1798.]

Mention has been made of the riot at Vienna which caused the departure of the French ambassador, Bernadotte. He was not replaced by the Directory, and long negotiations took place on the subject of the compensation due to the Republic for this insult. But neither party was in earnest. Both the French Directory and the Emperor Francis were preparing for the contest. The first overt act of war took place at the commencement of 1799, when the Austrian troops, under the command of the
[Sidenote: The Outbreak of War. 1799.]

Archduke Charles, occupied the passes of the Grisons, and it was in this quarter that before war was actually declared the first engagements were fought. In Italy General Schérer was attacked at Verona by the Austrian General Kray, and in Germany General Jourdan fell back into the Black Forest. In both of these quarters many skirmishes took place, and eventually on the 25th of March 1799 the Archduke Charles defeated Jourdan in a pitched battle at Stockach. A few days later, on the 5th of April, Schérer was defeated at Magnano. Meanwhile the Congress of Rastadt was still sitting, and Austria was nominally at peace with France. The conclusion of a treaty between France and the Empire, which was the subject of the deliberations at Rastadt, was necessarily a difficult matter to negotiate, for it involved nothing less than the entire reconstitution of the Holy Roman Empire, a reconstitution which could only be carried out by the secularisation of the bishoprics. Eventually, in the month of April 1799, after the engagements of Stockach and Magnano, the French plenipotentiaries at Rastadt understood that it was hopeless to expect to conclude a treaty with the Empire. They therefore asked for their passports to France. These passports were refused. As they left Rastadt the French plenipotentiaries were attacked by some Austrian hussars; two of them, Roberjot and Bonnier d'Alco, were killed, and the other, Jean Debry, left for dead. This odious violation of international law and the rights of ambassadors took the place of a formal declaration of war, and roused not only the Directory but the French people to the most strenuous exertions. Meanwhile the Emperor Paul of Russia declared war against France, and ordered three armies to be despatched to the scenes of action.

*Battles of Stockach and Magnano, 25th March and 5th April.*

The campaign of 1799 was fought out in three localities, in all of which the Russians played a most prominent part. In Italy a Russian army, under the command of one of the most famous generals in Europe, Suvórov, reinforced the Austrians after the battle of

*The Campaign in Italy. 1799.*

Magnano. Suvórov forced the passage of the Adda at Cassano on the 27th of April, and rapidly drove Moreau, who had succeeded Schérer in command, across northern Italy. On the 28th of April Suvórov entered Milan, and the Cisalpine Republic at once expired. On the 27th of May he entered Turin, and after leaving besieging armies before Mantua and Alessandria, shut up the remnants of Moreau's army in Genoa. But the army of Moreau was not the only French army in the Italian Peninsula. Several powerful divisions, under the name of the Army of Naples, were concentrated in Rome and Naples to support the newly-formed Roman and Parthenopean Republics. Macdonald, who had succeeded Championnet in the command of this army, rapidly concentrated and threatened to take the Austro-Russian army in flank. Suvórov withdrew from Turin and turned to his left to meet his new assailant. On the banks of the Trebbia a three days' battle was fought from the 17th to the 19th of June. The issue of the battle itself was doubtful, but Macdonald, finding himself unsupported by Moreau from Genoa, was obliged to retreat into Tuscany. Fearing to be cut off, he then forced his way along the difficult passage between the mountains and the sea, and joined Moreau, after collecting every French soldier from the garrisons in the south of Italy. The retreat of the French was followed by an outburst against the Italian republicans. *Battle of the Trebbia. 17th-19th June.*

The Parthenopean Republic was at once overthrown, and King Ferdinand of the Two Sicilies wreaked cruel vengeance on his subjects. Pope Pius VI. had been removed from his retreat near Florence to Valence, and the French Directors had some idea of keeping him prisoner as a hostage in the same way as Napoleon afterwards imprisoned his successor. But the old Pope could not bear the sufferings of his imprisonment, and died at Valence on the 29th of August 1799. Rome, deprived of the presence of the Pope and the Cardinals, fell under the dominion of the Roman nobles, who followed the example of the King of the Two Sicilies in persecuting the republicans. Meanwhile the *Death of Pope Pius VI. 29th Aug. 1799.*

French Directory appointed General Joubert, who was believed to be the best of the former subordinates of Bonaparte, to take command at Genoa of the relics of the armies of Moreau and Macdonald. With these soldiers he burst out of Genoa to raise the siege of Alessandria, but on the 15th of August he was utterly defeated by Suvórov at Novi in a great battle, in which Joubert himself was killed. In spite of these defeats the Directory refused to believe that Italy was lost. A new army was formed, and placed under the command of Championnet, who, however, was defeated at Genola on the 4th of November by the Austrians, under Melas, and driven back into France.

<small>Battle of Novi. 15th August.</small>

While Suvórov was conquering Italy and destroying the recollection of the victories of Bonaparte in that country, Masséna, who was in command of the French army in Switzerland, was engaged in a most difficult task. The Archduke Charles, who also had under his command a Russian army under Korsakov, forced his way slowly into Switzerland, driving the French before him, and in August 1799 left Korsakov in command at Zurich. The Archduke was then ordered to take the bulk of his army to the Rhine in order to invade France. Korsakov, abandoned to his own resources, showed himself far inferior in military ability to Suvórov. Masséna, with singular boldness, refused to remain on the defensive, and on the 26th of September drove the Russians out of Zurich. His victory was won just in time, for Suvórov, after defeating Joubert at Novi, had determined, in spite of the terrible weather, to cross the Alps. It was on the 24th of September, two days before Masséna's victory at Zurich, that the main Russian army arrived at the summit of the St. Gothard Pass. General Lecourbe, one of the finest mountain generals of his day, occupied the St. Gothard, and with a few battalions kept the whole Russian army at bay. Suvórov nevertheless persevered and hoped to turn Masséna's flank. But it was several weeks before he could reach the village of Altdorf. Being unable to

<small>The Campaign in Switzerland. 1799.</small>

<small>Battle of Zurich. 26th Sept.</small>

find boats to cross the lake, he had now to retreat, and when he reached the Grisons his army was practically destroyed by starvation and the stress of the weather. Masséna, thus relieved of his most formidable enemies, took possession of Constance, and by threatening the flank of the Archduke Charles forced the main Austrian army to fall back to the Danube.

The third campaign of 1799 was fought in Holland. In this quarter it had been arranged that the English and Russians were to act in concert. On the 27th of August the English fleet had successfully reached the Dutch coast, and had captured the relics of the Dutch fleet, defeated at Camperdown, in the Texel. After this operation an English army, under the Duke of York, and a Russian army, under General Hermann, disembarked at the Helder. General Brune was hurriedly despatched to take command of the few French troops in Holland, and co-operated with the army of the Batavian Republic under General Janssens. The campaign consisted of a succession of fierce but indecisive battles in the neighbourhood of Bergen. The English and Russians did not act harmoniously together; the country was unsuited for field operations; and supplies were not adequately provided. As a result of the operations, though he had not been really defeated, the Duke of York signed the Convention of Alkmaar on the 18th October, by which he agreed to surrender all prisoners on being allowed to evacuate Holland. *The Campaign in Holland. 1799.* *Battles of Bergen.*

The results of the campaigns of 1799 were decidedly favourable to France. Though Italy was lost, and more than one French army had been defeated, the victories of Masséna and of Brune more than compensated for these disasters. Not only had France not been invaded, but she had been able to retain her position in Switzerland and in Holland, and to hold the whole of the right bank of the Rhine. England, in spite of the Convention of Alkmaar, could point to the victory of the Nile and the capture of the Dutch fleet in the Texel as real successes, and Pitt and *Results of the Campaigns.*

Grenville did not despair of ultimate victory. The King of Prussia, who, when the affairs of France seemed to be desperate, had begun to assume an attitude of opposition, and demanded the evacuation of the Prussian provinces on the Rhine, speedily repented of his indiscretion, and made excuses for his behaviour. The Austrian ministers evinced no desire to continue the war; they resented the high-handed conduct of Suvórov, and showed themselves more afraid of their powerful ally, Russia, than of their declared enemy, France. They implored the English government to bring about the withdrawal of the Russian troops, and the Emperor Paul was only too glad to comply. The retreat of the Russians left Italy practically in the hands of Austria. The Grand Duke Ferdinand of Tuscany was restored to his dominions, but the King of Sardinia was not recalled, and Piedmont remained in the occupation of the Austrian troops. Genoa alone was held by a French garrison, which was closely besieged by the Austrians on the land side, and blockaded by the English Mediterranean fleet. It was under the influence of Austria and under the protection of Austrian troops that the Conclave met at Venice in November 1799 to elect a new Pope.

The significant feature of the campaigns of 1799 was the intervention of Russia. Mention has been made of the abandonment of the policy of the great Catherine by her successor. This change in the attitude of Russia was due mainly to the influence of England, but partly to the encouragement given by the French Directory to the Poles. The restoration of Poland to its place among the nations had long been a favourite idea among French republicans. Kosciuszko had been enthusiastically welcomed at Paris, and the first of the Polish legions which were to do good service under Napoleon was raised by Dombrowski in 1797. The Emperor Paul had met this attitude by welcoming the pretender Louis XVIII. to Russia, where he lent him the palace of Mittau and gave him a considerable pension. He also took into Russian pay the armed corps of *émigrés* under the command of the Prince de Condé. But fear of French assistance to Poland would not alone have induced the Emperor Paul to declare war. He was particularly offended by the French occupation of the Ionian Islands and of Malta. By the Treaty of Campo-Formio the Ionian Islands had been ceded to France, and the Russians regarded this cession as an indication that the Directory was going to interfere actively in the affairs of the East. The bad impression created by the occupation of the Ionian Islands had been increased by the conquest of Malta and the expedition to Egypt. Though Russia quite intended to destroy the power of Turkey, she had no idea of allowing any western nation to share the spoils. It was for this reason that the Emperor Paul accepted the title of Grand Master of the Knights of St. John, which the expelled Knights of Malta offered to him, and that he occupied the Ionian Islands with a Russian force in 1798. The foreign policy of the Emperor was so far popular in Russia in that it maintained the sole right of Russia to interfere in the East, but it was unpopular in that it seemed by the despatch of the armies under Suvórov and Korsakov to bolster up the power of Austria. Suvórov and his officers returned to Russia with a feeling of respect for their enemies, but with a feeling of intense disgust at the behaviour of their allies. Suvórov, indeed, went so far as to accuse the Austrians of playing the part of traitors, and the anger of Paul was raised to its height by the capture of Ancona, which was delivered by a secret compact to the Austrian general in spite of the assistance of Russian troops. He was equally angry with England on account of the failure of the expedition to Holland. Every thing at the close of 1799 conduced to make the Emperor Paul seek for a pretext to make peace, if not an actual alliance, with the French Republic.

While these important campaigns were being fought out in Europe, Bonaparte had not been idle in the East. The Battle of the Pyramids had made him master of Egypt, and though cut off by the English fleet from communication with France,

he remained master of the country. His internal administration made him excessively popular among the
Egyptians. He removed the Turks and Mamelukes
from office, and called on the Egyptians to govern
themselves. But the Turks did not intend to lose Egypt
without striking another blow, and a powerful army was sent
for its reconquest. Bonaparte determined to meet this army
half way, and in February 1799 he advanced into Syria. He
speedily reduced Palestine and took Jaffa, and then laid siege
to the strong fortress of Acre. Assisted by the English sailors of
Sir Sidney Smith, the garrison of Acre made a gallant defence.
The Turkish army advancing to its relief was defeated by
Bonaparte at Mount Tabor on the 16th of April. In spite
of his victory, he had, nevertheless, to abandon the siege of
Acre, and on the 20th of May he commenced his retreat to
Egypt. He there found the position to be extremely critical.
The Mamelukes had reorganised their army and reoccupied
Cairo, and a Turkish army had been disembarked by the
English fleet at Aboukir. Meanwhile Desaix, whom he had left
in command in Egypt, had gone up the Nile for the conquest
of the interior. Bonaparte soon re-established his power; he
defeated the Mamelukes at Cairo, and drove the Turkish army
into the sea. At this juncture he heard the news of the events
of the campaigns in Europe, and, what affected him more, of
the course of politics at Paris. He determined, therefore, to
return to France, and leaving Kléber in command in Egypt,
he set sail with a few personal friends. The ship on which he
embarked escaped the English cruisers, and he landed at
Fréjus on the 9th of October 1799 after a perilous voyage of
forty-seven days.

*Campaign in Syria. 1799.*

The varying issues of the campaigns of 1799 had profoundly
affected the situation of the Directors, and the disasters in Italy had turned the hopes both of the
army and of the French people towards Bonaparte.
At the annual change in the composition of the Directory
and the Councils which took place in 1799 a considerable

*Quarrel between the Councils and the Directory.*

alteration had been made. The new third of the Councils consisted almost entirely of men who, without being either Jacobins or Clichians, longed to see the establishment of a strong government in order to secure peace. The Directory, which had seemed so strong after the revolution of the 18th of Fructidor, had been considerably weakened by the behaviour of the Directors themselves. The election of none but civilians to the highest offices in the State was disliked by the army, and the characters of the Directors themselves had suffered. Reubell was the Director designed by lot to retire in May 1799; he was perhaps the ablest and most experienced of them all, but had been discredited by the bad conduct of his relative, Rapinat, in Switzerland. Sieyès was elected to succeed Reubell. This choice, and the acceptance of Sieyès, testified to a new condition of affairs. The former abbé might have been a Director on at least two former occasions, in 1795 and 1798, and his acceptance at this juncture was very significant. He had failed in his embassy to Berlin to induce the new King of Prussia to become the active ally of France, and had been convinced by his diplomatic experiences that the government of France must become frankly military, since the monarchical powers of Europe would not accept the possibility of a peaceable French Republic. From an internal point of view the acceptance of Sieyès indicated an increase of power for the Legislature, of which he was the idol.

The election of Sieyès was followed by a bloodless revolution. He maintained that the failure of the Constitution of the Year III. was due to the usurpation of the functions of the Legislature by the Directory, and, therefore, when the Councils declared Treilhard and Merlin of Douai to have been illegally chosen Directors, and called for the resignation of Revellière-Lépeaux, they found a powerful ally in Sieyès. The attacked Directors yielded without a struggle, and on 30th Prairial, Year VII. (18th June 1799), they were replaced by three personal friends of Sieyès, Gohier, Roger Ducos, and General Moulin. Barras was thus

Coup d'etat of 30th Prairial (18th June 1799).

the only member left of the original Directory. The Councils, not satisfied with this victory, began to usurp the executive functions of the Directory, and a general change of ministry took place. The new ministers were Reinhard, Robert Lindet, Cambacérès, Quinette, Bernadotte, replaced on 14th September by Dubois-Crancé, Fouché, and Bourdon de Vatry, who succeeded Talleyrand and his colleagues as Ministers of Foreign Affairs, the Finances, Justice, the Interior, War, Police, and the Marine respectively. It is worthy of note that four of the new ministers were formerly leading members of the Convention. But the administration of the Councils was not more effective than that of the Directory, and the news of the disembarkation of Bonaparte at Fréjus was received with a feeling of general satisfaction throughout France.

Bonaparte reached Paris on the 16th of October, and his assistance was sought by men of all parties. He allied himself with none, but there can be little doubt that he took the advice mainly of Talleyrand, Fouché, and Sieyès. Nevertheless he did not repulse the leaders of the Councils, and to show their attachment for him the Council of Five Hundred, on the 22d of October 1799, elected his brother Lucien Bonaparte to be their president, and the whole Legislature gave him a grand banquet on 6th November. The first stage of the revolution of Brumaire was a decree by which the Council of Ancients, or rather certain of its members, who had been initiated into the project of a *coup d'état*, taking advantage of a clause in the Constitution applicable to circumstances of popular agitation, resolved in the early morning of the 18th Brumaire, Year VIII. (9th November 1799), that the two Councils should leave Paris and meet at Saint-Cloud; and the execution of this decree was intrusted to General Bonaparte. In the palace of Saint-Cloud it was easy to surround the legislators by a body of troops faithful to Bonaparte, since the command of the troops in Paris was in the hands of one of his friends, General Lefebvre, who was discontented at not having been elected a Director instead of Moulin. Sieyès and Roger Ducos, who were in the plot, at once declared their resignations; Barras was induced to acquiesce; and the other two Directors were guarded as prisoners in the palace of the Luxembourg by General Moreau. On the following morning, the 19th of Brumaire, Bonaparte entered the Councils, escorted by soldiers; the Ancients listened to him quietly; but the Five Hundred were in a tumult; a proposal was made to declare the general and his supporters *hors la loi* or outlaws; and after a stormy scene the deputies were driven from the hall by the grenadiers. In the evening a few deputies, who were in the secret of the general's plans, met and decreed the suppression of the Directory and the creation of a provisional government, consisting of three Consuls. The three men chosen for this office were Bonaparte, Sieyès, and Roger Ducos. Commissions were appointed to revise the Constitution and to draw up with the Consuls new fundamental laws for the Republic. By this revolution Bonaparte practically became ruler of France, for Sieyès had no influence with the army, and Roger Ducos no influence with anybody. It was a military revolution like that of the 18th Fructidor; it was a bloodless revolution like that of the 18th Fructidor; but it differed in that, instead of establishing the power of five men, it established the power of one. And that one man was the idol of the army, and generally acknowledged to be the greatest general of France. The preponderance of Bonaparte was quickly recognised by his colleagues. 'Who shall preside?' said Sieyès at the first meeting of the provisional Consuls on 20th Brumaire. 'Do you not see that the general is in the chair?' replied Roger Ducos. And Sieyès, who was the chief epigram maker as well as the constitution-monger of the Revolution, is said to have summed up the situation with the remark to his friends on the same evening: 'Messieurs, nous avons un maître; il sait tout, il peut tout, il veut tout.'

# CHAPTER VII

## 1799-1804

Constitution of the Year VIII.—The Consulate—The Council of State—The Tribunate—The Legislative Body—The Senate—Internal Policy of the Consulate—General Reconciliation—The Code Civil—Ministers of the Consulate—Foreign Policy of the Consulate—Russia—Prussia—The Pope—Campaign of Marengo—Campaign of Hohenlinden—Winter Campaign of Moreau and Macdonald—The Treaty of Lunéville—Arrangements in Italy—Policy and Murder of the Emperor Paul of Russia—The Neutral League of the North—Battle of Copenhagen—War between Spain and Portugal—Treaty of Badajoz—Campaign of 1801 in Egypt—Peace of Amiens between England and France—Reconstitution of Germany—Secularisation of the German ecclesiastical dominions—Reconstitution of Switzerland—Concordat between the Pope and Bonaparte—Internal Organisation of France under the Consulate—The new Departments—Annexation of Piedmont—The Préfectures—System of National Education—Constitutional Changes in France—Bonaparte First Consul for life—Recommencement of War between England and France—Causes—Position of Affairs on the Continent—Plot of Pichegru and Cadoudal—Execution of the Duc d'Enghien—Bonaparte becomes Emperor of the French—Francis II. resigns the title of Holy Roman Emperor for that of Emperor of Austria.

THE revolution of the 18th of Brumaire had placed supreme power in the hands of Bonaparte; that power was speedily legalised and defined in the Constitution of the Year VIII. The chief political problem was once more how to regulate the relation between the legislative and executive authorities. The Constitution of 1791, and still more that of 1793, had entirely subordinated the executive to the legislative authority; the Constitution of the Year III. (1795) had endeavoured to co-ordinate them; the Constitution of the Year VIII. (1799) entirely subordinated the legislative to the executive. It fell once more to Sieyès, one of the

*The Constitution of the Year VIII.*

principal authors of the Constitutions of 1791 and 1795, as Second Provisional Consul, to define the new arrangements. His attempt at co-ordinating the two powers in the State in 1795 had failed in its operation: as was inevitable, the two authorities declined to preserve their legal relations to each other. On the 18th of Fructidor, Year v. (4th September 1797), the executive in the form of the Directory had usurped and partially destroyed the power of the Legislature, and on the 30th of Prairial, Year VII. (18th of June 1799) the Legislature had acted in the same way towards the executive. By the Constitution of the Year VIII., therefore, the executive power was frankly acknowledged to be supreme. In its details it was entirely the work of Sieyès, though his main idea—the appointment of a Grand Elector who should nominate to fill all offices, but should exercise no power—was rejected by Bonaparte. The new Constitution was soon ready; it was submitted to the primary assemblies of the people on the 14th December 1799, and was accepted by them by 3,011,107 votes against 1567, and was officially proclaimed on the 24th of December.

The keystone of the new Constitution was the Consulate. There were to be three Consuls nominated for ten years, but these officials were not to be equal in authority, as had been the case with the Directors. On the contrary, the First Consul was to be perpetual president and perpetual representative of the governing triumvirate. All administrative power was placed in his hands, and the Second and Third Consuls were little more than his chief assistants. The Consuls acting together nominated the Ministers, and also the Council of State, which was intended to be at the same time an administrative tribunal of appeal, and the originating source in matters of legislation. *The Consulate.*

In the work of legislation the Council of State was supplemented by the Tribunate and the Legislative Body. All laws prepared by the Council of State were first submitted to the Tribunate, which was composed *The Legislature.*

of one hundred members. The Tribunate could neither reject nor amend a law, but decided whether to support or oppose the project before the Legislative Body. The Legislative Body consisted of three hundred deputies chosen by certain electoral assemblies formed by a complicated scheme out of the taxpayers of the departments. By this scheme, after three series of elections, what was termed a 'National List' was drawn up. From this national list the Senate chose the members both of the Legislative Body and the Tribunate. The Legislative Body alone voted the taxes. In legislative matters it played the part of a national jury, listening to the arguments for or against brought forward by the Tribunate on every project prepared by the Council of State, and deciding in every case without discussion. The Legislative Body alone could give a project of the Council of State the character of a law. The Senate was composed of eighty members nominated for life by the Consuls. Its duties were to choose the members of the Tribunate and Legislative Body from the National List, and to decide whether any law or measure of the government was contrary to the Constitution. If it decided that such law or measure was unconstitutional it had the authority to annul it.

The Consulate was composed of Bonaparte as First Consul, with Cambacérès and Le Brun, both famous jurists, as his associates. Their policy was one of general reconciliation. The individuals deported after the revolution of the 18th of Fructidor were allowed to return to France if they had not, like Pichegru, become declared royalists. They were even taken into favour; while Carnot was appointed Minister of War, Portalis and Barbé-Marbois were nominated to the Council of State. The lists of emigration were closed; no longer could persons be declared to have emigrated on mere suspicion, and the First Consul, as an administrative measure, annulled the decrees excluding relations of *émigrés* and former nobles from filling executive offices. More than 150,000 *émigrés* were also allowed to return, mostly priests, who were no longer

*Internal Policy of the Consulate.*

regarded as rebels, and who, whether they had taken the oath to observe the Civil Constitution of the Clergy or not, were allowed to resume their sacred functions on simply promising to obey the new Constitution of the State. The Consulate did even more than this for the cause of religion; many churches which had been appropriated for civil purposes were restored to their original uses. Brigandage was sternly put down, and Bonaparte, at last, pacified La Vendée by negotiating a treaty of amnesty with the remaining Vendéan leaders at Montluçon, on the 17th of January 1800. A special effort was made to put the finances in order, and Gaudin, who held office as Minister of the Finances throughout the Consulate and the Empire, first proved his extraordinary powers. His financial reforms may be roughly summed up by the mention of his two most important measures. The decrees of the Directory in favour of forced loans from the rich, which had been arbitrarily and unfairly carried out, were abrogated and replaced by a general income-tax of twenty-five per cent. This established some justice in the collection, which partly compensated for the heaviness of the tax. The second measure was the appointment of receivers-general of taxes in every department. These men had to give heavy security, and were allowed a fair measure of profit in the form of a percentage on what they collected. They were strictly supervised, and the scandalous dilapidations which had signalised the period of the Directory were made impossible for the future. Further, in order to secure the support of the capitalists, the Bank of France was founded under the guarantee of the State. Finally, the First Consul decided to carry into effect the projects of the legal reformers of the Constituent Assembly and the Convention. Their labours had made possible the formation of a uniform code of law for France. Bonaparte appointed a Commission, consisting of Tronchet, Portalis, and Bigot de Préameneu, to examine the labours of their predecessors, and with their help to draw up the admirable civil code, which was afterwards known as the Code Napoléon.  *The Code Napoléon.*

In no respect was the administrative ability of the Consuls better manifested than in the selection they made of their ministers. It has already been noticed that Gaudin, the greatest financier of France, was appointed Minister of the Finances. Talleyrand and Fouché once more took possession of the portfolios of Foreign Affairs and of Police, which they held for many years. Their first Minister of the Marine, Forfait, did not remain long in office, but his successor, Decrès, held that post from 1801 till 1814. The same may be said with regard to the Ministry of Justice. Abrial, the first occupant of this post, gave way to Regnier in 1802, but he likewise remained in office till 1814. The Ministries of War and of the Interior were more difficult to fill; Carnot soon resented the tone of Bonaparte, and was succeeded by Berthier, afterwards Prince of Neufchâtel, who had been Chief of the Staff to Bonaparte in Italy. La Place, the great astronomer, had been appointed Minister of the Interior by the Provisional Government in November 1799. He did not show himself very efficient, and was succeeded by Lucien Bonaparte, the First Consul's ablest brother, in the following month. He too failed to carry out the wishes of the Consuls, and was succeeded in 1800 by one of the most distinguished administrators of the period, Chaptal.

Of foreign affairs Bonaparte, as First Consul, assumed the entire management; in internal matters he laid down the main principles indeed, but he allowed his colleagues some share in the government. He found France once more at war, as she had been before the Treaty of Campo-Formio, with Austria and England. But another redoubtable enemy had been added in Russia. Fortunately for France, for reasons which have already been indicated, the Emperor Paul was profoundly dissatisfied with his allies. From an unreasoning hatred for France, the Russian Emperor had now altered his sentiments to one of profound admiration for the person of the First Consul. Bonaparte was soon notified of this disposition at the Court of St. Petersburg. He sent his most intimate friend, Duroc, on a special mission to Russia, and the idea was already suggested that Russia and France ought to be the arbiters of Europe. He offered to recognise Paul not only as Grand Master of the Knights of Malta, but as the sovereign of that island, and promised in every way to forward Russian interests. In return, Paul, with his usual exaggeration, declared Bonaparte to be his dearest friend, surrounded himself with his portraits, drank publicly to his health, and ordered Louis XVIII. to leave Mittau. The Russian ambassador in Paris, Kolichev, on behalf of his master, proposed that Bonaparte should take the title of King of France, and make the crown hereditary in his family. Next in importance to the commencement of good relations with Russia, was the First Consul's effort to make the King of Prussia his declared ally. For this purpose he sent Duroc also to Berlin. But Frederick William III. was a different type of monarch from the Emperor Paul; he could not so readily alter his policy. Personally, he too admired the First Consul, and regarded him as the restorer of order and as a monarch in embryo; but, in spite of his admiration, he refused to comply with the wishes of Bonaparte, as he had rejected the propositions of the Directory, and insisted on the maintenance of his consistent attitude of strict neutrality. The last point to be noticed in the foreign policy of Bonaparte was his attitude towards the Pope. He not only allowed the body of Pope Pius VI. to be removed from Valence to be buried at Rome, but he recognised the new Pope, Pius VII., although he had been elected at Venice under Austrian influence: he even offered to restore him to his temporal dominion at Rome, and promised to enter into negotiations with him with regard to the re-establishment of the Catholic Church in France.

With the two great enemies of France, Austria and England, the First Consul had no desire to treat. Though unable to strike at England, owing to the weakness of the French navy, he could yet attack the Austrians in two quarters. Two powerful armies were prepared,

*The Campaign of Marengo, 1800.*

the one the Army of the Danube, which was placed under the command of Moreau, and the other the Army of the Interior, soon to become famous as the Second Army of Italy. Of all the conquests in Italy made by the French in 1796 and 1797, only Genoa remained in their possession. Masséna, fresh from his victories in Switzerland, had taken command of the besieged army. His defence is one of the most famous in history, and does no less honour to the general than his victory at Zurich. Bonaparte desired to relieve Genoa; and he resolved not to advance along the coast, as he had done in 1796, but by crossing the Alps, and descending upon Piedmont, to cut off the Austrian army occupying that province.

In the month of May Bonaparte crossed the Great Saint Bernard Pass at the head of 40,000 men, and fell at once on the Austrian flank. He was too late to relieve Genoa, which surrendered on the 4th of June, when but few of the soldiers were still able to stand, but he was in time to close the retreat of the Austrians upon Lombardy. On the 9th June 1800 General Lannes defeated the Austrian advanced guard at Montebello, and Bonaparte then barred the road from Alessandria to Piacenza. General Melas, though not yet joined by the troops which had taken Genoa, had a larger army than Bonaparte; on June 14 he forced his way out of Alessandria, and drove back the French columns which occupied the village of Marengo. The battle was practically lost by the French, when Desaix, who had been detached to the left with 6000 men, fell upon the Austrian flank. Desaix was killed, but the vigour of his attack practically cut the Austrian army in two. The dragoons of Kellermann completed the victory, and General Melas signed the Convention of Alessandria, by which he surrendered Genoa, Piedmont, and the Milanese to the French, and promised to withdraw the Austrian garrisons from all cities to the west of the Mincio. Bonaparte then attended a *Te Deum* sung in honour of his victory in the cathedral of Milan, and returned to Paris, leaving the Army of Grisons, under the command of General Macdonald, to follow up the Austrians.

While Bonaparte was winning the battle of Marengo, and reconquering Italy by a single blow, Moreau was again face to face with his old opponent, the Archduke Charles. The French advance was very slow. Fierce battles were fought at Engen, Mœskirchen, and Biberach in May 1800, and by the close of the summer Moreau had his headquarters at Augsburg, and his advanced guard at Munich. The slowness of Moreau's progress dissatisfied the First Consul, as did the want of success of the Archduke Charles dissatisfy the court of Vienna. Augereau was sent with 20,000 men to the assistance of Moreau, who was ordered, in spite of the severity of the winter, to continue his advance; and the Archduke John was appointed to succeed his brother, and ordered to take the offensive. The crowning event of this winter campaign was the great victory of Hohenlinden, which was won by Moreau on the 3d of December 1800. The Austrians lost the whole of their baggage and artillery and 12,000 prisoners. *Campaign of Hohenlinden.*

The First Consul from Paris ordered Moreau and Macdonald to advance into the home districts of the House of Austria. Moreau accordingly pushed along the Inn, the Salz, the Traun, and the Ens, driving the disorganised and discouraged Austrians before him until he was within twenty leagues of Vienna. Macdonald, at the same time, crossed the Splügen Pass in spite of the avalanches, and penetrated into the Tyrol, thus turning the Austrian forces on the Mincio and the Adige. On arriving at Trent, Macdonald turned to the right and was joined by Brune, who had occupied the territory of Venice, and the united French army marched upon Vienna. Under these circumstances, with Italy lost, and Vienna threatened from two quarters, the Emperor Francis sued for peace, which was concluded at Lunéville on the 9th of February 1801. *The Winter Campaign of 1800.*

The Treaty of Lunéville was more important from its

destruction of the old Holy Roman Empire than as the treaty of peace between France and Austria. From the latter point of view the Emperor Francis once more, as in the Treaty of Campo-Formio, recognised the Rhine as the limit of France. In Italy the Cisalpine Republic was once more constituted with the Adige as its frontier, Modena was to be compensated with the Breisgau, and Venice was again left to the House of Austria. Tuscany was taken from its Austrian Grand Duke, and erected into a kingdom of Etruria in favour of the Prince of Parma, a relative of the King of Spain, and Piedmont was annexed to France; but the King of the Two Sicilies was allowed to retain his dominions, and the Pope was restored to all his possessions except the Legations of Bologna and Ferrara. The Cisalpine Republic was reorganised, and granted a Constitution on the model of that of the Year VIII., in which Bonaparte was appointed First Consul. The Ligurian Republic was maintained, with the alteration that its Doge was nominated by France instead of being elected. The result of the new arrangements in Northern Italy was that both France and Austria had a foothold by their occupation of Piedmont and Venice, with the Cisalpine Republic as a buffer between them. The principle of secularising the German bishoprics was also again recognised in the Treaty of Lunéville, and the actual manner in which it should be carried out was referred to a special commission, whose conclusions were not adopted till 1803. The principal result of the treaty in Austria was the retirement of the minister Thugut, who was succeeded as State Chancellor by Count Louis Cobenzl, the diplomatist, who had negotiated the treaties both of Campo-Formio and of Lunéville.

The admiration of the Emperor Paul for Bonaparte increased daily, and it was the Russian Czar, not the French First Consul, who proposed an invasion of India across Asia, in order to strike a blow at the English power in the East. Indeed, the English had taken the place of the French in the mind of

Paul, who, not satisfied with forming once again the Neutral League of the North, determined to send his best troops against them. The Emperor's proposition was that one expedition should consist of 35,000 Frenchmen and 35,000 Russians, under the command of Masséna. This column was to go down the Danube, and then up the Don to a point whence it would be but a short march to the Volga. It was then to proceed down the Volga to Astrakhan, thence across the Caspian Sea to Astrabad, and then to march by Herat and Kandahar to the Punjab. Another column was to move by Khiva and Bokhara, and to invade India by the north of Afghanistan. These grandiose plans were not entirely accepted by Bonaparte, and the death of the Emperor prevented an attempt being made to see if they were practicable. The madness of Paul had steadily increased during his short reign. His nobility disapproved heartily of his war policy, both against France and later against England; his adoption of the Neutral League and its policy had done much to ruin the wealthy nobles of Northern Russia by forbidding the exportation of Russian commodities on English ships. To the discontent of the nobility, of the politicians, and of the capitalists must be added the fears of the courtiers. Even the heir to the throne, his eldest son Alexander, perceived that the rule of the maniac could not be borne much longer. It is hardly necessary to particularise all the causes of his unpopularity; it is enough to say that his behaviour was that of a madman. Certain courtiers, of whom the leaders were Count Pahlen, a Livonian nobleman; Benningsen, a Hanoverian general; Plato Zubov, the last favourite of the Empress Catherine, and his brother Nicholas, and the Prince Jachvill, determined to put an end to the tyranny of the Czar. In the night of the 23d of March 1801 he was attacked by these conspirators and ordered to sign an act of abdication; he refused; the lamp went out, and the Emperor was struck down and strangled by an unknown hand among his assailants.

When Bonaparte first entered office he recognised that

England was a more formidable, because a less approachable, enemy than Austria. Knowing that the French navy was unable to meet the English, he hoped to counterbalance the maritime preponderance of England by a league against her commerce. Owing to the long period of war, nothing was to be gained by solemn decrees forbidding the importation of goods into France, it was necessary to strike through the neutral nations. The three great commercial seats of English trade were the Levant, the Baltic, and Portugal. The failure of the expedition to Egypt proved that it was impossible to destroy the English trade in the Levant, and Bonaparte therefore resolved to strike in the other two directions. Acting mainly through the Emperor Paul, the Armed Neutrality of the North, or the Neutral League of 1780, was re-established between the Baltic powers of Russia, Prussia, Sweden, and Denmark. The real intention of Paul and of Bonaparte was to exclude English commerce entirely from the Baltic; but for the second time the Baltic powers nominally made themselves the guarantors of the rights of neutrals. They protested against the right assumed by England to search neutral ships, and to confiscate as contraband of war all the goods of belligerent powers found in them, and also against the prohibition against neutral ships trading between different enemies' ports. The Emperor Paul, like the Empress Catherine twenty years before, made himself the patron of the Neutral League.

*The Neutral League of the North, 1800-1.*

The English government naturally refused to accede to the demands of the Neutral League, and when the Baltic was closed to them an English fleet was ordered to force the blockade. This fleet was placed under the command of Sir Hyde Parker, with Nelson as second in command. On the 30th of March 1801 the fleet sailed down the Sound, in spite of the Danish batteries at Elsinore, and on the 2d of April Copenhagen was bombarded and a large part of the Danish fleet destroyed. This victory, and still more the death of the Emperor Paul, caused the

*Battle of Copenhagen. 2d April 1801.*

dissolution of the Neutral League of the North, and Bonaparte had to adjourn for some years his schemes for the annihilation of English commerce.

In the Iberian peninsula the designs of Bonaparte against English trade were more successful. Spain still remained the ally of France in spite of the sufferings that alliance had brought upon her, but Portugal had hitherto continued the faithful friend of England. Through Portugal English goods entered Spain and the south of France, and Bonaparte resolved to put an end to the neutrality of Portugal. For this purpose, in the year 1800, he despatched his ablest brother, Lucien Bonaparte, as ambassador to Madrid, with orders to negotiate with the Prince Regent of Portugal. The terms offered were that the Portuguese ports were to be closed to English trade, that special commercial advantages were to be given to French merchants, that French Guiana was to be extended to the river Amazon, and that a portion of Portuguese territory was to be ceded to Spain until Trinidad and Minorca were recovered by the latter power. The Prince Regent of Portugal rejected these hard terms; Spain declared war in the beginning of 1801, and 22,000 veteran French soldiers, under the command of General Leclerc, Bonaparte's brother-in-law, were sent to the assistance of Spain. The campaign was a very short one. The French troops never came into action; but the Portuguese were twice defeated in pitched battles, and lost some of their fortresses. The Prince Regent sued for peace, and a treaty was signed between Spain and Portugal at Badajoz on the 6th of June 1801. By this treaty the city and district of Olivenza were ceded to Spain, and, by a subsequent arrangement, the limits of French Guiana were extended to the river Amazon. Bonaparte was much disgusted with these treaties, and especially with the continued refusal of Portugal to close her ports to English commerce, and it was many months before he consented to ratify them. England refused to recognise Portugal as an enemy; but an English force occupied the

*Spain and Portugal. 1800-1.*

*Treaty of Badajoz.*

island of Madeira, and the East India Company's troops garrisoned Goa.

When Bonaparte left Egypt he was unable, owing to the stringency of the blockade maintained by the English fleet, to take more than a few companions with him. Kléber, who, as has been said, succeeded him in the command of the French army, soon found himself confronted by a powerful Turkish and Mameluke army. This army he defeated at the battle of Heliopolis on the 20th of March 1800, after which success Egypt again submitted to French rule. On the 14th of June 1800, the very day on which his former comrade Desaix met a soldier's death at the battle of Marengo, Kléber was assassinated by a Muhammadan fanatic in Cairo. Menou, the new French general in Egpyt, was in every way Kléber's inferior, and concentrated the French troops in the two cities of Cairo and Alexandria. Isolated entirely from the mother country, and unable to receive reinforcements or ammunition, the English government regarded the French in Egypt as an easy prey. On the 19th of March 1801 a powerful English army disembarked at Aboukir, under the command of Sir Ralph Abercromby, and defeated the French before Alexandria two days later in a pitched battle, in which Abercromby was killed. Siege was then laid to Alexandria and Cairo, and both cities surrendered to the English general, Lord Hutchinson, before the arrival of a division from India, which, under the command of Sir David Baird, had sailed up the Red Sea, marched across the Soudan desert, and descended the Nile to Cairo in boats. As a result of these operations, a convention was signed between the French and English generals in Egypt on the 2d of September 1801, by which the French garrisons evacuated all remaining posts, and were conveyed to France in English ships.

*Campaign in Egypt. 1800-1.*

. Though neither Bonaparte nor the leaders of English political opinion believed it possible for a permanent peace to be agreed to in the interests of their respective countries, the

outcry of both the English and the French people against the
prolonged war made it necessary for their rulers  The Peace
to conclude some kind of a truce. Pitt had   of Amiens.
in 1801 gone out of office, and his successor   1802.
Addington, afterwards Lord Sidmouth, declared in favour of
a peace policy. The treaty, which is known as the Peace of
Amiens, was really nothing more than a truce. Only a very
general agreement was come to, and many essential points
were left undecided. Both nations needed a rest, and neither
government looked upon the Peace of Amiens as affording a
permanent solution of their differences. Many loopholes were
left, which were certain to afford pretexts for renewing the war
to both contracting powers, and of these the most notable
was the question of the possession of Malta.

Far more important than the temporary Peace of Amiens
was the reconstitution of Germany, which was finally accepted
by the Diet at Ratisbon on the 25th of February  The Recon-
1803. The Holy Roman Empire which had  stitution of
lasted so many centuries ceased to exist. The  Germany.
ancient division of the Empire into circles was abolished, and
the three colleges which formed the Diet were profoundly
affected. Instead of the eight electors, three ecclesiastical and
five lay, that formerly existed, ten electors, one ecclesiastical
and nine lay, were created. The Archbishops of Cologne
and Trèves, whose states being on the left bank of the
Rhine were absorbed into France, lost their electoral dignity.
The Archbishop-Elector of Mayence was retained as Arch-
Chancellor of the Empire, and he received as his dominions
the Bishopric of Ratisbon, the Principality of Aschaffenburg,
and the County of Wetzlar. The nine lay electors were the
five princes who had formerly enjoyed the dignity, namely,
the Electors of Bohemia, Brandenburg, Saxony, Bavaria, and
Hanover, and four new Electors, the Margrave of Baden, the
Duke of Würtemburg, the Landgrave of Hesse-Cassel, and
the Grand Duke Ferdinand, brother of the Emperor, and
former Grand Duke of Tuscany, who was appointed Elector

of Salzburg. By this new arrangement, and by the abolition of two-thirds of the ecclesiastical electorate, the majority in the College of Electors passed from the Catholics to the Protestants. In the College of Princes there was the same result, for by the secularisation of the Catholic bishoprics the majority passed to the Protestant rulers. More sweeping still was the alteration in the third College—that of the Free Cities. Instead of fifty-two constituent members of this College only six were retained, and their maintenance was due to the intervention of France. These six cities were Augsburg, Bremen, Frankfort-on-the-Main, Hamburg, Lübeck, and Nuremberg. By these changes the constitution of the Empire was entirely altered; but still more notable was the change in the position of the various princes in Germany, for the tendency of the secularisation of the ecclesiastical states was to diminish the number of ruling princes and to increase the extent of their dominions.

The great war with France had shown the weakness of the Empire as an organisation, and had also proved the advantages to the inhabitants of the existence of large and powerful states.

**The Secularisations in Germany.** It was, therefore, the already existing kingdoms which received the greatest addition of territory under the new arrangements. Nominally, the secularised bishoprics were intended to compensate those German princes whose territories on the left bank of the Rhine had been ceded to France; practically, the powerful states only were increased. Austria, whose new possession of Venice in place of the Milanese had been reaffirmed by the Treaty of Lunéville, only acquired in Germany the Bishoprics of Brixen and Trent, but two Austrian princes received independent states, namely, the Grand Duke of Tuscany, Ferdinand, who, as has been said, was given the Archbishopric of Salzburg, with the title of Elector, and the Duke of Modena, who received the Breisgau. Nevertheless, the power of Austria was greatly weakened, for under the old arrangement the ecclesiastical electors and the Catholic bishops had always been partisans of Austria. Prussia was the country which profited the most, though she had suffered the least in the war against France. In exchange for part of the Duchy of Cleves, the Duchy of Guelders, and the County of Moers, Prussia received the large and wealthy Bishoprics of Hildesheim, Paderborn, Erfurt, and part of Münster, together with a number of abbeys, of which the largest were Herford, Quedlinburg, Elten, Essen, and Werden, and several free cities. Hanover received the Bishopric of Osnabrück, to which the King of England, as Elector of Hanover, had previously possessed the alternate nomination. Bavaria was made into a powerful and concentrated state. In exchange for the Palatinate, the Duchy of Deux-Ponts (Zwei-Brücken), the Principalities of Juliers, Simmern and Lautern, she received the Bishoprics of Würtzburg, Bamberg, Augsburg, Freisingen, and part of Passau, together with a large number of abbeys and free cities. Baden received the portion of the Bishoprics of Spires, Strasbourg, and Basle, situated on the right bank of the Rhine, the Bishopric of Constance, the cities of Heidelberg and Mannheim, and many abbeys and free cities. Finally, the Duchy of Würtemburg, in exchange for the Principality of Montbéliard, received abbeys and free towns, which increased its population by a hundred thousand inhabitants. It is not necessary to describe the various accessions granted to the Princes of Hesse-Cassel, Hesse-Darmstadt, Nassau, and the rest; but, it may be noted that the Prince of Orange, the former Stadtholder of Holland, received the Bishopric of Fulda. These changes remodelled Germany, and in the result were most prejudicial to France; for instead of there existing a series of buffers in the shape of small and weak states, France was brought almost directly into contact with Prussia and Austria.

At the same time that the ancient federal Holy Roman Empire was reconstituted, the ancient federal Republic of Switzerland was likewise reorganised. The reasons which had induced the Directory to intervene in Swiss affairs still existed; the revolutionary party

*The Reconstitution of Switzerland.*

which opposed the federal idea, and desired to form a united Switzerland, remained in direct opposition to the supporters of the former government of the cantons. It was essentially the question of government which divided the two parties, and there was no suggestion of restoring the feudal system, or the privileges of certain towns and certain cantons over others. The breath of the French Revolution had swept away political inequalities as completely in Switzerland as in France. Soon after the Treaty of Amiens, Bonaparte withdrew the French troops from the new Helvetic Republic. Civil war, as he expected, recommenced, and the Helvetic Government was driven from Berne by the federalists. Bonaparte therefore despatched an army to restore order, and summoned the leading Swiss statesmen to Paris. To them he propounded a new scheme of federal government, which was accepted, and the Act of Mediation, which was promulgated on the 19th of February 1803, established the new Constitution, and recognised the First Consul as Mediator. By the Act of Mediation Switzerland was divided into nineteen cantons, each of which had its own local government and special laws and taxes. The thirteen old cantons were maintained; six of them were democratic—Appenzell, Glarus, Schwyz, Unterwalden, Uri, and Zug; seven were oligarchical —Basle, Berne, Friburg, Lucerne, Schaffhausen, Soleure, and Zürich. The six new cantons added by Bonaparte comprised five territories which had formerly been subject; the Pays de Vaud and Aargau were made independent of Berne; Thurgau was separated from Schaffhausen, and Ticino from Uri and Unterwalden, and the canton of Saint-Gall was formed out of certain districts formerly belonging to Appenzell, Glarus, and Schwyz; finally, the Grisons, which had hitherto been an independent mountain republic, was declared a canton of Switzerland. Geneva had some years before been added to France as the Department of the Leman, and the Valais was now declared independent—a preliminary step to its ultimate annexation by France. The Federal Diet was to consist of twenty-five deputies, two from the six largest cantons, Aargau, Berne, the Grisons, Saint-Gall, the Pays de Vaud, and Zurich, and one from each of the others. The Diet was to meet every year in the capital of a different canton, and the Landamman of that canton was for that year the President of the Confederation. The Federal Act once more declared the entire abolition of feudalism, and of all privileges of birth, etc., and forbade for the future all internal customs-duties. Bonaparte proclaimed that he would not allow the interference of any other power in Switzerland, and took the title of Mediator of the Confederation of Switzerland.

It has already been stated that Bonaparte desired to stand well with the Catholic Church, and had recognised the advantages of a state religion. One of his most important measures during the Consulate was to put an end to the schism which had lasted since the promulgation of the Civil Constitution of the Clergy in 1790, with the assistance of the Pope, Pius VII. *The Concordat. 1801-2.* All the bishops elected under the Civil Constitution of the Clergy, and most of those who had emigrated, sooner than take the oath of allegiance to it, resigned, and the leaders of both sections were nominated and instituted to different dioceses. A new circumscription of sees was agreed to, and France was divided into fifty bishoprics and ten archbishoprics. It was agreed by the Concordat, which was signed between the Pope and the First Consul on the 15th of July 1801, and solemnly proclaimed on the 18th of April 1802, after being sanctioned by the Legislative Body, that the First Consul should nominate all bishops, and the Pope should institute. The government of the Consulate recognised the Catholic, Apostolic and Roman religion as that of the majority of the French people, and ordained that its public worship should be carried on freely so long as the police regulations were observed. All ecclesiastics were to swear fidelity to the government, which promised to pay a suitable salary to all bishops and curés. In return, the Pope promised that neither he nor his successors would lay any claim to the ecclesiastical estates which had been alienated, and that all such property should be held the indisputable possession of its purchaser.

The recognition of the frontier of the Rhine by the Treaty of Lunéville and the Diet of Ratisbon largely increased the territory of France. The First Consul proceeded to organise the additions on the bases laid down by the Constituent Assembly, Convention, and Directory. Belgium was divided into nine departments. The Rhenish territories, including the Palatinate, the Diocese of Trèves, etc., were divided into four departments, of which the headquarters were Aix-la-Chapelle, Coblentz, Mayence, and Trèves. Further south, the Department of the Mont-Terrible, which had been formed by the Convention out of the Republic of Mulhouse and the District of Porentruy, was merged into the Department of the Haut-Rhin, and the Principality of Montbéliard was united to the Department of the Doubs. The Republic of Geneva, as has been said, formed the Department of the Leman. Savoy was constituted as the Department of Mont-Blanc, and the County of Nice that of the Alpes-Maritimes. These were the recognised limits of France in 1801, and were defensible on geographical grounds; but, on the 11th of September 1802, Bonaparte went further, and declared the union of Piedmont with France. Instead of being amalgamated with the Cisalpine Republic, Piedmont was divided into six departments, and the island of Elba was detached from Tuscany and declared, like Corsica, to be a French island.

*The Prefectures.* At the head of each department a Préfet was appointed, to take the place of the national agents maintained by the Directory. At the head of each subdivision, now called an arrondissement instead of a district, was placed a Sous-Préfet, also nominated by the supreme executive, and at the head of each commune was the Maire, who was also nominated and not elected. Préfets, Sous-Préfets, and Maires were assisted by nominated councils in administrative matters, and appeals from their decisions lay to the Council of State.

Just as Bonaparte had built up the new Code of Law on the bases laid by the Legislative Committee of the Convention, so, too, he made use of the labours of its Committee of Public Instruction to establish a scheme of national education. In every commune which could afford the expense, he maintained the primary school established by the Convention; but he feared to burden the National Treasury with the expense of schools in the poorer communes, and preferred to leave their establishment to local endeavour. In secondary education, he suppressed the central schools of the Convention, and replaced them by twenty-nine lycées, specially intended for the education of the middle classes. For higher education, he founded ten schools of law and six of medicine; he improved the Polytechnic School, and started a school of mechanics, which became later the famous École des Arts et Métiers. The key-stone of the whole educational system, the foundation of the University, was, however, not laid till some years later.

*Education.*

The great administrative reforms of Bonaparte made him as popular among all classes of the population as his victories had made him in the army. Not only in France, but throughout Europe, he was looked upon as the restorer of order and good government. This sentiment appeared most vividly at the time when a plot against his life was discovered on the 24th of September 1800. This plot, which is known as the Conspiracy of the Infernal Machine, is said to have been the work of the Jacobin party; the explosion took place in the Rue Sainte-Nicaise, too late to do him any harm, but it was used as a pretext to exile the most vigorous republicans. So great was his popularity, that rumours were already heard of making him monarch. The first step in this direction was taken in 1802, when the Council of State proposed that the primary assemblies should be summoned to decide whether Bonaparte should not be made First Consul for life. In May 1802 this proposal was laid before the people, and was carried by more than

*Constitutional Changes.*

3,500,000 votes to 8000. Some slight changes were made at the same time, of which the most important were that the First Consul was enabled to nominate his successor, that the lists of candidates for public functions were replaced by electoral colleges appointed for life, and that the Senate was given the right to dissolve the Tribunate and the Legislative Body.

The First Consul clearly understood that the Peace of Amiens was not likely to last, and that war would soon break out again with England. He knew that England derived much of her influence from her navy and her colonies; he therefore spared no efforts to restore the French navy, and to make France once more a colonial power. His first essays in this direction were to obtain Louisiana from Spain in exchange for the kingdom of Etruria, formed in Italy for Prince Louis of Parma, and the extension of the limits of French Guiana to the Amazon extorted from Portugal. But his main project was to restore the French power in the West Indies. Guadeloupe and Martinique and the French Antilles had been restored to France by the Treaty of Amiens, and the First Consul resolved to make them the starting-point for the reconquest of San Domingo. This island had, as a result of the policy of Sonthonax and Polverel, the proconsuls of the Convention, been entirely lost to France; the planters and other whites had fled; and the revolted slaves and mulattoes were masters of the island. Toussaint Louverture, the leader of the negroes, refused to hold any communications with Bonaparte, and the First Consul therefore, as soon as the Peace of Amiens had opened the sea, sent an expedition of 20,000 men against him, commanded by his brother-in-law, General Leclerc. The island was reconquered by May 1802; but the victorious army was practically destroyed by yellow fever. Toussaint Louverture was taken prisoner and sent to France: but nevertheless, as soon as war with England again broke out, and the arrival of reinforcements was prevented by English cruisers, the negroes rose afresh under new leaders and destroyed the

*Bonaparte's Colonial Policy.*

remnant of the garrison. It may be added that the French Antilles were recaptured by the English in 1809 and 1810.

It has been said that the Treaty of Amiens was practically only a truce, and that many points of interest to the two nations were left undecided. Of these the most important regarded Malta. The English ministry positively refused to surrender this island to the Knights of Saint John, under the protectorate of the Emperor Alexander, which would leave it at the mercy of France. Bonaparte demanded the evacuation of Malta with much insistance as one of the conditions of the Treaty of Amiens; but the English government in reply pointed to the annexation of Elba, Parma and Piacenza, and Piedmont, and the interference in Switzerland, as also being breaches of the treaty. The First Consul was also very exasperated at the personal attacks made on him in the irresponsible English press. He failed to understand that by the English law the government could not prevent the publication of libels against him, and regarded their refusal to punish the libellers as personal insults to himself. The French ambassador in London prosecuted Peltier, the chief libeller, before the Court of King's Bench. He was brilliantly defended by Sir J. Mackintosh, and only ordered to pay a small fine. A public subscription was raised to pay his fine and costs, and the First Consul regarded this as adding a further insult to the injuries he had received. In truth, both governments felt that war was inevitable, and in May 1803 the rupture was complete. The English navy began to seize the French trading vessels, and the First Consul, as a reprisal, arrested all the English travellers he could find in France, and ordered Mortier to occupy Hanover.

<small>Recommencement of the War between England and France. 18th May 1803.</small>

The First Consul entered upon a fresh war with England with a light heart, for he believed that she would be unable to obtain any allies. Austria was exhausted by the terrible wars she had undergone, and the State Chancellor, Cobenzl, held that she needed time

<small>Position of Foreign Affairs.</small>

to recuperate. Prussia persisted in her attitude of strict neutrality; Haugwitz was dismissed from the Secretaryship of State for Foreign Affairs as being too French in his sympathies, after the occupation of Hanover, and was succeeded by Hardenberg, the maker of the Treaty of Basle. Spain was Bonaparte's faithful and hopeful ally; and Russia, the most formidable of the continental powers, inclined to his side. The attitude of the Emperor Alexander at this period was of the greatest importance. Educated by a Swiss publicist who sincerely loved France, La Harpe, the Emperor of Russia was inclined to admire the results of the French Revolution and the French people. His sentiments for the person of Bonaparte were nearly as full of enthusiastic admiration as those of his father, the Emperor Paul. He made the French ambassadors at St. Petersburg, Duroc and Caulaincourt, his personal friends, and wrote letters to Bonaparte expressing his feelings. But the Emperor's relatives, especially his mother, with his ministers and his courtiers, were opposed to France and in favour of a close alliance with England, or at the very least of the maintenance of strict neutrality. England practically commanded the Russian trade, and war with England meant the loss of the only market for Russian raw material, the consequent impoverishment of the Russian people, and the ruin of the Russian capitalists. Nevertheless the Emperor Alexander was an autocrat, and Bonaparte counted upon his friendship even though he could not secure his alliance.

On the outbreak of war the numerous French exiles in England offered their services to the English Government. It is significant of the change which had come over the state of affairs that, instead of endeavouring to raise a counter-revolution, they proposed to attack the person of the First Consul. The leaders of the new plot were Pichegru, now a declared royalist and partisan of the Bourbons, and Georges Cadoudal, the celebrated Chouan leader. Both had the audacity to go to Paris and to enter into relations with General Moreau. Moreau, though

*The Plot of Pichegru and Cadoudal.*

he resented the lofty position of Bonaparte and refused to serve him, would be no party to an assassination, more especially an assassination which would restore the Bourbons, and Cadoudal and Pichegru had to act with the assistance of certain French noblemen and some former Chouans. A plot was formed to murder the First Consul on the road from Malmaison to Paris, but it was discovered by the French police, and Bonaparte in terror ordered the gates of Paris to be closed as in the most terrible days of the Revolution, and proclaimed the pain of death against all who sheltered the conspirators. After some daring adventures the leaders were seized; Georges Cadoudal was executed; Pichegru was strangled in prison; and Moreau, who was condemned to two years' imprisonment, was allowed to go into exile in the United States. The French noblemen implicated were treated with more leniency, and the lives of their two chiefs, Armand de Polignac and Charles de Rivière, were spared.

The discovery of this plot against his life, which was undoubtedly fostered by the Bourbon princes, made the First Consul determined to wreak his vengeance against that unfortunate family. Being unable to seize the persons of the pretender, Louis XVIII., and his brother, the Comte d'Artois, who resided in England, he carried off a young Bourbon prince, the eldest son of the Prince de Condé, who was quite innocent of the conspiracy of Pichegru. The Duc d'Enghien was at this time living at Ettenheim in the Grand Duchy of Baden. He was arrested there by French soldiers, contrary to all international law, and taken to Vincennes. He was at once tried by a military commission as an *émigré* who had borne arms against France, and was condemned to death. The sentence was immediately carried out in spite of the demands of the young prince for an interview with the First Consul. This execution was a great political mistake. Bonaparte expected that it would terrify the Bourbon princes, but it reacted to his own prejudice. The Court of Saint-Petersburg went into mourning; the King

*Execution of the Duc d'Enghien. 21st March 1804.*

of Prussia, who had at last almost resolved to make an alliance with France, began to negotiate with Russia; the royal family of Austria looked upon the execution as a pendant to that of Marie Antoinette; and the English Government made use of the horror caused by it to endeavour to form a fresh coalition against France.

Directly after this tragedy, which proved that Bonaparte was practically an absolute monarch, he decided to take upon himself the rank of Emperor of the French. The Senate offered this title to the First Consul at Saint-Cloud on the 18th of May 1804, and the people ratified it by a majority of more than 3,500,000 votes. By the *senatus consultum* which made him Emperor the office was made hereditary to his direct descendants. As he had no children he was given the power to adopt, a power which it was undoubtedly expected would be used in favour of his stepson, Eugène de Beauharnais. A few months after the Corsican soldier of fortune was declared Emperor of the French, the last Holy Roman Emperor, Francis II., resolved to rid himself of what was now but an empty title. The new Constitution of the Holy Roman Empire had destroyed the imperial authority by depriving it of the votes of the ecclesiastical members in the Diet, and increasing or consolidating the dominions of the principal German states. Francis II. acknowledged the new order of things. On the 11th of August 1804, he erected the Austrian dominions into an hereditary empire, and on the 7th of December following, five days after the coronation of Bonaparte as the Emperor Napoleon by the Pope at Paris, the last Holy Roman Emperor proclaimed himself Emperor of Austria under the title of Francis I. This then was the result of fifteen years of revolution, the disappearance of the ancient figurehead of Europe, and the creation of a new Empire founded on the power of the sword.

# CHAPTER VIII

## 1804-1808

Napoleon, Emperor of the French—His Coronation as Emperor and as King of Italy—The Imperial Court—The Grand Dignitaries, Marshals, and Imperial Household—Institutions of the Empire—Ministers and Government—The Camp at Boulogne—Pitt's last coalition—Campaign of 1805—Capitulation of Ulm—Battles of Austerlitz and Caldiero—Battle of Trafalgar—Treaty of Pressburg—Death of Pitt—Prussia declares War—Campaign of Jena—Campaign of Eylau—Campaign of Friedland—Interview and Peace of Tilsit—The Continental Blockade—Capture of the Danish Fleet by England—French Invasion and Conquest of Portugal—State of Sweden—The Rearrangement of Europe—Louis Bonaparte King of Holland—Italy—Joseph Bonaparte King of Naples—Battle of Maida—Rearrangement of Germany—Bavaria—Würtemburg—Baden—Jerome Bonaparte King of Westphalia—Murat Grand Duke of Berg—Saxony—Smaller States of Germany—Mediatisation of Petty Princes—Confederation of the Rhine—Poland—The Grand Duchy of Warsaw—Conference of Erfurt.

NAPOLEON'S elevation to the rank of Emperor of the French only legalised in a more striking fashion the possession of power which he had long held. It did not make his authority any greater, for he had been practically the absolute monarch of France ever since 1799, but it gave promise of permanency, and that was what the French people most needed after the series of successive governments which had run their course since 1789. It is a mistake to regard Napoleon as having been made supreme ruler of France by the army alone; the legalisation of his power was even more enthusiastically received by the peaceful part of the population. The few ardent republicans who were left had been terrified out of resistance by the wholesale deportation of the principal Jacobins after the affair of the Infernal Machine. The adherents of the Bourbons were equally discouraged by the severe punishment dealt out to Pichegru and Georges Cadoudal. Every section of both the military and civil communities was ready to hail Napoleon as Emperor. But in the institution of the Empire he appealed to more than men's interests, he appealed to their imaginations. This he did in two ways. He created a Court, with all the magnificent apparatus of the great officers of the household, stately ceremonies and ancient customs, which gave to the people of Paris the spectacle of royal pomp which they had long regretted. On the other hand, he called to his assistance the most powerful engine for influencing the imagination of men, namely, religion. He determined to be consecrated with a ceremony which should exceed in splendour all the coronation ceremonies of the Bourbons. He summoned the Pope to France, and instead of being crowned at Rheims by the Archbishop and Primate, he received his crown at Paris from the hands of the Holy Father himself. At the very moment of his coronation he showed a pride of bearing at least equal to that of any of his predecessors upon the throne of France. After the Pope had anointed him, girded the sword of empire about him, and given him the sceptre, he prepared to place the crown upon the head of the new Caesar. But Napoleon gently took the crown from the hands of Pius VII., and after replacing it on the altar, raised it and crowned himself. The presence of the Pope in Paris for this great ceremony following upon the Concordat, caused Napoleon to be looked upon as the restorer of the Catholic religion, and greatly strengthened his position. Not satisfied with the crown of France, he accepted that of Italy also on the 20th of May 1805, and proceeded to Milan, where he placed upon his head the Iron Crown of the old Lombard Kings. He at once declared his intention of not personally administering his Italian kingdom, and appointed his stepson, Eugène de Beauharnais, to be Viceroy of Italy.

It has been said that Napoleon created a new Court, which

was intended to efface the recollection of the magnificence of the old Court of Versailles. At the head of this Court he created a hierarchy of Grand Dignitaries of the Empire, who were designed to form a Council of Regency in case of necessity. The chief of them was the Grand Elector, whose duty was to convoke the Senate, the Legislative Body, and the Electoral Colleges,—this post was conferred on the Emperor's elder brother, Joseph Bonaparte. Next ranked the Arch-Chancellor of the Empire, who was the chief of the judicial body,—this post was conferred on Cambacérès, the former Second Consul. Third came the Arch-Chancellor of State, whose business it was to receive foreign ambassadors and ratify treaties—this post was conferred upon Eugène de Beauharnais. Next came the Arch-Treasurer of the Empire, which post was first filled by Le Brun, the former Third Consul, and the remaining Grand Dignitaries were the Constable of the Empire, Louis Bonaparte, the Grand Admiral, Marshal Murat, and the Grand Judge, Regnier. In the same way as the Grand Dignitaries were at the head of the civil administration of the Empire, Napoleon created Marshals of France to be the representatives of the army. The first marshals were eighteen in number, and included all the most famous generals of the revolutionary period except Pichegru and Moreau, whose fate has been related. It was indispensable for the rank of Marshal of France to have commanded an army in the field, or at least a detached corps, and the office was surrounded with so many privileges as to make it the object of ambition to every colonel of a French regiment. The third hierarchy consisted of the great officers of the Emperor's household, who comprised a Grand Marshal, Duroc; a Grand Almoner, his uncle, Joseph Fesch, whom he had induced the Pope to make a cardinal; a Grand Chamberlain, Talleyrand; a Grand Huntsman, Marshal Berthier; and a Grand Equerry, Caulaincourt; and most of the first occupants of these offices were personal friends and former comrades in arms of the Emperor.

The Senate remained under the Constitution of the Empire, as under that of the Consulate, the most important and dignified political body. It was extended by the addition of the Grand Dignitaries, of the members of the Emperor's family, and of those whom he specially wished to reward; its seats were conferred for life; but it did little but congratulate the Emperor on all his proceedings. The Tribunate was reduced to fifty members, and the Legislative Body was allowed to discuss laws, but only in closed committees. These institutions, carefully devised though they were to maintain a semblance of free discussion, were really reduced to impotence by the autocratic power of the Emperor. The Council of State became more and more the real keystone of the administration of France. It was the one institution of the Consulate which developed under the Empire. But it did not develop collectively, but rather as a convenient administrative centre and a court of appeal for administrators in every branch of the government. Though the ministries were maintained, they were, as the government became more bureaucratic in its form, and more concentrated into the hand of Napoleon, infinitely subdivided, and the head of each subdivision had a seat in the Council of State. By this arrangement the Emperor was able to keep a check on his ministers, and to prevent the administration from being thrown out of gear by the death or retirement of a single man. Nevertheless, the ministries, as in all highly organised states, were of vast importance, and Napoleon was fortunate in the men he placed at their head. It is worthy of note that three of the ministers who had served him during the Consulate remained in office throughout the Empire, namely, Gaudin, afterwards created Duke of Gaeta, Minister of Finance, who had several assistants in the Council of State, of whom the most notable were Defermon, a former deputy in the Constituent Assembly and the Convention, and Louis; Decrès, also created a duke, Minister of the Marine; and Regnier, Duke of Massa and Grand Judge, Minister of Justice. At the War Office, the Emperor retained his chief of the staff, Marshal Berthier, until 1807, when he was succeeded by General Clarke, Duke of Feltre; and the various sections were presided over by able administrators, of whom the best were perhaps Lacuée de Cessac and Daru. At the Foreign Office, Talleyrand remained supreme until after the Treaty of Tilsit, in 1807, when he was replaced by Champagny, Duke of Cadore, who in his turn gave way to Maret, Duke of Bassano. At the Ministry of the Interior a change was made at the beginning of the Empire by the retirement of Chaptal, who had held that post with singular distinction throughout the Consulate, and the appointment of Champagny. But this department was overshadowed by the existence of the Ministry of General Police. Napoleon abolished this office in 1803, in the hope, doubtless, of dispensing with the services of Fouché; but that astute minister was a necessity, and in 1804 he was again appointed to his old office, which he held until 1810.

In the midst of the *fêtes* which accompanied his acceptance of the Empire, Napoleon did not forget that he was engaged in war with England. He declared that as he had crossed the Alps, so, too, he could cross the Channel. For this purpose he collected a flotilla of flat-bottomed boats at Boulogne, and encamped picked soldiers from the Armies of the Rhine and of Italy upon the coast. But he felt that it would be impossible for his flotilla to cross the Channel while the English fleets were masters of the sea. He therefore determined to unite the two French fleets, which were concentrated at Toulon and Brest, and summoned his allies, the Dutch and the Spaniards, to prepare fleets also. He kept 120,000 veterans continually at work practising embarkation and disembarkation, and it was commonly believed, not only in Europe, but in England itself, that the invasion would he carried into effect. The army was equipped in a very thorough fashion, and carefully organised as the Grand Army under the most experienced generals in

France, and it became one of the most efficient fighting machines ever known in the history of the world, its discipline being perfect and its enthusiasm unbounded.

While making these preparations for the invasion of England, Napoleon struck at other more accessible branches of the British power. In 1803 he occupied Hanover, the hereditary dominion of George III., in spite of its being covered by the Prussian line of demarcation. In 1804 he sent a division into the kingdom of Naples, in order to close the Neapolitan ports to English trade; and once more he threatened Portugal. He also endeavoured to stir up a maritime foe to the English, and sold to the United States the province of Louisiana, which he had annexed from Spain, in the hope of obtaining their alliance. It was only necessary for Napoleon to be master of the Channel for a few hours, and to have a fine day, for his project of invading England to succeed. According to his instructions, Admiral Villeneuve left Toulon in March 1805, eluded Nelson, joined the Spanish fleet, and made his way to the West Indies, where he expected to meet the fleet from Brest. But the Brest fleet could not break through the blockade; Villeneuve had to return, and, after an action with an English squadron under Sir Robert Calder on 22nd July, he put into Ferrol. At Napoleon's command, the admiral set out *Villeneuve's* for Brest on 11th August, but meeting with bad *Failure.* weather, he lost heart and sailed away to Cadiz. Thus foiled in his great scheme for bringing up an overpowering French fleet to cover his invading army, Napoleon dared not leave the harbour of Boulogne.

While threatened by the Boulogne flotilla, the English Government did all in its power to raise enemies on the Continent against Napoleon. Prussia, as usual, insisted on *Pitt's New* her neutrality; but Russia and Austria were not un-*Coalition.* willing to try their strength once more with France. *1805.* The Emperor Alexander of Russia was personally inclined to admire Napoleon, but he was induced by his Court, his family, and his ministry, who pointed out to him the importance of remaining on good terms with England, to sign an alliance with Pitt; he was further profoundly irritated by the violent scene which Napoleon, as First Consul, had had with his ambassador, Count Morkov, and was horrified at the execution of the Duc d'Enghien. The Emperor Francis of Austria was even more willing to fight Napoleon. He had spent the period of peace since the Treaty of Lunéville in re-organising his army, and believed that he would be more successful now that he was freed from the incubus of his position as Holy Roman Emperor. The State Chancellor, Cobenzl, was also keenly in favour of war, for he was a sincere believer in the might of Russia, and had imbibed a desire to please the Court of St. Petersburg, at which he had long held the post of Austrian ambassador. To induce these powerful allies to attack in force, Pitt, who was once more Prime Minister, did not grudge the wealth of England. Large subsidies were offered both to Russia and Austria, which supplied the means for commencing the campaign; and strenuous efforts were made to win the assistance of Prussia.

In the second line, Pitt counted on the assistance of Sweden and Naples. Napoleon's promptitude in invading the latter country destroyed any chance of its effecting a diversion in Italy, and Gustavus IV. of Sweden, though, like his father, a violent enemy of France, was unable to bring any active assistance, while Prussia remained neutral. A pretext for war was found in the annexation of Lucca and Genoa to the French Empire, and the Austrians and Russians resolved to strike at once. General Mack, with a powerful Austrian force, invaded Bavaria before the declaration of war, and, by the occupation of Ulm, he believed he had secured the valley of the Danube. Meanwhile the principal Austrian army of 120,000 men, under the Archduke Charles, invaded Italy, and a powerful force of Russians kept close to the Prussian frontier, in the hope of inducing Prussia to declare war against France.

Napoleon, despairing of success in his projected invasion of

England, resolved to turn promptly upon England's principal
<small>Campaign</small> ally, and directed the Grand Army to break up
<small>of 1805.</small> from Boulogne and enter Germany. Mack regarded it as certain that the French, as in the campaigns of Moreau, would advance through the Black Forest. Napoleon encouraged his illusion by showing him a few French troops in that quarter. Meanwhile, the Grand Army advanced in two portions through Würtemburg and Franconia, and, on reaching the Danube, after violating the Prussian neutrality by marching through Anspach, cut off Mack's retreat on Vienna. The Austrian general made an effort to break through the French army, but he was defeated by Ney at Elchingen, and surrendered on the 20th of October 1805 with
<small>Surrender</small> 33,000 men. The capitulation of Ulm did more
<small>of Ulm.</small> than deprive Austria of a serviceable army,—it left
<small>20th Oct. 1805.</small> open the road to Vienna. Napoleon rapidly followed up his success. He marched past a united Russian and Austrian army, which was quartered in Moravia, to influence Prussia, occupied Vienna, crossed the Danube, and
<small>Battle of</small> eventually faced the army of the two emperors at
<small>Austerlitz.</small> Austerlitz. On the 2d of December 1805, the
<small>2d Dec. 1805.</small> anniversary of his coronation, the Grand Army utterly defeated the Austrians and Russians. The allies lost 15,000 men killed and wounded, 20,000 prisoners, and 189 guns; and the Emperor Francis found himself defenceless, for his only other army, that in Italy, had been defeated at Caldiero by Eugène de Beauharnais and Masséna on the 30th of October. While the rapid campaign of Austerlitz,—perhaps
<small>Battle of</small> the most glorious of Napoleon's military career,—
<small>Trafalgar.</small> was taking place, he lost the navy which he had
<small>21st Oct. 1805.</small> prepared with so much care, and which had been intended to cover his invasion of England. The French admiral, Villeneuve, left Cadiz at the head of the united French and Spanish fleet, consisting of thirty-three ships of the line and five frigates. He had not gone far when he was met by Nelson at the head of the English squadron of twenty-seven

ships off Cape Trafalgar. The victory of Trafalgar, which was won on the 21st of October, was as complete as that of Austerlitz. The French and Spanish fleet was as entirely destroyed as the Austrian and Russian army. The allies at Trafalgar lost 7000 men in killed and wounded, and the English only 3000, among whom, however, was Nelson himself.

The result of the battle of Austerlitz was the Treaty of Pressburg, which was signed by Austria and France on the 26th of December 1805. The Russians had only lost one army, and their territory had not been invaded, so that they were still enabled to remain in arms. *Treaty of Pressburg. 26th Dec. 1805.* But Austria was completely crushed. By the Treaty of Pressburg, Venice, Istria, and Dalmatia were ceded to the Kingdom of Italy; but Napoleon kept the two latter provinces under his direct rule, and gave the command of them to General Marmont. The Tyrol and part of Swabia were ceded to Bavaria, and the Elector of that State took the title of King. The same title was conferred on the Duke of Würtemburg; the Duke of Baden became a Grand Duke; many small German principalities were suppressed, and, on 12th of July 1806, the Confederation of the Rhine was formed under the protectorate of the French Emperor. England could not blame Austria for making a separate treaty with France, for she herself had been saved from invasion by the departure of the Grand Army from Boulogne, not less than by the victory of Trafalgar. The news of Austerlitz was followed on the 23d of January 1806 by the death of Pitt, and the new English ministry of Fox and Grenville, now that the fear of invasion was over, desired to enter into negotiations with Napoleon.

The overthrow of Austria was followed by the overthrow of Prussia. Frederick William III. had prided himself on the manner in which, in spite of many temptations, he had maintained his attitude of strict neutrality. *Overthrow of Prussia.* Neither the offers of the Directory or of Napoleon, nor the subsidies lavishly promised by England, had been able to disturb his determination. The Prussian ministry proudly pointed to the fact that, while the rest of Europe had been torn by disastrous wars, Prussia had remained at peace ever since the Treaty of Basle in 1795. She had profited by her peace policy as much as France and Austria by their war policy. The rearrangement of Germany in 1803 had converted Prussia from a collection of scattered states into a united kingdom. She had even, up to the year 1803, maintained the freedom of the whole of the north of Germany from the terrible French invaders by the observation of the line of demarcation settled in 1795. The northern states of Germany looked to Prussia as their leader, and since the destruction of the Holy Roman Empire the Prussian policy had been completely victorious over the Austrian. The maintenance of the line of demarcation was the favourite scheme of the Prussian King, and as long as it was observed, nothing short of invasion would have disturbed his neutrality. But the occupation of Hanover in 1803, as one of the measures taken by Napoleon against England, had infringed the line of demarcation, and from that moment Frederick William III. inclined towards war.

In this warlike attitude he was encouraged by Russia and England, and still more by his own army. The Prussian army, the creation of Frederick the Great, represented in more than an ordinary fashion the Prussian nation. Relying on the recollections of the Seven Years' War, and confident in the proverbial discipline of their soldiers, the Prussian generals believed that they would be able to defeat the conquerors of the rest of Europe. With the utmost ardour the young Prussian noblemen shouted for war; they resented the long peace, and applauded the new attitude of the king. He was stimulated likewise by the hatred for France, which was openly encouraged by his beautiful Queen Louisa, and he met with opposition only from a few of his more experienced ministers, and from the old Duke of Brunswick, who well knew the excellence of the French troops. Undecided and hesitating, Frederick William refused to join the coalition of Austria and Russia in 1805, when his assistance would have been of the greatest service. He signed, indeed, the Treaty of Potsdam on 3d November 1805, undertaking to mediate, and to join the coalition with 180,000 men if Napoleon refused the terms he offered. But the proposed intervention came to nothing. Haugwitz, the Prussian minister, awaited at Napoleon's headquarters the result of the battle of Austerlitz, and on December 15 he signed the Treaty of Schönbrunn, by which Prussia ceded Cleves to France and Anspach to Bavaria, and received provisional possession of Hanover. Two months later, on February 15, Prussia was compelled by a supplementary treaty to definitely accept Hanover from Napoleon, an arrangement which was tantamount to declaring war with England.

The long neutrality of Frederick William III. was thus broken, and, as it soon appeared, in vain. For Napoleon almost immediately offered to restore Hanover to England, with which country he was induced to enter into negotiations for peace by the accession of Fox to office. At this news Frederick William mobilised his troops and prepared for war with France. In October 1806 he ordered the victor of Austerlitz to at once retire behind the Rhine, and slowly concentrated his army in Thuringia without waiting for the succour promised by the Russians. The Prussian officers applauded their king's conduct, for they desired to have the glory of defeating the French entirely to themselves. On the 14th of October 1806 the two corps of the Prussian army, which were advancing along the river Saale, were defeated by Napoleon himself at Jena, and by Marshal Davout at Auerstädt. The triumph was as complete as that of Austerlitz; and on the 25th the French army entered Berlin. *Campaign of Jena. Oct. 1806.*

It was now necessary for the Grand Army to attack the Russians. Napoleon, after occupying nearly the whole of Prussia and laying siege to Dantzic, entered Poland. He was received with an enthusiastic welcome by the Poles, whose independence he hinted at restoring. Polish troops had long served in his armies, *Campaign Eylau.*

and the sympathy of the French people for the oppressed Poles was known throughout Poland. On the 15th of December 1806 Napoleon occupied Warsaw and sent his army into winter quarters upon the Russian frontier. The Russian general, Benningsen, one of the murderers of the Emperor Paul, conceived the idea of surprising part of the French army in its winter quarters. He drove back the division of Bernadotte; but when he reached the neighbourhood of Königsberg he found that Napoleon had received information of his movement and had collected the bulk of his army. It was now Napoleon's turn to pursue the Russians. At the head of 60,000 men he found 80,000 Russians intrenched in the village of Eylau, and attacked them during a snowstorm on the 8th of February 1807. The battle was long disputed. The Russians had to retire, but it was estimated that the loss of both armies was about the same, namely, 35,000 men. This loss was far more severe to the French than to the Russians, for the French soldiers slain at Eylau were veterans of the Grand Army, and their place could only be taken by raw conscripts.

The result of the battle of Eylau was to allow the French army to remain undisturbed in its winter quarters. In the Russian camp, meanwhile, important diplomatic negotiations had been going on. Frederick William cemented his friendship with the Emperor Alexander, and appointed the most able of his servants, Hardenberg, to be State Chancellor in the place of Haugwitz. Prussia could indeed give but little real help, for her army was destroyed, and her country almost entirely in the hands of the French; but Alexander, nevertheless, consented in April 1807 to sign the Treaty of Bartenstein with Frederick William, by which they formed an offensive and defensive alliance. But the hopes of the diplomatists, founded on the drawn battle of Eylau, were soon to be frustrated by the military successes of Napoleon. On the 24th of May 1807 Dantzic, which had withstood a desperate siege, surrendered to General Lefebvre, and the besieging troops were able to join the main army.

*Battle of Friedland. 14th June 1807.*

The summer campaign of 1807 was very short. Benningsen, accompanied by the Emperor Alexander in person, advanced to attack the French army on the 14th of June. The Russians foolishly crossed the Alle at Friedland, and with the river at their back were completely defeated with a loss of 25,000 men. The victory of Friedland was decisive; it did not destroy the Russian Empire, as the victories of Austerlitz and Jena had destroyed the Austrian Empire and the Prussian Kingdom; it did not extinguish the fighting power of Russia; it did not diminish the *morale* of the Russian army, which proudly boasted that it had made a better stand against the French than either the Austrians or the Prussians. It was not positively necessary for the very existence of his monarchy that the Emperor Alexander should treat with Napoleon, but his successive defeats justified him before his Court and his ministers in demanding peace. He could reply to their arguments in favour of an English alliance for Russia that he had loyally tried to carry out the terms of that alliance, but that under the circumstances he could maintain it no longer. He had always wished for peace with France and the friendship of Napoleon; he now considered himself free to follow his personal inclinations.

On the 25th of June 1807 the Emperor of the French and the Czar of Russia had their famous interview at Tilsit on a raft moored in the middle of the river Niemen. The personal magnetism of Napoleon and his glory as a great conqueror powerfully impressed the vivid imagination of Alexander, who had always felt the warmest admiration for him. During this interview Napoleon spread before the eyes of the Emperor of Russia his favourite conception of the re-establishment of the old Empires of the East and of the West. They were to be faithful allies. France was to be the supreme power over the Latin races and in the centre of Europe; Russia was to represent the Greek Empire and to expand into Asia. These grandiose views charmed the Emperor Alexander, who believed that in

[margin note: Interview at Tilsit, 25th June 1807.]

adopting them he was following out the policy of Peter the Great and of the Empress Catherine. The one enemy to be feared and to be crushed according to Napoleon was England. And Alexander, in spite of the loss which his subjects would suffer, promised to enter into Napoleon's policy for the exclusion of England's commerce from the Continent, and to accept the doctrine of the Continental Blockade. But, at the same time, Alexander did not dare to go so far as to promise to declare war against England, in spite of the pressure put upon him by Napoleon. The first interview at Tilsit was followed by others, and eventually by the Peace of Tilsit. **Peace of Tilsit,** By this treaty Russia ceded the Ionian Islands **7th July 1807.** and the mouths of the river Cattaro in the south of Dalmatia, which had been occupied by the Russians since 1799, to France. Napoleon, on his part, promised that he would not restore the independence of Poland, and advised Alexander to obtain compensation for the growth of the power of France from Sweden and from Turkey. In pursuance of this policy a division of the French army invaded Swedish Pomerania and took Stralsund, while the Russians occupied Finland. Alexander was pressed by Napoleon to invade Turkey, and was promised the assistance of France in obtaining the cession of the Danubian principalities. The Emperor of Russia made loyal efforts to obtain a favourable peace for his ally, the King of Prussia. But Napoleon, though willing to humour Alexander, and desirous of making Russia his firm ally, did not hesitate to show his contempt for Frederick William III. He thought for a time of entirely extinguishing Prussia, but on the representations of Alexander he contented himself by taking possession of the Rhenish and Westphalian provinces of Prussia, and forming them with the principality of Hesse-Cassel into the kingdom of Westphalia. He also included Prussian Poland in his new Grand Duchy of Warsaw.

The Peace of Tilsit left Napoleon face to face with only one enemy, and that was England. The destruction of the

French fleet at Trafalgar and the diminution of the strength of the Grand Army from the losses suffered at Austerlitz, Jena, and Eylau, proved to the Emperor of the French that he had better abandon his project of invading England. But if he could not cross the Channel in force or meet the English fleets at sea, he believed he could ruin England by excluding her from the markets of the Continent. The English ministry, in pursuance of its reading of international law, had closed all neutral seaborne commerce from the mouth of the Elbe to the extremity of the French coast. Napoleon answered this measure by his Berlin Decree, which was issued in that city on the 21st of November 1806, and declared the British Islands to be in a state of blockade. All English merchandise was to be confiscated, as well as all ships which had touched either at a British port or at a port in the British Colonies. He followed up this measure by the Milan Decree of the 17th of December 1807, by which he declared that any ship of any country which had touched at a British port was liable to be seized and treated as prize. The entry of Russia into the scheme of the Continental Blockade would, Napoleon hoped, entirely ruin the English trade. But, in reality, it did nothing of the sort. English commerce was as active and enterprising as ever, and the risks it encountered in running the Continental Blockade only increased the profits of the English merchants. **The real sufferers were the inhabitants of the Continent, who had to pay enhanced prices for such articles of prime necessity as sugar.** Napoleon's expectation that the carrying trade of the world would desert England and fall into the hands of France and her allies was not fulfilled, because the English war fleets remained complete masters of the sea, and effectually prevented the rise of any other commercial power. The result of the Continental Blockade was therefore the impoverishment of the allies of France and their consequent hatred of Napoleon, while it increased rather than diminished the commercial prosperity of England.

The English ministers were not afraid of Napoleon's Conti-
**Bombardment** nental Blockade. But his occupation of Northern
**of Copen-**
**hagen.** Germany made them fear that his next step would
**Sept. 1807.** be to seize the Danish fleet as the Directory had
in former days appropriated the Dutch fleet. ·Secret stipulations were indeed made at Tilsit, by virtue of which the
Danish fleet was to be seized by France. *Information of
this scheme was given to the English ministers, and a secret
expedition was planned to prevent its being carried into effect.
Denmark was a neutral nation, and had given no pretext for
war to either France or England. But Denmark was a weak
nation and unable to defend itself. Under these circumstances the English struck first. A powerful expedition
anchored before Copenhagen in September 1807; the city
was bombarded; the small Danish army was defeated at
Kioge by a division under the command of Sir Arthur
Wellesley; and the whole Danish fleet was appropriated or
destroyed by England. By this rapid blow one of Napoleon's
most cherished schemes came to nought, and his hope of
getting another serviceable navy effectually extinguished.

The two most faithful allies of England were the small
**French In-** kingdoms of Portugal and Sweden. The Russians
**vasion of**
**Portugal.** were left to deal with the latter; Napoleon re-
**1807.** solved to attack the former himself. The French
Emperor, like the Directory before him, insisted on regarding
Portugal as an outlying province of England, and, indeed,
there was some ground for this view, as owing to the Methuen
Treaty the relations between the two countries were very
close. Yet the Prince Regent of Portugal in 1806 had
declined to declare himself the open ally of England, and
insisted on the maintenance of his position of neutrality.
Nevertheless, Napoleon resolved to ruin Portugal because the
Prince Regent declined to become a party to the Continental
Blockade. He at first resolved to act with Spain as he had
done in 1801, and on the 29th of October 1807 the Treaty
of Fontainebleau was signed, by which it was agreed that

the combined armies of France and Spain should conquer Portugal. The little kingdom was then to be divided into three parts; the northern provinces were to be given to the King of Etruria in exchange for his dominions in Italy which Napoleon desired to annex; the southern districts were to be formed into an independent kingdom for Godoy, the Prince of the Peace, the lover of the Queen of Spain, and the most powerful man in that kingdom; and the central portion was to be temporarily held by France. In pursuance of this secret treaty a French army under General Junot marched rapidly across the Peninsula, and on the news that it was close to Lisbon, the Prince Regent, with his mother, the mad queen, Maria I., and his two sons sailed for Brazil with an English squadron. Hardly had the Regent left the Tagus when Junot entered Lisbon on the 20th of November 1807. The French were favourably received in Portugal. The Portuguese resented the departure of the Prince Regent; democratic principles had made considerable progress; and no idea was entertained that there was a secret design to dismember the kingdom. Junot had little difficulty in occupying almost the whole of Portugal; he sent the picked troops of the Portuguese army under the name of the Portuguese Legion to join the Grand Army in Germany; and he promised a Constitution to the country. On the 1st of February 1808 he issued a proclamation that the House of Braganza had ceased to reign, and after the fortresses had been surrendered he proceeded to administer Portugal as a conquered country.

Gustavus IV. of Sweden, who had taken the power into his own hands from his uncle the Regent Duke of Sudermania and had married the sister-in-law of the Emperor Alexander of Russia, in 1797, had inherited the hatred for France, which had been, after 1789, one of the guiding principles of his father, Gustavus III. He had been the ready ally of England in all the coalitions against both the French Directory and Napoleon, and after the rupture of the Peace of Amiens in 1803, he became the key-stone of the

Anglo-Russian alliance. In 1805 he promised to place himself at the head of an English, Russian, and Swedish army which was to invade Hanover, and occupy Holland; but he failed to set sail on the appointed day, and caused the expedition to lead to no result. Nevertheless, he remained faithful to England, and at the time of the Treaty of Tilsit refused to abandon the English alliance. As has been already said, Swedish Pomerania was occupied by a division of the Grand Army, under Marshal Brune, and Sweden never recovered the ancient conquest of Gustavus Adolphus. In 1808, on the obstinate refusal of the Swedish King to accede to the Continental Blockade, the Emperor Alexander, as had been agreed at Tilsit, invaded Finland. England was ready to assist Sweden, and a powerful army, under Sir John Moore, was sent to Stockholm. At this crisis the King showed signs of insanity. The English expedition retired, and at the beginning of 1809 Gustavus IV. was dethroned.

After he had made himself Emperor, and still more after his victories over Austria and Prussia and his alliance with Russia, Napoleon began to assure his power on the Continent by establishing vassal kings in the neighbourhood of France. Just as the French Directory had surrounded the French Republic with smaller republics governed after its own model, so Napoleon surrounded his frontiers with subject kingdoms. The Batavian, the Cisalpine, and the Parthenopean Republics were succeeded by the kingdoms of Holland and of Naples and the vice-royalty of Italy. The form of the Batavian Republic had altered with every change in the Constitution of France. From a democratic Republic in the time of the Convention it had become a Directory and a Consulate, and in 1805, after the French Empire had been established, it received a new Constitution. By this arrangement Count Schimmelpenninck, a distinguished Dutch statesman, was appointed Grand Pensionary for life, but in June 1806 he was induced to resign, and Louis Bonaparte, the favourite brother of the French Emperor, was made King of Holland. The Dutch people had no objection to these changes. The introduction of the French system of administration consolidated the country from a group of federal states into a united nation. Its trade prospered, though it lost its fleet at Camperdown in 1797, and in the Texel in 1799, and it became more wealthy than ever, in spite of the conquest of all its colonies by England, by the close communication established with Paris and the abolition of the vexatious transit-duties in Belgium. Louis Bonaparte, the first King of Holland, showed himself a sagacious monarch. He caused the Civil Code to be introduced into his dominions in the place of the old cumbrous system of Dutch law. He encouraged literature and art, and he moved the capital from the Hague to Amsterdam. But the introduction of the Continental Blockade caused profound discontent. The Dutch merchants were ruined by its rigorous application; riots took place in many districts; and since Napoleon found the Continental Blockade was being evaded he caused French troops to enter Holland and occupy the mouths of the rivers. Louis Bonaparte protested against this conduct, and in 1810 he resigned the crown which his brother had given him.

It has been said that when Napoleon made himself Emperor he likewise assumed the title of King of Italy, and that he did not undertake the government, but conferred it upon his step-son, Eugène de Beauharnais, as Viceroy. The original Kingdom of Italy only comprehended the dominions of the Cisalpine Republic,—that is to say, Lombardy, the Duchies of Modena and Parma, and the former Papal Legations of Bologna and Ferrara. By the Treaty of Pressburg in 1806 the Kingdom of Italy was increased by the addition of Venice and of the former Venetian territories on the mainland. Genoa, Lucca, Piedmont, and Tuscany, were, however, directly administered by France, and the city of Rome and the Campagna was added to the French Empire in the year 1810. In the south

*Italy.*

*Rome.*

of the Italian peninsula Naples was erected into an independent kingdom, which was intended to include
the island of Sicily. This kingdom was conferred
upon the elder brother of Napoleon, Joseph Bonaparte, on
the 30th of March 1806. Joseph, like King Louis of Holland,
tried to act as a good king. He formed an able ministry, consisting almost entirely of Neapolitans, and containing but two
Frenchmen,—Miot de Melito, Minister of War, and Saliceti,
Minister of Police. He introduced good laws, and made
efforts to put down the brigandage which ravaged the southern
districts of his kingdom. The island of Sicily meanwhile resisted all the attempts of the French. It acknowledged the
rule of Ferdinand, King of the Two Sicilies, who had retired
to Palermo, and it was garrisoned by an English army. This
army kept Joseph in perpetual embarrassment. The English
encouraged the brigands of Calabria, and in the summer of
1806 they made a descent upon the mainland, and on the 3d
of July the English general, Sir John Stuart, defeated the
French general Reynier at Maida. This victory, however,
was followed by the capitulation of Gaeta on the 18th of
July, after which event the French army in Calabria was
strengthened to such an extent that the English were unable
to do more than defend Sicily. The internal administration
of Joseph Bonaparte deserves every praise; he abolished
feudalism; he endeavoured to introduce honesty and up-
rightness in the collection of the taxes; he declared the
equality of all citizens before the law; and by the suppression of many monasteries he improved the finances of the
country and largely increased the number of peasant proprietors. Lastly, must be noticed the Illyrian
provinces of Dalmatia and Istria, which had
been ceded by the Treaty of Pressburg. They were directly
administered by General Marmont, who reported to Napoleon
himself and not to the Viceroy of Italy. After the Treaty
of Tilsit they were augmented by the Ionian Islands, and
Napoleon kept a powerful army in this quarter to threaten

the Turks. It is probable, indeed, that he dreamt of restoring the independence of Greece, and his Illyrian army was well placed for carrying out such a project.

In his re-arrangement of the states of Germany and of the balance of power in Central Europe, Napoleon, like the Directory, followed out the traditional policy of Richelieu and Mazarin. He held it to be an advantage for France that there should be a number of small German states between the Rhine and the hereditary dominions of the House of Austria, but he considered that the very small size of the states maintained by the Treaty of Westphalia in 1648 made them inadequate buffers. He, therefore, enlarged the Western German states and endeavoured to unite their interests with those of France. The reconstitution of Germany after the Peace of Lunéville in 1803 destroyed the old Holy Roman Empire. Napoleon worked on the same lines, and his measures have had almost the same permanence as the arrangements of 1803. The changes took place gradually in accordance with the Treaties of Pressburg and of Tilsit, but their final results may be considered as a whole. *Napoleon's Reorganisation of Germany.*

Maximilian Joseph, the Elector of Bavaria, had, by hereditary right, united the Electorates of the Palatinate and of Bavaria with the Duchy of Deux-Ponts. *Bavaria.* He had been educated at the Court of Versailles, but nevertheless he approved of the doctrines of the French Revolution and became one of the earliest allies of Napoleon. The arrangements after the Treaty of Lunéville, which had deprived him of the Palatinate and of the Duchy of Deux-Ponts, had given him a powerful and concentrated state. By the Treaty of Pressburg he received in addition the Tyrol and the cities of Nuremberg and Ratisbon with the title of King. In 1809 he further received the Principality of Salzburg, which made his kingdom one of the most powerful in Germany. Possessing the whole of the upper valley of the Danube, and the valleys of its affluents, Bavaria formed a strong frontier state against Austria, and to the north marched with the kingdom of Saxony. King Maximilian Joseph felt that he owed his power to the French Emperor, and to seal the friendship he gave his daughter, the Princess Augusta, in marriage to Napoleon's step-son, the Viceroy Eugène de Beauharnais.

**Würtemberg.** On the western frontier of Bavaria, in order to check that state if it became too powerful, Napoleon erected the smaller kingdom of Würtemberg. Frederick, Duke of Würtemberg, like Maximilian Joseph of Bavaria, had shown himself ready to recognise the authority of the French Republic and of Napoleon. He had received considerable additions to his territories with the title of Elector in 1803, and after the Treaty of Pressburg he received the whole of Austrian Suabia except the Breisgau and Ortenau with the title of King. He, too, like the first King of Bavaria, entered into a personal alliance with Napoleon, and gave his daughter, the Princess Catherine, in marriage to Jerome Bonaparte, King of Westphalia. The

**Baden.** third south German state which deserves notice is Baden, whose Duke, Charles Frederick, was made an Elector in 1803, and in 1805 received the title of Grand Duke with the greater part of Ortenau and the Breisgau from Austrian Suabia. He, too, formed a family alliance with Napoleon by the marriage of his heir to Stéphanie de Beauharnais, Napoleon's step-daughter. The kingdom of

**Westphalia.** Westphalia, which was formed by Napoleon for his brother Jerome after the Treaty of Tilsit, was an entirely new creation, not an enlargement of a former German state like Bavaria and Würtemberg. It consisted of the Electorate of Hesse-Cassel, the Prussian territories on the left of the Elbe, including the bishoprics of Paderborn and Hildesheim, the Old Mark of Brandenburg, etc., the Duchy of Brunswick, a portion of Hanover, and other scattered districts. It thus contained the greater part of the valleys of the Ems, the Weser, and the Oder, but it did not reach the sea, and its only important fortress was Magdeburg. Jerome, who was appointed its first king, was not such a capable monarch as his brothers Joseph and Louis, but he formed an able ministry, of which the most conspicuous members were Siméon, the famous French jurist, as Minister of Justice, and the historian, Johann Müller as Minister of Public Instruction. The Westphalian people did not amalgamate so thoroughly as Napoleon had expected; but this was not the fault of Jerome's ministry, which abolished feudalism, introduced the Civil Code, and regularised the administration. The Grand Duchy of Berg, which he granted to his brother-in-law Murat in 1806, was another creation of Napoleon. It was formed out of the Duchy of Berg ceded by Bavaria, the County of the Mark and the Bishopric of Münster, detached from Prussia, and of the Duchy of Nassau. It formed a compact little state of a million inhabitants, commanding part of the course of the Rhine, with its capital at Düsseldorf. The key-stone of Napoleon's policy in Eastern Germany was Saxony. The Elector of that state had taken part with the Prussians in the campaign of Jena, but Napoleon nevertheless calculated that the ruler of Saxony, placed as he was between Prussia and Austria, must naturally be an ally of France. He, therefore, in spite of his behaviour in 1806, gave the Elector of Saxony the title of King and the Circle of Lower Lusatia. After the Treaty of Tilsit Napoleon did yet more for the King of Saxony, whom he created likewise Grand Duke of Warsaw. Of the smaller states of Germany maintained by Napoleon, the most important was Hesse-Darmstadt which separated the kingdom of Westphalia from the Grand Duchy of Berg. As a faithful ally of Napoleon, the Landgrave Louis X. received some accessions of territory with the title of Grand Duke. The fourth Grand Duchy after Baden, Berg, and Hesse-Darmstadt, was the Grand Duchy of Frankfort. This was conferred upon the Archbishop, Charles de Dalberg. This prelate had been coadjutor to the Archbishop Elector of Mayence in the time of the Revolution. He had succeeded to the Archbishopric in 1802, and in 1803, on the re-organisation of Germany, was the only ecclesiastical elector retained. He was then given the Bishopric of Ratisbon, and when that was transferred to Bavaria, was granted instead the Principalities of Fulda and Hanau and the territory of Aschaffenburg. The last Grand Duchy was that of Würtzburg, which was conferred on the Archduke Ferdinand, the former Grand Duke of Tuscany, in exchange for the Principality of Salzburg given to Bavaria in 1809. These territorial changes were supplemented by a wholesale destruction of the very small states. The Knights of the Empire lost their sovereign rights; all the petty dukes and princes whose territory was enclosed in the larger states which have been mentioned, were also mediatised, that is to say, while retaining their rights as lords and their titles, they lost their immediate sovereignty and became a sort of privileged aristocracy. This measure, which supplemented the arrangements of 1803, finally destroyed the ancient system of Germany. The little courts with but few exceptions disappeared, and Germany became a collection of powerful states instead of a congeries of feudal principalities.

Napoleon endeavoured to concentrate the power of the German princes as a whole by the formation of the Confederation of the Rhine, of which he was officially recognised as Protector. The original Confederation of the Rhine established in July 1805, consisted of only fifteen princes, but after Tilsit it comprised thirty-two. The Arch-Chancellor of the new confederation was Charles de Dalberg, the Grand Duke of Frankfort, the only ecclesiastic who was acknowledged as a member. It comprised in all the four kingdoms of Bavaria, Würtemberg, Westphalia, and Saxony, the five grand-duchies and twenty-three principalities. Its policy was conducted by a Diet sitting at Frankfort composed of two colleges,—the College of Kings and the College of Princes. The Confederation of the Rhine, which was mainly situated between the Rhine and the Elbe, contained a population of twenty million Germans, and was bound by

*Confederation of the Rhine.*

treaty to contribute a hundred and fifty thousand soldiers to the armies of Napoleon.

In no respect did Napoleon prove how thoroughly his idea of re-establishing the ancient Empires of the East and the West had taken possession of his imagination than in his treatment of Poland. In order to please the Emperor Alexander he did not insist upon re-establishing Polish independence. Not only did he neither dare nor wish to deprive Russia of her Polish provinces, but at Tilsit he even ceded to Alexander the two Polish circles of Salkief and Tloczow. But though he dared not establish a powerful independent Poland for fear of offending Russia, he nevertheless formed, in 1807, a small Polish state under the name of the Grand Duchy of Warsaw. By this half measure he failed to satisfy the Poles, who had looked to him to be the restorer of Polish independence, and at the same time offended the Emperor Alexander, who disliked the creation of a Polish state of any size or under any form. The Grand Duchy of Warsaw eventually contained the whole of Prussian and the greater part of Austrian Poland, and was placed under the rule of the King of Saxony as Grand Duke of Warsaw, just as in former days the Electors of Saxony had been Kings of Poland. In this half-and-half policy with regard to Poland was to be found the greatest peril to the newly-formed alliance between Alexander and Napoleon.

For more than a year the alliance between Russia and France, between Alexander and Napoleon, remained the most important fact of European polity; but causes of dissension soon arose. On the one hand, Alexander resented the existence of the Grand Duchy of Warsaw, and felt that his subjects had cause to grumble at the sufferings they endured owing to the Continental Blockade; on the other, there were not wanting signs that Napoleon's power had reached its height, and was now about to decline. The first symptoms of this decline were his quarrel with the Pope and his intervention in the affairs of Spain. The first blows struck at his military superiority were the defeat of the French troops in Portugal by Sir Arthur Wellesley at Vimeiro and the capitulation of General Dupont to the Spaniards. The Treaty of Tilsit marked the true zenith of Napoleon's power; but in spite of the misfortunes he suffered in 1808, and his wanton intervention in the affairs of Spain, he still seemed the greatest monarch in Europe. Feeling his prestige somewhat affected, and fearing the effect upon the mind of his imaginative ally, Napoleon, trusting in the magnetism of his presence and his conversation, had recourse to a personal interview with Alexander at Erfurt in September 1808. There the two masters of Europe discussed the state of affairs; Napoleon soothed Alexander's discontent, and again promised him the Danubian provinces. But the full confidence which had been established at Tilsit was not restored at Erfurt. Alexander, in spite of his admiration for the person of Napoleon, felt distrustful of his policy, and Napoleon deceived himself when he thought he had regained his ascendency over the mind of the Russian Emperor. The interviews between the two Emperors formed the important political side of the Congress of Erfurt; but the features which dazzled Europe were the grand *fêtes*, the pit full of kings which listened to Talma, the great French actor, and the obsequiousness of the high-born German princes to one who, a few years before but a general of the French Republic, was now master of Europe.

*Marginal note: Conference at Erfurt. Sept. 1808.*

# CHAPTER IX

## 1808-1812

Napoleon's two reverses between the Treaty of Tilsit and the Congress of Erfurt—England sends an army to Portugal—Campaign of Vimeiro and Convention of Cintra—The Revolution in Spain—Joseph Bonaparte King of Spain—Victory of Medina del Rio Seco and Capitulation of Baylen—Napoleon in Spain—Sir John Moore's advance—Battle of Corunna—The Resurrection of Austria—Ministry of Stadion—Campaign of Wagram—Treaty of Vienna—Campaign of 1809 in the Peninsula—Battle of Talavera—Expedition to Walcheren—Napoleon and the Pope—Annexation of Rome—Revolution in Sweden—Revolution in Turkey—Treaty of Bucharest—Greatest Extension of Napoleon's dominions—Internal Organisation of his Empire—The new Nobility—Internal reforms — Law — Finance — Education — Extension of these reforms through Europe—Disappearance of Serfdom—Religious Toleration—Reorganisation of Prussia—Reforms of Stein and Scharnhorst—Revival of German National feeling—Marriage of Napoleon to the Archduchess Marie Louise—Birth of the King of Rome—Steady opposition of England to Napoleon—Policies of Canning and Castlereagh—Campaigns of 1810 and 1811 in the Peninsula—Signs of the decline of Napoleon's power between 1808 and 1812.

THE Treaty of Tilsit marked the greatest height of Napoleon's power in Europe; at the Congress of Erfurt he seemed, indeed, to be as powerful as at Tilsit; but during the interval he had experienced two serious mishaps. The first of which was caused by the fact that England, which had hitherto fought the French upon the sea, and had met with only slight success in purely military expeditions, began in 1808 a serious effort to break the tradition of the invincibility of the French army.

The last important campaign upon the Continent in which an English army had taken part, was in 1793-1795. Since that time many English expeditions had been despatched to carry out isolated plans; some of these expeditions had been crowned with success, such as Abercromby's and Hutchinson's reconquest of Egypt in 1801, and Stuart's brilliant little campaign of Maida in 1806; others had been egregious failures, notably the Duke of York's campaign in Holland in 1799, and Lord Cathcart's landing in Hanover in 1805. Confident in their naval superiority, the English Ministers, ever since 1795, had paid more attention to the military occupation of islands than to the despatch of armies to the mainland. Acting on this policy, the English had conquered the French West Indies in 1793 and 1795, and again proceeded in 1809 to reoccupy those which had been restored to France at the Peace of Amiens. When Spain declared herself the ally of France, England occupied her chief West Indian possession, the Island of Trinidad; when the subjection of Holland to France became manifest, England conquered the Cape of Good Hope in 1797, and again after the Treaty of Amiens, in 1805. Nor did the English ministers neglect the more distant possessions of her various enemies. Ceylon and Java were taken from the Dutch in 1796 and 1807 respectively; the Mauritius was conquered from France in 1809, and an unsuccessful attempt was made to conquer Spanish South America, Monte Video and Buenos Ayres, in 1806. But England did not confine her policy of attacking islands to distant seas; she also established herself firmly in the Mediterranean. In 1797 Minorca was taken, in 1801 Malta, and eventually in 1805 an English army, as has been said, garrisoned Sicily. The policy of Fox was identical with that of Pitt, and favoured small, detached expeditions; some of these were failures, like the expedition to South America in 1806, and that to Egypt in 1808, but others attained their end. Now, however, a new policy began to make way. Instead of isolated expeditions and the occupation of islands which could be defended by the English fleets, it was resolved once more, as in 1793, to disembark a powerful English army on the Continent, and to try military conclusions with the French.

In order that England should act effectively on the Continent, it was necessary that her army should have a friendly base of operations. The failure of the expedition to Bergen in 1799, and of many similar expeditions, proved that it was impossible to expect complete success when the disembarking army had to fight from the moment of its landing, and had to secure its communications with the sea. An opportunity was afforded for obtaining such a base of operations as was necessary, by an insurrection breaking out in Portugal against the French invaders. It has been said that General Junot occupied the whole of Portugal without much difficulty, except the northern and southern provinces, which were held by Spanish armies. Junot partitioned out the country into military governments under French generals, whose oppressive behaviour exasperated the people. After the outbreak of the revolution against the French in Spain, the Spanish forces in Portugal retired, and Oporto at once declared itself independent of France, and elected a Junta of Government, headed by the Bishop. Isolated risings took place all over the country. Many French officers and soldiers were murdered, and the insurgents were punished with the most rigorous cruelty. The Junta of Oporto was, however, unable to make head against Junot, for the best regular troops of the Portuguese army had been despatched to join the Grand Army in Germany. The Junta had therefore to depend upon undisciplined militia, and feeling the impossibility of combating the French regular troops in the field, applied for help to England. This gave the English ministers their opportunity. A force which had been collected at Cork, under the command of Lieutenant-General Sir Arthur Wellesley, for an expedition to South America, was ordered instead to proceed to Portugal. He was joined by some other troops, and disembarked at the mouth of the Mondego river. He marched southwards towards Lisbon, and defeated a French division at Roriça on the 17th of August 1808. After receiving further reinforcements, he was attacked by Junot at Vimeiro on the 21st of August, and won a decisive victory. On the field of battle Wellesley was superseded by Sir Harry Burrard, and he in his turn by Sir Hew Dalrymple. Instead of following up the victory, the latter general concluded the Convention of Cintra, by which Junot agreed to evacuate Portugal. From a military point of view this was a poor sequel to the victory of Vimeiro; from a political point of view it was a signal success. Portugal was freed from the French as speedily as she had been conquered by them, and England thus secured a friendly base of operations. The three generals were all recalled, and Sir John Moore took command of the English army. A Council of Regency was established, and an English officer, General Beresford, was sent to organise a Portuguese army, partly under the command of English officers, and wholly paid by the English Government.

*Convention of Cintra. 30th August 1808.*

The loss of Portugal was the first serious reverse which Napoleon had met with from a trained and disciplined army. But at the same time he was made to feel the difficulty of overcoming even an unorganised national rising, with the very best of troops. It has been mentioned that the King of Spain and the Queen's favourite, Godoy, were partners to the Treaty of Fontainebleau, which arranged for the dismemberment of Portugal. Spain had been the consistent ally of France ever since the Treaty of Basle in 1795, and in the cause of France had lost not only the islands of Minorca and Trinidad, but two gallant fleets in the naval battles of Cape St. Vincent and Trafalgar. Nevertheless, Napoleon deliberately determined to dethrone his faithful ally Charles IV. It is said that after the expulsion of the Bourbons from Naples, Godoy had made overtures for joining the coalition against France, but after the victory of Jena the Court of Madrid, if it had ever thought of opposing the will of Napoleon, became more obsequious than ever. Court intrigues gave the French Emperor the opportunity he desired for interfering with the affairs of Spain. The heir to the throne, Ferdinand, Prince of the Asturias, hated his

*The Revolution in Spain, 1808.*

mother's lover, Godoy, and for sharing in a plot against the favourite was thrown into prison. He appealed for help to Napoleon, and Charles IV., his father, on his side also appealed to the French emperor. Napoleon began to move his troops across the Pyrenees, and a French army under the command of Murat approached Madrid. The King of Spain was rumoured to be about to follow the example of the Prince Regent of Portugal, and to leave the country. The population of Madrid rose in insurrection and maltreated Godoy, who fell into their hands. Charles IV. then abdicated in favour of his son, who proceeded to France to obtain the support of Napoleon. Charles IV. and his Queen followed Ferdinand, and when the Spanish royal family was assembled at Bayonne, Charles IV. was induced to cede the crown of Spain to Napoleon, who conferred it on his brother Joseph Bonaparte, King of Naples, on the 6th of June 1808. But it was one thing to proclaim Joseph King of Spain and the Indies; it was another to place him in power. *Joseph Bonaparte made King of Spain. 6th June 1808.* The patriotism of the Spanish people was stirred to its depths, and the Spaniards declined to accept a new monarch supported by French troops. In every quarter insurrections broke out and juntos were formed. Appeals were made to England for help, and money, arms, ammunition and English officers were disembarked at all the chief ports of Spain. In the month of May the mob of Madrid drove out the French soldiers of Murat, who had to retire behind the Ebro. But mobs and undisciplined militia can never stand against regular troops. Marshal Bessières defeated the best Spanish army under the command of General Cuesta at Medina del Rio Seco on the 14th of July 1808, and on the 20th of July Joseph entered Madrid. Before his arrival at his new capital, flying columns had been sent in every direction, and one of these on its way to Cadiz met with a serious disaster. This was the famous Capitulation of Baylen. The French division of *Capitulation of Baylen. 20th July 1808.* General Dupont was surrounded at that place and forced to capitulate. By the terms of the Capitulation, Dupont engaged that not only the soldiers under his immediate command, but also that two fresh divisions which were coming up should surrender. The Capitulation of Baylen deprived Napoleon of the services of 18,000 men, but the loss of prestige could not be estimated by numbers. The Spanish insurgents were greatly encouraged and rose in every quarter; a guerilla warfare was begun, which was in the end more fatal to the French army than regular defeats, and Napoleon had for the first time to fight a nation in arms. This was an exact reversal of the situation of affairs in the wars of the French Revolution; at that time it was the French nation in arms which defeated the disciplined soldiers of the Continental monarchs; now it was the Spanish nation in arms which counteracted the schemes of Napoleon. It is almost impossible to estimate the losses experienced by the French during the war in the Iberian Peninsula; the defeats inflicted on them by the Anglo-Portuguese army accounted for but a small portion of this loss; it was the harassing duty of maintaining garrisons in every town and almost in every posting-house which exhausted the French army.

It need hardly be said that Napoleon was far from expecting such disasters as the Capitulation of Baylen and the Convention of Cintra. He had been so accustomed to victory that he could not understand the change in his affairs. He looked upon these two events as having only a temporary importance, and proceeded to the Congress at Erfurt with a light heart. Though checked in Spain, he was none the less the master in Germany, and the monarchs of Central Europe did not know that he had reached his zenith and was about to decline. The Emperor Alexander alone seems to have had some suspicion of the truth, for he entered into fresh relations with England by means of the strong English party at his Court, which was headed by the Empress-mother. As soon as the Congress of Erfurt was over, Napoleon proceeded to Spain in person, accompanied by his Guard and his most experienced troops, and surrounded

*Napoleon in Spain.*

by his most famous generals. After the Capitulation of Baylen, Joseph Bonaparte had left Madrid, and with the bulk of the French army had retreated behind the Ebro. He was there joined by Napoleon, who had under his command no less than 135,000 men. He rapidly advanced upon Madrid; Marshal Soult defeated the Spanish Army of the Centre at Burgos on the 10th of November; Marshal Victor the Spanish Army of the Left at Espinosa on the 11th of November; and Marshal Lannes the Army of the Right at Tudela on the 3d of November. In spite of the snow, the Emperor in person forced the pass of the Somo Sierra, and on the 13th of December received the capitulation of Madrid. The victories of his lieutenants and his own rapid and successful advance on the capital, convinced Napoleon that the difficulties of the Spanish war had been exaggerated, and the result of this impression was that he neglected in after years to strengthen his armies in Spain sufficiently, and attributed all failures to the incompetence of his generals, instead of to the obstinate tenacity of his opponents.

After occupying Madrid, the Emperor next determined to turn his strength against the English forces in the Peninsula. Sir John Moore, who was in command of the English army in Portugal, could not believe that the Spanish armies were too weak to face the French; but when he heard that Napoleon was at Madrid, he resolved to make a diversion in order to prevent him from conquering Andalusia, and to give time for the Junta of Seville to organise the defence of that province. Leaving a small division to protect Portugal under Sir John Cradock, Moore, with the bulk of the English army, invaded north-west Spain and advanced as far as Salamanca and Toro. Napoleon, as Moore had expected, put off the invasion of Andalusia and turned against the English. Moore having thus effected his purpose, then fell back into Galicia. In the midst of most terrible weather he effected one of the most famous retreats in history, turning occasionally to face his

*Sir John Moore's advance.*

pursuers, and fighting several brilliant rear-guard actions. Napoleon conducted the pursuit in person for some time, but hearing that Austria was preparing for war, he handed over the command to Soult and suddenly returned to France. Soult did not come up with the English army until it had reached Corunna, and was waiting there to embark. A battle was fought to protect the embarkation of the English, in which Sir John Moore was killed, and Soult, whose losses during the rapid pursuit had been very great, turned southwards to occupy Oporto.

*Battle of Corunna. Jan. 16, 1809.*

The Treaty of Pressburg had made a very painful impression, not only upon the mind of Francis I. of Austria, but also on the Austrian people. The indignation aroused by the cession of Dalmatia and the loss of Venice, which had been given to the House of Austria as compensation for the Milanese, had exasperated the Austrian people. But, on the other hand, the Hungarians were inclined, like the Poles, to look to Napoleon as the possible restorer of their national independence. The policy of the Emperor Francis had been to treat the Hungarians, whom he had placed under the rule of his brother, the Archduke Joseph, as semi-independent, and to make as little change as possible in the Hungarian Constitution. He regarded his German provinces as the really important portion of his dominions, and gave them his undivided attention. After the Treaty of Pressburg, the Emperor dismissed his chancellor and prime minister Cobenzl, and replaced him by Count Philip Stadion. The new Chancellor was a thorough German, though descended from a Grisons family, and the main point of his policy was to rouse the patriotism of the Germans as a nationality against the French. In fact, from 1805 until the outbreak of war in 1809, Stadion endeavoured to arouse the national spirit which afterwards made Germany successful in the final war of liberation against Napoleon. He circulated patriotic literature, and formulated the idea of German unity, which he saw must take the place of the extinct notion of the Holy Roman Empire.

*Austria. 1805-1809.*

He was successful in rousing the German popular feeling to the greatest height in the German provinces of Austria; but the time was not yet ripe for the expression of a similar sentiment throughout the whole of Germany. The weight of the Continental Blockade was not experienced in its fullest form until after 1809. And the patriotic feeling which was to have so full a development could not be stirred up in a moment. But in the German territories of Austria Stadion was completely successful. The Emperor Francis himself was a thorough German, and during the progress which he made through his states in 1808, with his beautiful second wife, the Empress Ludovica, a princess of Modena, roused the utmost enthusiasm. Ever since the Peace of Pressburg the Archduke Charles, as Commander-in-Chief, had been organising the military power of Austria; regiments of volunteers were formed in Vienna and all the large cities; and the militia for the first time were disciplined and trained for offensive war, and not maintained merely for the preservation of the peace. While the smaller princes of Germany were obsequiously doing honour to Napoleon at Erfurt, the Emperor of Austria was preparing for war. The successful insurrection of the Spaniards, and the Capitulation of Baylen, encouraged Stadion in his belief that if a national feeling could be roused against the French domination, it would be as successful in Germany as in Spain. The English Ministry encouraged the attitude of the Austrian Emperor, and promised not only large subsidies if an Austrian army would take the field, but also that a powerful diversion should be made in the Netherlands by an English army. Napoleon heard of this disposition of Austria in 1808, but at first paid very little heed to it. During his winter campaign in the Peninsula, however, it became obvious that the Austrians were in a hurry to come to conclusions with him, and he therefore hastened back from Spain to make his preparations for this new war, instead of pursuing the English to Corunna.

From both the political and the military point of view,

Napoleon was justified in believing in 1809 that he had little to fear from the intervention of Austria. The South German princes, like the Kings of Bavaria and Würtemberg, had been too much favoured by him to desire to oppose him, and willingly sent their contingents to serve in his ranks. From the population of his new creation, the kingdom of Westphalia, he looked for assistance, not opposition, and what remained of Prussia was occupied by French armies. The Emperor Alexander of Russia, still under the glamour of the interview at Erfurt, and the grand promises for the division of the world repeated to him there, showed no inclination to assist Austria. Indeed, the feeling of opposition between Austria and Russia, which had shown itself in 1799 and 1800, had been augmented by the unfortunate campaign of Austerlitz. Each ally blamed the other for that disaster; the Austrian officers openly declared that they hated a Russian more than a Frenchman, and the Russians reciprocated this feeling. Austria's only ally, therefore, was England. From a military point of view, the Austrian army had not yet been sufficiently reorganised, in spite of the efforts of Stadion and the Archduke Charles, to make a successful resistance to the French; but, as the event of the campaign showed, it was able to make a better stand than it had ever made before.

*Campaign of Wagram. 1809.*

In April 1809 the Archduke Charles, amid the greatest enthusiasm of the Austrian people, issued a manifesto to the German race, and at the head of 170,000 men advanced into Bavaria. At the same time another army, under the Archduke John, invaded Italy. At that moment Napoleon had only two *corps-d'armée* in Southern Germany, one under the command of Marshal Davout at Ratisbon, and the other under Marshal Masséna at Augsburg. The Archduke Charles intended to get between the two marshals and defeat them separately. But Napoleon arrived in person, with some of the finest troops he had been employing in Spain, before the Archduke could complete his operations. On the 20th of April he defeated the Austrian left at Abensberg, and on the

22d he routed the Austrian right under the Archduke in person at Eckmühl. In the five days' fighting, which included these battles, the Austrians lost 7000 men in killed and wounded, and 23,000 prisoners. In the result it was the Austrians, not the French, who were cut in two, and Napoleon rapidly followed the Austrian left to Vienna. The capital surrendered on the 12th of May, and Napoleon then resolved to cross the Danube and attack the main body of the Austrian army under the Archduke Charles. He attempted to pass the river at the point where is situated midway the island of Lobau. When the greater part of his army had reached the island he pushed across to the other bank, and on the 21st and 22nd of May stormed the villages of Aspern and Essling. But on the evening of the second fight he found it necessary to withdraw into the island of Lobau, for his bridges of boats which connected the island with the right bank of the river had been swept away, and his ammunition had fallen short. The Tyrolese, too, had risen under Hofer, and Napoleon's position was most critical. Nevertheless he determined not to retreat; the island of Lobau became an entrenched camp; stronger bridges were thrown from it to the right bank of the Danube; and reinforcements were summoned from different quarters.

<small>Battle of Aspern. 21st and 22nd May 1809.</small>

The most important of these reinforcements were supplied by the French Army of Italy, which reached Napoleon in the island of Lobau on the 2nd of July. This army was commanded by the Viceroy of Italy, Eugène de Beauharnais, whose military adviser and principal subordinate was General Macdonald. The Viceroy had, before Macdonald reached him, been checked at Sacilio by the Archduke John, but after Macdonald's arrival he pushed on rapidly. A decisive victory, which prevented the Archduke John from pursuing, was won over the Hungarians at Raab on the 14th of June, after which Eugène de Beauharnais was enabled safely to join the Emperor in the island of Lobau. With his army

PERIOD VII.   S

thus increased, Napoleon crossed to the left bank of the Danube on the morning of the 5th of July, at the head of 180,000 men, many of whom were Westphalians, Bavarians, and Italians. On the following day he completely defeated the Archduke Charles at the battle of Wagram, at which the Austrians lost more than 30,000 men. Though defeated, the Austrian army was not disgraced, and Napoleon himself said, when blamed for not following up his victory, 'If I had had my veterans of Austerlitz I should have carried out a manœuvre which, with my present troops, I dare not execute.' Had the Archduke John come up in time and placed himself under his brother's command, the battle might have had a different result, and as it was, the Austrian Emperor need not have considered himself forced to conclude peace.

*Battle of Wagram. 6th July 1809.*

The Emperor Francis, however, did not dare to risk the further event of war, and on the 14th of October 1809 he signed the Treaty of Vienna. By this treaty Austria ceded Trieste, Carniola, Istria, and a large part of Croatia to Napoleon, who added them to Dalmatia, which he had acquired at the Treaty of Pressburg, and made out of them the Government of the Illyrian Provinces. Francis also abandoned the Tyrolese, and ceded the greater part of Salzburg to the King of Bavaria, whose army, along with the Saxon contingent under Bernadotte, had played a great part in winning the victory of Wagram. He had to give up the whole of Western Galicia; the greater part of this province was added to the Grand-Duchy of Warsaw, but certain districts were ceded to the Emperor Alexander, who in reply to the demands of Napoleon had despatched an army to act in that quarter against the Austrians. This action had still further incensed the Emperor of Austria against the Emperor of Russia, while it did not satisfy Napoleon, who complained that the Russians had not acted with sufficient vigour, and had been waiting to hear the result of the main campaign in the neighbourhood of Vienna. In Austria itself the most

*Treaty of Vienna. 14th October 1809.*

important result of the war was the retirement of Count Philip Stadion, who was succeeded as Chancellor of State by Count Metternich.

During the campaign of Wagram the French armies left in Spain had been continuing their operations. Before the actual outbreak of war with Austria, Saragossa had been captured on the 21st of February 1809, after an obstinate siege, which proved to the French the mettle of their new opponents. The most important operations had been carried out in three quarters of the Peninsula. In Arragon and Catalonia, General Gouvion-Saint-Cyr acted with considerable skill in a campaign of which the main feature was the reduction of small fortresses, and his successor, General Suchet, steadily pursued the same policy. Both of these generals invariably defeated any Spanish army which met them in the field. From Madrid King Joseph had acted in two different directions. Marshal Moncey took Valencia; Marshal Victor defeated the Spanish army of the South, which was under the command of Cuesta, at Medellin; and General Sebastiani approached the frontiers of Andalusia. But in Portugal the French had again to meet the English, who had in the previous year defeated them at Vimeiro, and drawn them away to Corunna. After the departure of Sir John Moore's army, Marshal Soult had invaded Portugal from the north and occupied Oporto. There is no doubt that if he had acted boldly he might have captured Lisbon, which was only guarded by a feeble division under Sir John Cradock. But Soult wasted his time in intriguing, it is said, for the throne of Portugal, until the English Ministry had time to reinforce Cradock, and to send Sir Arthur Wellesley to command the army in Portugal. Wellesley speedily dislodged Soult from Oporto, and drove his army in disorder back into Galicia. He then, following the example of Moore, invaded Spain, in the expectation of saving Andalusia. He met the French army in Spain, under the command of Marshal Victor, at Talavera. He repulsed the French

*The Peninsular War. 1809.*

*Battle of Talavera. 28th July 1809.*

attack on his position on the 28th of July, and had he been efficiently assisted by the Spaniards under Cuesta he might have won a great victory. As it was, his success prevented the French from invading Portugal, but it was not sufficiently decisive to save Andalusia. The French army was reorganised; the Spaniards were routed at the battle of Ocana, on the 12th of November, and the whole of the fertile province of Andalusia, with the exception of Gibraltar and Cadiz, fell into the hands of the French.

Unfortunately the English Ministers failed to understand immediately the greatness of the opportunity given to them by Napoleon's behaviour in the Peninsula, and instead of concentrating all their military strength for the support of Sir Arthur Wellesley, who was made Viscount Wellington for his victory of Talavera, they despatched one of the finest armies that ever left England on the Walcheren Expedition. They had promised to assist the Emperor of Austria by making a diversion in the north of Europe. The object of this diversion was Antwerp, on which city Napoleon was spending vast sums of money in the hope of making it the commercial rival of London. This expedition, which was placed under the command of the Earl of Chatham, the elder brother of the younger Pitt, never reached Antwerp. It was landed in the island of Walcheren, and took Flushing in August 1809. It met no French army worthy of the name, but was destroyed as a fighting machine by the pestilences and fevers of the unhealthy island in which it was quartered. The expedition took place too late to be of any service to Austria, for the English army did not disembark until a month after the battle of Wagram had been fought, and in the want of energy with which it was conducted, it may almost be classed with the disastrous expedition to Bergen in 1799. At sea, however, the English fleet maintained its pre-eminence. In this year Guadeloupe, Martinique, and the Mauritius were conquered, and an attempt was made to burn the French fleet in the Basque Roads by Lord Cochrane, which might have

*Expedition to Walcheren. 1809.*

been completely successful if he had not been thwarted by the admiral in command, Lord Gambier.

It has been said that one of the measures by which Napoleon secured his ascendency over the minds of the French people was the conclusion of the Concordat by which the schism which had divided the French Church was closed. He had at the commencement of his tenure of power treated the new Pope, Pius VII., with much respect, and the Pope had in return made the Emperor's uncle, Fesch, a Cardinal, and had come to Paris to crown him Emperor. But troubles soon arose between Napoleon and Pius VII. The Emperor proclaimed himself the successor of Charlemagne, and wished to restrict the Pope entirely to spiritual affairs. The terms of the Concordat were not thoroughly carried out. The Pope would not give Napoleon the supreme authority over the French bishops, which he desired, and His Holiness looked on the transformation of the priesthood in France from an independent body into salaried officials with extreme disfavour. On the Pope's return to Rome in 1805, he requested that the French troops should evacuate the whole of the former States of the Church. Napoleon did not comply with this request, and not satisfied with ordaining the cession of the Legations of Bologna and Ferrara to the Kingdom of Italy, he occupied Ancona, and confiscated the principalities of Ponte Corvo and Benevento, which he bestowed on Bernadotte and Talleyrand. The declaration of the Continental Blockade increased the dissatisfaction of the Pope, who declined to obey it, as he also did a further order in 1806 to expel from Rome all English, Russian, Swedish, and Sardinian subjects. After some months of perpetual bickering Napoleon directed General Miollis to occupy Rome on the 2nd of February 1808. Pius VII., in the cause of peace, dismissed Cardinal Consalvi, his Secretary of State, but he could not satisfy the demands of the Emperor, and on the 17th of May 1809 the States of the Church in Italy were declared united to the French Empire, and Rome was officially decreed to be the Second City of that

Empire. Exasperated by this open insult, Pius VII. excommunicated the French Emperor. Napoleon, who was at that time in his camp in the island of Lobau, ordered that the Pope should be removed from Rome. He was arrested by General Radet on the 6th of July, the day of the victory of Wagram, and forcibly removed to Savona, near Genoa, where he was kept as a State prisoner. Pius VII. in his exile consistently protested against the usurpations of Napoleon, and refused from this time to give canonical institution to the bishops nominated by the Emperor. In 1811 Napoleon attempted to put ecclesiastical affairs in France on a new footing, and summoned a national council or synod of bishops to meet at Paris. But the Pope refused to negotiate with the synod, and he was accordingly removed to Fontainebleau in 1812. While there Napoleon pretended that His Holiness agreed to a new and revised Concordat which was promulgated as a law on the 13th of February 1813. Pius VII. always denied that he had given his consent to the new arrangement, which would have deprived him of his most valued prerogatives, and stated that he had always regarded himself as a prisoner since his removal from Rome. By his conduct towards the Pope Napoleon committed a great mistake. He lost the support of the faithful body of Catholics in France whom he had conciliated in 1801, and he gave a pretext for his enemies to declare him the enemy of religion. The Caesarism which had infected his imagination after his great victories in 1806 and 1807 appeared in his behaviour towards Pius VII. as well as in his intervention with the affairs of Spain.

The year 1809, which witnessed the campaign of Wagram and the overthrow of the Pope, was also signalised by a revolution in Sweden, which was followed by very important results. It has been said that Gustavus IV. remained faithful to the coalition against Napoleon even after the Peace of Tilsit. By that peace it was arranged that the Emperor of Russia should annex Finland. This was carried out in 1808, after a very weak opposition on the part

*The Revolution in Sweden. 1809.*

of the Swedes, and in the same year Swedish Pomerania was occupied by the French. In spite of these losses the King of Sweden declared war against Denmark, and then quarrelled with the general of the English army sent to his assistance. For this conduct, which seemed conclusive as to the loss of sanity by the King, the Swedes resolved to dethrone him. At the commencement of 1809 the Baron Adlersparre, the commander-in-chief of the army sent to invade Norway, concluded a secret armistice with the Danes, and marched on Stockholm. On the 13th of March 1809 the King was arrested, and on the 29th he was forced to sign a deed of abdication. This act was ratified by the States of Sweden on the 10th of May, and the King's uncle, the Duke of Sudermania, was elected King as Charles XIII. A new constitution of an aristocratic type, restoring the power of the Swedish nobles which had been severely curtailed by Gustavus III., was promulgated, and on the 18th of January 1810 the States elected as heir to the throne, since the new King had no sons, the Prince Christian of Holstein-Augustenberg. This young prince died in May of the same year, and the question then arose as to his successor. There was no possible prince of the reigning family, and the king was old and in bad health. It happened that in 1806 the Swedish officers employed in Hanover had made the acquaintance of Marshal Bernadotte, who commanded in that quarter, and it was suggested that he should be elected as Prince Royal. This choice was dictated by a hope that it would please the French Emperor, for Bernadotte was not only one of his most distinguished marshals, but was connected with his family, for both he and Joseph Bonaparte had married daughters of Monsieur Clary, a tradesman of Marseilles. Bernadotte received the consent of Napoleon; on the 19th of October 1810 he abjured Catholicism; and on the 5th of November he was elected Prince Royal by the Swedish Diet. He was at once charged with the direction of foreign affairs and with the reorganisation of the Swedish army, and he played an important part in the overthrow of the French Emperor.

With Sweden and Poland, Turkey had for a long time been considered as the third barrier against the advance of Russia.

Turkey. Bonaparte, like earlier French statesmen, had held this view, but after the Peace of Tilsit he expressed himself as ready and willing to abandon all three countries to the encroachments of Russia. The loss of Finland and Pomerania had reduced Sweden to a minor state; the Grand-Duchy of Warsaw was a poor substitute for the Kingdom of Poland, and it is now necessary to observe the effects upon Turkey of her abandonment by France. The Sultan, Selim III., had been thrown into a close alliance with England by Napoleon's occupation of Egypt when he was but a general of the French Republic, and still more by his daring march into Syria. When he became First Consul, Napoleon endeavoured to destroy the unfavourable opinion entertained of him at Constantinople, and sent thither as his ambassador one of the ablest of the French diplomatists, General Sebastiani, who managed to ingratiate himself with the Porte. The English monopoly of the commerce of the Levant was displeasing to the Porte, and Pitt failed to induce the Sultan to enter into the coalition against France in 1805. In 1807 an English fleet under Sir John Duckworth was sent to compel the Sultan to give up his friendship with the French. After forcing the passage of the Dardanelles, it had to retire without achieving its object, and suffered great loss while sailing down the Straits. This behaviour of England threw the Turks entirely on the side of France. French officers were employed to reorganise the Turkish army, and a regular militia was established. Sultan Selim was a monarch in advance of his times, and endeavoured to introduce certain reforms, but he roused against him both the Muhammadan Ulemas and the Janissaries. The former disliked his civil reforms, the latter his establishment of the militia. Selim was dethroned, and replaced by Mustapha IV. on the 21st of July 1807. But the reign of Mustapha was but of short duration. The Pasha of Rustchuk marched to Constantinople, and when he found that the Sultan Selim had been assassinated, he dethroned Mustapha and placed his nephew, Mahmoud II., on the throne of Turkey. The first event of the new reign was a violent battle between the Janissaries and the freshly organised militia in the streets of Constantinople, after which Mahmoud executed his own brother and most of his relations, and established himself firmly on the throne. The new Sultan, who was a man of extraordinary vigour, was at once attacked by the Russians, as had been arranged by the the Treaty of Tilsit. Napoleon had pointed out to Alexander that he could easily annex the Danubian principalities, and he hoped that the Turks would afford enough occupation to the Russian army to prevent it from interfering with his projects in Europe. The Russian attack on Turkey was followed by a treaty of peace between England and the Porte, in spite of the efforts of the French diplomatists; but the English, as usual, considered it enough to send subsidies in money without supplying troops. In 1809 the Turks were defeated at Braila and Silistria, and by the close of 1810 the Russian army under the command of Prince Bagration occupied the whole of Wallachia, Moldavia, and Bessarabia. In 1811 the Russian general Kutuzov crossed the Danube, and occupied both Silistria and Shumla, and the way was opened to Constantinople. But, fortunately for the existence of the Turkish power, Napoleon in 1812 was preparing to invade Russia; the efforts of the French diplomatists to induce the Sultan Mahmoud to continue the war were fruitless; the Porte said that it had too often proved the worthlessness of the French offers of help, and on the 28th of May 1812 a treaty of peace was signed between Russia and Turkey at Bucharest. By this treaty the Turks ceded part of Bessarabia and Moldavia to Russia, and acknowledged the Principality of Servia, but its chief importance in European history is that it relieved the Emperor Alexander from an important enemy at a moment of crisis, and allowed him to turn all his strength against the French invaders.

*Treaty of Bucharest. 28th May 1812.*

The period from 1809 to 1812, that is, from the Peace of Vienna to the invasion of Russia, witnessed the greatest extension of the dominions of Napoleon. But this enormous increase of territory did not strengthen France; new difficulties appeared with each fresh advance; and although in 1811 the boundaries of the French power were far more distended than they were in 1808, the Empire was not so strong. By his annexations Napoleon abandoned the principle which he had formerly set before himself. He had declared that the natural boundaries of France were the Rhine and the Alps, and every annexation beyond those natural limits was a distinct act of defiance to Europe. From 1806 to 1808 his policy was to surround France with a belt of subject kingdoms; by his annexations from 1809 to 1812 his borders touched those of the great Continental powers. In the north Napoleon accepted the abdication of his brother Louis, who had protested against the measures taken for maintaining the Continental Blockade, and on the 9th of July 1810 he declared Holland an integral part of the Empire. Holland was divided into eight departments, and lost its existence as an independent nation. Then in pursuance of the Continental Blockade, Napoleon, on the 13th of December 1810, annexed the districts in North Germany from the borders of Holland to the mouth of the Weser. By this step he united the whole coast-line from Friesland to Denmark, and hoped to close entirely the English trade with North Germany. The districts annexed were the Duchy of Oldenburg, the sea-coast of Hanover, the territories of the Princes of Salm and Aremberg, and the free cities of Bremen, Hamburg, and Lübeck. These districts were divided into four departments, the Ems-Supérieur, the Lippe, the Bouches-du-Weser, and the Bouches-de-l'Elbe, with their capitals at Osnabrück, Münster, Bremen, and Hamburg. These annexations showed what persistent opposition Napoleon met in Germany to the Continental Blockade, when his own brother Louis could not maintain it in Holland, and he was afraid to trust the coast-line of Westphalia to his brother Jerome. Turning further south, Napoleon in 1810 annexed the Valais, which he had declared independent of Switzerland, under the name of the Department of the Simplon. In Italy the most flagrant breach of the former French system was committed. When the kingdom of Italy was formed in 1805, the Emperor had kept Piedmont under his own control in order to command both sides of the Alps, and in 1810 he preferred to amalgamate the Ligurian Republic, Parma, the Kingdom of Etruria, and the States of the Church with his directly-governed departments in Piedmont, rather than to unite them to the Kingdom of Italy. These districts were divided into nine departments, and it is curious to notice such cities as Rome, Genoa, Parma, Florence, Siena, and Leghorn as capitals of French departments. In all, the French Empire at its greatest consisted of one hundred and thirty departments directly administered from Paris, excluding from consideration the Illyrian provinces and the Ionian Islands, which were not treated as departments. Mention has already been made of the subject kingdoms, and it is only to be noted here that Murat, the famous cavalry general and brother-in-law of Napoleon, was made King of Naples when Joseph Bonaparte was promoted to the throne of Spain, and that the infant son of Louis Bonaparte, the former King of Holland, received Murat's Grand-Duchy of Berg. Napoleon also made his favourite sister, Elisa, Grand Duchess of Tuscany and Princess of Lucca and Piombino; his second sister, Pauline, Duchess of Guastalla; and his Chief of the Staff and most trusted subordinate, Marshal Berthier, independent Prince of Neufchâtel.

The administration of this vast empire was purely bureaucratic. Napoleon endeavoured to establish a hierarchy of civil officials, who should be as completely under his direct control as the officers of his army. He ruled the Empire like a general. Implicit obedience to orders was the only means to promotion in his civil, as

*Internal Organisation of the Empire.*

well as in his military, organisation. He delighted in insisting on this comparison. The Legion of Honour was not a military order, but was conferred with equal freedom on civil officials, and in all matters the Emperor's will could be consulted and was supreme. No subjects were too minute for his supervision. He reorganised the ancient theatrical company of the Comédie Française with the same attention to detail as a matter of State administration. The development of a bureaucracy dependent on absolutism was in curious contrast to the Constitution of 1791, and the theories which had prevailed at the beginning of the French Revolution. Freedom of petition, freedom of the press, individual liberty, representative institutions, and all the liberties won by the French people were entirely abolished. The censorship of the press was re-established, and carried out with more rigour than it had been even under the Bourbon monarchy. All manuscripts had to be revised before being sent to the printer, and perfectly innocent allusions, which might be interpreted into applying condemnation of the existing order of things, brought upon their authors immediate imprisonment, and the destruction of their books. Individual liberty ceased to exist; for the Emperor exiled and imprisoned at his will. The secret police, which had been organised by Fouché, exercised a minute inquisition into the most private affairs, and a crowd of spies kept the Emperor informed of every current of opinion in Paris and throughout the Empire. The arbitrariness of his government was greatly due to his sensitiveness to public opinion, and it is narrated that during his enforced residence in the island of Lobau he was far more exercised in mind by his spies' reports of the conversations on the subject in the Faubourg St. Germain than by the movements of the Austrians. Representative institutions had been practically superseded by the Constitution of the Year VIII., but the last vestige of a power which could criticise the Emperor's will, the Tribunate, was suppressed in 1808. The Senate became merely a dignified body to congratulate the Emperor on his victories, and the Legislative Body registered, without murmuring, all his decrees. It is a curious fact that, in 1811, Napoleon imitated the most arbitrary measure of the Committee of Public Safety, and, when the price of corn rose, he fixed a maximum price for its sale in Paris.

Next to his own absolutism Napoleon believed in the principle of heredity. He showed this primarily in the treatment of his own family. He not only brought his mother to Paris, and under the title of Madame Mère en- dowed her with a large income, but bestowed on his brothers and sisters, in spite of the marked incapacity of many of them, the most important posts. The kingdoms given to Joseph, Louis, and Jerome Bonaparte were accompanied by the intimation that they were to rule subject to his will, and he exercised an autocratic power over all the members of his family. For instance, he insisted that Jerome should divorce his wife, an American lady named Patterson, because his own consent had not been obtained, and forced him to marry a Würtemberg princess. His own lack of children greatly grieved him, and he made various arrangements as to his successor. At one time it was thought he would nominate his step-son, Eugène de Beauharnais; at another he selected an infant son of his brother Louis to be his heir, and had him baptized by the Pope just after his own coronation in 1805; and when the infant died, he issued a decree, arranging the succession among his brothers and their children in order of seniority. He created his brothers, sisters, and step-children Princes of the Empire, and gave them honorary seats in the Senate and Council of State, and he insisted upon his wife Josephine surrounding herself with all the pomp of a monarchical Court. The desire of creating a Court which should outshine that of the Bourbons caused Napoleon to bid high for the support of the ancient noble families of France. By bestowing large incomes, rapid promotion, and repeated favours he was able to get men and women bearing the oldest names in France to accept office as

*The Hereditary Principle.*

chamberlains and lords and ladies-in-waiting, while many scions of former sovereign families in Germany and the Netherlands did not hesitate to request admission to such Court offices. But he did not trust solely to the old nobility to form the splendour of his Court; he always suspected that they were sneering at him, and endeavoured to counterbalance them by creating a new nobility. This new nobility was formed entirely from the men who did him good service, whether in military or civil departments. By the side of his marshals, most of whom he created dukes, he ranked his chief diplomatists and ministers, and the example was followed into inferior ranks. Good service as the *préfet* of a department led to a barony as certainly as gallant service in the field at the head of a regiment, and former members of the Convention, who, as Deputies on Mission, had exerted unlimited authority, were content to accept the title of Chevalier of the Empire, the lowest in his new peerage. The peerage of the Empire was strictly hereditary, though in many instances the Emperor assumed the right exercised by former kings of granting permission to adopt an heir. But the new peerage was purely ornamental; it conferred no political power whatever. Napoleon never dreamt of creating a House of Lords; he only conceived the notion of balancing the influence of the old aristocracy by the creation of one dependent entirely on himself. In his desire to maintain the dignity of his new nobles, he granted many of them large incomes and vast estates; his marshals were encouraged to live in the most extravagant fashion by the repeated payment of their debts; and the grant of a peerage was in many cases accompanied by what he called a *dotation*, which supplied an income sufficient to maintain the dignity. Some of these 'dotations' were of princely magnificence. They were largely situated in Italy and Poland, and were intended to make the new possessors independent barons, like the famous paladins of Charlemagne. Among the most important of these grants, after the Principality of Neufchâtel, which was a semi-

[margin: Napoleon's Aristocracy.]

independent sovereignty, may be noted the Principalities of Benevento, Ponte Corvo, Parma, Piacenza, and Gaeta, which were conferred upon Talleyrand, Bernadotte, Cambacérès, Le Brun, and Gaudin. By these means Napoleon hoped to keep his subordinates faithful to him, while their influence on opinion would rival that exercised by the old nobility.

But while wielding an undisputed absolutism, Napoleon looked on his position in a spirit similar to that of the benevolent despots of the eighteenth century. Though he would do nothing by the people, he was ready to do much for them. In the path of legal reform he followed up the measure taken by the formation of the Civil Code. He had plenty of learned jurists to carry out his instructions, and the Civil Code was succeeded, in 1806, by the Codes of Civil and Criminal Procedure, in 1808 by the Commercial Code, and finally by the Penal Code. These great codes form an epoch in the legal history of Europe, and have earned for Napoleon the title of the modern Justinian, though they were only carried out by his directions, and based on the principles laid down, and the work done, by the Constituent Assembly and the Convention. Their great advantage was their simplicity and universality, which checked the tedious delays inherent in all systems of common or uncodified law. In jurisdiction Napoleon also followed the example of the statesmen of the Revolution. He encouraged rapidity in procedure and in the execution of judgments, and he greatly extended the powers of the commercial tribunals in which practical men of business had a voice. In financial matters, as in his legal reforms, Napoleon's great aim was to attain simplicity, and he reduced the loss in the passage of taxes from the taxpayer to the Treasury to a minimum. His creation of the Bank of France has been mentioned, and by its side he established the Caisse d'Amortissement, which consisted of the pecuniary guarantees of all the collectors of the taxes merged into one fund. These guarantees formed an

*Internal Reforms. Law.*

*Finance.*

important sum of money for immediate use as well as a valuable security. Napoleon further managed to pay off that portion of the debt left to him by the Republic, which represented the sums due for the suppression of the old courts of judicature, etc. With regard to the ordinary debt, he preserved Cambon's great creation of the Grand Livre, which enabled every creditor to become a fund-holder, while the Emperor knew the exact extent of the public debt. The Emperor's first steps towards the formation of a national system of education have been described, but it was not until after the campaign of Wagram that the system was completed. In 1806 he had organised the Imperial University, but it did not take its final form until 1811. This university was not a university in the English sense. It consisted of the chief professors and teachers, and was intended to include all the professors and teachers throughout France. It was placed under the superintendence of a Grand Master, a celebrated man of letters, Fontanes, and its duty was to superintend the whole course of higher education. In the Emperor's own words, he wished to create a teaching profession organised like the judicial or the military profession, of which all the professors scattered throughout the country might feel themselves an integral part. In 1808 he granted the university an income of 400,000 livres, in addition to the fees, etc., and declared in favour of the irremovability of its members. To recruit this new teaching profession, Napoleon established the Normal School of Paris for the instruction of those who desired to become professors or teachers.

*Education.*

These great reforms in law, in finance, and in education outlasted Napoleon's reconstitution of Europe. Their effect spread far beyond the actual limits of France. As a direct result of the French Revolution serfdom disappeared in Switzerland, in Belgium, and in Northern Italy. Napoleon carried on the work further to the east. In the Kingdom of Westphalia, and in all the states of Germany which he created or enlarged, serfdom was entirely

*Extension of the system to Germany.*

abolished. The feudal system was suppressed wherever the influence of the French extended. Maximilian Joseph, King of Bavaria, and his minister, Montgelas, carried out the principles of the French Revolution by abolishing the privileges of the nobility and the clergy. In every direction the French codes were either adopted or imitated; the course of justice was made simple and cheap; education was organised; and the economical rules of the French administration introduced. In more distant countries the same reforms were carried out. By the constitution of the Grand Duchy of Warsaw the Polish serfs, perhaps the most miserable of all serfs, were freed from their bondage, and absolute equality before the law decreed. In Naples Joseph Bonaparte and Murat, and in Spain Joseph Bonaparte by himself, carried out the same great reforms; and though the reaction after 1815 tended to replace matters on their former footing, it proved to be impossible to restore the old evils in their entirety. Not less admirable was Napoleon's vindication of the great principle of religious toleration. In Catholic states such as Bavaria Protestants received the priceless boon of religious liberty; in Protestant states like Saxony it was the Catholics who profited by the broad-mindedness of the French Emperor; and in every country the Jews were relieved from the degrading position in which they had been kept. In military organisation the reforms which had made the French army master of the world were introduced by Napoleon. With the disappearance of the petty German states disappeared also the feudal armies. Conscription may, indeed, appear a heavy burden on a state, but in Germany, at any rate, it created for the first time national armies to take the place of the ill-disciplined mercenaries who had hitherto been hired by the petty princes.

The most curious feature in the creation of a new Germany, which was the result of Napoleon's reforms as much as of his victories, was the formation of new Prussia. In Germany proper, that is, in Germany between the Rhine and the Elbe, reforms were introduced

The Organisation of Prussia.

under French supervision, if not always by French agents. In Prussia the reforms came on the initiative of a great minister. The speedy overthrow of the famed Prussian army in the campaign of Jena convinced Prussian statesmen of the necessity for sweeping changes. By the Treaty of Tilsit Prussia was shorn of all the acquisitions in Central Germany which she had received as the price of her consistent neutrality, and was thrust behind the Elbe. On the other side she lost her Polish provinces. Even the small Prussia thus left was occupied by French troops, and was forced to pay a war contribution of a hundred and forty millions as well as to maintain an army of 42,000 men for the service of Napoleon. It would seem that Prussia was to be driven back into the position of a second-rate state, but at this juncture Frederick William III. summoned to his ministry two remarkable men—the Freiherr vom Stein, a Knight of the Holy Roman Empire and a native of Nassau, and Scharnhorst, a Hanoverian officer. Neither of these men were Prussians, but they were both enthusiastic Germans. They believed that Prussia would yet form the key-stone on which German emancipation from the power of Napoleon could be reared. They understood that Prussia must be entirely reconstituted, and that an old-fashioned Prussia could neither combat Napoleon nor lead the new Germany which he had created. Stein, therefore, as Minister of the Interior, adapted the reforms of the French Revolution and of Napoleon to Prussia. He established equality before the law by the abolition of serfdom, he suppressed the territorial privileges of the nobility, and he gave permission to the bourgeois and the peasants to purchase land. He encouraged municipal life by introducing a system of election to municipal offices, and, as far as he could, abolished the social privileges of the nobility. Scharnhorst, as War Minister, reorganised the Prussian army on the French model. He changed it from an entity independent of the people into a national army. Since Prussia was only permitted to maintain an army of

42,000 men, he arranged that as many as possible should obtain a military training by passing through the ranks for a short period. He went further than Napoleon. He did not adopt a system of conscription by which a portion of the population designed by lot should enter the ranks, but insisted that every citizen was bound to military service. Between 1807 and 1810, and the system was continued after his retirement until 1813, Scharnhorst passed a large proportion of the youth of Prussia through the ranks of the army, and thus formed—what Napoleon so greatly needed at the crisis of his career—an effective reserve. It is interesting to observe that it was in the country most maltreated by Napoleon that the French reforms were most successfully initiated. Napoleon perceived the danger, and in 1808 he insisted on the dismissal of Stein, and in 1810 on that of Scharnhorst.

It is a curious sequel to the benefits conferred upon Germany by Napoleon directly and by the influence of French principles that their result was to rouse in Germany, for the first time for many centuries, a truly national feeling. This was caused chiefly by the suppression of the Holy Roman Empire, and its being replaced by states large enough to arouse national patriotism; but it was partly due also to a sense of national degradation inspired by the presence of French armies, and to the fact that the benefits conferred were the gift of a foreign sovereign and not the result of national progress. A universal feeling of opposition to the French grew up in the hearts of the German people. The individualist doctrines, which found favour in the eighteenth century and reached their highest expression in philosophers and poets, such as Herder and Goethe, gave way to a new national sentiment, inspired by a new school of poets and political thinkers represented by Körner and Arndt, by Jahn and Friedrich von Gentz. The new spirit was mainly developed among the German youth. Secret societies and clubs were formed to obtain by force the freedom of Germany from the French, and the dissatisfied

*The revival of German national feeling.*

souls forgot the benefits they had received individually in their resentment at their being granted by France. Austria under the administration of Count Philip Stadion, who was largely inspired by Gentz, endeavoured, in 1809, to take advantage of the revival of German national feeling. But Austria was universally considered as a foreign power whose military prowess was derived from Hungary, and the Emperor Francis in taking the new title of Emperor of Austria gave countenance to this idea. The House of Hapsburg was not regarded as thoroughly German; it was looked on as a foreign dynasty, whose dominions were mainly inhabited by non-German races; its loyalty to the Roman Catholic religion caused it to be suspected by the Protestants; it was blamed for the disorganisation of past centuries; and contemned for its repeated defeats by the French and its selfish policy at the time of the treaties of Campo-Formio and Lunéville.

Prussia, on the other hand, though, like Austria, it was not a truly German state, seemed fitted by history and tradition to embody the idea of German nationality. Even after the defeat of Jena, Frederick the Great and his victory over the French at Rossbach were recalled as distinctively German glories, and the eyes of patriotic Germans were turned to the diminished power of Prussia as the natural lever for the creation of a free Germany. The administrative system of Prussia and its strongly concentrated political theory of the essential unity of the State, as opposed to the new French idea of the omnipotence of the people, which was condemned in German eyes as having led to the absolutism of an adventurer, had always exercised a peculiar fascination over the best intellects of Germany. It was by means of statesmen of foreign birth that Prussia was reorganised and prepared to cope successfully with the power of Napoleon. Stein and Hardenberg, Scharnhorst and Gneisenau, York and Lombard were none of them native Prussians; yet they were all in turn attracted into the Prussian service, and were instrumental in bringing about her resurrection as a German power. The war of 1809 first showed Napoleon that he was soon to have a national feeling to deal with in Germany as well as in Spain. While Napoleon was in the neighbourhood of Vienna a Prussian lieutenant of the name of Katt attempted to seize Magdeburg; a Prussian major named Schill pillaged the arsenal and treasury of the Duke of Anhalt, who had often expressed his outspoken admiration for the French Emperor, and invaded Saxony; and the fourth son of the Duke of Brunswick, the heir to the duchy which had been absorbed in the kingdom of Westphalia, raised his Black Legion, which he termed the Army of Vengeance, and carried on a partisan war. Even the person of Napoleon was not safe in Germany. A lad named Staps was shot for imagining an attack on his life at Schönbrunn in 1809, and many other conspiracies were discovered by the French police. Napoleon despised this ebullition of popular feeling in Germany, just as he did in Spain, and the measures which he took against it, such as arbitrary arrests, and the shooting of the bookseller Palm, only exasperated the new national patriotism.

The Emperor, as has been said, was a great believer in the hereditary idea, and his not having children to succeed him was more than a personal, it was a political subject of grief to him. The campaign of Wagram had raised him to the height of his power, and he wished to establish his dynasty on a firm foundation. It was therefore for personal, for political, and for European motives, that he resolved on his return from Vienna in 1809 to divorce his wife, the Empress Josephine. It was from no dislike for his wife, but from a stern conviction of political necessity that he took this step. He insisted, that Josephine should preserve her title of Empress, he granted her Malmaison as her palace, with a large income, and he continued his favours to his step-children, Eugène de Beauharnais, and Hortense, the wife of his brother Louis Bonaparte. On the 15th of December 1809 the divorce was pronounced on the ground that the religious marriage, *Marriage of Napoleon with Marie Louise, 2nd April 1810.*

which had taken place on the day before his coronation as Emperor, was not valid because of the absence of witnessses. The Emperor's first intention was to wed a Russian grand-duchess. He was still enamoured of his idea of dividing the world with the Emperor Alexander, and considered that a relationship with that monarch would best ensure his power. But the Emperor Alexander was beginning to throw off his infatuation for Napoleon. He now perceived, that in the alliance he had made, he gave more than he got, and various causes of discontent were sedulously fomented by his Court and his family. It was further the custom of the Russian Court for the mothers to have the chief choice in the disposing of their daughters' hands. Now the Empress-mother was a princess of the House of Würtemburg, and had imbibed a profound hatred for the French Emperor. She persuaded her son to throw various delays in the path of the Emperor's desires without actually rejecting his offer. Under these circumstances, Napoleon abruptly changed his mind, and at the suggestion, it is said, of Prince Schwartzenberg, the Austrian ambassador at Paris, demanded the hand of an Austrian archduchess. The Emperor Francis thought it necessary to yield, and on the 2nd of April 1810, the marriage took place between the French Emperor and the young Archduchess Marie Louise. The ceremony was of the utmost magnificence, and a new Court was formed for the new Empress, which contained many French nobles who had refused to wait on Josephine. On the 20th of March 1811, a son was born to the French Emperor who was created in his cradle King of Rome, and this birth was regarded by Napoleon as finally cementing his power, both in France and in Europe.

During the period from the Treaty of Vienna in 1809 to the invasion of Russia in 1812, Napoleon had but one declared enemy. The English Ministers, despite the overthrow of Austria and Prussia, and the alliance between France and Russia, persisted in opposing

*The Peninsular War, 1810-1812.*

France. Just as Pitt and Grenville could not believe in the stability of the various French revolutionary governments, and therefore maintained the impossibility of concluding permanent peace with France, so their successors, Wellesley and Castlereagh, also declined to believe in the stability of Napoleon's Empire, and argued that no permanent peace could be made with him. It is just possible, that while Fox was in office in 1806, a peace might have been concluded, but the succession of his victories had inspired Napoleon with a belief in his own invincibility, and he had no idea of negotiating on any basis but the complete recognition of his reconstitution of Europe. Finding it impossible to break the naval power of England, he endeavoured to ruin her commerce by the Continental Blockade, with the result of increasing England's prosperity, and turning the people of the Continent against him.

Two methods of carrying on the war were supported by Castlereagh and Canning, who were Secretaries of State in the Portland administration from 1807 to 1809. Canning believed in rousing the national feeling of invaded states against the universal conqueror, and for this purpose sent large sums of money to Spain; Castlereagh, on the other hand, thought that as France could no longer meet England at sea, England must meet France on the land. This was the theory which lay at the bottom of the despatch of the first Portuguese and of the Walcheren Expeditions, and in spite of the failure of the latter, it has since been recognised as a correct theory. The victory of Wellington at Talavera, though it had but little actual result on the course of the war in Spain, kept Portugal free from French invasion during the year 1809. But it did more, it inspired the English governing class with the belief that they had at last discovered the right way of fighting Napoleon, and that they had also found a general. Lord Wellesley, the elder brother of Wellington, who was Foreign Secretary from 1809 to 1812, supported the new system with all his might, and under his encouragement

Wellington slowly formed the Anglo-Portuguese army by a series of campaigns into a magnificent fighting machine, which, though smaller in numbers than the Grand Army of France, equalled it in discipline and military efficiency.

Napoleon, after his successes in 1808, despised the Spanish levies and the English army. He therefore declined to go in person to the Peninsula, and sent his greatest marshal, Masséna, to drive the English out of Portugal. A plan of campaign was formed, by which Masséna was to penetrate Portugal from the north-east, while Soult was to advance from Andalusia in the south-east. The two marshals were to meet at Lisbon. Fortunately for Wellington, not only did Soult not agree with Masséna, but the latter marshal found it impossible to control his subordinates, Ney, Junot, and Reynier. Masséna nevertheless marched in the summer of 1810, and Wellington had to fall back before him. On September 27th, Masséna was repulsed in an attack upon the Anglo-Portuguese position at Busaco, but the English general felt it necessary to retreat further, to the lines which he had fortified in the neighbourhood of Lisbon, which are known as the lines of Torres Vedras. As Wellington retired, the Portuguese devastated their country, and when Masséna came to a halt in front of the lines of Torres Vedras, he found it most difficult to maintain himself on account of the scarcity of provisions. Soult did not come to his help as he had expected, but only advanced as far as the city of Badajoz, which he captured. Throughout the winter of 1810-11, Masséna remained in front of Wellington, but, in spite of reinforcements, he was unable to attack the Anglo-Portuguese lines, and in the spring of 1811, had to retreat into Spain.

*Campaign of 1810.*

Wellington then divided his army; with one portion he followed Masséna, and laid siege to Almeida, the other he despatched under Marshal Beresford to form the siege of Badajoz. In the south of Spain, the only city which held for the Junta was Cadiz, which was

*Campaign of 1811.*

defended by an Anglo-Spanish army. Marshal Victor was in charge of the besieging force, which was defeated at Barrosa on the 5th of March 1811. In spite of this diversion, Wellington had to meet fresh advances by the main armies of Soult and Masséna. On the 5th of May 1811, he repulsed Masséna at Fuentes de Onor after a hard-fought battle, which Masséna might have won had he been properly supported by Marshal Bessières. In the south, Soult was repulsed by Beresford at the battle of Albuera on May 16th. After having thus once more freed Portugal from French invasions, Wellington laid siege successively to Ciudad-Rodrigo and Badajoz. Though these border fortresses remained in French hands, the valour of the Anglo-Portuguese army surprised Napoleon, who recalled Masséna in disgrace. But in the east of Spain his generals met with some success. Suchet in 1810 and 1811 reduced Arragon and Valencia, took many fortresses, and destroyed the Spanish army in that quarter, under the command of General Blake, at the battle of Albufera. Throughout central Spain, though no regular Spanish armies took the field, the French were harassed by the Spanish guerillas. These patriotic brigands destroyed the morale of the French troops in Spain and sapped the strength of Napoleon. All the benefits conferred by Joseph Bonaparte, the abolition of feudalism and of the Inquisition, religious tolerance and good laws, counted for nothing. The Spaniards would receive no benefits from a French monarch imposed on them by Napoleon, and it was in Spain that Napoleon first felt the effect of a national opposition, which was at a later date in Russia and in Germany to destroy his power.

The period from the Conference of Erfurt to the invasion of Russia seemed to mark the height of Napoleon's power, but during it are to be perceived the symptoms of the changes which led to his fall. At Erfurt, Alexander of Russia was still his firm ally. His power was bounded by subject kingdoms, and divided by them from the great states of Europe. In France he was still regarded

Conclusion.

as the restorer of order and the supporter of religion. By 1812 the situation had changed. The Emperor Alexander was no longer his admirer and faithful ally. The vast extension of the Empire had weakened his power, and the French people were beginning to discover how dearly they were paying in the sacrifice of their individual liberty for the glory of one man. His wanton interference in Spain had raised a new force against him in the shape of the resistance of a nation, and had afforded the English an opportunity to meet him on land. In Germany, too, a national spirit was rising, and Prussia, which he had maltreated, was reorganised, and ready to set itself at the head of Germany. But there was one cause yet more significant which was developed during this period — the character of his soldiers was altered. The Grand Army, which had consisted of veterans trained in the wars of the Revolution, had wasted away at Austerlitz and Jena, Eylau and Friedland, and in the Spanish campaigns. At Wagram he felt how different were the men under his command, and was forced to depend largely on foreign contingents, of whose fidelity he could not be certain; and he was to find in 1812 that the conscripts of the Empire, though full of military ardour and desirous of rivalling the fame of their predecessors, had not the physical strength, the solidity, and the experience of the veterans who had made him Emperor of the French and Master of Europe.

# CHAPTER X

## 1812-1814

Causes of Growing Disagreement between Alexander and Napoleon—Intervention of Castlereagh and Bernadotte—The Attitude and Internal Policy of Prussia—Invasion of Russia by Napoleon—Battle of Borodino—Retreat of the French from Russia—Campaign of 1812 in the Peninsula—Battle of Salamanca—Policy of Bernadotte—Prussia declares War—First Campaign of 1813 in Saxony—Armistice of Pleswitz—Convention of Reichenbach—Congress of Prague—Austria declares War—Second Campaign of 1813 in Saxony—Battle of Dresden—Treaty of Töplitz—Battle of Leipzig—General Insurrection of Germany against Napoleon—Campaign of 1813 in the Peninsula—Battle of Vittoria—Wellington's Invasion of France—Negotiations for Peace—Proposals of Frankfort—The Allies invade France—Napoleon's first Defensive Campaign of 1814—Other Movements against Napoleon—Bernadotte—Holland—Battle of Orthez—Italy—Congress of Châtillon—Attitude of France towards Napoleon—Treaty of Chaumont—Napoleon's Second Defensive Campaign of 1814—Occupation of Paris by the Allies—The Policy of Talleyrand—The Provisional Government—Alexander's Speech to the French Senate—Napoleon declared to be no longer Emperor—Abdication of Napoleon—Provisional Treaty of Paris—Battle of Toulouse—Arrival of Louis XVIII., and his Assumption of the Throne of France—First Treaty of Paris.

THE causes of the disagreement between Napoleon and the Emperor Alexander dated back to the Treaty of Tilsit. At that time, though personally full of enthusiasm for the French conqueror, Alexander looked with suspicion on the formation of the Grand Duchy of Warsaw as a possible first step towards the restoration of Poland. Napoleon pointed out to him that he could obtain compensation in the direction of Sweden and of Turkey—a suggestion which led to the conquest of Finland and eventually of Bessarabia. Though Alexander carried out the projects proposed to him, he continued to resent the

*Gradual disagreement between Alexander and Napoleon.*

creation of the Grand Duchy of Warsaw, and still more the maintenance of French troops in that quarter. At the Congress of Erfurt Napoleon to some degree allayed the suspicions of his ally, but on his return to Russia there can be no doubt that Alexander looked upon himself as duped and badly treated. The war of 1809 widened the breach. Napoleon complained that the Russian troops promised for his assistance had not acted with vigour, and Alexander regarded with open discontent the cession of part of Austrian Galicia to the Grand Duchy of Warsaw. The dethronement of the Duke of Oldenburg, who had married Alexander's favourite sister, the Grand Duchess Catherine, and the absorption of his Duchy into the French Empire, in 1810, was another and more personal cause of disagreement. The delay in granting a Russian grand duchess to him in marriage was looked on by Napoleon as a personal slight, and his interference in Spain appeared to the Russian Emperor a sign that Napoleon could maltreat even his most faithful ally. The carrying out of the Continental Blockade embittered the situation. Napoleon complained that the Russians did not adhere loyally to the arrangement for the exclusion of English commerce. Alexander on his side complained that his country was being ruined by the blockade, while the French Emperor granted many licences to Frenchmen to trade with England.

To these political reasons must be added the personal characters of the two emperors. Napoleon, though he had spoken at Tilsit of dividing Europe between France and Russia, began, as his power increased, to devise schemes for securing the Empire of Europe for himself and the exclusion of Russia from any share. Instead of restoring the Empires of the East and West, Napoleon arrogated to himself the position of ruler of Europe, and spoke of thrusting Russia back into Asia. In these views he was encouraged by many of those surrounding him. His marshals, finding no profits to be got from Spain, looked forward to enriching themselves in Russia. His statesmen, either from motives of their own or to please his personal wishes, declared that France could not be safe until Russia was crushed. Alexander on his side was surrounded by bitter enemies of Napoleon. His ministers never wearied of emphasizing the ruin caused to Russia by the Continental Blockade. The King of Prussia, whom he had made his personal friend, pleaded for the complete restoration of his dominions. His family, and especially his mother, regarded Napoleon as the enemy of the human race; English agents were perpetually inciting the Russians to declare for commercial freedom; and three of the most accomplished and most able statesmen in Europe constantly urged him to war with France, namely, Stein, whom Napoleon had ordered the King of Prussia to dismiss; Pozzo di Borgo, a Corsican, who had known Napoleon in his youth, and who hated him as a personal enemy; and Nesselrode, a skilled diplomatist and an intimate friend of Metternich.

These various causes, both political and personal, might not then have led to war had it not been for the direct intervention of the English by means of the new Prince Royal of Sweden, Bernadotte. Lord Castlereagh, in January 1812, returned to office. He advocated the carrying on of the war against Napoleon, not only by reinforcing Wellington in the Peninsula, but by subsidizing the monarchs of the Continent. He therefore despatched three diplomatists to the three chief courts of the Continent, to endeavour to form a fresh coalition against Napoleon. These were his brother, Sir Charles Stewart, ambassador to Berlin, Lord Aberdeen to Vienna, and Lord Cathcart to St. Petersburg. Lord Cathcart was a distinguished military officer, and strenuously urged Alexander to declare war, and he brought with him several English officers to assist in reorganizing the Russian army, of whom the best known is Sir Robert Wilson. But it was rather through Sweden than directly that Castlereagh influenced the Emperor Alexander. Bernadotte, on being elected Prince Royal, had applied to Sweden the Continental Blockade against England, but he soon perceived how ruinous that policy was to his new country, and inclined to make some arrangement with England. Being unable to break with Napoleon by himself, Bernadotte acted as the intermediary between England and Russia, and in April 1812 signed a secret treaty with Alexander at Abo, by which Sweden renounced all claims on Finland on condition that Russia should promise Norway in its stead. Both England and Russia approved of this scheme. Frederick VI. of Denmark, who had succeeded his father, Christian VII., in 1808, had, after the capture of the Danish fleet in 1807, formed a most intimate alliance with Napoleon, and Alexander at Abo held out to Bernadotte, not only a hope that he might have the whole of Denmark as a result of successful war against the French, but even an expectation that he might eventually receive the throne of France as a reward for his services. Not less important than the English intervention in Sweden was the effect of English influence in Turkey; for it was through English mediation that the Treaty of Bucharest was signed in May 1812, which allowed the Emperor of Russia to concentrate all his military power against Napoleon.

Between France and Russia there remained, however, Austria, Poland, and Prussia. Though Napoleon's direct do-

*Prussia. The Ministry of Hardenberg.* main extended to Lübeck along the coast, he had not ventured to annex Germany proper, which lies between the Elbe and the Rhine, or to accept the title of German Emperor, in addition to that of the Emperor of the French and King of Italy, as had been suggested by the Prince Primate, Dalberg. Yet Germany proper, owing to his creation of the Confederation of the Rhine and the Kingdom of Westphalia, was so thoroughly under his influence that, from a military point of view, it might be regarded as part of his Empire. Austria, Poland, and Prussia were, however, more independent, and his first effort, when he decided to attack Russia, was to secure their active co-operation. The Emperor Francis, since the campaign of Wagram, had abandoned the idea of resistance. He feared and disliked the Russians;

Napoleon was his son-in-law, and he did not intend to oppose his wishes. He therefore promised willingly enough that an Austrian army should invade Russia to the south of the direct French invasion. In the Grand Duchy of Warsaw the Poles cared little for their Grand Duke, the King of Saxony; they looked to Napoleon for the restoration of their complete independence, and delighted in the thought of striking a blow at their old foes, the Russians. In Prussia the position was more complicated. Reduced as the kingdom was, the reforms of Stein and Scharnhorst had created a national feeling, which could not as yet be utilised in attacks on the French soldiers who occupied the Prussian fortresses. Stein himself had been driven from Prussia by Napoleon's orders, but a successor, Hardenberg, completed his work. It is significant that when Hardenberg was reappointed State Chancellor in 1810, he did not undertake the Foreign Office, as he had done in 1806, but the ministries of the Finance and the Interior. It was Hardenberg who in 1810 made the nobles subject to taxation, and brought Stein's promised Representative Assemblies into partial use; who, on 23rd January 1811, suppressed the Teutonic Order, and made its possessions part of the national domain; and who, on 11th September 1811, achieved the logical result of Stein's edict abolishing serfdom by granting the peasants power to become absolute proprietors of two-thirds of their holdings on surrendering the other third to the lords in full recognition of all feudal dues and servitudes.

Hardenberg's most ardent coadjutor was William von Humboldt. As Stein and Hardenberg had done the work of the French Revolution in Prussia by abolishing feudalism and securing equality before the law, so William von Humboldt established a national system of education in many respects similar to Napoleon's creation in France, and reformed the whole department of public instruction. At the head of the system was founded the University of Berlin. Prussia had deeply felt the loss of the University of Halle when that city was separated from Prussia by the Treaty of Tilsit. Königsberg, though made famous by Kant, was too distant from the centre of the reduced kingdom to fill its place, and the new national spirit was concentrated in the new University of Berlin. Learned men came from all parts of Germany. Savigny, Fichte, Wolf, Buttmann, Boeckh, Schleiermacher, and Niebuhr all enrolled themselves as professors; and Germany, not merely Prussia, found a worthy representative in the world of thought.

In the resurrection of Prussia King Frederick William III. merely acquiesced in the reforms of Stein and Hardenberg. But his former leaning to neutrality had given place to a desire for revenge on the French. In July 1810 he lost his patriotic wife, Queen Louise, and her death only exasperated his feelings. Nevertheless, he refused to declare himself on the side of Russia in 1812. The Emperor Alexander announced his policy of allowing the French to invade, and his intention of thus drawing Napoleon far from his base, and Frederick William felt that he was not strong enough to openly oppose the French Emperor. He was even constrained by the occupation of his fortresses to go further, and, on 24th February 1812, he signed an offensive and defensive alliance with Napoleon. By this treaty Prussia was not only to feed the French armies passing through her dominions to invade Russia, but to send an army of 30,000 men to act with them. Alexander was not displeased by this behaviour. He knew that Prussia could not help itself; he felt a sincere friendship for the hapless king; he understood that beneath the surface, not only Prussia, but all Germany was boiling with indignation against the French; and in 1812, when war was at hand, he summoned the inspirer of German national feeling, the great Prussian minister, Stein, from his exile in Austria to become his adviser and coadjutor in his German policy.

Without any actual declaration of war, Russia entered into negotiations with England, and Napoleon assembled a vast army

## Napoleon Invades Russia

on the banks of the Vistula. In May 1812 he entered Germany to take the command, and at Dresden had interviews with the King of Prussia and the Emperor of Austria. Of the 325,000 men with whom he crossed the river Niémen and invaded Russia only 155,000 were French; the remainder were foreign contingents. *The Invasion of Russia. May 1812.* He detached to his left Marshal Macdonald, with the Prussian contingent and some Westphalians and Poles, to attack Riga and advance on St. Petersburg, with the hope of joining Bernadotte and the Swedes; he was supported on his right by the Austrian subsidiary force, and with the centre of his army he advanced in person into Lithuania. That province being occupied, Napoleon crossed the Dnieper, and on the 18th of August he took Smolensk, in spite of the efforts of a Russian army of 80,000 men to cover the city. On his extreme right the Austrian army, under Prince Schwartzenberg, was checked by the arrival of the Russian army, set free by the Peace of Bucharest. The Russian generals, Barclay de Tolly and Bagration, in the centre, steadily retreated.

This military policy soon reduced the efficiency and numbers of the French army; for it was drawn further from its base into a barren country, in which it was harassed by peasants and guerillas, and it was necessary to leave large divisions to protect the communications. The Emperor Alexander had approved of this policy, and as the Russian army retired the people abandoned their villages, as the Portuguese had done during the invasion of Masséna in 1810. But the Russian soldiers grumbled at this politic retreat, and the Emperor Alexander resolved to strike one blow for his capital. Barclay de Tolly was replaced by Kutuzov, and the Russian army suddenly halted on the banks of the Mosková. On the 7th of September a most terrible battle was fought there, which is known as the battle of Borodino. The Russians are said to have lost 50,000 men, including General Bagration, and it is certain that the French lost more than 30,000. Nevertheless, the *Battle of Borodino. 7th Sept. 1812.*

PERIOD VII. U

French loss was proportionately the most; for Napoleon was far away from any reinforcements, whereas the Russians were fighting in their fatherland. On the 14th of September the French army occupied Moscow. On the 16th, either by accident or on purpose, fire broke out in the Russian capital. It raged for three days and three nights, and more than three-fifths of the city was utterly destroyed. The Emperor Alexander then entered into negotiations with Napoleon, and, whether he intended it or not, he kept the French Emperor from moving until too late for his safety. It was not until the 15th of October that Napoleon saw that negotiating was waste of time, and started from Moscow. The winter was an early one. Snow fell heavily. When Smolensk was reached, it was found that all the provisions stored there had been destroyed. The retreating army, now in a state of disorganisation, was hunted through the country, not only by the Russian soldiers, but by the peasantry returning to their homes. Marshal Ney covered the retreat, and won on this occasion his title of 'the bravest of the brave.' Napoleon, on being informed that a conspiracy against him, headed by General Malet, had been discovered in Paris, left the retreating army early in December. After his departure the cold increased. The retreat became a rout; Murat, who succeeded to the command, could not keep the army together; and but very few of the 155,000 Frenchmen who had invaded Russia recrossed the river Niémen.

While Napoleon was wrecking one army in Russia, Wellington was defeating another French army in Spain. Marmont, who had succeeded Masséna, failed to prevent the fall of Ciudad Rodrigo in January, or that of Badajoz in April, and after a long course of intricate manœuvres, gave Wellington the opportunity to attack and defeat him at the battle of Salamanca, July 22, 1812. The victory was complete. Joseph Bonaparte evacuated Madrid, and withdrawing all his troops from Andalusia fell back behind the Ebro. Wellington occupied Madrid on August 12, and then with his main army

*Campaign in the Peninsula. 1812.*

*Battle of Salamanca. 22d July 1812.*

advanced on Burgos. Burgos, however, resisted all his assaults. The Anglo-Portuguese army had to retire once more into Portugal, and Joseph Bonaparte for the last time returned to his capital. While this campaign was being fought Lord William Bentinck, who commanded the English garrison in Sicily, was requested to send troops to the eastern coast of Spain to effect a diversion. But the operations were badly combined; Sir John Murray was driven from before Tarragona; and at a subsequent date Lord William Bentinck himself failed to make an impression on Suchet's army at Alicante. The victory of Salamanca was a proof of the insecure foundation on which the throne of Joseph Bonaparte rested. Owing to it alone he had to leave Madrid, and evacuate the whole of southern Spain; the military policy of the English ministers was justified; and though Salamanca cannot be compared with the disasters in Russia, it yet had its effect in showing the increasing weakness of the French military power.

The retreat of the French and their passage of the Niémen enabled Prussia to throw off the mask of alliance with France. The Prussian contingent, amounting to 18,000 men, had been placed under the command of Marshal Macdonald, and was occupied in the siege of Riga. Napoleon had hoped that this detached army upon his left would be joined by Bernadotte at the head of the Swedes. But Bernadotte, as has been seen, had forgotten his French nationality in accepting the position of heir to the Swedish throne. His first idea was to make himself popular in Sweden by securing the conquest of Norway to take the place of Finland, and behind it lay the hope of possibly succeeding Napoleon himself. In his original communications with the Emperor Alexander, he had demanded the assistance of a Russian army for the conquest of Norway as the price of his adhesion to the coalition against Napoleon. When Alexander would not make a definite promise, Bernadotte applied to his former sovereign in June 1812, and promised to assist in the French invasion of Russia, if Napoleon would

*Prussia declares war. 16th March 1813.*

guarantee to him the possession of Norway. But the French Emperor would make no compact with his former marshal, and hoped that he would lend his assistance to the occupation of St. Petersburg in return for vague promises. Bernadotte therefore remained neutral, and Macdonald, without the expected help from Sweden, could get no further than Riga. The retreat of the main French army from Moscow made it necessary for Macdonald likewise to fall back, and in the course of his retreat the Prussian contingent, under the command of General York, deserted, and that general signed the Convention of Tauroggen, on 30th December 1812, by which he abandoned France without definitely declaring himself upon the side of Russia. Macdonald, with his Westphalians and Poles, managed to leave Russia in safety, and to join the remnants of the main army. But the desertion of York was a symptom of what was to follow. Stein summoned the Estates of East Prussia at Königsberg; the Prussians rose *en masse*, and the French army, pursued by the Russian troops and these new enemies, retreated behind the Vistula.

Frederick William of Prussia at last threw off the mask, and, on the 7th of February 1813, he called out the reserve which had been formed by the skilful military policy of Scharnhorst, and ordered the Landwehr and the Landsturm to join the colours; on 27th February he signed the Treaty of Kalisch with Russia, promising alliance; on 16th March he declared war against France; and he joined the headquarters of his friend Alexander, and lived in his company until the termination of the war. Prussian enthusiasm grew to its height; the reserves fell in from every city and district, and the broken French army, which was now left under the command of Eugène de Beauharnais, retreated first behind the Oder and then behind the Elbe, leaving powerful garrisons in Dantzic, Stettin, and the chief Prussian fortresses. The Russians of the army of the right pursued vigorously, and after driving the French from Berlin, the Russian generals, Chernishev and Tetterborn, took Hamburg. The resurrection of Prussia and the rapid retreat of the French caused Bernadotte to declare himself openly on the side of the allies, and he crossed the Baltic and entered Germany at the head of a Swedish army of 12,000 men. The King of Prussia's declaration of war with France was received with enthusiasm. Two separate Prussian armies were formed, the first under Bülow to act with the Swedes, and the Russian army of the right, and to defend Berlin, the other under Blücher in Silesia to co-operate with the second invading army of the left from Russia. The command in chief of this latter army was, after the death of Kutuzov in May, conferred on Barclay de Tolly, while Wittgenstein commanded the Russian contingent.

In the spring of 1813 Napoleon started for Germany to face the new coalition. His Westphalian, Bavarian, and Saxon allies were still true to him and increased their contingents. He called to his assistance the old soldiers who were employed in the garrisons of Holland and Northern Germany, and he raised a large number of fresh conscripts, who, in spite of their youth and inexperience, were at once directed upon Germany. At the head of 250,000 men, eventually increased to 300,000, he invaded Saxony. He defeated Wittgenstein at Lutzen or Gross Görschen on the 2d of May, at which battle his friend, Marshal Bessières was killed, and Scharnhorst was mortally wounded, and re-occupied Saxony. He defeated the whole of the allied army of Silesia at Bautzen on the 20th of May, and established his headquarters at Dresden. Meanwhile Vandamme had recaptured Hamburg, and, after placing it in a state of defence, joined the Emperor in Saxony. After these vigorous blows both sides desired a rest, and on the 3d of June the Armistice of Pleswitz was signed, and it was agreed that a congress should be held at Prague to consider if terms of peace could not be arranged. The important point to be decided at Prague was the position to be adopted by Austria; and both sides prepared to offer a high price for her active assistance, for her intervention would probably settle the result of the war. Napoleon trusted that his father-in-law, the Emperor Francis, would not abandon him, and counted upon the assistance of an Austrian army. He relied also upon the hereditary hatred of Austria for Prussia, and promised his father-in-law, as the price of his active assistance, not only the restoration of the Illyrian provinces, but of the whole of Silesia, which Frederick the Great had torn from Maria Theresa. Napoleon was even sanguine enough to count upon the former friendship which the Emperor Alexander had felt for him, and he hoped that the invasion of Russia would be forgiven if he guaranteed the possession of the whole of Poland. The country which would be sacrificed by these arrangements was Prussia. Napoleon projected the entire extinction of the Prussian kingdom, and suggested that the kingdom of Westphalia should be extended to the Oder. That he should venture to offer such terms showed how entirely Napoleon misunderstood his position. The Emperor Francis, although his daughter was Napoleon's wife, could not forget the humiliations that Austria had undergone, and allowed his feelings as an Austrian to outweigh his sentiments as a father. The Emperor Alexander had been entirely cured by the invasion of Russia of his former infatuation, and now distrusted the French Emperor as much as he had formerly believed in him; he had struck up an intimacy with the King of Prussia, and had promised him his restoration to the whole of his dominions.

Meanwhile the rulers of Austria, Russia, and Prussia signed a treaty at Reichenbach on 17th June 1813, by which Austria assumed the position of a mediator and promised to declare war against France, if the conditions of peace, which she should offer, were rejected. In return for this attitude, Austria was given a free hand to negotiate with the South German States, and the idea of rousing a national German feeling against France, which was strongly advocated by Stein, was abandoned. Metternich had no liking for the national idea; it seemed to him to bear the

*Convention of Reichenbach. 17th June 1813.*

imprint of the spirit of the French Revolution, and could only end in disaster to Austria. The rising of Prussia had indeed been a success, but if it spread through Germany, it might end in a united Germany with Prussia at its head, and the consequent depreciation of the Austrian power. The example of Spain, which Stein and patriotic Germans pointed to, seemed to cut in two ways; if, on the one hand, it had raised a people in arms against Napoleon, on the other it had encouraged revolutionary ideas. Both the Emperor Alexander and King Frederick William felt the weight of these arguments, and the conception of the war changed from a national uprising to a coalition of the usual type. Under these circumstances, Napoleon's propositions were ignored, and proposals were made to him on the other hand that he should be content with the natural limits of France, namely, the Rhine and the Alps; that he should restore the Bourbons to Spain and the independence of Holland; that he should abandon his position as head of the Confederation of the Rhine and allow the Pope to return to Rome. Murat was to remain at Naples, and Jerome on the throne of Westphalia, and the terms offered were by no means unfavourable to France, though perhaps hardly justified by the military position of the allies. Metternich, who perceived that Austria held the key to the position, brought these terms to Napoleon's headquarters at Dresden, and informed the Emperor that if they were not accepted, Austria would join the coalition against him.

Napoleon refused with scorn; Castlereagh, through the English ambassador, Lord Aberdeen, promised large subsidies to Austria; and on the 1st of August 1813, the Emperor of Austria promised definitely to join the allies with 200,000 men if Napoleon refused to accept the terms offered to him. The Congress met at Prague. Caulaincourt, the French plenipotentiary, stated that he had no power to accept the terms offered by Francis, and Austria, on the 12th of August, declared war against France. On the 14th of August, when it was too late, Napoleon declared his acceptance of the terms, and received the answer that the whole matter must be referred to the allied monarchs. War in fact was inevitable, and the Armistice of Pleswitz was at an end.

The intervention of Austria not only deprived Napoleon of

*Second Campaign of 1813 in Germany.*

an expected ally, but endangered his military position in Saxony, as a strong Austrian army was being concentrated in Bohemia under the command of Prince Charles von Schwartzenberg. Nevertheless the French Emperor refused to retire, and prepared at the head of 300,000 men to make face against the allies in spite of their great superiority in number. The plan of campaign of the allies was drawn up by Moreau, who had been induced to leave America and give the advantage of his advice to the Czar of Russia. There was also upon the staff of the Russian army one of the ablest strategists in Europe who, like Moreau, had formerly been an officer in the French army, General Jomini. The plan was to direct an army from the north, of Prussians, Russians and Swedes, under Bülow, Chernishev, and Bernadotte, an army from the east of Russians, called the Army of Poland, which was being formed under Benningsen, an army from Silesia, of Prussians under Blücher, and Russians under Wittgenstein, and finally an army of Austrians under Schwartzenberg, assisted by the Russian main army of Barclay de Tolly, and the Russian Imperial Guard under the Grand Duke Constantine, upon Dresden. But Napoleon with his accustomed rapidity of action determined to strike first, and he detached three corps under Oudinot, Macdonald and Vandamme, against Bernadotte, Blücher, and Schwartzenberg; Benningsen was too far in the rear to be dangerous. Oudinot and Macdonald were defeated by Bernadotte and Blücher at Gross Beeren and the Katzbach respectively, on the 23d and 25th of August, and Schwartzenberg, instead of waiting for the other armies, attacked the French centre at Dresden. On the 26th and 27th of August a terrible battle was fought, in which Moreau was mortally wounded. Napoleon was successful, but he suffered severe losses which he was unable

## The Treaty of Töplitz 313

to repair. Three days later he received the news that Vandamme's army, which had penetrated into Bohemia to cut off Schwartzenberg's communications, had been forced to capitulate at Kulm to the Russians under Barclay de Tolly. The battle of Dresden proved to the allies that it was impossible for one of their armies to overthrow Napoleon unassisted, and they therefore recurred to their original plan. Napoleon once more endeavoured to break from his defensive position and struck at Berlin; but Marshal Ney was defeated by Bernadotte and Bülow at Dennewitz, on 6th September, and he had to wait while the ring formed round him. The Emperor's losses during the first part of this campaign had been immense. He had lost over 10,000 men by the capitulation of Kulm; his young soldiers had been decimated at the Katzbach and Dennewitz; and the troops of the German contingents deserted *en masse*. In fact when the operations of the allies were completed and their armies had concentrated around Leipzig, to which place he had withdrawn, he had not more than 160,000 men, whose confidence was shaken by repeated defeats, to oppose to more than double that number.

After the battle of Dresden, the army of Schwartzenberg retired into Bohemia, and the allied monarchs determined to define their position as to the future. The enormous armies they were concentrating made them feel sure of success, if they held together. On 9th September the important Treaty of Töplitz was signed. By this treaty it was agreed that Prussia and Austria should be restored as nearly as possible to the limits they had held in 1805, that the Confederation of the Rhine should be dissolved, and that entire independence should be granted to the states of southern and western Germany. This decision overcame the lingering hesitation of the south German monarchs, who had feared retaliation from the allies for their consistent adhesion to Napoleon. Of these states, Bavaria was the chief, and on 8th October the Treaty of Ried was signed

Treaty of Töplitz. 19th Sept. 1813.

between Austria and Bavaria, by which Bavaria promised the aid of 36,000 men in return for complete indemnity and the recognition of complete sovereignty in her dominions. Then the allies in their full strength attacked Napoleon. For three days, from the 16th to the 19th of October, the terrible battle of Leipzig was fought. The result was a foregone conclusion, and even without the desertion of the Saxons in the course of the battle, the ruin of the French army was certain. Napoleon's forces were not only defeated, they were destroyed, and in the utmost disorder the routed French divisions fled in a state of disorganisation across Germany. At this moment Maximilian Joseph of Bavaria, whom Napoleon had made a king, declared against him as he had promised, and not only withdrew the Bavarian contingent, but endeavoured to check the French retreat. At the battle of Hanau on October the 30th, however, the remnant of the French army broke through the Bavarians, and it eventually found safety behind the Rhine.

*Battle of Leipzig. 16th—19th October 1813.*

*Battle of Hanau.*

The battle of Leipzig was followed by a general rising throughout central Europe against the French. The secret societies which had been formed to promote the idea of the freedom of Germany acted in every direction. Many isolated regiments of the French army were cut off and the French garrisons in the various German cities were closely besieged. The benefits which had been conferred by French administration were forgotten and the people thought only of the humiliation of the French occupation. Nor was this spirit confined to Germany. The Dutch rose in rebellion, and declared in all the chief cities of Holland for the Prince of Orange. That prince at once left England and set himself at the head of the insurgents, and Lord Castlereagh a few months later sent to his assistance an English force under the command of Sir Thomas Graham to reduce the few Dutch fortresses still occupied by French garrisons. In Italy also an almost universal insurrection

*Insurrection of Germany against Napoleon 1813.*

broke out against the French domination. Lord William Bentinck, who commanded the English army which occupied Sicily, sailed to Genoa with a powerful force and encouraged the insurgents in that quarter. Meanwhile an Austrian army under General Hiller invaded Italy from the north-east and defeated Eugène de Beauharnais at Valsarno on the 26th of October. Against this unanimity of national opposition Napoleon could make but little headway; the French people were tired of the conscription; they had not approved of the invasion of Russia; and were indisposed at the moment of crisis to support the Emperor.

While the French armies were suffering the succession of disasters which expelled them from Germany, a similar series of catastrophes occurred in Spain. Wellington broke up from his quarters in the summer of 1813, and marching in a north-easterly direction attempted to cut off all communication between France and Madrid. This movement completely overthrew the French domination in Spain. Joseph Bonaparte with all the troops he could collect fled from Madrid. He was unable to defend himself behind the Ebro as in 1812, for the positions on that river had been skilfully turned. Wellington eventually came up with the French army at Vittoria. There Marshal Jourdan, who commanded for King Joseph, endeavoured to resist, but he was completely defeated by the Anglo-Portuguese army on the 21st of June 1813. This victory drove the French back into France, for Suchet was likewise obliged to abandon his conquests in Valencia, and to retire into the mountains of Arragon and Catalonia. The victory in the field was followed as in Germany by a burst of national enthusiasm. The Spanish guerillas destroyed every isolated French post, and even managed to place some serviceable divisions at the disposition of Wellington. The English general took up a position on the French frontier between Pampeluna and San Sebastian, blockading the former and besieging the latter place. To face him Soult was sent to the

*Campaign in the Peninsula 1813.*

*Battle of Vittoria. 21st June.*

south-west of France to defend the frontier. On the 31st of August San Sebastian was stormed; Pampeluna speedily fell; and Wellington was able to establish a new base of operations, and to invade France. On the 10th of November the Anglo-Portuguese army drove Soult from his positions on the Nivelle, and after the battles of the Nive or Saint Pierre from the 9th to the 13th of December Wellington invested Bayonne.

*Wellington invades France. Oct. 1813.*

These repeated disasters in different quarters induced Napoleon to consider the advisability of concluding a peace. He was now only too ready to accept the terms offered to him at the Congress of Prague. The allies were by no means so united as they seemed. The Austrian Minister Metternich, in particular, was not desirous of destroying the power of France. England had no wish to come to any conclusion which should disproportionately increase the strength of Russia, and the aim of all the allied monarchs was to allow France to develop in her own way as long as she withdrew her pretensions to interfere in Europe. Metternich's proposals, in November 1813, were that France should preserve her natural limits of the Rhine and the Alps, but should restore all former rulers in Holland, Italy, and Spain. Napoleon gave evidence of his desire for peace at this period by the dismissal of his Foreign Secretary, Maret, Duc de Bassano, and the appointment of Caulaincourt, Duc de Vicenza, who was known to be in favour of peace and was also a personal friend of the Emperor Alexander, at whose Court he had been ambassador during the palmy days of the alliance between France and Russia. The terms of peace offered by Metternich, which are known as the Proposals of Frankfort, at which city the allied monarchs were residing, were confided to M. de Saint Aignan, a French diplomatist who had been taken prisoner during the advance of the allies and who was the brother-in-law of Caulaincourt. The proposals were definitely acceded to by Lord Aberdeen on the part of England and by Hardenberg on the part of Prussia. The

*Negotiations for Peace.*

favourable nature of them was dictated by the fear entertained by the allied monarchs that France would rise in her might as she had done in 1793 if her borders were invaded. For this reason the allies remained for some weeks upon the right bank of the Rhine, concentrating their forces and hesitating to advance. Napoleon, however, could not understand that he was beaten. Instead of replying at once to the Proposals of Frankfort, which were dated the 9th of November, it was not until late in December that he instructed Caulaincourt to go to the allied quarters and discuss them. His instructions to Caulaincourt showed how little he appreciated the position of affairs. He demanded that, in addition to the natural limits of France, he should hold the cities of Wesel, Cassel opposite Mayence, and Kehl opposite Strasbourg on the right bank of the Rhine, which fairly signified that he did not abandon his projects on Germany. He further demanded that a kingdom should be formed for his brother Jerome in Germany, and for Eugène de Beauharnais in Italy. Before these counter-propositions reached the headquarters of the allied monarchs, they had resolved to invade France, and the opportunity was gone for ever for France to attain her natural limits under the sanction of Europe.

The attitude of the allies, as indicated in the Proposals of Frankfort, was mainly dictated by Metternich, who did not desire to see his Emperor's son-in-law dethroned or to see France greatly weakened. But the Emperor Alexander and his friend, the King of Prussia, soon repented of the assent they had given to Metternich's ideas. Alexander desired to invade France as a reply to the invasion of Russia in 1812, and hoped to occupy Paris as Napoleon had occupied Moscow. The King of Prussia, and still more his generals and ministers, had felt most keenly the humiliating condition to which Prussia had been degraded, and desired to wreak their vengeance on France. It was therefore agreed that since the Proposals of Frankfort had not been promptly accepted, the result of a

*The Invasion of France 1814. First Campaign.*

successful invasion of France should be the return of that country into the limits she possessed at the beginning of the wars of the Revolution. The attitude of Russia and Prussia was that adopted by England. Lord Castlereagh heard with dismay, that it was intended to allow France the limits of the Rhine, for by that concession she would hold Belgium and Antwerp, which it had been the consistent policy of all English Ministers for many generations to keep independent of France. The barrier treaties of former days, and the wars against Louis XIV. had been sustained for the purpose of keeping France out of the Belgian Netherlands, and the English cabinet resolved to continue this classic policy. For this purpose, Lord Castlereagh was in person despatched to the headquarters of the allied monarchs, with the greatest powers ever granted to a British statesman. He was given 'full powers to negotiate and conclude of his own authority, and without further consultation with the government, all conventions or treaties, either for the prosecution of war or for the restoration of peace.'[1]

Lord Castlereagh sailed from Harwich on the 31st of December 1813, on which day Blücher with the main Prussian army, known as the Army of Silesia, crossed the Rhine in three columns at Coblentz, Mannheim, and Mayence. Blücher was supported by three Russian *corps d'armée*, but it was further south that the main Russian army in conjunction with the Austrians invaded France under the command of Schwartzenberg. It was not without some difficulty that the Emperor Alexander was induced to consent to the violation of the neutrality of Switzerland. But the military arguments put forward by his generals overcame his scruples. By marching through Switzerland, Schwartzenberg's army was enabled to turn the mountains of the Jura, and to leave the French fortresses on the Rhine, behind him. This invasion on two distinct lines gave Napoleon the opportunity

[1] Alison's *Lives of Lord Castlereagh, and Sir Charles Stewart*, vol. ii p. 241.

of carrying out one of the military manœuvres of which he was most fond. He concentrated between the two invading armies a force of between 50,000 and 70,000 men. This was a terrible falling off from the vast armies with which he had invaded Russia in 1812, and fought the allies in Saxony in 1813; it was a falling off not only in numbers, but in military efficiency, for with the exception of the remnant of the Guard, he had only under his command some regiments of conscripts and national guards untrained to war. At this period Napoleon bitterly repented the mistake he had made, in leaving over 150,000 veteran soldiers as garrisons in the various fortresses in Europe. The presence of these men would very likely have turned the scale. He had left, for instance, 12,000 men in Hamburg under the command of Marshal Davout, 16,000 in Magdeburg, 8000 in Dantzic, and large garrisons in other distant cities, such as Stettin. These fortresses were blockaded by local militia; their occupation did not withdraw many regular troops from the allied armies, while it fatally weakened the resources of France.

Nevertheless, with his boy conscripts and his Guard, Napoleon fought one of his greatest campaigns. Blücher foolishly scattered his troops, after his entry into Champagne. Napoleon quickly took advantage of his mistake. He cut up division after division of Blücher's army at Brienne, Champaubert, Montmirail, and Vauchamps, between the 29th of January and the 14th of February, and then turning against Schwartzenberg, who had also scattered his forces, he defeated a Russian division at Nangis, and an Austrian division at Montereau on the 17th and 18th of February. These rapid blows startled and disconcerted the allies. Blücher's army was practically destroyed; Schwartzenberg fell back, and asked for an armistice; and proposals were made for the evacuation of France. It was only the constancy of the Emperor Alexander and the determination of Lord Castlereagh which induced the allies to persist. Two *corps d'armée*, one of Prussians under Bülow, the other of

Napoleon's Victories in France. 1814.

Russians under Wintzingerode, were on Lord Castlereagh's sole authority detached from Bernadotte's army and ordered to reinforce Blücher. Meanwhile, Alexander insisted that Schwartzenberg should concentrate instead of retiring. In reality, Napoleon's successes were more fatal to himself than to the allies, for they induced him to break off the negotiations at the Congress of Châtillon.

While the first campaign of 1814 was being fought out in Other movements against Napoleon. 1814. France, the movement against Napoleon was becoming general. Bernadotte had after the victory of Leipzig been placed in command of the army in northern Germany. Full of the idea which had been suggested to him by the Emperor Alexander in 1812, that he might succeed Napoleon on the throne of Bernadotte. France, Bernadotte did not wish to appear before his own countrymen in the light of an invader. He had occupied himself for some weeks after the battle of Leipzig with blockading Davout in Hamburg, and fighting the Danes in Holstein. Even if he could not obtain the throne of France, he was quite resolved to win Norway, and for this purpose he attacked the Danes, and after some fighting, compelled Frederick VI. of Denmark to sign the Treaty of Kiel on 14th January 1814, by which Denmark ceded Norway to Sweden, in exchange for Swedish Pomerania. Bernadotte even went so far as to negotiate with Davout, to whom he promised a free passage to France with all his troops as the price of the surrender of Hamburg. But the Emperor Alexander would not submit to this, and Bernadotte was imperiously ordered only to leave a blockading force before Hamburg, and to advance to the French frontier.

It was at this juncture that Bernadotte was deprived of his two finest *corps d'armée*, which were ordered up to the assistance of Blücher. But in addition to the danger threatened Holland. by Bernadotte's army, Napoleon also met with serious opposition in the Netherlands. The Dutch people declared for the Prince of Orange, and Holland was quickly lost. A force under the command of the Prince marched into Belgium, and besieged Antwerp, which was defended by the former member of the Committee of Public Safety, Carnot, who, though neglected by Napoleon in the days of his greatness, had come to the help of France in the time of her distress. To assist the Prince an English division under Sir Thomas Graham had, as has been said, been despatched to Holland. Graham failed to take Bergen-op-Zoom on the 20th of February, but his presence in the Netherlands not only encouraged the Dutch, but prevented Napoleon from obtaining help from that quarter.

In the south, Marshal Augereau, whom the Emperor had placed in command at Lyons, was, as he himself said, no longer the Augereau of Castiglione. He had been directed to make a diversion against the Austrian left as it entered France with some conscripts and troops drawn from the former Army of Spain, but he remained inactive, and his operations were of no assistance to the Emperor. In the south-west corner of France, Soult was unable to do more than make head against Wellington and the Anglo-Portuguese army. After the battles of the Nive or of Saint Pierre, Bayonne was completely invested, and Wellington, leaving the left of his army to carry on the siege, marched eastwards against Soult. That marshal had been weakened by the detachments he had been ordered to send to Augereau, and to Napoleon himself. Nevertheless, he made a gallant stand at Orthez on the 27th of February, but was defeated and forced to fall back further into France. *Augereau.* *Wellington wins battle of Orthez. 27th February 1814.*

In Italy the Viceroy, Eugène de Beauharnais, who in the retreat from Russia had given evidence that he was a general of the very first order, offered a gallant resistance to the Austrians under General Hiller. But the defection of the King of Bavaria, his father-in-law, opened the passes of the Tyrol to the Austrians, and Eugène de Beauharnais was then compelled to retreat. At the *Italy.*

commencement of 1814, Metternich entered into negotiations with Murat, the King of Naples. Through the influence of his wife, Caroline Murat, sister of Napoleon, with whom Metternich had been in most intimate relations when he was ambassador at Paris, Murat, in the hope of preserving his kingdom, issued a violent proclamation against his benefactor, Napoleon, and advanced to the banks of the Po, at the head of a Neapolitan army of 80,000 men. This movement caused Eugène de Beauharnais, whose fidelity to his stepfather shines out in bright contrast to the treachery of Murat, to fall back still further. He defeated the Austrians under Marshal Bellegarde on the Mincio on the 8th of February, but was unable to follow up his success owing to the position of Murat. In his rear, Lord William Bentinck had landed at Genoa and issued a proclamation promising independence to that city, and the support of England in securing the independence and unity of Italy. Napoleon at one time thought of calling Eugène de Beauharnais to his side, but his rapid victories over the isolated *corps d'armée* of the allies in February caused him to abandon this wise project.

It has been said that one effect of Napoleon's victories was to break up the Congress of Châtillon. It had been suggested that a congress should meet at Mannheim at the time of the Proposals of Frankfort, but Napoleon's delay prevented it from assembling until after the invasion of France was an accomplished fact. The success of this invasion altered the attitude of the allies towards France. They saw that the French nation was not going to arise in its might as it had done in 1793. They heard through sure hands that the people were almost in open rebellion against the Emperor. The Legislative Body had dared to oppose his wishes. Everywhere the conscription was evaded, and there was a muttered feeling throughout France that the country had had enough of war and that it was time that the blood-tax on the French youth should cease. Even the army itself was beginning to

The Congress of Châtillon. 3d Feb.-19th March 1814.

despair. The Emperor had lost his prestige in Russia and at Leipzig. His soldiers were not the veterans of his former wars; his generals and his marshals began to murmur and to fear that a war à *outrance* would end in their personal ruin. Under these circumstances the Congress of Châtillon met on the 3d of February 1814. The French plenipotentiary was Caulaincourt, the most upright of Napoleon's statesmen. The other powers nominated, not their chief ministers, Metternich, Nesselrode, Hardenberg, and Castlereagh, although they were all at headquarters, but subordinate diplomatists, namely, Count Philip Stadion, the predecessor of Metternich, for Austria, William von Humboldt for Prussia, Razumovski for Russia, and Lord Cathcart, Lord Aberdeen, and Sir Charles Stewart for England.

At Châtillon very different conditions from the Proposals of Frankfort were offered. The main stipulation was that France should return to her limits before the Revolution. England haughtily declared that the naval question with regard to the rights of neutrals was not to be mentioned, and everything was made subject to the great question of the French limits. Caulaincourt disputed the proposals on the ground that it was unfair that France should be reduced to the limits she had held in 1789 while the other powers had been so vastly increased by the rearrangement of Germany and the partition of Poland. Nevertheless he was most anxious that Napoleon should accept these proposals. He granted that they were worse than the Proposals of Frankfort, but argued that if the war continued they were likely to be worse still. Napoleon, however, looked upon the Congress as an opportunity for gaining time. He believed that by his military successes he would avert the disasters which threatened him, and on the day of the battle of Montereau, the 18th of February, he wrote that he was only willing to agree to a peace on the basis of the Frankfort Proposals, and in his own handwriting he added to his despatch to Caulaincourt, 'Sign nothing.'[1] It

[1] Fain, *Manuscrit de l'An* 1813, pp. 297, 298.

is worthy of note that in the Proposals of Châtillon nothing was said about Napoleon himself. The Emperor Francis assumed that his son-in-law would remain upon the throne of France, and Lord Castlereagh expressed no view to the contrary. But the English Minister was absolutely determined not to yield to Napoleon's demand for the natural limits of France. England was the paymaster of the coalition, and Castlereagh having just promised £10,000,000 to pay the military expenses of 1814 felt that he had the right to insist on his demand. Napoleon in after years declared that his persistence in retaining Belgium was the reason for his refusal to accede to the Proposals of Châtillon. 'Antwerp,' he said to Las Cases, 'was to me a province in itself; it was the principal cause of my exile to Saint Helena, for it was the required cession of that fortress which made me refuse the terms offered at Châtillon. If they would have left it to me peace would have been concluded.'[1] Metternich wrote to Caulaincourt pressing the acceptance of the Proposals of Châtillon, but Napoleon obstinately refused, and the Congress had practically failed by the beginning of March, though it did not actually break up until the 19th of that month.

The fact that the French nation did not rise in arms against the invaders has been mentioned as the primary cause for the difference between the terms offered at Frankfort and at Châtillon.

*Attitude of France towards Napoleon.*

Nothing proves more completely how thoroughly Napoleon had extinguished the spirit of the Revolution than the lukewarmness with which his call to arms was received in 1814. In 1793 the invasion of France had caused a frenzy of patriotism. The people had submitted to the Reign of Terror, because it meant a strong government which could expel the English, Prussians, and Austrians. France was at that time hemmed in by difficulties infinitely greater than those which she had to face in 1814. Then she had no great general. In 1814 she possessed one of the greatest generals

---

[1] Las Cases, *Mémorial de Sainte-Hélène*, vol. vii. pp. 56, 57.

the world has ever seen. In 1793 she was torn by civil war in La Vendée and by brigands in every sparsely populated district. In 1814 she had enjoyed fifteen years of internal tranquillity. In 1793 her finances were utterly disordered, her industries were destroyed, and the whole country a prey to anarchy. In 1814 she had been for years the chief nation in Europe, and the wealth of other countries had been drained to enrich her. But the difference was that in 1793 and the succeeding years the French people felt that they were fighting to ward off the interference of foreign nations in their internal affairs, whereas in 1814 they were called on to defend the power of a single man who had infringed the rights and the freedom of other nations. By his bureaucratic system Napoleon had crushed out the power of popular initiative which had been the strength of the Republic; by his suppression of individual liberty he had made the majority of the French people disaffected to his Empire.

There must be considered also the exhaustion of actual physical resources. In the campaigns of 1812 and 1813, it is estimated that nearly 750,000 Frenchmen were either killed, wounded, or taken prisoner. Before that time the Grand Army had been slowly destroyed on many a field of battle, and there simply were not sufficient men of military instinct and physical strength to fill the ranks. In 1813 Napoleon enrolled the conscripts whose turn would have come in 1815—mere boys of sixteen, who had melted away after the battle of Leipzig—and the men he called to the ranks in 1814 were those who had been passed over by the conscription in previous years, and were too long inured to civil life to be willing to serve as soldiers.

To the feeling that resistance to the invaders was not a national duty, must be added a general indisposition to support the Empire. The opinions which had found vent during the French Revolution had not been extinguished by the Empire; they had only been suppressed; and all the educated part of the nation was united in desiring representative institutions so as to exercise a share in directing the policy of the government. This opinion showed itself in the Legislative Body which was summoned in December 1813. Napoleon had announced that his cause was the cause of France; but in return the leaders of the Legislative Body only begged him to make peace. A paragraph was inserted in the report of the Legislative Body upon the Proposals of Frankfort, which contains the following words : 'It belongs to the Government according to the Constitution to propose the most effectual means to repel the enemy and secure peace. These means will only be effectual if the French people are convinced that their blood will be shed only to defend the country and our protective laws. It appears, therefore, indispensable that at the same time that His Majesty shall propose the most prompt and efficacious measures for the safety of the State, the Government should be besought to maintain the entire and constant execution of the laws which guarantee to the French people the rights of liberty, security, and property, and to the nation the complete enjoyment of its political rights. That guarantee appears the most effectual means for restoring to the French people the energy necessary for their defence in the present crisis.' Napoleon was much irritated by this attack on his arbitrary authority, and although this paragraph was expunged from the report by 254 votes to 223 he nevertheless dissolved the Legislative Body in a rage.

Neither at the Congress of Châtillon nor in the Legislative Body was a single word said about restoring the Bourbons. They had lost all credit during their exile. The French people did not want them. The allied powers did not care about them. By Lord Castlereagh's orders Wellington received the Duc d'Angoulême, son of the Comte d'Artois, in his camp in the south of France, but he distinctly refused to recognise him in any way whatever. The English general went further and issued a proclamation in which he declared that the war was being waged for security to Europe, not for a change of dynasty in France, and that no interference was

*The Bourbons.*

either intended or would be permitted in the free decision of the French people with regard to their internal government. When the Duc d'Angoulême was favourably received in Bordeaux and the Mayor of that city hoisted the white flag, Wellington wrote to the Bourbon prince defining his attitude and censuring the assertion in the Duke's proclamation, that he was supported by England.

In spite of his real weakness Napoleon was so infatuated by his successes in February 1814 that, as has been said, the Congress came to an end, but he was not far wrong in his estimation of the effect of his victories upon the allied monarchs. So profoundly was Schwartzenberg terrified by the destruction of Blücher's army and the victories of Nangis and Montereau that he wished to retreat from France. Differences between the powers at this juncture threatened to break up the coalition, and it was only the determination of Lord Castlereagh that kept them together. The English minister on the 1st of March 1814 concluded the secret Treaty of Chaumont. By this treaty the relations of the allied monarchs to each other on several points were defined, and though many fresh causes of dissension arose at a later date, it was the Treaty of Chaumont which kept the powers together until the overthrow of Napoleon, and which laid the basis of the final settlement at Vienna. By this treaty the four great powers, England, Russia, Austria and Prussia, bound themselves, if France refused to return within her ancient limits, to form an offensive and defensive alliance. Each member of the coalition was to maintain 150,000 men in the field, and England bound herself, in addition to paying her own contingent and maintaining her navy, to contribute a subsidy of £5,000,000 a year to be divided equally amongst the other three contracting parties. As England by this arrangement offered more than twice as much as any other country, Castlereagh practically became the master of the coalition. After peace was concluded each of the powers was to furnish a contingent of 60,000 men if any

*Treaty of Chaumont. 1st March 1814.*

one of them were attacked. The resettlement of Europe was to be arranged on the following bases: that the German Empire should be restored as a federal union; that Holland and Belgium should be united into a monarchy under the House of Orange; that Spain should be restored to its ancient sovereign; that Italy should be divided into independent states; and that Switzerland should be guaranteed as independent and neutral by all the great powers.

The result of the Treaty of Chaumont was to stiffen the attitude of the allies in France. All thought of retreat was abandoned and both the Austrians under Schwartzenberg, and the Army of Silesia under Blücher recommenced their advance upon Paris. Napoleon pursued the tactics which had been crowned with success in the month of February, and prepared to strike at each of the invading armies in turn. His first movement as before was against Blücher. The Army of Silesia had been reduced by the actions of Champaubert, Montmirail, etc., from 60,000 to 30,000 men, but it was now increased to more than its former number by the arrival of Saint Priest's Russians and of the two corps of Bülow and Wintzingerode which had been detached from Bernadotte by Lord Castlereagh. Napoleon was not aware of the extent of these reinforcements, and he therefore with his army of barely 30,000 men ventured to attack Blücher. On the 7th and 9th of March, the severe actions of Craonne and Laon were fought. Neither side won victories, but Napoleon failed to repeat his former successes, which was tantamount to a defeat. After the battle of Laon both Blücher and Napoleon reviewed the armies at their disposal, and the disparity of their strength is shown by the fact that whereas Blücher reviewed 109,000 men, Napoleon found that including all reinforcements, he had but 46,000. Having failed to check the Prussians, Napoleon turned to attack Schwartzenberg's army. On the 20th of March he fought an action at Arcis-sur-Aube, in which the Russians repulsed the French attack. The Emperor then

*Napoleon's Second Campaign in France. March 1814.*

resolved on a final effort. He determined to attack the lines of communication of the invaders, and marched towards the Vosges Mountains. But the invaders were in too strong force to be terrified by this manœuvre. A few divisions only were left to watch him, and the main armies continued their advance on Paris. On March the 30th, Schwartzenberg and Blücher arrived in front of the French capital. They had under their command about 200,000 men, whereas Marshals Marmont and Mortier, who had been charged with the defence of Paris, could not get under arms more than 28,000 including the National Guard. In spite of this enormous difference of strength the two marshals took up a position and prepared to defend Paris. But after the most obstinate resistance the allies carried the French position after ten hours' fighting on the 30th of March, and on the following day the Emperor Alexander and the King of Prussia entered Paris. Napoleon rapidly followed the allied army, but the occupation of Paris was fatal to his cause. He was ready to continue the war, but his marshals were not. On the 4th of April Ney, Macdonald, Oudinot, and Lefebvre had an interview with the Emperor, and told him that the army would fight no more. Napoleon was obliged to give heed to their remonstrances, and he sent Ney, Macdonald, and Caulaincourt to make what arrangements might be possible with the allied monarchs.

*Battle of Paris. 30th March 1814.*

*Occupation of Paris by the Allies.*

On entering Paris the Emperor Alexander and King Frederick William proceeded at once to the residence of Talleyrand. That astute statesman quickly decided upon a definite policy. He understood that the allies had hitherto treated with Napoleon, and that they were not favourably disposed to the Bourbons. He knew that the French nation did not desire the return of the former dynasty. But he felt that the only method which would enable France to take up a logical position on the Continent was by the restoration of the Bourbon monarchy. If Louis XVIII. were accepted as King of France, it would be a

*The Provisional Government at Paris.*

contradiction in terms to their professed belief in hereditary rights, and their hatred for the results of the Revolution, for the allied monarchs to attack the unity of France. For this reason Talleyrand persuaded Alexander that it would be inadmissible either to accept the government of the Empress Marie Louise in the name of her son, the King of Rome, or still less to recognise Alexander's candidate, Bernadotte. In his own words to the Emperor: 'Any attempt to create a Regency or to appoint Bernadotte is a mere intrigue; nothing remains but Bonaparte or the Bourbons.' Alexander then declared that he would no longer treat with Napoleon, and Talleyrand as Vice-Arch-Chancellor of the Empire summoned the Senate to meet upon the 1st of April.

The Senate at once elected a Provisional Government consisting of Talleyrand as President and the Comte de Bournonville, former War Minister of the Republic, the Comte de Jaucourt, a former leader of the Legislative Assembly, the Abbé de Montesquiou, a former leader of the Constituent Assembly, and the Duc de Dalberg, nephew of the Prince Primate of Germany. The Senate then resolved that, whatever government should be adopted, the sale of the national and ecclesiastical estates in the days of the Revolution should be ratified, the liberty of worship and of the press established, and a general amnesty declared. On the following day the Emperor Alexander addressed the Senate. He said: 'It is neither ambition nor the love of conquest which has led me hither; my armies have only entered France to repel unjust aggressions. Your Emperor carried war into the heart of my dominions when I only wished for peace. I am a friend of the French People; I impute their faults to their chief alone; I am here with the most friendly intentions; I wish only to protect your deliberations. You are charged with one of the most glorious missions which generous men can discharge,—that of securing the happiness of a great people, in giving France institutions, at once strong and liberal, with which she cannot dispense in the advanced state of civilisation to which she has attained.' Alexander in conclusion, as a sign of his goodwill, declared that he would release the 150,000 French prisoners of war then in Russia.

That evening the Senate solemnly declared Napoleon to be no longer Emperor, and formed a Provisional Ministry, including Comte Beugnot, Minister of the Interior, Baron Louis, Minister of Finance, and General Dupont, who had been disgraced for the Capitulation of Baylen, Minister for War. Matters had reached this stage when Napoleon's emissaries Ney, Macdonald, and Caulaincourt, arrived at the headquarters of the allied monarchs. These faithful adherents proposed that Napoleon should abdicate in favour of his infant son. This offer, which would have been gladly received some days before, was now rejected, owing to the influence of Talleyrand, and on April the 6th, when Napoleon received the news of this rejection, he unconditionally abdicated at Fontainebleau. This step was made necessary by the fact that the faithful marshals could not even speak in the name of the whole army on behalf of Napoleon. Marshal Marmont, who had distinguished himself in the great battle before Paris, had made separate terms for himself and placed his army at the disposal of the allies. The desertion of Marmont deprived Napoleon of the greater part of the forces on which he relied, and rendered his unconditional abdication necessary. *Abdication of Napoleon. 6th April 1814.*

The abdication of Napoleon was followed by the arrival of Lord Castlereagh in Paris. The English minister had since the breaking up of the Congress of Châtillon remained at the headquarters of the Emperor of Austria at Dijon. It was there that he had entered into intimate relations with Metternich, relations which were to lead to most important results. On the 11th of April 1814, the Provisional Treaty of Paris was signed. It was essentially a treaty between the Emperor Napoleon, through his plenipotentiaries, and the allied monarchs. It was not a treaty with France, for Louis XVIII. *Provisional Treaty of Paris. 11th April 1814.*

had not arrived from England, or been recognised as king, and the Provisional Government could only enter into provisional arrangements. By this treaty, which was signed by Caulaincourt, Macdonald, Ney, Metternich, Nesselrode, Hardenberg, and Castlereagh, Napoleon renounced for himself and his descendants the Empire of France and the Kingdom of Italy. He was, however, to retain the title of Emperor; the island of Elba was erected into an independent principality for him, and an income of £180,000 a year was granted to him. The duchies of Parma and Piacenza were secured in full sovereignty to the Empress Marie Louise, and after her decease to the King of Rome, and the divorced Empress Josephine was given an annuity of £40,000 a year.

**Battle of Toulouse. 10th April 1814.** On the day before this treaty was signed, April 10th, 1814, the Battle of Toulouse was fought. Wellington after his victory of Orthez had rapidly followed Soult into the heart of Southern France. When he attacked the French positions in front of Toulouse, he was ignorant of the great events which had been passing at Paris and at Fontainebleau, and it was only after his entrance into the city that he perceived the white cockade was being worn.

On the 20th of April 1814, Napoleon bade farewell to the **Arrival of Louis XVIII.** Guard at Fontainebleau, and started for Elba, and on the 24th his successor, Louis XVIII., who had not entered France since his escape in 1791, landed at Calais. The new King was eminently fitted by his natural character, which had been matured by his long exile, for a constitutional monarch, but unfortunately he was surrounded by men who had shared his exile, and who did not share his placable disposition. On the 2d of May, when he had reached the neighbourhood of Paris, Louis XVIII. published what is known as the Declaration of St. Ouen. In this declaration, he promised a constitution to the French people, which should provide among other things for a representative government with two chambers, complete liberty of worship and the press, the right of the representatives to grant taxation, the inviolability of all property, including national and ecclesiastical estates, which had been sold during the Revolution, the responsibility of the ministers, irremoveability of the judges, and complete equality before the law. On the following day, he entered Paris amid general rejoicings, for the French people had forgotten their grievances of olden time in the memory of their more recent sufferings in the latter years of Napoleon. He was not in any way treated with by the Provisional Government; his return was tacitly accepted as inevitable; and he returned to the Tuileries as of divine right, without any bargain being made with him.

The first important duty which fell to Louis XVIII. was the signature of a definitive treaty of peace with the allies. The evacuation of French territory by the invaders had been arranged with the Provisional Government on the 23d of April, and the foreign troops were already beginning to retire. By the definitive Treaty of Paris, which was negotiated by Talleyrand on behalf of Louis XVIII., it was agreed that France should return to her limits of 1792. By this arrangement, the early annexations of the Revolution before the outbreak of war were secured to France. These additions included Avignon and the County of the Venaissin, which had formerly belonged to the Pope, and several districts in Alsace, of which the most noteworthy were the Principality of Montbéliard formerly the property of the King of Würtemberg, and the Republic of Mulhouse. France also received Chambéry, and part of Savoy, with certain rectifications of the frontier in the neighbourhood of Geneva, and on the north-eastern border. All the former French colonies, except the islands of the Mauritius, Tobago, and Saint Lucia, were restored to France. With regard to other countries, it was agreed, as had been laid down in the Treaty of Chaumont, that Germany was to become a Confederacy instead of an Empire, that Holland and Belgium were to be united, that Italy was to be divided into independent states,

*First Treaty of Paris. 30th May 1814.*

and that the independence of Switzerland was to be guaranteed by all the great powers. At the same time that this treaty was signed, a secret treaty was agreed to between the four invading powers, without consulting France. This secret treaty dealt largely with the future apportionment of the territories on the left bank of the Rhine which had been administered by France ever since 1794. It was roughly agreed that these provinces should be annexed to Prussia, and it was further laid down, that Austria should possess the whole of Lombardy, and that Genoa should be united to Sardinia. The details of this arrangement, and the many other questions which were certain to arise were adjourned, and it was settled that they should be considered at a great congress which was to meet at Vienna.

The two nations which had done the most to overthrow the excessive power of Napoleon were England and Russia, and the two men most conspicuously concerned were the Emperor Alexander and Lord Castlereagh. The two rival German powers, Austria and Prussia, naturally inclined to different sides. Prussia was the declared ally of Russia; the Emperor Alexander and the King Frederick William had formed one of the romantic personal friendships which Alexander loved; and the Russian and Prussian ministers were in perfect accord in desiring to punish France and her allies, and to aggrandise themselves. Austria on the other hand naturally inclined to support England. Both feared the increasing preponderance of Russia; both felt that enough had been done in deposing Napoleon, and did not desire to wreak vengeance on France; both were inclined to be moderate in their demands. This rivalry between Russia with Prussia, and Austria with England had appeared in its incipient stages before the Treaty of Chaumont, and it was to rise to its height during the Congress of Vienna. The return of the Bourbons to France was to have an important result on the rivalry between the allies, and it is a significant proof of the inherent power of France, and of the greatness of the ascendency which she had won, that she was enabled at Vienna to act the most decisive part. The overthrow of Napoleon had not really weakened France; she had lost her natural territorial limits of the Rhine and the Alps which she might have obtained but for the stubbornness of Napoleon; nevertheless, she was still strong enough to be feared, and in the day of her greatest disaster she was able to exert a greater influence in the affairs of Europe than she had ever done since the time of Louis XIV.

# CHAPTER XL

## 1814-1815

The Congress of Vienna—Monarchs and Diplomatists present—History of the Congress—Treaty between France, Austria, and England—The Questions of Saxony and Poland—The German Confederation—Disposition of the provinces on the left bank of the Rhine—Mayence and Luxembourg —Reconstitution of Switzerland—Rearrangements in Italy—Questions of Murat, Genoa, and the Empress Marie Louise—Sweden—Denmark— Spain—Portugal—England's share of the spoil—The Questions of the Slave Trade and the Navigation of Rivers—Close of the Congress—Preparations against Napoleon—The first reign of Louis XVIII. in France— Napoleon's return from Elba—The Hundred Days—The Campaign of Waterloo—Occupation of Paris—Second Treaty of Paris—Napoleon sent to Saint Helena—The Holy Alliance—Return of Louis XVIII.—Government of the Second Restoration—The Chambre Introuvable—Reaction in Spain and Naples—Territorial Results of the Congress of Vienna—The Principle of Nationality—Permanent Results of the French Revolution in Europe—The Problem of harmonising the Principles of Individual and Political Liberty with that of Nationality.

**Congress of Vienna.** ON the 1st of November 1814 the diplomatists who were to resettle Europe as arranged by the definitive Treaty of Paris met at Vienna. But many of the monarchs most concerned felt that they could not give their entire confidence to any diplomatist, however faithful or distinguished, and they therefore came to Vienna in person to support their views. The final decision of disputes obviously lay in the hands of the four powers which by their union had conquered Napoleon. These four powers solemnly agreed to act in harmony and to prepare all questions privately, and then lay them before the Congress. In fact they intended to impose their will upon the smaller states of Europe just as Napoleon had done.' That they did not succeed and that

## The Congress of Vienna 337

their concert was broken was due to the extraordinary ability of Talleyrand, the first French plenipotentiary. The history of the Congress is the history of Talleyrand's skilful diplomacy, and the resettlement of Europe which it effected was therefore largely the work of France.

The Emperor Francis of Austria acted as host to his illustrious guests. The royalties present were the Emperor Alexander of Russia, with his Empress, the Grand Duke Constantine, and his sisters, the Grand Duchesses Marie of Saxe-Weimar and Catherine of Oldenburg; the King of Prussia with his nephew Prince William; the King and Queen of Bavaria, the King and Crown Prince of Würtemburg, the King of Denmark, the Prince of Orange, the Grand Dukes of Baden, Saxe-Weimar, and Hesse-Cassel, the Dukes of Brunswick, Nassau, and Saxe-Coburg. The King of Saxony was a prisoner of war and absent. *Monarchs and Diplomatists present.*

The plenipotentiaries of Russia were Count Razumovski, Count von Stackelberg, and Count Nesselrode, who were assisted by Stein, the former Prussian minister, and one of Alexander's most trusted advisers, by Pozzo di Borgo, the Corsican, now appointed Russian ambassador to Paris, by Count Capo d'Istria, the future President of Greece, by Prince Adam Czartoryski, one of the most patriotic Poles, and by some of the most famous Russian Generals, such as Chernishev and Wolkonski. The Austrian plenipotentiaries were Prince Metternich, the State Chancellor, the Baron von Wessenberg-Ampfingen, and Friedrich von Gentz, who was appointed to act as Secretary to the Congress.

England was represented by Lord Castlereagh, Lord Cathcart, Lord Clancarty, and Lord Stewart, Castlereagh's brother, who as Sir Charles Stewart had played so great a part in the negotiations in 1813, and who had been created a peer for his services. The English plenipotentiaries were also aided by Count von Hardenberg, and Count von Münster, who were deputed to represent Hanoverian interests. The Prussian plenipotentiaries were Prince von Hardenberg, the State

Chancellor, and William von Humboldt, who in military matters were advised by General von Knesebeck. The French representatives, whose part was to be so important, were Talleyrand, Prince of Benevento, the Duc de Dalberg, nephew of the Prince Primate, the Marquis de la Tour du Pin, and the Comte Alexis de Noailles. These were the representatives of the great powers. Among the representatives of the lesser powers may be noted from the importance of their action, Cardinal Consalvi, who represented the Pope, the Count of Labrador for Spain, Count Palmella for Portugal, Count Bernstorf for Denmark, Count Löwenhielm for Sweden, the Marquis de Saint-Marsan for Sardinia, the Duke di Campo-Chiaro for Murat, King of Naples, Ruffo, for Ferdinand King of the Two Sicilies, Prince von Wrede for Bavaria, Count Wintzingerode for Würtemburg, and Count von Schulemburg for Saxony. In addition to these plenipotentiaries representing powers of the first and second rank, were innumerable representatives of petty principalities, deputies for the free cities of Germany, and even agents for petty German princes mediatised by Napoleon in 1806.

When Talleyrand with the French legation arrived in Vienna he found, as has been said, that the four great powers had formed a close union in order to control the Congress. His first step therefore was to set France forth as the champion of the second-rate states of Europe. The Count of Labrador, the Spanish representative, strongly resented the conduct of the great powers in pretending to arrange matters, as they called it, for the Congress. Talleyrand skilfully made use of Labrador, and through him and Palmella, Bernstorf and Löwenhielm managed to upset the preconcerted ideas of the four allies, and insisted on every matter being brought before the Congress as a whole, and being prepared by small committees specially selected for that purpose. His next step was to sow dissension amongst the great powers. As the champion of the smaller states he had already made France of considerable importance, and he

*History of the Congress.*

then claimed that she too had a right to be treated as a great power and not as an enemy. His argument was that Europe had fought Napoleon and not France; that Louis XVIII. was the legitimate monarch of France; and that any disrespect shown to him or his ambassadors would recoil on the heads of all other legitimate monarchs. He claimed that France had as much right to make her voice heard in the resettlement of Europe as any other country, because the allied monarchs had distinctly recognised that she was only to be thrust back into her former limits and not to be expunged from the map of Europe. Having made his claim good on the right of the legitimacy of his master to speak for France as a great power equal in all respects to the others, he proceeded to sow dissension among the representatives of the four allied monarchs. This was not a difficult thing to do, for the seeds of dissension had long existed. The difference he introduced was that in speaking as a fifth great power, and as the champion of the smaller states, France became the arbiter in the chief questions before the Congress.

The division between the great powers was caused by the desire of Russia and Prussia for the aggrandisement of their territories. The Emperor Alexander wished to receive the whole of Poland. His idea, which was inspired by his friend, Prince Adam Czartoryski, was to form Poland into an independent kingdom ruled, however, by himself as Emperor of Russia. The Poles were to have a new Constitution based on that propounded in 1791, and the Czar of Russia was to be also King of Poland, just as in former days the Electors of Saxony had been Kings of Poland, but he was to be an hereditary, not an elected, sovereign. To form once more a united Poland, Austria and Prussia were to surrender their gains in the three partitions of Poland. Austria was to receive compensation for her loss of Galicia in Italy; Prussia was to be compensated for the loss of Prussian Poland by receiving the whole of Saxony. As it had been already arranged that Prussia was to receive the bulk of the Rhenish territory on the left bank of the Rhine in addition to her great extensions of 1803, the result would be to make Prussia by far the greatest power in Germany. Talleyrand was acute enough to perceive that Lord Castlereagh did not approve of the extension of the influence of Russia, and that Metternich was equally indisposed to allow Prussia to obtain such a wholesale aggrandisement. Saxony had been the faithful ally of France to the very last, and Talleyrand felt that it would be an indelible stain on the French name if it were thus sacrificed. He was cordially supported in this view by his new master, for though the King of Saxony had been the faithful ally of Napoleon, Louis XVIII. did not forget that his own mother was a Saxon princess. Working, therefore, on the feelings of Castlereagh and Metternich, he induced England and Austria to declare against the scheme of Russia and Prussia.

The Emperor Alexander and Frederick William blustered loudly; they declared that they were in actual military possession of Poland and of Saxony, and that they would hold those states by force of arms against all comers. In answer, Talleyrand, Castlereagh, and Metternich signed a treaty of mutual alliance between France, England, and Austria, on the 3d of January 1815. By this secret treaty the three powers bound themselves to resist by arms the schemes of Russia and Prussia, and in the face of their determined opposition the Emperor Alexander gave way. Immediately Napoleon returned from Elba he found the draft treaty between the three powers on the table of Louis XVIII. and at once sent it to Alexander. That monarch, confronted with the danger threatened by Napoleon's landing in France, contented himself with showing the draft to Metternich and then threw it in the fire. The whole of this strange story is of the utmost interest; it proves not only the ability of Talleyrand, but the inherent strength of France. It is most significant that within a few months after the occupation of Paris by the allies for the first time France should again be recognised as a great power, and form the main factor in breaking up the cohesion of the alliance, which had been formed against her.

## Alliance between England, Austria, and France 341

The result of Talleyrand's skilful policy was thus to unite England, Austria, and France, supported by many of the secondary states, such as Bavaria and Spain, against the pretensions of Prussia and Russia. Powerful armies were immediately set on foot. France in particular raised her military forces from 130,000 to 200,000 men, and her new army was in every way superior to that with which Napoleon had fought his defensive campaigns in 1814, for it contained the veteran soldiers who had been blockaded in the distant fortresses or had been prisoners of war. England too was enabled to make adequate preparations, for on December the 24th, 1814, a treaty had been signed at Ghent between the United States and England which put an end to the war which had been proceeding ever since 1812 on account of England's naval pretensions. Bavaria also promised to put in the field 30,000 men for every 100,000 supplied by Austria. Although the secret treaty of January 3d was not divulged until after the return of Napoleon from Elba, the determined attitude of the opposition caused the Emperor Alexander to give way. It was decided that instead of the whole of Saxony, Prussia should only receive the district of Lusatia, together with the towns of Torgau and Wittenberg; a territory which embraced half the area of Saxony and one-third of its population. The King of Saxony, who had been treated as a prisoner of war, and whom the Emperor of Russia had even threatened to send to Siberia, was released from captivity, and induced by the Duke of Wellington, who succeeded Lord Castlereagh as English plenipotentiary in February 1815, to agree to these terms. The salvation of Saxony was a matter of great gratification to Louis XVIII., who remembered that though the king had been the faithful ally of Napoleon, he was also his own near relative.

*Secret Treaty of 3d Jan. 1815.*

*Treaty of Ghent. Dec. 24, 1814.*

*Settlement of Saxony.*

Since Prussia was obliged to give up her claim to the whole of Saxony, Russia also had to withdraw from her scheme of uniting the whole of Poland. Nevertheless, Russia retained the lion's share of the Grand Duchy of

*Settlement of Poland.*

Warsaw; in 1774 her frontier had reached the Dwina and the Dnieper; in 1793 she obtained half of Lithuania as far as Wilna; in 1795 she annexed the rest of Lithuania and touched the Niémen and the Bug; in 1809 Napoleon had granted her the territory containing the sources of the Bug; and now in 1815 her borders crossed the Vistula, and by the annexation of the Grand Duchy of Warsaw, including that city, penetrated for some distance between Eastern Prussia and Galicia. Prussia received back its share of the two first partitions of Poland, with the addition of the province of Posen and the city of Thorn, but lost Warsaw and its share in the last partition; while Austria received Cracow, which was to be administered as a free city. Alexander was deeply disappointed by the frustration of his Polish schemes, but he nevertheless kept his promise to Prince Adam Czartoryski and granted a representative constitution and a measure of independence to Russian Poland.

Though the great diplomatic struggle arose over the combined question of Saxony and Poland, the most important work of the Congress was not confined to it alone. Committees were appointed to make new arrangements for Germany, Switzerland, Italy, and to settle other miscellaneous questions. Of these committees the most important was that which reorganised Germany. It had been arranged by the secret articles of the Treaty of Paris that a Germanic Confederation should take the place of the Holy Roman Empire. The example of Napoleon and his institution of the Confederation of the Rhine was followed and developed. Instead of the hundreds of small states which had existed at the commencement of the French Revolution, Germany, apart from Austria and Prussia, was organised into only thirty-eight states. These were the four kingdoms of Hanover, Bavaria, Würtemburg, and Saxony; the seven grand duchies of Baden, Oldenburg, Mecklenburg-Schwerin, Mecklenburg-Strelitz, Hesse-Cassel, Hesse-Darmstadt, and Saxe-Weimar; the nine duchies of Nassau, Brunswick, Saxe-Gotha,

*The Germanic Confederation.*

## The Germanic Confederation

Saxe-Coburg, Saxe-Meiningen, Saxe-Hildburghausen, Anhalt-Dessau, Anhalt-Bernburg, and Anhalt-Köthen; eleven principalities, two of Schwartzburg, two of Hohenzollern, two of Lippe, two of Reuss, Hesse-Homburg, Liechtenstein, and Waldeck, and the four free cities of Hamburg, Frankfort, Bremen, and Lübeck. The number of thirty-eight was made up by the duchies of Holstein and Lauenburg, belonging to the King of Denmark, and the grand duchy of Luxembourg, granted to the King of the Netherlands. In its organisation the Germanic Confederation resembled the Confederation of the Rhine. The Diet of the Confederation was to be always presided over by Austria and was to consist of two Chambers. The Ordinary Assembly was composed of seventeen members, one for each of the larger states, one for the free cities combined, one for Brunswick, one for Nassau, one for the four duchies of Saxony united, one for the three duchies of Anhalt united, and one for the smaller principalities. This Assembly was to sit permanently at Frankfort and to settle all ordinary matters. In addition there was to be a General Assembly to be summoned intermittently for important subjects, consisting of sixty-nine members returned by the different states in proportion to their size and population. Each state was to be supreme in internal matters, but private wars against each other were forbidden as well as external wars by individual states on powers outside the limits of the Confederacy. In the territorial arrangements of the new Confederation, the most important point is the disappearance of all ecclesiastical states. The Prince-Primacy, which Napoleon had established in his Confederation of the Rhine, was not maintained, and Dalberg, who had filled that office throughout the Empire, was restricted to his ecclesiastical functions.

The most difficult problem to be decided was the final disposition of the districts on the left bank of the Rhine, which had been ruled by France ever since 1794. It had been settled by the secret articles at Paris that these dominions should be used for the

*Territorial arrangements on the Rhine.*

establishment of strong powers upon the borders of France. The main difficulty was as to the disposition of the important border fortresses of Mayence and Luxembourg. Prussia laid claim to both these places, but was strongly resisted by Austria, France, and the smaller states of Germany. It was eventually resolved that Prussia should receive the northern territory on the left bank of the Rhine, stretching from Elten to Coblentz, and including Cologne, Trèves, and Aix-la-Chapelle. In compensation for the Tyrol and Salzburg, which she was forced to return to Austria, and in recognition of her former sovereignty in the Palatinate, Bavaria was granted a district from the Prussian borders to Alsace, including Mayence, which was designated Rhenish Bavaria. Finally, Luxembourg was formed into a grand duchy, and given as a German state to the House of Orange. It was not united to the new kingdom of the Netherlands, which was formed out of Holland and Belgium, but was to retain its independence under the sovereignty of the King of the Netherlands. The union of the provinces of the Netherlands was one of the favourite schemes of England, and was carried into effect in spite of the well-known feeling of opposition between the Catholic provinces of Belgium and the Protestant provinces of Holland.

As in its re-organisation of Germany, so in the settlement of Switzerland, the Congress of Vienna followed the example set by Napoleon. The Emperor had quite given up the idea which had fascinated the French Directory of forming Switzerland into a Republic, one and indivisible. He had yielded to the wishes of the Swiss people themselves, and organised them on the basis of a confederation of independent cantons. The Congress of Vienna continued Napoleon's policy of forbidding the existence of subject cantons in spite of the protests of the Canton of Berne. Napoleon's cantons of Argau, Thurgau, Saint-Gall, the Grisons, the Ticino, and the Pays de Vaud were maintained, but the number of the cantons was raised from nineteen to twenty-two by the formation of the three new cantons of Geneva, the Valais, and Neufchâtel, which had formed part of the French Empire. The Canton of Berne received in reply to its importunities the greater part of the former Bishopric of Basle. The Swiss Confederation as thus constituted was placed under the guarantee of the great powers and declared neutral for ever. The Helvetic Constitution, which was promulgated by a Federal Act dated the 7th of April 1815, was not quite so liberal as Napoleon's Constitution. Greater independence was secured in that the constitutions of the separate cantons and organic reforms in them had not to be submitted to the Federal Diet. The prohibition against internal custom houses was removed. The presidency of the Diet was reserved to Zurich, Berne, and Lucerne alternately, and the Helvetic Diet became a Congress of Delegates like the Germanic Diet rather than a Legislative Assembly. It is to be noted that in spite of the declaration of the Congress of Vienna, Prussia refused to renounce her claims on her former territory of Neufchâtel, the independence of which as a Swiss canton was not recognised by her until 1857.

The resettlement of Italy presented more than one special problem. The most difficult of these to solve was caused by the engagements entered into by the allies with Murat in 1814. Talleyrand, on behalf of the King of France, insisted on the dethronement and expulsion of Murat, while Metternich from friendship for Caroline Murat wished to retain him in his kingdom. The Emperor Alexander, who ever prided himself on his fidelity to his engagements, wished to protect Murat, and had at Vienna struck up a warm friendship with Eugène de Beauharnais, Napoleon's Viceroy of Italy. Murat, ungrateful though he was personally toward Napoleon, had yet imbibed his master's ideas in favour of the unity and independence of Italy. During the campaign of 1814, he had led his army to the banks of the Po, and he persisted in remaining there after the Congress of Vienna had met. But the diplomatists at Vienna had no wish to accept the great idea of Italian unity. Murat's aspirations in this direction were most annoying to them, and it was with real pleasure that they heard after the landing of Napoleon from Elba that Murat had by an indiscreet proclamation given them an excuse for an open declaration of war. The Duke di Campo-Chiaro, Murat's representative at Vienna, had kept him informed of the differences between the allied powers, and an indiscreet note asking whether he was to be considered as at peace or at war with the House of Bourbon gave the plenipotentiaries their opportunity. War was immediately declared against him; an Austrian army defeated him at Tolentino on the 3d of May 1815, and he was forced to fly from Italy. The acceptance of Murat's ambassador, who spoke in his name as King of the Two Sicilies, made it difficult for the Congress to know how to treat with Ruffo who had been sent as ambassador by Ferdinand, the Bourbon King of the Two Sicilies, who had maintained his power in the island of Sicily through the presence of the English garrison. Acting on the ground of legitimacy, it was difficult to reject Ferdinand's claims, which were warmly supported by France and Spain, but Murat's ill-considered behaviour solved the difficulty, and after his defeat Ferdinand was recognised as King of the Two Sicilies. Murat, later in the year, landed in his former dominions, but he was taken prisoner and promptly shot.

Another Italian question which presented considerable difficulty was the disposal of Genoa and the surrounding territory. When Lord William Bentinck occupied that city, he had in the name of England promised it independence and even hinted at the unity of Italy. Castlereagh unfortunately felt it to be his duty to disavow Bentinck's declaration, and Genoa was united to Piedmont as part of the kingdom of Sardinia. The third difficult question was the creation of a state for the Empress Marie Louise. An independent sovereignty had been promised to her. She was naturally supported by her father, the Emperor Francis of Austria, and was ably represented at Vienna by her future husband, Count

Neipperg. It was eventually resolved that she should receive the duchies of Parma, Piacenza, and Guastalla, but the succession was not secured to her son, the King of Rome, but was granted to the rightful heir, the King of Etruria, who, until the succession fell in, was to rule at Lucca. The other arrangements in Italy were comparatively simple. Austria received the whole of Venetia and Lombardy, in the place of Mantua and the Milanese, which she had possessed before 1789. The Grand Duchy of Tuscany, with the principality of Piombino, was restored to the Grand-Duke Ferdinand, the uncle of the Emperor Francis of Austria, with the eventual succession to the Duchy of Lucca. The Pope received back his dominions including the Legations of Bologna and Ferrara, and Duke Francis, the grandson of Hercules III., was recognised as Duke of Modena, to which duchy he would have succeeded had not Napoleon absorbed it in his kingdom of Italy.

The arrangements with regard to the other states of Europe made at the Congress of Vienna were comparatively unimportant, and did not present the same difficult problems as the resettlement of Germany, Switzerland, and Italy. Norway in spite of its disinclination was definitely ceded to Sweden, but Bernadotte had to restore to France the West-Indian island of Guadeloupe, which had been handed over to him by England in 1813, as part of the price of his alliance. Denmark had by the Treaty of Kiel with Bernadotte been promised Swedish Pomerania in the place of Norway. This promise was not carried out. Denmark like Saxony had been too faithful an ally of Napoleon not to be made to suffer. Swedish Pomerania was given to Prussia, and Denmark only received the small Duchy of Lauenburg. By these arrangements both Sweden and Denmark were greatly weakened, and the Scandinavian States, by the loss of Finland and Pomerania, surrendered to their powerful neighbours, Prussia and Russia, the command of the Baltic Sea. Spain, owing to the ability of the Count of Labrador,

*Other States.*

*Sweden.*

*Denmark.*

*Spain.*

and the support of Talleyrand, not only lost nothing except the island of Trinidad, which had been conquered by England, but was allowed to retain the district round Olivenza, which had been ceded to her by Portugal in 1801. The desertion of Portugal by England in this particular is the chief blot on Lord Castlereagh's policy at Vienna. The Portuguese army had fought gallantly with Wellington, and there was no reason why she should have been forced to consent to the definite cession of Olivenza to Spain when other countries were winning back their former borders. Portugal was also made to surrender French Guiana and Cayenne to France. England, though she had borne the chief pecuniary stress of the war and had been more instrumental than any other power in overthrowing Napoleon, received less compensation than any other country. She kept Malta, thus settling the question which led to the rupture of the Peace of Amiens; she received Heligoland, which was ceded to her by Denmark, as commanding the mouth of the Elbe; and she was also granted the protectorate of the Ionian Islands, which enabled her to close the Adriatic. Among colonial possessions England took from France the Mauritius, Tobago, and Saint Lucia, but she returned Martinique and the Isle of Bourbon, and forced Sweden and Portugal to restore Guadeloupe and French Guiana. With regard to Holland, England retained Ceylon and the Cape of Good Hope, but she restored Java, Curaçao, and the other Dutch possessions. In the West Indies also, she retained, as has been said, the former Spanish island of Trinidad.

One reason for Castlereagh's moderation at Vienna is to be found in the pressure that was exerted upon him in England to secure the abolition of the slave-trade. It is a curious fact that while the English plenipotentiary was taking such an important share in the resettlement of Europe, the English people were mainly interested in the question of the slave-trade. The great changes which were leading to new combinations in Europe, the aggrandisement of

Prussia, the reconstitution of Germany, the extension of Austria, all passed without notice, but meetings, in Lord Castlereagh's own words, were held in nearly every village to insist upon his exerting his authority to abolish the trade in negro slaves. Castlereagh therefore lent his best efforts, in obedience to his constituents, to this end. The other ambassadors could not understand why he troubled so much about what seemed to them a trivial matter. They suspected a deep design, and thought that the reason of England's humanity was that her West Indian colonies were well stocked with negroes, whereas the islands she was restoring were empty of them. The plenipotentiaries of other powers possessing colonies in the tropics therefore refused to comply with Castlereagh's request and it was eventually settled that the slave-trade should be abolished by France after five, and by Spain after eight years. Castlereagh had to be content with this concession, but to satisfy his English constituents he got a declaration condemning the slave-trade assented to by all the powers at the Congress. Another point of great importance which was settled at the Congress of Vienna was with regard to the navigation of rivers which flow through more than one state. It had been the custom for all the petty sovereigns to impose such heavy tolls on river traffic that such rivers as the Rhine were made practically useless for commerce. This question was discussed by a committee at the Congress, and a code for the international regulation of rivers was drawn up and generally agreed to.

*The Navigation of Rivers.*

These matters took long to discuss, and might have taken longer had not the news arrived at the beginning of March 1815 that Napoleon had left Elba and become once more undisputed ruler of France. In the month of February the Duke of Wellington had succeeded Lord Castlereagh as English representative at Vienna, for the latter nobleman had to return to London to take his place in Parliament. At the news of the striking event of Napoleon's being once more at the head of a French army

*Close of the Congress of Vienna. June 1815.*

all jealousies at Vienna ceased for the time. The Duke of Wellington was taken into consultation by the allied monarchs, and it was resolved to carry into effect the provisions of the Treaty of Chaumont. The great armies which had been prepared for a struggle amongst themselves were now turned by the allies against France. A treaty of alliance was signed at Vienna between Austria, Russia, Prussia, and England, on the 25th of March 1815, by which those powers promised to furnish 180,000 men each for the prosecution of war, and stipulated that none of them should lay down arms until the power of Napoleon was completely destroyed. It was arranged that three armies should invade France, the first of 250,000 Austrians, Russians, and Bavarians under Schwartzenberg across the Upper Rhine, the second of 150,000 Prussians under Blücher across the Lower Rhine, and the third of 150,000 English, Hanoverians and Dutch from the Netherlands. Subsidies to the extent of £11,000,000 were promised by England to the allies. These arrangements made, the allied monarchs and their ministers left Vienna. But the final general Act of the Congress was not drawn up and signed until the 8th of June 1815, ten days before the battle of Waterloo.

It has been said that the allied armies after the abdication of Napoleon at Fontainebleau had retired and left France to the rule of Louis XVIII. That King on returning to France had made most liberal promises in the declaration known as the Declaration of Saint Ouen. These principles were embodied in a Charter, which was granted on the 4th of June 1814. By this Charter representative institutions and entire individual liberty were promised, and also the maintenance of the administrative creations of the Empire. Under the new Constitution there were to be two chambers, the one of hereditary peers, the other of elected representatives. The promises of the Charter were very fair, and had they been duly carried out, France might have been entirely contented, but unfortunately for himself Louis XVIII

*The First Reign of Louis XVIII.*

had not learned experience in his exile. In spite of the Charter he regarded himself as a ruler by right divine. Emigrés, even émigrés who had borne arms against France and consistently abused their fatherland, were promoted to the highest offices in the State. The King surrounded himself with reactionary courtiers, and what was worse with reactionary ministers. The favour shown to returned émigrés, the haughty attitude of the Princes of the blood, and the violent proclamations of the returned bishops and clergy made the people of France fear that the promises made in the Charter were but a sham, and that the next step would be that the estates of the Church and of the Crown which had been sold during the Revolution would be resumed. The feeling of distrust was universal. The rule of Louis XVIII. had been accepted only as a guarantee of peace. It was never popular, and the former subordinates of Napoleon began to regret the Imperial *régime*. If this was the feeling among the civil population, it was still more keenly felt in the army. Prisoners of war, and the blockaded garrisons, who had returned to France, felt sure that Napoleon's defeat in 1814 had been but accidental and wished to try conclusions once more with Europe. In all ranks a desire was expressed to wipe out the disgrace of the occupation of Paris by the allies.

On the 1st of March 1815, Napoleon, who had been informed of the universal feeling in France, landed in the Gulf of San Juan, and began the short reign which is known as the Hundred Days. He was accompanied by the 800 men of the Guard whom he had been allowed to have at Elba, and was received with the utmost enthusiasm by all classes. His journey through France was a triumphal procession. The King's brother, the Comte d'Artois, vainly attempted to organise resistance at Lyons. Marshal Ney, who had promised to arrest his patron, joined him with the army under his command on the 17th of March, and on the 20th Napoleon re entered Paris and took up his quarters at the Tuileries. Louis XVIII. had fled on the

Napoleon's return from Elba. March, 1815.

news of Ney's defection, and escaping from France took shelter at Ghent. Napoleon had learnt bitter lessons from his misfortunes. He declared that he would grant full and complete individual liberty, and also the freedom of the press, and on the 23d of April he promulgated what he called the Additional Act consecrating these principles. He felt his error in depending too entirely upon his bureaucracy, and he appealed on the ground of patriotism to the men of the Revolution whom he had in the days of his power carefully kept from office. These men rallied round him, and he appointed their most noteworthy representative, Carnot, his Minister of the Interior. He declared his acceptance of the two chambers ordained by the Charter, and most of the peers created by Louis XVIII. took the oath of allegiance once again to Napoleon.

After rousing national enthusiasm by appeals to patriotism and by the liberal provisions of the Additional Act, Napoleon organised his army, and in his favourite fashion decided to strike before any invasion of France took place. Of the three armies prepared for the invasion the one nearest within reach was that commanded by the Duke of Wellington. That General on leaving Vienna had been placed at the head of a miscellaneous force of English, Hanoverians, Dutch, and Belgians. He greatly regretted the absence of most of his veterans of the Peninsula who were still in America, and complained of the number of raw troops under his command. He agreed to act in harmony with the Prussians under Blücher, who brought his army into the Netherlands. Napoleon determined to strike before Wellington and Blücher had united. He crossed the frontier at the head of 130,000 men, and by his skilful and rapid movements practically surprised the allied generals. On the 16th of June 1815, he defeated Blücher at Ligny, while Ney with his left fought a drawn battle with the English advanced divisions at Quatre-Bras. By these engagements the English and Prussian armies were separated. Napoleon then resolved

*Campaign of Waterloo. June 1815.*

## Battle of Waterloo

to attack the English with the bulk of his army, and detached Marshal Grouchy to pursue the Prussians. Blücher, however, promised to come to Wellington's assistance if the English were attacked, and Wellington relying on this promise took up his position at Waterloo. On the 18th of June the battle of Waterloo was fought. The English army held its position in spite of repeated and furious attacks, until Blücher came up on the French right. Unable to continue the struggle against two foes, the French army was obliged to give way, and after the repulse of the Guard, which might have covered his retreat, Napoleon recognised that he was completely routed. He fled to Paris, and on the 22d of June he abdicated in favour of his son, the King of Rome. He nominated an executive commission of government, and then went on board ship in the hope of escaping to America. In this project he failed, and on 15th July he surrendered to Captain Maitland on board H.M.S. *Bellerophon*. The army of Wellington and Blücher pursued the defeated foe, but the rout had been too complete for the French to make another stand. Cambrai the only place that attempted to resist was easily taken, and on the 3d of July Wellington and Blücher re-occupied Paris. Meanwhile the grand army of Schwartzenberg had also invaded France, and the country was once more in the possession of the allies.

The terms of the second Treaty of Paris proved that the allied monarchs understood the difference between the opposition made by France to Europe in 1814 and 1815. In 1814 the Treaty of Paris which was then concluded was, if not particularly liberal to France, at least perfectly just. The allied monarchs and their ministers had appreciated the fact that in 1814 they were fighting Napoleon and not France. The campaign of 1815 had been of a different character. The French nation and not merely the French army had given proof of their attachment both to the Empire and to Napoleon's person. It was therefore considered necessary, not only to impose harsher terms upon France, but to exact securities for the future.

Second Treaty of Paris. 20th Nov. 1815.

PERIOD VII.                                                                 Z

Several schemes were proposed, of which one was to detach Alsace, Lorraine, and French Flanders, if not the whole of Picardy, and to reduce the limits of France to what they were before the conquests of Louis XIV. This scheme, which was earnestly supported by Prussia, who hoped to get the lion's share of the districts taken from France, was warmly opposed by Austria and England. The latter power was not to be bribed by the proposed extension of the frontier of its new creation, the Kingdom of the Netherlands. And the former objected entirely to any increase of the power of Prussia. Lord Castlereagh in his opposition to these extravagant suggestions of Prussia was supported by the Emperor Alexander and his minister, Nesselrode, and eventually it was agreed that France should be reduced to its exact limits of 1789. This meant that France lost all the cessions made to it in 1814, except Avignon and the Venaissin. Chambéry and the part of Savoy then granted to France were restored to the King of Sardinia; the districts in the neighbourhood of Geneva were also returned to that canton, and the fortress of Huningen on the borders of Switzerland was ordered to be dismantled; and the various rectifications of the frontier on the eastern and north-eastern borders were no longer sanctioned. A war contribution of 700,000,000 francs was laid upon France, in addition to which she was to maintain, at the cost of 250,000,000 francs a year, an army of 150,000 men in the possession of her chief frontier fortresses for a period of five years.

These were the most important conditions of peace contained in the second Treaty of Paris, which was signed on 20th of November 1815. But what France felt more bitterly than pecuniary contributions, or even the loss of territory, was the decision of the allied powers that the numerous pictures and works of art, which had been accumulated in Paris during the wars of the Revolution and the Empire, should be returned to their former owners. The Prussians were not satisfied with this, they wished to punish Paris more severely. Blücher was only prevented by the intervention of Lord Castlereagh and the Duke of Wellington from exacting a contribution of a 110,000,000 francs from the inhabitants of Paris alone. The Prussians even made preparations to blow up the Bridge of Jena, whose name perpetuated their greatest military humiliation, and were only prevented from their purpose by the expressed determination of Louis XVIII. to stand upon the bridge and be blown up with it if they persisted, and Blücher had to be satisfied with the alteration of the name of the bridge from the Bridge of Jena to the Bridge of the Military School. The question of the disposition of the person of Napoleon was one of some difficulty. He reached Torbay on board the *Bellerophon* on the 24th of July 1815, and the English Ministers did not know what to do with their illustrious prisoner. They dared not trust him in any part of Europe or America from which he could repeat his expedition from Elba. Blücher loudly declared that he ought to be shot at Vincennes like the Duc d'Enghien, but the English Government thought it would be sufficient to confine him on an isolated island. For this purpose they borrowed the island of Saint Helena from the East India Company, and on the 8th of August, Napoleon set sail for his place of exile on board H.M.S. *Northumberland*. Napoleon sent to St. Helena.

A month after the departure of Napoleon for St. Helena, the Emperor Alexander, the Emperor Francis, and King Frederick William signed the treaty which is known as the Holy Alliance. By this treaty it was declared that the Christian religion was the sole base of government, and the contracting monarchs promised to aid each other on all occasions like brothers, and to recommend to their peoples the exercise of the duties of the Christian religion. Lord Castlereagh declined on behalf of the Prince Regent to join the Holy Alliance, but on the 28th of November 1815, after the signature of the Peace of Paris, he agreed to an alliance that should include all the four powers, of which the aims were to keep from the throne of France either Napoleon or any relation of his, to combine together for the security of their separate states, and the general tranquillity of Europe, and to hold at fixed dates congresses for the settlement of disputed questions.

The second restoration of Louis XVIII. differed from the first as the second Treaty of Paris differed from its predecessor. After the events of the Hundred Days, the Bourbon King could no more delude himself with the idea that he was welcome to the people of France. He owed his seat upon the throne only to the absence of Napoleon and the presence of the allied armies in France, and he prepared on this occasion to punish those who had deserted him. He refused to grant an amnesty, and on the 24th of July 1815, he proscribed fifty-seven of the leading men in France, of whom nineteen were ordered to be tried by court-martial, and thirty-eight were banished. The most illustrious of the victims who perished under this proscription was Marshal Ney, who was shot at Paris on the 7th of December, after being condemned to death by the Chamber of Peers. This procedure was rendered necessary because it would have been difficult to find a court-martial to condemn the bravest of the French marshals. Marshal Moncey, who was nominated to preside over such a court-martial, refused in an eloquent letter which caused him to be sent to prison for three months. Far worse than these executions was the result of the outbreak of brigandage in the south of France. Under the pretext of being Royalists, the Companies of Jehu, which had ravaged the south of France in the days of the Thermidorians and of the Directory, again set to work. Political, religious, and personal passions excited to massacre. Pillage and murder were rife throughout the south of France, and among the victims who were slain in this White Terror of 1815 were Marshal Brune, and Generals Ramel and Lagarde. Special courts were formed by a law voted on the 12th of December 1815, to punish political offences. These provost's courts were as severe and almost as unjust as the revolutionary tribunals in the provinces during the Reign of Terror, and many hundreds of executions took place. Finally, in January 1816, what was ironically called a Law of Amnesty was passed. This law, from the list of its exceptions, was practically a gigantic proscription. Among others, all surviving members of the Convention who had voted for the death of Louis XVI. were exiled if they had in any way accepted the authority of Napoleon during the Hundred Days, which most of them had done. Under this Law of Amnesty most of the great statesmen who had been concerned in the government of France since 1793 were driven into exile. Conspicuous among them were Carnot, Merlin of Douai, Sieyès, Cambacérès, and David, the greatest painter of his time.

Restored for a second time to the throne of France, Louis XVIII. declined to take warning from the result of his former policy. He again showered his favours on returned *émigrés*, and pursued a thoroughly reactionary policy. As soon as he was firmly seated at the Tuileries, with the Prussians and the English encamped round Paris, he dismissed Talleyrand and Fouché from office and formed a new and strongly Royalist ministry under the presidency of the Duc de Richelieu, who had spent the last twenty years of his life in exile as one of the chief administrators of Russia. The king avowed his intention of keeping the promises he made in the Charter of 1814, but those promises were carried out in such a way as to make them absolutely illusory. He took advantage of the general adhesion given to Napoleon on his return from Elba to exclude from the Upper Chamber or House of Peers most of the leading men in France, leaving the majority entirely in the hands of former *émigrés*, and of men who by the excess of their royalism wished to palliate their offence in not having emigrated. The Lower House, or Chamber of Representatives, even exceeded the House of Peers in its violent royalism. The deputies, chiefly elected under the direct pressure of threats of vengeance, were ready to adopt any reactionary measure suggested to them. Louis XVIII. gave this Assembly the name of the 'Chambre Introuvable,' which he intended as a compliment, but which has survived as a term of derision. Among the first laws voted were the suspension of individual liberty, and of the liberty of the press, and the request was then made that the King, in his goodness, would revise fourteen articles of the Charter which were too liberal. But even this chamber, aided by the presence of foreign armies, could not make France revert to the condition in which it had been before 1789. A hint of the resumption of ecclesiastical or national domains would have set the whole country in an uproar, and the Chamber had to be satisfied with voting a large sum of money out of the ordinary taxes as compensation to the *émigrés* for their sufferings in exile.

The spirit of reaction went much further in Spain than in France. Ferdinand VII., on returning to his capital in May 1814, issued a proclamation attacking the Cortes, which had done so much to recover the country from the hands of the French. In his own words: 'A Cortes convoked in a manner never before known in Spain has been profiting by my captivity in France, and has usurped my rights by imposing on my people an anarchical and seditious Constitution based on the democratic principles of the French Revolution.' The King of Spain then proceeded to annul by his own absolute authority everything that had been done during his absence. He re-established the Inquisition, and proscribed and condemned to death all who had taken part in reforming the institutions of Spain, whether under the authority of Joseph Bonaparte or under that of the National Cortes. Many hundreds, if not thousands, of Spanish patriots were put to death in a vain attempt of Ferdinand VII. to restore things as they had been in former days. The attempt to carry out a complete reaction resulted in utter failure. Insurrections broke out in all directions, and the Spanish colonies in South America took advantage of the troubles in the fatherland to strike a blow for their own freedom. It is satisfactory to be able to state that the head of the third reigning branch of the House of Bourbon behaved with more moderation and wisdom than Ferdinand VII. of Spain or Louis XVIII. of France. Ferdinand IV., King of the Two Sicilies, returned to his capital at Naples in June 1815. He can hardly be blamed for ordering the execution of Murat whom he had always regarded as a usurper, and it is greatly to his credit that he made some endeavour to retain the excellent administration on the French system which had been established by Joseph Bonaparte and Murat.

The final overthrow of Napoleon and his exile to St. Helena allowed the new system for the government of Europe as laid down by the Congress of Vienna to be tried. That system may be roughly designated as the system of the Great Powers. Before 1789, certain states, such as France and England and Spain, were, from fortuitous circumstances, or the course of their history, larger, more united, and therefore more fitted for war, than others, but the greater part of the Continent was split up into small, and in the case of Germany, into very small states. Several of these small states, such as Sweden and Holland, had at different times exercised a very considerable influence, and the policy of Frederick the Great had added another to them, in the military state of Prussia. At the Congress of Vienna the tendency was to diminish the number and power of the secondary states, and to destroy minute sovereignties. Sweden and Denmark were relegated to the rank of third-rate powers; the petty principalities of Germany were built up into third-rate states. Austria and Prussia were established as great powers, but the increase of their territory brought with it dissimilar results. Prussia became the preponderant state of Germany, while Austria, whose Imperial House had so long held the position of Holy Roman Emperor, became less German, and now depended for its strength on its Italian, Magyar, and Slavonic provinces. The irruption of Russia into the European comity of nations was another significant feature. By its annexation of the greater part of the Grand Duchy of Warsaw, Russia thrust itself between Prussia and Austria territorially, while its leading share in the overthrow of Napoleon made its place as a European power unassailable. It may be doubted if the policy of Peter the Great and the Empress Catherine was thus carried out. The tendency of those rulers was to make the Baltic and the Black Sea Russian lakes, and to build up an Empire of the East; affairs in Central Europe only interested them in so far as they prevented interference with their Eastern designs, and did not lead to the erection of powerful states on the Russian border.

Nothing is more remarkable in the settlement of Europe by the Congress of Vienna than the entire neglect of the principle of nationality. Yet it was the sentiment of national patriotism which had enabled France to repulse Europe in arms, and had trained the soldiers with whom Napoleon had given the law to the Continent and had overthrown the mercenary armies of his opponents. It was the principle of nationality which had crippled Napoleon's finest armies in Spain, and which had produced his expulsion from Russia. It was the feeling of intense national patriotism which had made the Prussian army of 1813, and enabled Prussia after its deepest humiliation to take rank as a first-class power. But the diplomatists at Vienna treated the idea as without force. They had not learnt the great lesson of the French Revolution, that the first result of rousing a national consciousness of political liberty is to create a spirit of national patriotism. The Congress of Vienna trampled such notions under foot. The partition of Poland was consecrated by Europe; Italy was placed under foreign rulers; Belgium and Holland, in spite of the hereditary opposition of centuries, were united under one king. The territories on the left bank of the Rhine, which were happy under French rule, and had been an integral part of France for twenty years, were roughly torn away, and divided between Prussia, Bavaria, and the House of Orange, under the fancied necessity, induced by the

*The Principle of Nationality.*

exploded notion of maintaining the balance of power in Europe, of building up a bulwark against France. Such short-sighted policy was certain to be undone. Holland and Belgium separated; Italy became united; Poland maintained the consciousness of her national unity, and has more than once endeavoured to regain her independence; France has never ceased to yearn after her 'natural' frontier, the Rhine; the states of Germany have developed a national German patriotism which has led to the creation of the modern German Empire. This feeling of conscious nationality was the result of the French Revolution and the wars of Napoleon; its existence is the strength of England, France, Russia, and Germany, its absence is the weakness of Austria. In so far as the spirit of nationality was neglected at the Congress of Vienna, its work was but temporary; in its resurrection, which has filled the history of the present century, the work of the French Revolution has been permanent.

But after all, the growth of the spirit of nationality is only a secondary result of the French Revolution upon Europe; it did not arise in France until foreign powers attempted to interfere with the development of the French people after their own fashion; **Permanent results of the French Revolution.** it did not arise in Europe until Napoleon began to interfere with the development of other nations. The primary results of the French Revolution,—the recognition of individual liberty, which implied the abolition of serfdom and of social privileges; the establishment of political liberty, which implied the abolition of despots, however benevolent, and of political privileges; the maintenance of the doctrine of the sovereignty of the people, which implied the right of the people, through their representatives, to govern themselves,—have also survived the Congress of Vienna. When Europe tried to interfere, the French people sacrificed these great gains to the spirit of nationality, and bowed before the despotism of the Committee of Public Safety and of Napoleon; they have since regained them. The French taught these principles to the rest of

Europe, and the history of Europe since 1815 has been the history of their growth side by side with the idea of nationality. How the two, liberty and nationality, can be preserved in harmony is the great problem of the future; the history of Europe from 1789 to 1815 affords many examples of the difficulty of the problem and of the dangers which beset its solution.

# APPENDICES

THE RULERS AND MINISTERS OF THE

*(Capitals indicate Rulers; small capitals, Chief*

| | Holy Roman Empire; after 1805, Austria. | Great Britain. | France. |
|---|---|---|---|
| 1789. | JOSEPH II. (Emperor since 1765; ruler of Austria since 1780.) KAUNITZ (since 1756.) *Philip Cobenzl* (since 1780.) | GEORGE III. (since 1760). WILLIAM PITT (since Dec. 1783). *Duke of Leeds* (since Dec. 1783). | LOUIS XVI. (since 1774). *Comte de Montmorin* (since 1787). |
| 1790. 1791. | LEOPOLD II. (Feb.) .................. | ...*Lord Grenville* (June) | ...*A. de Valdec de Lessart* (Nov.) |
| 1792. | FRANCIS II. (March). | .................. | REPUBLIC (Sept.) *Dumouriez* (March). *Chambonas* (June). *Bigot de Ste. Croix* (Aug). *Lebrun Tondu* (Aug.) |
| 1793. 1794. 1795. | COLLOREDO............ *Thugut* (June). .................. | .................. .................. | ...*Deforgues* (June) ..(Ministry abolished— April '94—Oct. '95). DIRECTORY (Oct.) *Delacroix* (Nov.) |
| 1796. 1797. | *Louis Cobenzl* (April) | .................. | ...*Talleyrand* (July). |
| 1798. 1799. | *Thugut* (Jan.)... *Lehrbach*(Oct.) | .................. | CONSULATE (Nov.) *Reinhardt* (July). *Talleyrand* (Nov.) |
| 1800. 1801. | LOUIS COBENZL. | .. HENRY ADDINGTON (March). *Lord Hawkesbury* (March.) | |
| 1802. 1803. 1804. | .................. | .. WILLIAM PITT (May). *Lord Harrowby* ,, | |
| 1805. 1806. | .................. PHILIP STADION...... | ...*Lord Mulgrave*(Jan.) .. LORD GRENVILLE(Feb.) *Charles James Fox* (Feb.) *Viscount Howick* (Sept.) | NAPOLEON, Emperor. |
| 1807. | .................. | .. DUKE OF PORTLAND (March). *George Canning* (March.) | .,..*Champagny* (Aug.) |
| 1808. | | | |
| 1809. 1810. | METTERNICH......... | .. SPENCER PERCEVAL (Dec.) *Lord Bathurst* (Oct.) *Lord Wellesley* (Dec.) | |
| 1811. 1812. | .................. .................. | .................. *Lord Castlereagh* (March). EARL OF LIVERPOOL (June). | ...*Maret* (April). |
| 1813. 1814. | .................. .................. | ........ ......... .................. | ...*Caulaincourt* (Nov.) LOUIS XVIII. *Talleyrand* (April). |

# DIX I.

## GREAT POWERS OF EUROPE, 1789-1815.

*Ministers; and italics, Foreign Ministers.*)

| Prussia. | Russia. | Spain. | |
|---|---|---|---|
| FREDERICK WILLIAM II. (since 1786). *Hertzberg* (since 1756). | CATHERINE II. (since 1762). *Ostermann* (since 1775). | CHARLES IV. (since Dec. 1788). FLORIDA BLANCA (since 1773). | 1789. |
| *Schulemburg* (May). | | | 1790. 1791. |
| HAUGWITZ (Oct.) | | ARANDA (July). GODOY (Nov.). | 1792. |
| | | | 1793. 1794. |
| | | | 1795. |
| | PAUL I. (Nov.) OSTERMANN. *Panine.* | | 1796. |
| FREDERICK WILLIAM III. (Nov.) | | | 1797. |
| | | *Saavedra* (March). *Urquijo* (August). | 1798. |
| | | GODOY (Dec.). | 1799. 1800. 1801. |
| | ALEXANDER I. (Mar.). PANINE. *Kotchoubey.* | | |
| | VORONZOV. | | 1802. 1803. |
| HARDENBERG (Aug.) | *Adam Czartoryski* (May). | | 1804. |
| HAUGWITZ (Feb.) HARDENBERG (Nov.) | *Baron Budberg* (Aug.) | | 1805. 1806. |
| STEIN (July) *Goltz* (July). | *Roumianzov* (Sept.) | | 1807. |
| | | JOSEPH BONAPARTE. AZANZA. | 1808. |
| | | | 1809. |
| HARDENBERG (July). | ROUMIANZOV *Nesselrode.* | | 1810. 1811. 1812. |
| | | FERDINAND VII. | 1813. 1814. |

## The Rulers of the Second-rate

| | Sweden. | Denmark. | Turkey. | Portugal. |
|---|---|---|---|---|
| 1789 | Gustavus III. (Since 1771.) | Christian VII. (Since 1766.) | Abdul Hamid. (Since 1774.) Selim III. (April.) | Maria I. (Since 1777.) |
| 1790 | | | | |
| 1791 | Gustavus IV. (March.) | | | |
| 1792 | | | | |
| 1793 | | | | |
| 1794 | | | | |
| 1795 | | | | |
| 1796 | | | | |
| 1797 | | | | |
| 1798 | | | | |
| 1799 | .................. | .................. | .................. | *Prince John, Regent.* |
| 1800 | | | | |
| 1801 | | | | |
| 1802 | | | | |
| 1803 | | | | |
| 1804 | | | | |
| 1805 | | | | |
| 1806 | | | | |
| 1807 | .................. | .................. | Mustapha IV. (May.) | |
| 1808 | .................. | Frederick VI. (March.) | Mahmoud II. (July.) | |
| 1809 | Charles XIII. (May.) | | | |
| 1810 | *Bernadotte, Prince Royal (Aug.)* | | | |
| 1811 | | | | |
| 1812 | | | | |
| 1813 | | | | |
| 1814 | | | | |
| 1815 | | | | |

## POWERS OF EUROPE, 1789-1815.

| Sardinia. | The Two Sicilies. | Bavaria. | Würtemburg. | |
|---|---|---|---|---|
| Victor Amadeus III. (Since 1773.) | Ferdinand IV. (Since 1759.) | Charles Theodore. (Since 1777.) | Charles Eugène. (Since 1735.) | 1789 |
| | | | | 1790 |
| | | | | 1791 |
| | | | | 1792 |
| | | | | 1793 |
| | | | | 1794 |
| | | | Frederick Eugène. (Oct.) | 1795 |
| Charles Emmanuel IV. (Oct.) | ............ | ............ | ............ | 1796 |
| | | | Frederick I. (Dec.) | 1797 |
| | | | | 1798 |
| | | Maximilian Joseph. | ............ | 1799 |
| | | | | 1800 |
| | | | | 1801 |
| Victor Emmanuel I. (June.) | ............ | ............ | ............ | 1802 |
| | | | | 1803 |
| | Naples. | | | 1804 |
| | | | | 1805 |
| | Joseph Bonaparte. (March.) | ............ | ............ | 1806 |
| | | | | 1807 |
| | Joachim Murat. (August.) | ............ | ............ | 1808 |
| | | | | 1809 |
| | | | | 1810 |
| | | | | 1811 |
| | | | | 1812 |
| | | | | 1813 |
| | Ferdinand IV..... | ............ | ............ | 1814 |
| | | | | 1815 |

# European History

APPEN-

THE FAMILY

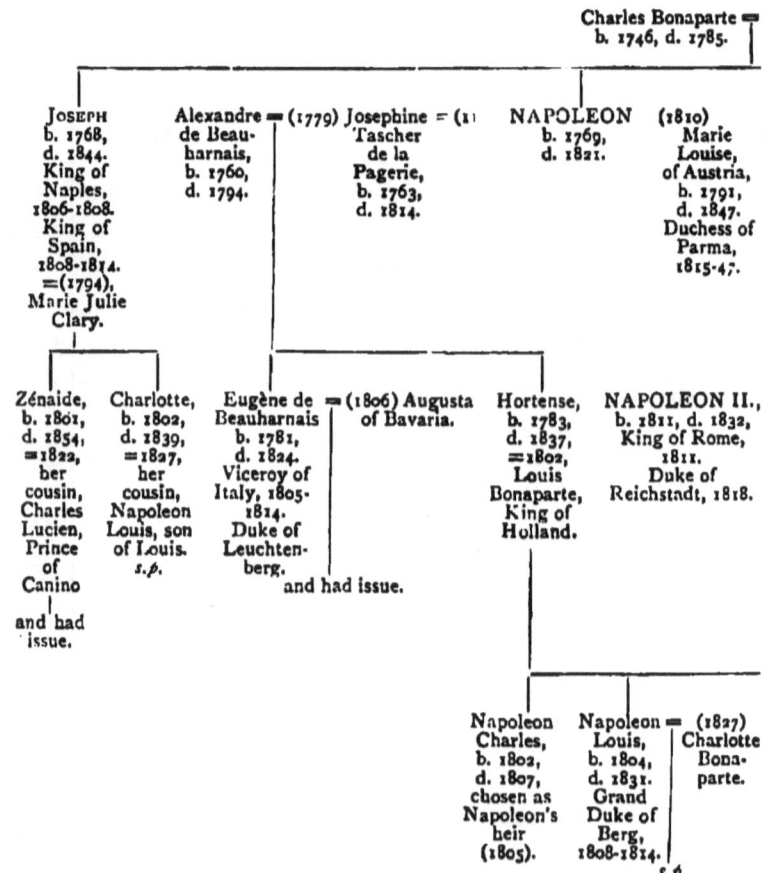

*European History* 369

## DIX III.

### OF NAPOLEON.

Letizia Ramolino,
b. 1750, d. 1839.

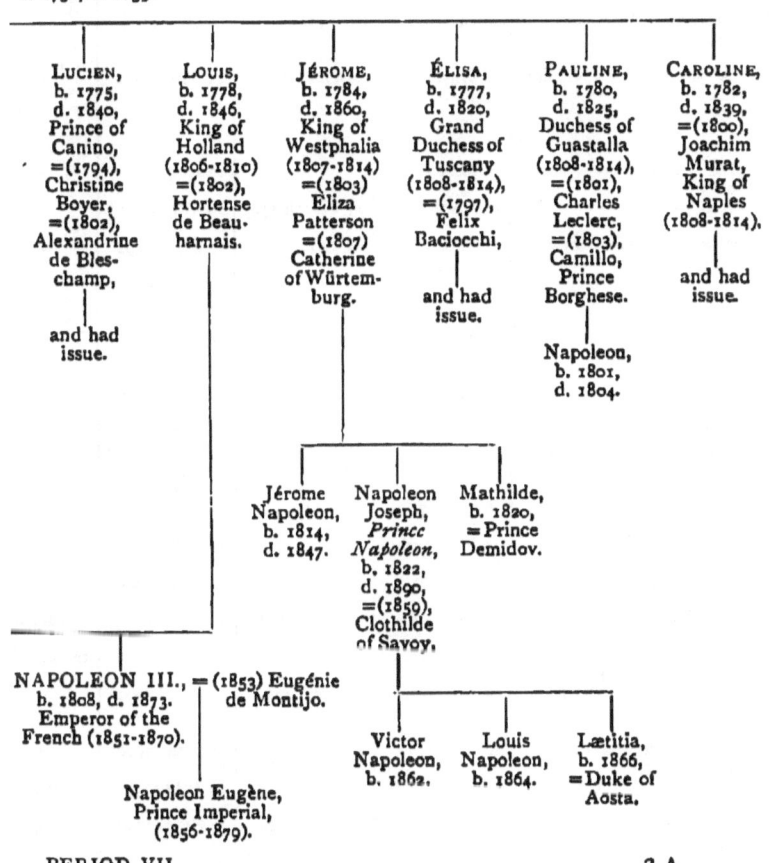

| LUCIEN, | LOUIS, | JÉROME, | ÉLISA, | PAULINE, | CAROLINE, |
| b. 1775, | b. 1778, | b. 1784, | b. 1777, | b. 1780, | b. 1782, |
| d. 1840, | d. 1846, | d. 1860, | d. 1820, | d. 1825, | d. 1839, |
| Prince of | King of | King of | Grand | Duchess of | =(1800), |
| Canino, | Holland | Westphalia | Duchess of | Guastalla | Joachim |
| =(1794), | (1806-1810) | (1807-1814) | Tuscany | (1808-1814), | Murat, |
| Christine | =(1802), | =(1803) | (1808-1814) | =(1801), | King of |
| Boyer, | Hortense | Eliza | =(1797), | Charles | Naples |
| =(1802), | de Beau- | Patterson | Felix | Leclerc, | (1808-1814). |
| Alexandrine | harnais. | =(1807) | Baciocchi, | =(1803), | |
| de Bles- | | Catherine | | Camillo, | |
| champ, | | of Würtem- | | Prince | |
| | | burg. | and had | Borghese. | and had |
| | | | issue. | | issue. |
| and had | | | | Napoleon, | |
| issue. | | | | b. 1801, | |
| | | | | d. 1804. | |

Jérome   Napoleon   Mathilde,
Napoleon,  Joseph,    b. 1820,
b. 1814,   *Prince*   =Prince
d. 1847.   *Napoleon*, Demidov.
           b. 1822,
           d. 1890,
           =(1859),
           Clothilde
           of Savoy,

NAPOLEON III., =(1853) Eugénie
b. 1808, d. 1873.   de Montijo.
Emperor of the
French (1851-1870).

                Victor      Louis      Lætitia,
                Napoleon,   Napoleon,  b. 1866,
                b. 1862.    b. 1864.   =Duke of
                                       Aosta.

Napoleon Eugène,
Prince Imperial,
(1856-1879).

PERIOD VII.

| Names. | Born. | General of Brigade. | General of Division. | MARSHAL. |
|---|---|---|---|---|
| BERTHIER, Louis Alexandre. | 20 Nov. 1753 | 22 May 1792 (Maréchal de Camp) | 13 June 1795 | 19 May 1804 |
| MURAT, Joachim. | 25 March 1767 | 10 May 1796 | 25 July 1799 | " |
| MONCEY, Bon Adrien Jeannot. | 31 July 1754 | 18 Feb. 1794 | 9 June 1794 | " |
| JOURDAN, Jean Baptiste. | 29 April 1762 | 27 May 1793 | 30 July 1793 | " |
| MASSÉNA, André. | 6 May 1756 | 22 Aug. 1793 | 20 Dec. 1793 | " |
| AUGEREAU, Charles Pierre François. | 21 Oct. 1757 | .. | 25 Dec. 1793 | " |
| BERNADOTTE, Jean Baptiste Jules. | 26 Jan. 1763 | 26 June 1794 | 22 Oct. 1794 | " |
| SOULT, Jean de Dieu Nicolas. | 29 March 1769 | 11 Oct. 1794 | 21 April 1799 | " |
| BRUNE, Guillaume Marie Anne. | 13 May 1763 | .. | 17 Aug. 1797 | " |
| LANNES, Jean. | 11 April 1769 | 17 March 1797 | 10 May 1799 | " |
| MORTIER, Adolphe Édouard Casimir Joseph. | 13 Feb. 1768 | 23 Feb. 1799 | 25 Sept. 1799 | " |
| NEY, Michel. | 10 Jan. 1769 | 1 Aug. 1796 | 28 March 1799 | " |
| DAVOUT, Louis Nicolas. | 10 May 1770 | 24 Sept. 1794 | 3 July 1800 | " |
| BESSIÈRES, Jean Baptiste. | 6 Aug. 1768 | 18 July 1800 | 13 Sept. 1802 | " |
| KELLERMANN, François Christophe. | 28 May 1735 | 9 March 1788 (Maréchal de Camp) | 19 March 1792 (Lieut.-General) | " |
| LEFEBVRE, François Joseph. | 15 Oct. 1755 | 2 Dec. 1793 | 10 Jan. 1794 | " |
| PÉRIGNON, Dominique Catherine de. | 31 May 1754 | .. | 25 Dec. 1793 | " |
| SÉRURIER, Jean Mathieu Philibert. | 8 Dec. 1742 | 22 Aug. 1793 | 13 June 1795 | " |
| VICTOR, Victor Claude Perrin, called. | 7 Dec. 1764 | 20 Dec. 1793 | 10 March 1797 | 13 July 1807 |
| MACDONALD, Jacques Étienne Joseph Alexandre. | 17 Nov. 1765 | 26 Aug. 1793 | 28 Nov. 1794 | 12 July 1809 |
| OUDINOT, Nicolas Charles. | 25 April 1767 | 14 June 1794 | 12 April 1799 | " |
| MARMONT, Auguste Frédéric Louis Viesse de. | 20 July 1774 | 10 June 1798 | 9 Sept. 1800 | " |
| SUCHET, Louis Gabriel. | 2 March 1770 | 23 March 1798 | 10 July 1799 | 8 July 1811 |
| GOUVION-SAINT-CYR, Laurent. | 13 April 1764 | 10 June 1794 | 2 Sept. 1794 | 27 Aug. 1812 |
| PONIATOWSKI, Joseph, Prince. | 7 May 1762 | .. | .. | Oct. 1813 |
| GROUCHY, Emmanuel de. | 23 Oct. 1766 | 7 Sept. 1792 | 13 June 1795 | 17 Apr. 1815 |

# DIX IV.

## MARSHALS.

| Titles | Notes. |
|---|---|
| Prince-Duke of Neufchâtel 15 March 1806; Prince of Wagram 31 Dec. 1809. | Peer of France 1814; committed suicide or was murdered at Bamberg 1 June 1815. |
| Prince 1 Feb. 1805; Grand Duke of Berg 15 March 1806; King of Naples 1 Aug. 1808. | Shot at Pizzo in Italy 13 Oct. 1815. |
| Duke of Conegliano 2 July 1808. | Governor of the Hôtel des Invalides 1833-42; died at Paris 20 April 1842. |
| Count 1 March 1808. | Peer of France 1814 and 1819; Governor of the Hôtel des Invalides 1830-33; died at Paris 23 Nov. 1833. |
| Duke of Rivoli 24 April 1808; Prince of Essling 31 Jan. 1810. | Died at Paris 4 April 1817. |
| Duke of Castiglione 26 April 1808. | Peer of France 1814; died at La Houssaye 12 June 1816. |
| Prince of Ponte Corvo 5 June 1806; Crown Prince of Sweden 21 Aug. 1810. | King of Sweden 5 Feb. 1818; died at Stockholm 8 March 1844. |
| Duke of Dalmatia 29 June 1808. | Minister for War Dec. 1814—March 1815; Peer of France June 1815; exiled 1815-19; Peer of France 1827; Minister for War 1830-34, 1840-45; Marshal-General 1847; died at Saint Amans 26 Nov. 1851. |
| Count 1 March 1808. | Peer of France 2 June 1815; murdered at Avignon 2 Aug. 1815. |
| Duke of Montebello 15 June 1808. | Mortally wounded at the battle of Aspern; died at Vienna 31 May 1809. |
| Duke of Treviso 2 July 1808. | Peer of France 1814 and 1819; Ambassador to Russia 1830-31; Chancellor of the Legion of Honour 1831; Minister for War 1834-35; killed by the explosion of an infernal machine at Paris 28 July 1835. |
| Duke of Elchingen, 5 May 1808; Prince of the Moskowa 25 March 1813. | Peer of France 1814; shot at Paris 7 Dec. 1815. |
| Duke of Auerstädt 2 July 1808; Prince of Eckmühl 28 Nov. 1809. | Minister for War 1815; Peer of France 1819; died at Paris 1 June 1823. |
| Duke of Istria 28 May 1809. | Killed at Lutzen 1 May 1813. |
| Count 1 March 1808; Duke of Valmy 2 May 1808. | Peer of France 1814; died at Paris 13 Sept. 1820. |
| Count 1 March 1808; Duke of Dantzic 10 Sept. 1808 | Peer of France 1814 and 1819; died at Paris 14 Sept. 1820. |
| Count 6 Sept. 1811. | Peer of France 1814; created a Marquis 1817; died at Paris 25 Dec. 1818. |
| Count 1 March 1808. | Governor of the Hôtel des Invalides, 1804-15; Peer of France 1814; died at Paris 21 Dec. 1819. |
| Duke of Belluno 10 Sept. 1808. | Peer of France 1815; Minister of War 1821-23; died at Paris 1 March 1841. |
| Duke of Taranto 9 Dec. 1809. | Peer of France 1814; Chancellor of the Legion of Honour 1815-31; died at Courcelles 7 Sept. 1840. |
| Count 2 July 1808; Duke of Reggio 14 April 1810. | Peer of France 1814; Chancellor of the Legion of Honour 1839-47; Governor of the Hôtel des Invalides 1842-47; died at Paris 13 Sept 1847. |
| Duke of Ragusa 28 June 1808. | Peer of France 1814; Ambassador to Russia 1826-28; died at Venice 22 July 1852. |
| Count 24 June 1808; Duke of Albufera 3 Jan. 1813. | Peer of France 1814 and 1819; died near Marseilles 3 Jan. 1826. |
| Count 3 May 1808. | Peer of France 1814; Minister for War July-Sept. 1815, 1817-19; created a Marquis 1819; died at Hyères 17 March 1830. |
| .... | Drowned in the Elster at the battle of Leipzig 19 Oct. 1813. |
| Count 28 Jan. 1809. | Exiled 1815-20; restored as Marshal 1831; died 29 May 1847. |

APPEN-

NAPOLEON'S MINISTERS DURING THE

|  | Foreign Affairs. | Interior. | Finances. | War. |
|---|---|---|---|---|
| 1799. | 9 Nov. Charles Maurice de TALLEYRAND-PÉRIGORD. (Prince of Benevento 5 June 1806.) | 12 Nov. Pierre Simon LAPLACE. (Count 24 April 1808.) | 10 Nov. Martin Michel Charles GAUDIN. (Count 26 April 1808; Duke of Gaeta 15 Aug. 1809.) | 10 Nov. Louis Alexandre BERTHIER. |
| ,, | ,, | 25 Dec. Lucien BONAPARTE. | ,, |  |
| 1800. | ,, | ,, | ,, | 12 April. Lazare Nicolas Marguerite CARNOT. |
| ,, | ,, | 6 Nov. Jean Antoine CHAPTAL. (Count 26 April 1808; Count of Chanteloup 25 March 1810.) | ,, | 8 Oct. Louis Alexandre BERTHIER, (Prince of Neufchâtel 13 March 1806; Prince of Wagram 31 Dec. 1809.) |
| 1801. | ,, | ,, | ,, | ,, |
| 1802. | ,, | ,, | ,, | ,, |
| 1803. | ,, | ,, | ,, |  |
| 1804. | ,, | 1 Aug. Jean Baptiste Nompère de CHAMPAGNY. | ,, | ,, |
| 1805. | ,, | ,, | ,, | ,, |
| 1806. | ,, | ,, | ,, |  |
| 1807. | 8 Aug. Jean Baptiste Nompère de CHAMPAGNY. (Count 24 April 1808; Duke of Cadore 15 Aug. 1809.) | 9 Aug. Emmanuel CRETET. (Count of Champmol 26 April 1808.) | ,, | 9 Aug. Henri Jacques Guillaume CLARKE. (Count of Hunebourg 24 April 1808; Duke of Feltre 15 Aug. 1809.) |
| 1808. | ,, | ,, | ,, | ,, |
| 1809. | ,, | 1 Oct. Jean Pierre Bachasson de MONTALIVET. (Comte 27 Nov. 1808.) | ,, | ,, |
| 1810. | ,, | ,, | ,, | ,, |
| 1811. | 17 April. Hugues Bernard MARET. (Count 3 May 1809; Duke of Bassano 15 Aug. 1809.) | ,, | ,, | ,, |
| 1812. | ,, | ,, | ,, | ,, |
| 1813. | 20 Nov. Armand Augustin Louis CAULAINCOURT. (Duke of Vicenza 7 June 1808.) | ,, | ,, | ,, |
| 1814. | ,, | ,, | ,, | ,, |

# DIX V.

## Consulate and Empire 1799-1814.

| Marine. | Justice. | Police. | Public Worship. | |
|---|---|---|---|---|
| 24 Nov. Pierre Alexandre Laurent FORFAIT. | 19 July. Jean Jacques Régis CAMBACÉRÈS. (Duke of Parma 24 April 1808.) | 20 July. Joseph FOUCHÉ. | .................. | 1799. |
| " | 25 Dec. André Joseph ABRIAL. (Count 26 April 1808.) | .................. | .................. | " |
| " | | | . | 1800. |
| " | | | | " |
| 1 Oct. Denis DECRÈS. (Count June 1808; Duke 28 April 1813.) | .................. | .................. | .................. | 1801. |
| " | 15 Sept. Claude Ambroise REGNIER. (Count 24 April 1808; Duke of Massa 15 Aug. 1809.) | 15 Sept. (*Ministry abolished.*) | .................. | 1802. |
| " | " | | | 1803. |
| " | " | 10 July. Joseph FOUCHÉ. (Count 24 April 1808; Duke of Otranto 15 Aug. 1809.) | July. Jean Étienne Marie PORTALIS. | 1804. |
| " | " | " | " | 1805. |
| " | " | " | " | 1806. |
| " | " | " | Aug. Félix Julien Jean BIGOT DE PRÉAMENEU. (Count 24 April 1808.) | 1807. |
| " | " | " | " | 1808. |
| " | " | " | " | 1809. |
| " | " | June 8. Anne Jean Marie René SAVARY. (Duke of Rovigo 1808.) | " | 1810. |
| " | " | " | " | 1811. |
| " | " | " | " | 1812. |
| " | " | " | " | 1813. |
| " | " | " | " | 1814. |

# APPEN-
## CONCORDANCE OF THE REPUBLICAN
(Extracted from Stephens' *History of the*

|  | YEAR II. 1793-1794. | YEAR III. 1794-1795. | YEAR IV. 1795-1796. |
|---|---|---|---|
| 1 Vendémiaire, | 22 September 1793. | 22 September 1794. | 23 September 1795. |
| 11    ,, | 2 October. | 2 October. | 3 October. |
| 21    ,, | 12 October. | 12 October. | 13 October. |
| 1 Brumaire, | 22 October. | 22 October. | 23 October. |
| 11    ,, | 1 November. | 1 November. | 2 November. |
| 21    ,, | 11 November. | 11 November. | 12 November. |
| 1 Frimaire,. | 21 November. | 21 November. | 22 November. |
| 11    ,, | 1 December. | 1 December. | 2 December. |
| 21    ,, | 11 December. | 11 December. | 12 December. |
| 1 Nivôse, | 21 December. | 21 December. | 22 December. |
| 11    ,, | 31 December. | 31 December. | 1 January 1796. |
| 21    ,, | 10 January 1794. | 10 January 1795. | 11 January. |
| 1 Pluviôse,. | 20 January. | 20 January. | 21 January. |
| 11    ,, | 30 January. | 30 January. | 31 January. |
| 21    ,, | 9 February. | 9 February. | 10 February. |
| 1 Ventôse, | 19 February. | 19 February. | 20 February. |
| 11    ,, | 1 March. | 1 March. | 1 March. |
| 21    ,, | 11 March. | 11 March. | 11 March. |
| 1 Germinal, | 21 March. | 21 March. | 21 March. |
| 11    ,, | 31 March. | 31 March. | 31 March. |
| 21    ,, | 10 April. | 10 April. | 10 April. |
| 1 Floréal, | 20 April. | 20 April. | 20 April. |
| 11    ,, | 30 April. | 30 April. | 30 April. |
| 21    ,, | 10 May. | 10 May. | 10 May. |
| 1 Prairial, | 20 May. | 20 May. | 20 May. |
| 11    ,, | 30 May. | 30 May. | 30 May. |
| 21    ,, | 9 June. | 9 June. | 9 June. |
| 1 Messidor, | 19 June. | 19 June. | 19 June. |
| 11    ,, | 29 June. | 29 June. | 29 June. |
| 21    ,, | 9 July. | 9 July. | 9 July. |
| 1 Thermidor, | 19 July. | 19 July. | 19 July. |
| 11    ,, | 29 July. | 29 July. | 29 July. |
| 21    ,, | 8 August. | 8 August. | 8 August. |
| 1 Fructidor, | 18 August. | 18 August. | 18 August. |
| 11    ,, | 28 August. | 28 August. | 28 August. |
| 21    ,, | 7 September. | 7 September. | 7 September. |
| 1st Complementary Day, or 'Sans-Culottide,' | 17 September. | 17 September. | 17 September. |
| 5th Complementary Day, or 'Sans-Culottide,' | 21 September. | 21 September. | 21 September. |
| 6th Complementary Day, or 'Sans-Culottide.' | .. | 22 September. | .. |

NOTE.—Each month in the Republican

## AND GREGORIAN CALENDARS.
*French Revolution*, vol. ii. (Longmans and Co.))

| YEAR V. 1796-1797. | YEAR VI. 1797-1798. | YEAR VII. 1798-1799. | YEAR VIII. 1799-1800. |
|---|---|---|---|
| 22 September 1796. | 22 September 1797. | 22 September 1798. | 23 September 1799. |
| 2 October. | 2 October. | 2 October. | 3 October. |
| 12 October. | 12 October. | 12 October. | 13 October. |
| 22 October. | 22 October. | 22 October. | 23 October. |
| 1 November. | 1 November. | 1 November. | 2 November. |
| 11 November. | 11 November. | 11 November. | 12 November. |
| 21 November. | 21 November. | 21 November. | 22 November. |
| 1 December. | 1 December. | 1 December. | 2 December. |
| 11 December. | 11 December. | 11 December. | 12 December. |
| 21 December. | 21 December. | 21 December. | 22 December. |
| 31 December. | 31 December. | 31 December. | 1 January 1800. |
| 10 January 1797. | 10 January 1798. | 10 January 1799. | 11 January. |
| 20 January. | 20 January. | 20 January. | 21 January. |
| 30 January. | 30 January. | 30 January. | 31 January. |
| 9 February. | 9 February. | 9 February. | 10 February. |
| 19 February. | 19 February. | 19 February. | 20 February. |
| 1 March. | 1 March. | 1 March. | 1 March. |
| 11 March. | 11 March. | 11 March. | 11 March. |
| 21 March. | 21 March. | 21 March. | 21 March. |
| 31 March. | 31 March. | 31 March. | 31 March. |
| 10 April. | 10 April. | 10 April. | 10 April. |
| 20 April. | 20 April. | 20 April. | 20 April. |
| 30 April. | 30 April. | 30 April. | 30 April. |
| 10 May. | 10 May. | 10 May. | 10 May. |
| 20 May. | 20 May. | 20 May. | 20 May. |
| 30 May. | 30 May. | 30 May. | 30 May. |
| 9 June. | 9 June. | 9 June. | 9 June. |
| 19 June. | 19 June. | 19 June. | 19 June. |
| 29 June. | 29 June. | 29 June. | 29 June. |
| 9 July. | 9 July. | 9 July. | 9 July. |
| 19 July. | 19 July. | 19 July. | 19 July. |
| 29 July. | 29 July. | 29 July. | 29 July. |
| 8 August. | 8 August. | 8 August. | 8 August. |
| 18 August. | 18 August. | 18 August. | 18 August. |
| 28 August. | 28 August. | 28 August. | 28 August. |
| 7 September. | 7 September. | 7 September. | 7 September. |
| 17 September. | 17 September. | 17 September. | 17 September. |
| 21 September. | 21 September. | 21 September. | 21 September. |
| .. | .. | 22 September. | .. |

Calendar consisted of *thirty* days.

# INDEX

The dates given in brackets are those of the birth and death of the person indexed; where only the date of death is known it is preceded by a †.
Full names and titles are given.
Proper names commencing with 'da,' 'de,' 'd',' are indexed under the succeeding initial letter.

ABDUL HAMID (1725-89), Sultan of Turkey, 44.
Abensberg, battle of (20 April 1809), 272.
Abercromby, Sir Ralph, English general (1735-1801), 224.
Aberdeen, George Gordon, Earl of, English diplomatist (1784-1860), 301, 311, 316, 323.
Abo, treaty of (April 1812), 302.
Aboukir Bay, French fleet defeated in, by Nelson (1 August 1798), 195.
Abrantes, Duke of. *See* Junot.
Abrial, André Joseph, Comte, French statesman (1750-1828), 216.
Acre, siege of (1799), 208.
Acton, Joseph, Neapolitan statesman (1737-1808), 23.
Adda, the, Bonaparte forces the passage of, at Lodi (1796), 174; Suvórov, at Cassano (1799), 203.
Addington, Henry, Viscount Sidmouth, English statesman (1757-1844), 225.
Additional Act, the, declared by Napoleon (23 April 1815), 352.
Adige, the, Italy up to, ceded to Austria by treaty of Campo-Formio (1797), 192; by treaty of Lunéville (1801), 220; Austrian positions on, turned by Macdonald (1800), 219.
Adlersparre, George, Baron, Swedish general (1760-1837), 279.
Aix-la-Chapelle, a free city of the Holy Roman Empire, 35, 150, 230, 344.
Albuera, battle of (16 May 1811), 297.

Albufera, battle of (26 Dec. 1811), 297.
—— Duke of. *See* Suchet.
Aldenhoven, battle of (2 Oct. 1794), 150.
Alessandria, fortress built at, by Victor Amadeus III., 27, 203, 204, 218.
Alexander I., Emperor of Russia (1777-1825), attitude at his accession, 234; joins coalition against France, 242, 243; defeated at Austerlitz, 244; at Eylau and Friedland, 248, 249; interview with Napoleon at Tilsit, 249, 250; makes treaty of Tilsit, 250; conquers Finland, 254, 278; acquisitions in Poland, and dislike of Grand Duchy of Warsaw, 261; interview with Napoleon at Erfurt, 262; conduct in 1809, 274; war with Turkey, 281; makes treaty of Bucharest, 281; refuses a sister to Napoleon, 294; causes of dissension with Napoleon, 299-301; makes treaty of Abo with Bernadotte, 302; summons Stein to his Court, 304; his policy of retreat before Napoleon (1812), 305; fights battle of Borodino, 305; negotiates with Napoleon, 306; forms friendship with Frederick William III. of Prussia, 308; distrust of Napoleon, 310; agrees to Proposals of Frankfort, 316; desires to invade France, 317; refuses to retreat, 319, 320; enters Paris, 329; influenced by Talleyrand, 329, 330; speech to the French Senate, 330,

377

331; greatness of his share in overthrowing Napoleon, 334; at the Congress of Vienna, 337; his desire for the whole of Poland, 339; forced to give way, 340, 341; gave constitution to Poland, 342; protected Murat and Eugène de Beauharnais, 345; signs treaty against Napoleon (1815), 350; opposes partition of France, 354; joins the Holy Alliance, 355.
Alexandria, 195, 224.
Alicante, Bentinck repulsed at (1812), 307.
Alkmaar, Convention of (18 Oct. 1799), 205.
Almeida, siege of (1811), 296.
Alps, French reach the summit of Mont Cenis (1795), 151; Suvórov crosses (1799), 204, 205; Bonaparte (1800), 218; Macdonald (1800), 219.
Alsace, rights of the Princes of the Empire in, 79; proposals of Mirabeau and Merlin, 80; letter of Leopold on, 89, 90; *conclusion* of the Diet of the Empire on, 108; invaded by Würmser, 130, 139; recovered by the French (1794), 140; proposal to detach from France (1815), 354.
Altdorf, Suvórov reaches (1799), 204.
Altenkirchen, battle of (20 Sept. 1796), 178.
Alton, Richard, Count d', Austrian general (1732-90), 43, 47, 48, 63, 64.
Alvensleben, Philip Charles, Count von, Prussian statesman (1745-1802), 153, 170, 179.
Alvinzi (Alvinczy), Joseph, Austrian general (1735-1810), 176.
America, South, 264, 358.
—— United States of. *See* United States.
*Ami du Peuple*, Marat's journal, 61.
Amiens, treaty of (1802), 225.
Amnesty, general, decreed by the Convention (1795), 166.
—— law of, promulgated (1815), 357.
Amsterdam, 32, 149, 255.
Ancients, Council of. *See* Council.
Ancona, 175, 207, 277.
Angoulême, Maria Thérèse Charlotte, Duchess of, daughter of Louis XVI. (1778-1851), 168.
—— Louis Antoine, Duke of, son of the Comte d'Artois (1775-1844), 326, 327.
Anhalt, the Dukes of, Princes of the Empire (1789), 34, 343.
Anhalt-Köthen, Louis, Duke of (1761-1819), 293.
Anhalt-Zerbst, the Empress Catherine, a princess of, 18.
Ankarström, John James, Swedish officer (1761-1792), 110.
Anselme, Jacques Bernard Modeste d', French general (1740-1812), 117.
Anspach, Napoleon violates Prussian neutrality by marching through (1805), 244.
Antwerp, riot against the Austrians suppressed at (1788), 47; abandoned to the Belgian patriots (1789), 64; Napoleon's buildings at, 276; Carnot's defence of (1814), 321; its retention cause of Napoleon's fall, 324.
Aoust, Eustache, Comte d', French general (1764-94), 140.
Appenzell, democratic canton of Switzerland, maintained by Bonaparte (1803), 228.
Aranda, Don Pedro Pablo Abaracay Bolea, Count of, Spanish statesman (1718-99), 4, 21, 126.
Archbishop-Electors of the Holy Roman Empire, 34, 39, 40.
Arcis-sur-Aube battle of (20 March 1814), 320.
Arcola, battle of (16 Nov. 1796), 176.
Aremberg, Louis Engelbert, Duke of (1750-1820), 93.
—— Prosper Louis, Duke of (1785-1863), 282.
Argau, canton of Switzerland, formed by Bonaparte (1803), 228; recognised by Congress of Vienna (1815), 344.
Aristocracy, Napoleon's, 286.
Armistices: Cherasco (1796), 174; Foligno (1796), 175; Giurgevo (1790), 88; Pleswitz (1813), 309.
Arndt, Ernest Maurice, German poet (1769-1862), 291.
Arragon, Suchet's campaigns in, 275, 295.
Arras, atrocities of Le Bon at (1794), 139.
Artois, Charles Philippe, Comte d', younger brother of Louis XVI., afterwards King Charles X. of

France (1757-1836), 55, 59, 102, 139, 167, 172, 351.
Aschaffenburg, principality of, granted to the Elector of Mayence, 225, 260.
Aspern or Essling, battle of (21, 22 May 1809), 273.
Assignats issued in France, 74; their effect, 98.
Aubert-Dubayet, Jean Baptiste Annibal, French general (1759-1797), 166, 182.
Auckland, William Eden, Lord, English diplomatist (1744-1814), 65, 93.
Auerstädt, battle of (14 Oct. 1806), 247.
—— Duke of. *See* Davout.
Augereau, Charles Pierre François, Duke of Castiglione, French general (1757-1816), 191, 219, 321; App. iv.
Augsburg, Bishop of, an ecclesiastical prince of the Holy Roman Empire, 34.
—— bishopric of, merged in Bavaria (1803), 227.
—— city of, a free city of the Empire (1789), 35; taken by Moreau (1800), 219; maintained as a free city (1803), 226; Masséna's headquarters (1809), 272.
Augusta, Princess, of Bavaria married to Eugène de Beauharnais, 258.
Augustus, Prince, of Prussia (1779-1843), 337.
Aulic Council, the, 35.
Austerlitz, battle of (2 Dec. 1805), 244.
Austria, position in 1789, 14-17; influence in the Empire, 35; obtained cessions by the treaty of Sistova (1791), 88; got nothing in the second partition of Poland (1793), 122; received Cracow, etc. at third partition of Poland (1795), 152; received Venice for Lombardy by treaty of Campo-Formio (1797), 199; and by treaty of Lunéville (1801), 220; obtained Trent and Brixen, but lost much influence in the resettlement of Germany (1803), 226; formed into an empire (1805), 236; lost Venice, Istria, the Tyrol, etc. by treaty of Pressburg (1805), 245; lost Trieste, Galicia, Salzburg, etc. by treaty of Vienna (1809), 274;
at Congress of Vienna (1814) got back Cracow, 342, and Lombardy and Venetia, 347. *See* Francis II., Joseph II., Leopold II.
Austrian Netherlands. *See* Belgium.
Auvergne, movement against the Convention in (1793), 131.
Avignon, city of, wishes to join France (1790), 76; secured to France by first treaty of Paris (1814), 333; and by second treaty of Paris (1815), 354.

BABEUF, FRANÇOIS NOËL (Gracchus), French socialist (1764-97), 181.
Badajoz, treaty of (1801), 223; taken by Soult (1810), 296; by Wellington (1812), 306.
Baden, condition in 1789, 37; made an electorate (1803), 225; increased by the secularisations (1803), 227; made a grand duchy (1806), 245; received Ortenau and the Breisgau (1809), 258; a state of the Confederation of the Rhine (1808), 260; of the Germanic Confederation (1815), 342. *See* Charles Frederick, Charles Louis Frederick.
Bagration, Peter, Prince, Russian general (1762-1812), 281, 305.
Bailly, Jean Sylvain, French statesman (1736-93), 53, 59, 138.
Baird, Sir David, English general (1757-1829), 224.
Ball, Sir Alexander John, English admiral (1759-1809), 195.
Baltic Sea, effort to exclude English commerce from, 222; command of, given to Russia and Prussia by the Congress of Vienna, 347.
Bamberg, Bishop of, an ecclesiastical prince of the Holy Roman Empire, 34.
—— bishopric of, merged in Bavaria (1803), 227.
Bank of France, founded by Bonaparte, 215.
Bantry Bay, French expedition to (1796), 185.
Barbé-Marbois, François, Comte de, French statesman (1745-1837), 188, 191, 214.
Barclay de Tolly, Michael, Prince, Russian general (1755-1818), 305, 309, 313.

Barentin, Charles Louis François de Paule de, French minister (1738-1819), 51.
Barère, Bertrand, French orator (1755-1841), 117, 133, 134, 145, 149, 155.
Barnave, Antoine Pierre Joseph Marie, French politician (1761-93), 100.
Barras, Paul François Jean Nicolas, Comte de, French statesman (1755-1829), 147, 164, 165; nominates Bonaparte to command the army of Italy, 174; his attitude as a Director, 181; co-operates in *coup d'état* of Fructidor 1797, 191; only original Director left (July 1799), 209, 210; resigns (Nov. 1799), 211.
Barrosa, battle of (5 March 1811), 297.
Bartenstein, treaty of (April 1807), 248.
Barthélemy, François, Marquis de, French diplomatist (1747-1830), 156, 188, 189, 191.
Basire, Claude, French politician (1764-94), 117.
Basle, Bishop of, an ecclesiastical prince of the Holy Roman Empire, 34, 41; with fiefs in Alsace, 79.
—— bishopric of, part ceded to Baden (1803), 227; part to canton of Berne (1815), 345.
—— canton of Switzerland, maintained by Bonaparte (1803), 228.
—— treaties of (1795), 156, 157.
Basque Roads, affair in the (1809), 276.
Bassano, Duke of. *See* Maret.
Bastille, capture of the (14 July 1789), 57, 58.
Batavian Republic founded (1795), 150; imitates the French constitutions, 193; turned into the kingdom of Holland (1806), 254, 255.
Battles: Abensberg (1809), 272; Albuera (1811), 297; Albufera (1811), 297; Aldenhoven (1794), 150; Alexandria (1801), 224; Altenkirchen (1796), 178; Arcis-sur-Aube (1814), 328; Arcola (1796), 176; Aspern (Essling) (1809), 273; Auerstädt (1806), 247; Austerlitz (1805), 244; Barrosa (1811), 297; Bautzen (1813), 309; Bergen (1799), 205; Biberach (1800), 219; Borodino (1812), 305; Braila (1809), 281; Brienne (1814), 319; Burgos (1808), 269; Busaco (1810), 296; Cairo (1799), 208; Caldiero (1796), 176; Caldiero (1805), 244; Camperdown (1797), 194; Cassano (1799), 203; Castiglione (1796), 175; Ceva (1796), 174; Champaubert (1814), 319; Copenhagen (1801), 222; Corunna (1809), 270; Craonne (1814), 328; Dego (1796), 174; Dennewitz (1813), 313; Dresden (1813), 312; Dubienka (1792), 122; Eckmühl (1809), 273; Elchingen (1805), 244; Engen (1800), 219; Espinosa (1808), 269; Essling (Aspern) (1809), 273; Ettlingen (1796), 178; Eylau (1807), 248; Famars (1793), 130; Figueras (1794), 150; First of June (1794), 145; Fleurus (1794), 144; Foksany (1788), 45; Friedland (1807), 249; Fuentes de Onor (1811), 297; the Geisberg (1793), 140; Genola (1799), 204; Giurgevo (1790), 88; Gross-Beeren (1813), 312; Gross-Gorschen (Lützen) (1813), 309; Hanau (1813), 314; Heliopolis (1800), 224; Hohenlinden (1800), 219; Hondschoten (1793), 140; Jemmappes (1792), 118; Jena (1806), 247; Kaiserslautern (1794), 144; the Katzbach (1813), 312; Kioge (1807), 252; Laon (1814), 328; Leipzig (1813), 314; Ligny (1815), 352; Loano (1795), 151, 173; Lodi (1796), 174; Lützen (Gross Gorschen) (1813), 309; Maciejowice (1794), 152; Magnano (1799), 202; Maida (1806), 256; Marengo (1800), 218; Matchin (1791), 96; Medellin (1809), 275; Medina del Rio Seco (1808), 267; the Mincio (1814), 322; Millesimo (1796), 174; Moeskirchen (1800), 219; Mondovi (1796), 174; Montebello (1800), 218; Montenotte (1796), 174; Montereau (1814), 319; Montmirail (1814), 319; Mount Tabor (1799), 208; Nangis (1814), 319; Neerwinden (1793), 127; Neumarkt (1797), 186; the Nile (Aboukir Bay) (1798), 195; the Nive (1813), 316; the Nivelle (1813), 316; Novi (1799), 204; Ocana (1809), 276; Orthez (1814), 321; Pacy-sur-Eure (1793), 131; Paris (1814), 329; the Pyramids (1798), 195; Quatre Bras (1815), 352; Raab (1809), 273; Raclawice (1794), 151; Rivoli (1797), 176; Roliça (1808),

265; the Rymnik (1788), 45; Sacilio (1899), 273; St. Vincent (1797), 183; Salamanca (1812), 306; Saorgio (1794), 144; Silistria (1809), 281; Stockach (1799), 202; Svenska Sound (1790), 95; Talavera (1809), 275, 276; Tobac (1788), 45; Tolentino (1815), 346; Toulouse (1814), 332; Trafalgar (1805), 245; the Trebbia (1799), 203; Tudela (1808), 269; Unzmarkt (1797), 186; Valmy (1792), 115; Valsarno (1813), 315; Vauchamps (1814), 319; Vimeiro (1808), 265, 266; Vittoria (1813), 315; Wagram (1809), 274; Waterloo (1815), 353; Wattignies (1793), 140; Zielence (1792), 121, 122; Zurich (1799), 204.

Bautzen, battle of (20 May 1813), 309.

Bavaria, the Emperor Joseph's designs on, 16, 17; its Elector also Elector-Palatine, 34; condition in 1789, 37; invaded by Moreau (1796), 178; treaty of Pfaffenhofen, 180; promised to Austria by Bonaparte (1797), 193; occupied by Moreau (1800), 219; increased by the secularisations (1803), 227; invaded by the Austrians (1805), 243; receives the Tyrol and becomes a kingdom (1806), 245; receives Salzburg (1809), 257; member of the Confederation of the Rhine, 260; invaded by the Austrians (1809), 272; great internal reforms, 289; member of the Germanic Confederation (1815), 342; receives Mayence for the Tyrol (1815), 344. *See* Charles Theodore, Maximilian Joseph.

Baylen, capitulation of (1808), 267, 268.

Bayonne besieged by the English (1813, 1814), 316, 321.

Beauharnais, Eugène de, stepson of Napoleon (1781-1824), 236, 238, 239, 244, 255, 256, 273, 308, 315, 321, 322, 345.

Beaulieu, Jean Pierre, Baron de, Austrian general (1725-1820), 174.

Beccaria, Cæsar Bonesana, Marquis de, Italian philosopher (1738-94), 26.

Belgium, opposition to the Emperor Joseph's reforms in (1788), 15; his apparent success, 43; armed resistance in, 47; abolition of Belgian liberties, 47, 48; the Austrians driven from (1789), 64; the Belgian Republic formed (Jan. 1790), 65; struggle between the Van der Nootists and Vonckists, 92, 93; reconquered by the Austrians (Dec. 1790), 94; conquered by the French under Dumouriez (1792), 118; annexed to the French Republic, 118; rises against the French (1793), 126; Dumouriez driven from (1793), 127; reconquered by the French (1794), 144; organised as part of the French Republic, 150; cession to France agreed to by Austria at Leoben, 186; and at Campo-Formio (1797), 192, 193; organised into nine French departments, 230; England insists on its separation from France, 318; invaded by the Prince of Orange (1814), 321; Napoleon refuses to give up, 324; united with Holland into the kingdom of the Netherlands (1815), 344, 360.

Belgrade, taken by the Austrians (1789), 45.

Bellegarde, Henri, Comte de, Austrian general (1755-1831), on the Mincio (1814), 322.

Belluno, Duke of. *See* Victor.

Bender, city of, taken by the Russians (1789), 45.

—— Blaise Colombeau, Baron, Austrian general (1713-98), 65, 93, 94.

Benevento, principality of, belonged to the Pope in 1789, 24; Talleyrand made prince of, 277.

Benezech, Pierre, French administrator (1745-1802), 166.

Benningsen, Levin Augustus Theophilus, Count, Russian general (1745-1826), 221, 248, 249, 311.

Bentinck, Lord William Charles Cavendish, English general (1774-1839), 307, 315, 322, 346.

Beresford, William Carr, Viscount, English general (1770-1856), 266, 297.

Berg, grand duchy of, created for Murat (1806), its extent, 252; member of the Confederation of the Rhine, 260; conferred on son of Louis Bonaparte (1808), 283.

Bergen, battles of (19 Sept. and 2 Oct. 1799), 205.

Bergen-op-Zoom, English repulsed from (1814), 321.
Berlin, occupied by Napoleon (1806), 247; decree issued at (1807), 251; University of, founded, 303, 304; the French driven from (1813), 308.
Bernadotte, Jean Baptiste Jules, Prince of Ponte Corvo (1806), Prince Royal of Sweden (1810), King Charles XIV. of Sweden (1818), (1764-1844), French ambassador to Austria (1798), 197; insulted at Vienna, 198; Minister of War (1799), 210; attacked by the Russians (1807), 247; commanded the Saxons at Wagram (1809), 274; Prince of Ponte Corvo, 277; elected Prince Royal of Sweden (1810), 279; signs treaty of Abo with Emperor Alexander (1812), 302; intrigues with Napoleon, 307, 308; invaded Germany (1813), 309; wins battle of Gross Beeren, 312; and of Dennewitz, 313; defeated the Danes and exchanged Pomerania for Norway (1814), 320; rejected for throne of France, 330; got Norway, but had to give up Guadeloupe (1815), 347; one of Napoleon's marshals, App. iv.
Bernard, Great St., Bonaparte crosses (1800), 218.
—— Little St., French reach the summit of (1795), 151.
—— of Saintes, Adrien Antoine, French politician (1750-1819), 139.
Berne, chief oligarchical canton of Switzerland in 1789, 41; occupies Geneva (1792), 125; occupied by the French (1798), 199; Vaud and Argau separated from (1803), 228; obtained part of the Bishopric of Basle (1815), 345.
Bernis, François Joachim de Pierre, Cardinal de, French statesman (1715-94), 19.
Bernstorf, Count Andrew, Danish statesman (1735-97), 32, 46, 120.
—— Count Christian, Danish statesman (1769-1835), 338.
Berthier, Louis Alexandre, Prince of Neufchâtel and Wagram, French general (1753-1815), 200, 216, 241, 239, 283, App. iv.
—— de Sauvigny, Louis Bénigne François, French administrator (1742-89), 59.
Bessarabia, conquered by the Russians under Potemkin (1789), 45; under Bagration (1810), 281; part of, ceded to Russia by treaty of Bucharest, 281.
Bessières, Jean Baptiste, Duke of Istria, French general (1768-1813), 267, 297, 309, App. iv.
Beugnot, Jacques Claude, Comte, French administrator (1761-1835), 331.
Biberach, battle of (9 May 1800), 219.
Bidassoa, the passage of, forced by the Spaniards (1739), 130; by the French (1794), 140.
Bigot de Préameneu, Félix Julien Jean, Comte, French jurist (1747-1825), 215.
Bilbao, taken by the French (1795), 151.
Billaud-Varenne, Jacques Nicolas, French statesman (1756-1819), 193, 134, 138, 139, 147, 149, 155.
Biron, Armand Louis de Gontaut, Duc de, French general (1747-93), 138.
Bischofswerder, Hans Rudolf, Baron von, Prussian statesman (†1803), 31, 87.
Bishops, the Princes of Germany, 34, 39.
Black Legion of Brunswick raised, 293.
Blake, Joachim, Spanish general (†1827), defeated at Albufera (1811), 247.
Blücher, Gebhard Lebrecht von, Prince of Wahlstatt, Prussian general (1742-1819), 309, 312, 318, 319, 328, 329, 350, 352, 353, 355.
Boeckh, Augustus, German scholar (1785-1861), 304.
Bohemia, opposition to Joseph's reforms in, 15; the reforms suspended, 66; pacified by Leopold, 84.
Boissy d'Anglas, François Antoine, Comte, French statesman (1756-1826), 155, 165, 168, 182.
Bologna, belonged to the Pope, 24; occupied by Bonaparte (1796), 175; merged in the Cisalpine Republic, 192; in the kingdom of Italy, 255; restored to the Pope (1815), 347.
Bonaparte, Caroline, Queen of Naples. *See* Caroline.

Bonaparte, Elisa (1777-1820), 283.
—— Jerome (1784-1860), King of Westphalia. *See* Jerome.
—— Joseph (1768-1844), 239 (1806), 255. *See* Joseph.
—— Louis (1778-1846), 239, 254, 255. *See* Louis.
—— Lucien (1775-1840), 210, 216, 223.
—— Napoleon (1769-1821) at the siege of Toulon (1793), 140 ; brings up artillery for the defence of the Convention (1795), 164 ; defeats the insurgents of Vendémiaire, 165 ; appointed to the command of the army of Italy (1796), 174 ; defeats the Sardinians, 174 ; conquers Lombardy, 174 ; makes armistice with the Pope, 175 ; defeats the Austrians at Castiglione, 175, at Arcola and Rivoli, 176 ; invades the Tyrol and signs Preliminaries of Leoben, 186 ; opposed the Clichians, 189 ; sends Augereau to Paris to help the Directors, 191 ; formed the Cisalpine Republic, 192 ; signs treaty of Campo-Formio (1797), 192 ; commands army of the Interior, 194 ; takes Malta and invades Egypt (1798), 195 ; campaign in Syria (1799), 208 ; returns to France, 208 ; makes *coup d'état* of 18 Brumaire, 210, 211 ; provisional First Consul, 211 ; First Consul, 214 ; internal policy, 215 ; forms the Bank of France and Code Civil, 215 ; foreign policy, 216, 217 ; wins battle of Marengo and conquers Italy, 218 ; First Consul of the Cisalpine Republic, 220 ; his Spanish policy, 223 ; concludes the treaty of Amiens (1802), 225 ; reorganises Switzerland, 228 ; Mediator of the Swiss Confederation, 229 ; makes Concordat with the Pope, 229 ; forms the prefectures, 230 ; educational reforms, 231 ; First Consul for life (1802), 232 ; arrests the English in France and occupies Hanover (1803), 233 ; execution of the Duc d'Enghien (1804), 235 ; Emperor of the French (1804), 236. *See* Napoleon.
—— Pauline, Princess Borghese (1780-1825), 283.
Bonn, the university of, 40, 150.

Bonnier - d'Alco, Ange Elisabeth Louis Antoine, French politician (1749-1799), 202.
Bordeaux, 131, 327.
Borodino, battle of (7 Sept. 1812), 305.
Bosnia, invaded by the Austrians (1788), 43.
Bouillé, François Claude Amour, Marquis de, French general (1739-1800), 72, 97, 98, 100.
Boulogne, Napoleon's camp at (1804-5), 241, 242.
Bourbon, Isle of (Réunion), restored to France (1815), 348.
Bourdon, Léonard Jean Joseph, French politician (1758-1816), 147.
Bourdon de Vatry, Marc Antoine, French administrator (1761-1828), 210.
Bourges, federalist army proposed to be formed at (1793), 131, 132.
Bournonville, Pierre de Riel, Comte de, French general (1752-1821), 330.
Brabant, Constitution of, abolished by the Emperor Joseph (1789), 47.
Braila, battle of (1810), 281.
Branicki, Francis Xavier, Polish statesman († 1819), 121.
Braschi, Giovanni Angelo. *See* Pius VI., Pope.
Breda, 48, 64.
Breisgau, the, granted to the Duke of Modena (1803), 226 ; to the Grand Duke of Baden (1805), 258.
Bremen, a free city of the Holy Roman Empire, 35 ; retained its independence (1803), 226 ; annexed to Napoleon's Empire (1810), 282 ; one of the four free cities of the Germanic Confederation (1815), 343.
Brescia formed part of the Cisalpine Republic, 192.
Brest, blockaded by English fleet, 184 ; French fleet at, unable to break the blockade (1805), 242.
Brienne, battle of (29th Jan. 1814), 319.
Brigandage rife in France under the Directory, 181 ; put down by the Consulate, 215 ; rife in Calabria, 256.
Brissot, Jean Pierre, French politician (1754-1793), 101, 105, 107, 116, 129.

384  European History, 1789-1815

Brissotin section of the Girondin party in the Convention, 116.
Brittany, opposition to the Convention in, 131; pacified by Hoche, 180, 181.
Brixen, bishopric of, united to Austria (1803), 226.
Broglie, Victor François, Duc de, French general (1718-1804), 56.
Bruges, 64.
Bruix, Eustache, French admiral (1759-1805), 196.
Brumaire, *coup d'état* of the 18th (1799), 210, 211.
Brune, Guillaume Marie Anne, French general (1763-1815), 199, 205, 219, 254, 356, App. iv.
Brunswick, Duchy of, merged in kingdom of Westphalia (1806), 258;. a member of the Germanic Confederation (1815), 342.
Brunswick-Lüneburg, Duke of. *See* Charles William Ferdinand.
Brunswick-Oels, Duke of. *See* Frederick William.
Brussels, 15, 47, 48, 64, 94, 118, 144.
Bucharest, 45, 281.
Buenos Ayres, 264.
Bülow, Frederick William von, Prussian general (1755-1816), 309, 312, 313; detached to join Blücher in France (1814), 319, 320, 328.
Burgos, battle of (10 Nov. 1808), 269; Wellington fails to take (1812), and retreats from, 307.
Burke, Edmund, English orator (1730-97), 120.
Burrard, Sir Harry, English general (1755-1815), 266.
Busaco, battle of (27 Sept. 1810), 296.
Buttmann, Philip Charles, German scholar (1764-1829), 304.
Buzot, François Nicolas Léonard, French politician (1760-94), 116.
Buzotins, a section of the Girondins, 116.

CABARRUS, FRANÇOIS, Spanish statesman (1752-1810), 21.
Cadiz, besieged by the French (1810-12), 296, 297.
Cadore, Duke of. *See* Champagny.
Cadoudal, Georges, Chouan leader (1771-1804), 234, 235.
Caen, army organised by the Girondins against the Convention at (1793), 131.
Caillard, Antoine Bernard, French diplomatist (1737-1807), 215.
Cairo, taken by Bonaparte (1798), 195; the Mamelukes defeated at (1799), 208; taken by the English (1801), 224.
Caisse d'amortissement founded, 287, 288.
Calabria, brigandage in, encouraged by the English, 256.
Calder, Sir Robert, English admiral (1745-1818), his action (1805), 242.
Caldiero, battle of (12 Nov. 1796), 176; battle of (30 Oct. 1805), 244.
Cambacérès, Jean Jacques Régis, Duke of Parma, French statesman (1753-1824), 156, 159, 166, 182, 210, 214, 239, 287, 357.
Cambon, Joseph, French statesman (1754-1820), 129, 133, 288.
Cambrai, 353.
Camperdown, battle of (11 Oct. 1797), 194.
Campo-Chiaro, Duke of, Neapolitan statesman, 338, 346.
Campo-Formio, treaty of (17 Oct. 1797), 192, 193.
Campomanes, Don Pedro Rodriguez, Count of, Spanish statesman (1723-1802), 21.
Canning, George, English statesman (1770-1827), 295.
Cantons of Switzerland, 228, 345.
Cape of Good Hope taken by the English (1805), 264; retained by them (1815), 348.
Capitulations: of Ulm (1805), 243; of Baylen (1808), 267, 268; of Kulm (1813), 313.
Capo-d'Istria, John, Count, Greek statesman (1776-1831), 337.
Carniola ceded to Napoleon (1809), 274.
Carnot, Lazare Nicolas Marguerite, French statesman (1753-1823), 133, 134, 140, 148, 165, 177, 181, 191, 214, 216, 321, 352, 357.
Caroline, Marie, Queen of the Two Sicilies (1752-1814), 23.
—— Murat, Queen of Naples (1782-1839), 322, 345.
Carrier, Jean Baptiste, French politician (1756-1794), 139, 141, 149.
Cassano, battle of (27 April 1799), 203.

# Index 385

Castiglione, battle of (15 Aug. 1796), 175.
—— Duke of. *See* Augereau.
Castlereagh, Robert Stewart, Viscount, Marquis of Londonderry, English statesman (1769-1822), his views on the way to carry on the war with Napoleon, 295; returns to office (1812); 301; his policy to form a fresh coalition, 301, 302; efforts to get Austria to join (1813), 311; sends expedition to Holland, 314; sent with full powers to France (1814), 318; persists in the war and calls up reinforcements for Blücher, 319, 320; opposition to the retention of Belgium by France, 324; signs treaty of Chaumont, 327; friendship with Metternich, 331; signs treaty of Paris, 332; one of the two men who did most to overthrow Napoleon, 334; English representative at the Congress of Vienna (1814), 337; signs treaty with France and Austria against Russia and Prussia, 340; disavows Bentinck's Italian proclamation, 346; gets the Slave Trade condemned, 349; succeeded by Wellington at Vienna, 349; opposes Prussia's schemes for punishing France (1815), 354; refuses to join the Holy Alliance; 355.
Catalonia, 144, 150, 151, 275.
Cathcart, William Schaw, Lord, English general (1755-1843), 264, 301, 323, 337.
Catherine II., Empress of Russia (1729-96) a benevolent despot, 4; attitude to other Powers of Europe (1789), 12, 13; alliance with Joseph II., 17; extension of Russia under, 18; policy in Poland, 18; internal policy, 19; war with the Turks (1789-90), 43-45; with the Swedes (1789-90), 45, 46; deprived of the Austrian alliance by Leopold, 95; makes peace with Sweden at Verela (1790), 95, 96; with the Turks at Jassy (1792), 96; attitude towards the French Revolution, 109, 121; invades Poland (1793), 121; signs second partition of Poland, 122; asserts she is fighting Jacobinism in Poland, 125; invades Poland (1795), 151; extinguishes independence of Poland, 152; receives the Comte d'Artois, 172; death (1796), 185.
Catherine, Grand Duchess of Oldenburg, Queen of Würtemburg (1788-1819), 300, 337.
—— Princess, of Würtemburg (1783-1835), marries Jerome Bonaparte, King of Westphalia (1807), 258.
Cattaro, mouths of the river, ceded by Russia to France at Tilsit (1807), 250.
Caulaincourt, Armand Augustin Louis de, Duke of Vicenza, French statesman (1772-1827), 234, 239, 311, 316, 317, 323, 324, 329, 331, 332.
Cayenne restored to France (1814), 348.
Ceva, battle of (16 April 1796), 174.
Ceylon, taken by the English (1796), 264; retained in 1815, 348.
Chabot, François, French politician (1759-94), 117.
Chalier, Marie Joseph, French politician (1747-93), 131.
Chambéry, annexed to France (1814), 333; restored to King of Sardinia (1815), 354.
'Chambre Introuvable' (1815), 357, 358.
Champagny, Jean Baptiste Nompère de, Duke of Cadore, French statesman (1756-1834), 241.
Champaubert, battle of (10 Feb. 1814), 319.
Champ de Mars, Paris, massacre of (17 July 1791), 101.
Championnet, Jean Etienne, French general (1762-1800), 200, 203, 204.
Chaptal, Jean Antoine, Comte, French administrator (1756-1832), 216, 241.
Charles III., King of Spain (1716-88), benevolent despot, his reforms, 4, 21; commenced his career as a reforming monarch at Naples, 23.
—— IV., King of Spain (1748-1819), 21, 77, 79, 193, 196, 157, 183, 223, 232, 252, 253, 267.
—— XIII., King of Sweden, formerly Duke of Sudermania (1748-1818), 46, 110, 120, 171, 253, 279.
—— II., King of Etruria (1799-1863), 253, 347.

PERIOD VII.  2 B

Charles Augustus, Duke of Saxe-Weimar (1757-1828), 38, 337, 342.
— Emmanuel IV., King of Sardinia (1751-1819), 200.
— Eugène, Duke of Würtemburg, (1728-93), 37, 38.
— Frederick, Margrave of Baden-Baden and Baden Durlach (1728-1811), 37, 79, 167, 180, 225, 227, 245, 258, 260.
— Louis Frederick, Grand Duke of Baden (1786-1816), 258, 337, 342.
— Theodore, Elector of Bavaria and Elector Palatine (1729-99), 37, 172, 180.
— William Ferdinand, Duke of Brunswick - Lüneburg, Prussian general (1735-1806), 32, 113, 114, 115, 116, 126, 246.
— Archduke, Austrian general (1771-1847), elected Grand Duke of Belgium (1790), 94; commands the Austrian army in Germany (1796), 177; repulses Jourdan and Moreau, 178; effect of his success, 180; commands Austrian army in the Tyrol (1797), 185; defeated by Bonaparte, and signs Preliminaries of Leoben, 186; defeats Jourdan (1799), 202; and advances to the Rhine, 204; forced to retreat, 205; campaign against Moreau (1800), superseded, 219; invades Italy (1805), 243; defeated at Caldiero, 244; reorganises Austrian army, 271; invades Bavaria (1809), 272; defeated at Eckmühl, 273; fights battle of Aspern, 273; defeated at Wagram, 274.
Charter, the, of 4 June 1814, 350.
Chatham, John Pitt, Earl of, English general (1756-1820), 276.
Châtillon, Congress of (1814), 323, 324.
Chaumette, Pierre Gaspard, French politician (1763-94), 141.
Chaumont, treaty of (1 March 1814), 327, 328.
Chauvelin, François Bernard, Marquis de, French politician (1766-1832), 120.
Cherasco, armistice of (28 April 1796), 174.
Chernishev, Alexander, Count, Russian general, 308, 312, 313, 337.
Chestret, M., elected burgomaster of Liége (1789), 49.

Chiaramonti, Gregorio Barnaba Luigi. *See* Pius VII., Pope.
Choczim, taken by the Austrians and Russians (1788), 43.
Choiseul, Etienne François, Duc de, French statesman (1719-85), made the 'Pacte de Famille' with Spain, 14.
Christian VII., King of Denmark (1749-1808), 32, 46, 171.
Cintra, Convention of (30 Aug. 1808), 266.
Circles, the executive divisions of the Holy Roman Empire, 36; abolished (1803), 225.
Cisalpine Republic, 192, 203, 220, 255.
Ciudad Rodrigo, taken by Wellington (Jan. 1812), 306.
Clancarty, Richard Trench, Earl of, English diplomatist (1767-1837), 337.
Clarke, Henri Jacques Guillaume, Duke of Feltre, French general (1765-1818), 241.
Clavière, Etienne, French politician (1735-93), 41, 114, 125.
Clement Wenceslas of Saxony, Archbishop-Elector of Trèves in 1789, 40.
Clementine Museum at Rome re-organised by Pope Pius VI., 24.
Clerfayt, François Sébastien Charles Joseph de Croix, Comte de, Austrian general (1733-98), 88, 150, 172.
Clichian party, 182, 187, 188, 189, 190, 191.
Club, Cordeliers. *See* Cordeliers.
— de Clichy, 182, 187.
— Jacobin. *See* Jacobin.
— of 1789, 101.
Cobenzl, Count Louis, Austrian statesman (1753-1808), 192, 220, 233, 243, 270.
— Count Philip, Austrian statesman (1741-1810), 126.
Coblentz, 150, 230, 344.
Coburg, Frederick Josias of Saxe-Coburg-Saalfeld, Prince of, Austrian general (1737-1815), 43, 44, 45, 88, 127, 130, 144.
Cochon de Lapparent, Charles, French administrator (1749-1825), 182, 191.
Cochrane, Thomas, Lord, Earl of Dundonald, English admiral (1775-1860), 276.

Code, Civil, bases of, laid by the Convention, 156; Bonaparte's commission to draw up, 215.
Codes of law promulgated by Napoleon, 287.
Colli, Louis Leonard Gaspard Venance, Baron, Sardinian general (1760-1811), 174.
Colloredo, Count Jerome, Prince-Archbishop of Salzburg in 1789, 39.
Collot-d'Herbois, Jean Marie, French politician (1750-96), 117, 133, 134, 138, 147, 149, 155.
Cologne, Archbishop of, an Elector in the Holy Roman Empire, 34.
—— archbishopric of, excellently ruled in 1789, 40; merged in France, 225; ceded to Prussia (1815), 344.
—— city of, a free city of the Holy Roman Empire, 35; taken by the French (1794), 150; ceded to Prussia (1815), 344.
Committee of General Defence, 127.
—— of General Security, 135, 136, 146, 148.
—— of Mercy, 143.
—— of Public Safety, the first chosen (April 1793), 127, 128; its work, 132, 133; formation of the Great, 133; growth of its power, 134; its system of government—the Reign of Terror, 135; its instruments—the Committee of General Security, 135, 136; the deputies on mission, 136, 137; laws of the Suspects and the Maximum, 137; the Revolutionary Tribunal, 137, 138; its power organised, 138, 139; its success, 139-141; opposition to, 141-143; overthrows the Hébertists, 142; the Dantonists, 145; its triumphs on land, 143, 144; failure at sea, 144, 145; Robespierre's position in, 146; renewed by a quarter monthly after Robespierre's fall, 148; its supremacy maintained, but its system changed, 148, 149; filled by members of the Plain, 156.
Commune of Paris overthrows the monarchy (Aug. 1792), 115; its energy, 114; insists on expulsion of the Girondins (June 1793), 129; becomes Hébertist and opposes the Committee of Public Safety, 141;

becomes Robespierrist, and is decimated by the Convention, 147.
Conclusum of the Empire, how arrived at, 33, 34.
Concordat between the Pope and Bonaparte (1802), 229, 230, 277.
Condé, taken by the Austrians (1793), 130.
Condé, Louis Joseph de Bourbon, Prince de, French general (1736-1818), 106, 167, 178, 206, 207.
Condillac, Étienne-Bonnot, Abbé de, French philosopher (1715-80), 25.
Conegliano, Duke of. See Moncey.
Confederation, Germanic. See Germanic.
—— of the Rhine. See Rhine.
—— of Switzerland. See Switzerland.
—— of Targovitsa, asks Catherine to intervene in Poland (1795), 121.
Conferences: Erfurt (1808), 262; Pilnitz (1791), 102; Reichenbach, (1790), 87; Tilsit (1807), 249, 250.
Congresses: Châtillon (1814), 323, 324; the Hague (1799), 93, 94; Prague (1813), 311; Rastadt (1798), 186, 192, 202; Reichenbach (1790), 87; Sistova (1790), 88; Vienna (1814-15), 336-350.
Consalvi, Hercules, Cardinal, Italian statesman (1757-1824), 277, 337.
Conscription, established in France (1798), 201; in Germany, 289.
Constance, Bishop of, an ecclesiastical Prince of the Holy Roman Empire, 34.
—— bishopric of, merged in Grand Duchy of Baden (1803), 227.
—— city of, taken by Massena (1799), 205.
Constantine, Grand Duke, brother of the Emperor Alexander (1779-1831), 312, 337.
Constantinople, great riot at (1807), 281.
Constituent Assembly: the Tiers État declares itself the National Assembly (June 1789), 53; oath of the Tennis Court, and Séance Royale, 54; session of 4 August, 60; makes the Constitution of

1791, 68-73; authority passed to, 97; discredited the executive, 98; dissolved (1791), 105.
Constitution, the French, of 1791, 68-73; revised, 101; completed, 103; compared with the Polish of 1791, 104, 105; its local arrangements confirmed by the Constitution of the Year III., 162.
—— the French, of 1793, 132, 138, 141.
—— the French, of the Year III. (1795), 156, 159, 160, 161, 162.
—— the French, of the Year VIII. (1799), 212-214; the Consulate, 213; the Legislature, 214, 215.
—— the French, of the Empire (1805), 240.
—— the French, promised by the Charter (1814), 350.
—— the Polish, of 1791, 104, 105; abrogated, 122.
Consulate, the, in France, 213.
Consuls, the (1799-1804), Bonaparte, Cambacérès, Le Brun, 214.
—— the Provisional (1799), Bonaparte, Sieyès, Roger Ducos, 211.
Continental Blockade against England, 250, 251, 255, 261, 282, 300, 301.
Convention, National, 116, 117, 118, 119, 120, 127, 132, 134, 147, 155, 163, 164, 165, 166.
Conventions: Alexandria (1800), 218; Alkmaar (1799), 205; Cintra (1808), 268; Leoben (1797), 186; Reichenbach (1790), 87, 88; Tauroggen (1812), 308.
Copenhagen, battle of (2 April 1801), 222; bombarded and the Danish fleet seized by the English (1807), 252.
Cordeliers Club at Paris, 101, 141.
Corfu, occupied by the French (1797), 192. *See* Ionian Islands.
Cornwallis, Charles, Marquis, English general (1738-1805), 197.
Corsica, ceded to France by Genoa (1768), 27; occupied by the English (1793), 145; abandoned by them (1796), 183.
Corunna, battle of (16 Jan. 1809), 270.
*Corvée*, or forced labour, 5, 6, 16.
Council of Ancients, established in France (1795), 161, 162, 189, 190, 209, 210, 211.
Council of Five Hundred, established in France (1795), 161, 162, 182, 189, 190, 209, 210, 211.
—— of State, established in France under the Consulate (1799), 213, 231, 240.
Court, Napoleon's, 238, 239, 285, 286.
Couthon, Georges Auguste, French politician (1756-94), 133, 135, 147.
Cracow, university of, reorganised, 104; Kosciuszko raises standard of Polish independence at (1794), 151; given to Austria at third partition of Poland (1795), 152; joined to Grand Duchy of Warsaw (1809), 274; given to Austria as a free city (1815), 342.
Cradock, Sir John Francis, Lord Howden, English general (1762-1839), 269, 275.
Craonne, battle of (7 March 1814), 328.
Croatia ceded to Napoleon (1809), 274.
Cuesta, Don Gregorio Garcia de la, Spanish general (1740-1812), 267, 275, 276.
Curaçao, restored to Holland by England (1815), 348.
Custine, Adam Philippe, Comte de, French general (1740-93), 118, 138.
Czartoryski, Prince Adam George, Polish statesman (1770-1865), 337, 339.

DALBERG, CHARLES THEODORE DE, German prelate (1744-1817), Coadjutor-Archbishop-Elector of Mayence in 1789, 39; retained as Arch-Chancellor of the Empire with new territory (1803), 225; Grand Duke of Frankfort (1806), 259; received Fulda and Hanau and became Prince Primate of the Confederation of the Rhine, 260; suggested that Napoleon should be Emperor of Germany, 302; lost his territorial sovereignty (1815), 343.
—— Emeric Joseph, Duc de, French statesman (1773-1833), 330, 338.

Dalmatia, belonged to Venice in 1789, 27; ceded to Austria (1797), 192; annexed by Napoleon (1805), 245. *See* Illyrian Provinces.
—— Duke of. *See* Soult.
Dalrymple, Sir Hew Whiteford, English general (1750-1830), 266.
Danton, George Jacques, French statesman (1759-94), 101, 107, 114, 117, 120, 127, 129, 133, 134, 135, 136, 142, 143.
Dantzic promised to Prussia by the treaty of Warsaw, 85; the Poles refuse to surrender, 87; given to Prussia at second partition of Poland (1793), 122; besieged and taken by the French (1806), 247, 248; French garrison left in 1812, 308; besieged (1812-14), 319.
—— Duke of. *See* Lefebvre.
Danubian Principalities, the, promised to Alexander by Napoleon (1807), 250.
Dardanelles, the, forced by an English fleet (1807), 280.
Daru, Pierre Antoine Noël Bruno, Comte, French administrator (1767-1829), 241.
Daunou, Pierre Claude François, French politician (1761-1840), 156.
Dauphiné, influence of the Assembly in (1788), on the elections to the States-General in France, 51.
David, Jacques Louis, French painter (1748-1825), 357.
Davout, Louis Nicolas, Duke of Auerstädt, Prince of Eckmühl, French general (1770-1823), 247, 272, 319, 320, App. iv.
Debry, Jean Antoine, French politician (1760-1834), 202.
Declaration of the Rights of Man (1789), 60.
—— of Saint-Ouen (1814), 332, 333.
Decrès, Denis, Duke, French admiral (1761-1820), 216, 240.
Defermon, Joseph, Comte, French administrator (1756-1831), 240.
Dego, battle of (15 April 1796), 174.
Delacroix, Charles, French politician (1740-1805), 166, 189, 190.
Demarcation, line of, protecting Northern Germany, agreed to at treaty of Basle between France and Prussia (1795), 157; its effect on the position of Prussia, 170; proposal to extend (1796), 179; violated by the occupation of Hanover (1804), 242; this violation leads Prussia to prepare for war, 246.
Denmark, under Russian influence in 1789, 13; its prosperity and reforms, 32; the king a member of the Holy Roman Empire as Duke of Holstein, 34; attacks Sweden (1788), but forced to make peace, 46; remains neutral during the general war with France, 120, 124, 171; joins League of the North and is attacked by England (1801), 222; Copenhagen bombarded and the Danish fleet seized by England (1807), 254; Sweden declares war against (1808), 279; a faithful ally of Napoleon, 302; invaded by Bernadotte and forced to exchange Norway for Swedish Pomerania (1814), 320; gets the Duchy of Lauenburg for Swedish Pomerania (1815), 347; cedes Heligoland to England (1815), 348.
Dennewitz, battle of (6 Sept. 1813), 313.
Deputies of the Convention sent on mission, 128; put down the Girondin movement, 131; an instrument of the Reign of Terror; their work —in the provinces, 136; with the armies, 136, 137.
Desaix, Louis Charles Antoine, French general (1768-1800), 178, 208, 219.
Desmoulins, Camille, French politician (1762-94), 56, 133, 142, 143.
Despots, the benevolent, of the eighteenth century, 4, 5; the Emperor Joseph II., 15, 16; the Empress Catherine of Russia, 19; Charles III. of Spain, 21; Leopold of Tuscany, 24; Ferdinand of Parma, 25; Frederick the Great of Prussia, 29; Gustavus III. of Sweden, 33; Charles Theodore of Bavaria and Charles Frederick of Baden, 37.
Deux-Ponts (Zweibrücken), duchy of, 38, 79; merged in France (1803), 227.
Diderot, Denis, French philosopher (1713-84), 4, 9, 19.
Diet, the Imperial, of the Holy Roman Empire (Reichstag), 33, 35.

Diet, the, of the Confederation of the Rhine (1806), 260.
—— the, of the Germanic Confederation (1815), 343.
Dignitaries, the Grand, of Napoleon's Empire, 239.
Dillon, Arthur, French general (1750-94), 115.
—— Theobald, French general (1743-92), 111.
Directors, the, of the French Republic (1795-99): elected Oct. 1795, Barras, Carnot, Letourneur, Revellière-Lépeaux, Reubell, 165, 166; May 1797, Barthélemy succeeds Letourneur, 188; Sept. 1797, François de Neufchâteau and Merlin of Douai succeed Barthélemy and Carnot, 191; May 1798, Treilhard succeeds François de Neufchâteau, 195; May 1799, Sieyès succeeds Reubell, 209; June 1799, Ducos, Gohier, and Moulin succeed Merlin of Douai, Revellière-Lépeaux, and Treilhard, 211.
Directory, the, its functions as established by the Constitution of the Year III., 160, 161; foreign policy left to Reubell, 169, 179; military affairs to Carnot, 177; its internal policy, 180, 181; struggle with the Clichians, 189, 190; *coup d'état* of Fructidor 1797, 191; interferes in the elections of 1798 to the Legislature, 196; its weakness (1799), 209; struggle with the Legislature (1799), 209; abolished 18 Brumaire (1799), 211.
Dombrowski, John Henry, Polish general (1755-1818), 206.
'Dotations,' 286.
Dresden, battle of (27 Aug. 1813), 312.
Drouet, Jean Baptiste, French politician (1763-1824), 168.
Dubienka, battle of (17 July 1792), 122.
Dubitza taken by the Austrians (1788), 43.
Dubois-Crancé, Edmond Louis Alexis, French politician (1747-1814), 210.
Duckworth, Sir John Thomas, English admiral (1747-1817), 280.
Ducos, Roger, French politician (1754-1816), 209, 211.
Dugommier, Jean François Coquille, French general (1721-94), 140, 144, 150, 151.
Dumont, André, French politician (1764-1836), 139.
Dumouriez, Charles François, French general (1739-1823), 110, 111, 112, 114, 115, 116, 118, 119, 120, 126, 127.
Duncan, Adam, Viscount, English admiral (1731-1804), 193, 194.
Dunkirk besieged by the Duke of (1793), 130; relieved by Houchard, 140.
'Duodecimo duchies' of Germany in 1789, 40.
Duphot, Léonard, French general (1770-97), 209.
Dupont de l'Étang, Pierre, Comte, French general (1765-1838), 267, 268, 331.
Dufort, Amédée Bretagne Malo, Comte de, French courtier (1770-1836), 99.
Duroc, Géraud Christophe Michel, Duke of Friuli, French general (1772-1813), 217, 234, 239.
Düsseldorf, 37, 172, 259.

ECCLESIASTICAL princes of the Holy Roman Empire, 34, 39, 40; their states secularised (1803), 170.
Eckmühl, battle of (22 April 1809), 273.
—— Prince of. *See* Davout.
Education, national system established before 1789 in Spain, 21; in Portugal, 22; in Tuscany, 24; in Parma, 25; in Lombardy, 26; in Denmark, 32; in Baden, 37; attempted in Poland, 104; reforms in, attempted by the Convention in France, 156; Bonaparte's scheme of, 231; Napoleon's system of, 258; established in Prussia by Humboldt, 303, 304.
Egypt, conquered by Bonaparte (1798), 195; his administration of, and reconquest (1799), 208; French expelled from, by the English (1801), 224; failure of English expedition to (1808), 264.
Ehrenbreitstein, fortress, taken by Marceau (1795), 172.
Elba, declared a French island, 230; granted to Napoleon (1814), 332; his escape from (1815), 349, 351.

*Index* 391

Elchingen, battle of (20 Oct. 1805), 244.
—— Duke of. *See* Ney.
Elections, the, to the States-General in France (1789), 50, 51.
Electors, the eight, of the Holy Roman Empire in 1789, 34; the ten established in 1803, 225.
Elizabeth, Madame, sister of Louis XVI. (1764-94), 61, 68.
Elliot, Hugh, English diplomatist (1752-1830), 78.
Elsinore, batteries at, passed by the English fleet (1801), 222.
Elten, abbey of, merged in Prussia (1803), 227; and again (1815), 344.
Elwangen, the Abbot of, an ecclesiastical Prince of the Holy Roman Empire, 34.
*Emigrés*, Belgian, strong measures taken against (1789), 48.
—— French, 59, 63, 81, 97, 106, 108, 109, 113, 137, 154, 166, 167, 169, 172, 188, 214, 215, 351, 357, 358. *See* Condé.
Emperor of the French, Napoleon declares himself (1804), 236; refuses to be Emperor of Germany, 302.
—— Holy Roman, position of, 34; Francis II. abandons the title of (1804), 236. *See* Francis II., Joseph II., Leopold II.
Empire, Holy Roman, 17, 33-36, 79-80, 108, 121, 193, 225-227.
—— Napoleon's, its establishment, 237, 238; Grand Dignitaries of, 239; institutions and administrative system, 240; greatest extension of (1810), 282, 283.
Engen, battle of (3 May 1800), 219.
Enghien, Louis Antoine Henri de Bourbon, Duc d' (1722-1804), shot at Vincennes, 235.
England, condition of, 8; Member of the Triple Alliance, 13, 32; alliance with Portugal, 21; condition in 1789, 27, 28; looks favourably on the French Revolution, 63; the affair of Nootka Sound, 77, 78; the Emperor Leopold appeals to, 86; attitude towards the French Republic, 120; France declares war against (1793), 120; paymaster of the coalition against France, 125, 126; occupies Toulon, 139; and Corsica, 145; withdrew subsidies from Prussia, 153; national feeling in, against France, 154; supported the French *émigrés*, 154, 166, 167; did not wish for peace with France, 169; Spain declares war against, 183; attempts at peace, 184, 190; blockades and defeats the Dutch fleet, 193, 194; takes Minorca and Malta, 195; forms the second coalition, 197; Bonaparte attacks her commerce through the Neutral League of the North, 222; drives the French out of Egypt, 224; the Peace of Amiens, 225; recommencement of the war with France, 233; Napoleon's project of invading, 241, 242; forms the third coalition, 243; the Continental Blockade against and its effect, 251; seizes the Danish fleet, 252; decides to actively intervene on the Continent, 263, 295; hitherto contented with taking colonies and detached expeditions, 264; sends an army to Portugal, 265, 266; promises subsidies to Austria (1809), 271; the Walcheren Expedition, 276; Castlereagh's and Canning's theories, 295; forms fresh coalition, 301, 302; greatness of her share in overthrowing Napoleon, 334; colonial gains made at the Congress of Vienna, 348; insists on abolition of the Slave Trade, 348, 349; refuses to join the Holy Alliance, 355. *See* Castlereagh, Pitt.
Erfurt, bishopric of, merged in Prussia (1803), 227.
—— conference at (1808), 262.
Erthal, Baron Francis Louis of, Prince-Bishop of Bamberg and Würtzburg in 1789, 39.
—— Baron Frederick Charles of, Archbishop-Elector of Mayence and Prince-Bishop of Worms in 1789, 39.
Espinosa, battle of (11 Nov. 1808), 269.
Essen, abbey of, merged in Prussia (1803), 227.
Essling or Aspern, battle of (21, 22 May 1809), 273.
—— Prince of. *See* Massena.
Esterhazy, Nicholas Joseph, Prince (1714-90), 91.
Etruria, kingdom of, 220, 253. *See* Louis.

Ettlingen, battle of (June 1796), 178.
Eugène de Beauharnais, Viceroy of Italy. *See* Beauharnais.
Ewart, Joseph, English diplomatist (1760-92), English representative at the Congress of Reichenbach (1790), 87.
Eylau, battle of (8 Feb. 1807), 248.

FABRY, M., elected burgomaster of Liége (1789), 49.
Famars, battle of (24 May 1793), 130.
Faypoult, Guillaume Charles, French administrator (1752-1817), 166, 182.
Felino, Marquis of. *See* Tillot.
Feltre, Duke of. *See* Clarke.
Féraud, Jean, French politician (1764-1795), killed in rising of 1 Prairial, 155.
Ferdinand, VII., King of Spain (1784-1833), 267, 358.
—— IV., King of the Two Sicilies (1751-1825), 23, 120, 121, 171, 200, 203, 256, 264, 346, 359.
—— III., Grand Duke of Tuscany, second son of the Emperor Leopold (1769-1824), 83, 120, 157, 171, 200, 206, 220, 225, 226, 260, 347.
—— Duke of Parma and Piacenza, 25, 174, 175.
—— Archduke, third son of Maria Theresa (1754-1806), 26.
Ferrara, Legation of, belonged to the Pope in 1789, 24; occupied by Bonaparte (1796), 175; part of the Cisalpine Republic (1797), 192; of the kingdom of Italy (1805), 255; restored to the Pope (1815), 347.
Ferrari, Raphael di, Doge of Genoa in 1789, 27. [152.
Fersen, Axel, Count (1759-1810), 113.
Fesch, Joseph, uncle of Napoleon (1763-1839), 239, 277.
Feudalism, 3, 6, 8, 28, 60, 199, 256, 259, 288, 289, 290, 297, 303, 361.
Fichte, John Theophilus, German philosopher (1762-1814), 304.
Figueras, battle of (20 Nov. 1794), 150, 151.
Filangieri, Gaetano, Neapolitan political writer (1752-88), 23.
Finance, Napoleon's system of, 287, 288.
Finland, belonged to Sweden (1789), 32; campaigns of Gustavus III. in

1788, 45, 46; (1790), 95; conquered by the Emperor Alexander (1808), 250, 254, 279; ceded to Russia by Bernadotte in exchange for Norway (1812), 302.
Firmian, Charles Joseph, Count, Austrian statesman (1716-82), 26.
Fitzherbert, Alleyne, Lord St. Helens, English diplomatist (1753-1839), 78.
Five Hundred, Council of. *See* Council.
Flanders, the Estates of, declare their independence of Austria (1789), 64.
Flesselles, Jacques de, French administrator (1721-89), 58.
Fleurus, battle of (26 June 1794), 144.
Florence, 200, 283. *See* Tuscany.
Florida Blanca, Joseph Monino, Count of, Spanish statesman (1728-1809), 21, 77, 78.
Flushing taken by the English (1809), 276.
Foksany, battle of (31 July 1789), 45.
Foligno, armistice of, between the Pope and Bonaparte (1796), 175.
Fontainebleau, treaty of (1808), 252, 253; Pope Pius VII. taken to, 278; Napoleon abdicates at (1814), 331.
Fontanes, Louis de, French writer (1757-1821), 288.
Forfait, Pierre Alexandre Laurent, French administrator (1752-1807), 216.
Fouché, Joseph, Duke of Otranto, French politician (1763-1820), 210, 216, 241, 357.
Foullon de Doué, Joseph François, French administrator (1715-89), 59.
Fox, Charles James, English statesman (1749-1806), 245, 247, 264.
France, serfdom and feudalism practically extinct, 6; why the Revolution broke out, 8; position in 1789, 19, 20; elections to the States-General (1789), 49, 51; result of the capture of the Bastille in (July 1789), 59, 60; divided into departments, 68, 69; state of, in 1791, 98; effect of the flight to Varennes on, 101, 102; wishes for war, 107; exasperated by Brunswick's proclamation, 113; invaded (1792), 114; (1793), 130; opposition to the Convention (1793), 131, 132; submits to the

## Index

Reign of Terror, 141; becomes a vast arsenal, 143; after the victory of Fleurus rejects the Terror, 148; detests the Convention because of the Terror (1795), 163; but would not rise against it, 164; internal peace established (1796), 180; state of (1796), 181; acquiesced in the *coup d'état* of Fructidor (1797), 191; state of (1798), weary of politics, 196; welcomed Bonaparte's return (1799), 210; pacified under the Consulate, 215; organisation into prefectures, 230; popularity of Bonaparte in (1802), 231; enthusiastically welcomes the Empire, 237; conduct to the Pope damaged Napoleon's popularity in, 278; Napoleon's autocratic rule in, abolition of individual liberty and representative institutions, 284; indisposed to support Napoleon (1813), 315; would not rise to defend France in 1814 as in 1793, 322; weary of the military policy of Napoleon and physically exhausted, 324-326; reduced to its limits of 1792, 333; distrusts Louis XVIII., 351; welcomes Napoleon back (1815), 351, 352; difference of its attitude in 1814 and 1815, 353, 354; reduced to its limits of 1789, 354; reactionary government of Louis XVIII., 357, 358.

Francis II., Holy Roman Emperor, I. Emperor of Austria (1768-1835), succeeded his father Leopold (1792), 110; elected and crowned Emperor, 112; war with France, 112, 113; loses Belgium, 118: regarded himself as duped by being left out of second partition of Poland (1793), 122; makes Thugut his Foreign Minister, 126; his armies invade France, 130, 139; repulsed, 140; receives Cracow and rest of Galicia at final partition of Poland (1795), 152; change in his attitude towards France, 153, 154; exchanges French prisoners for Madame Royale, 168; appealed to his people's patriotism against Bonaparte (1796), 176; signs Convention of Leoben (1797), 186; and treaty of Campo-Formio (1797), 192; again prepares for war with France (1798), 197, 201; was more afraid of Russia than France, 206; signs treaty of Lunéville and dismisses Thugut (1801), 220; declares himself Emperor of Austria (1804), 236; forms coalition with Russia and England, and invades Italy and Bavaria (1805), 243; signs treaty of Pressburg, 245; prepares for a fresh war, and tries to rouse a national German spirit, 270, 271; invades Italy and Bavaria (1809), 272; makes treaty of Vienna, and dismisses Stadion, 274; appoints Metternich State-Chancellor, 275; gives his daughter Marie Louise to Napoleon, 294; invades Russia as Napoleon's ally (1812), 303; attempts to mediate between Napoleon and the allies, 310; declares war against Napoleon (1813), 311; does not want to overthrow Napoleon (1814), 316, 317, 324; signs treaty of Chaumont, 327; inclined to side with England against Russia and Prussia, 334; receives the allied monarchs at Vienna (1814), 337; signs secret treaty with England and France (3 Jan. 1815), 340; obtains the duchy of Parma for his daughter Marie Louise, 346, 347; joins the Holy Alliance, 355; greatly weakened actually if not territorially by the great war, 359.

Francis IV., of Este, grandson of Hercules III., Duke of Modena (1779-1846), 347.

—— Prince, of Prussia, (1797), 189.

François de Neufchâteau, Nicolas, Comte, French politician (1750-1828), 190, 191, 195, 196.

Franconia invaded by Jourdan (1796), 177, 178; by Napoleon (1805), 244.

Frankenberg, Cardinal, Archbishop of Malines, 47, 65.

Frankfort-on-the-Main, a free city of the Holy Roman Empire, 35; Leopold crowned Emperor at (1790), 89; Francis crowned Emperor at (1792), 112; held to ransom by Custine (1792), 118; taken by Jourdan (1796), 177; maintained as a free city (1803), 226; the Proposals of (1813), 316; maintained as a free city and member of the

Germanic Confederation (1815), 343.
Frankfort, Grand Duchy of, created (1806), 259, 260.
Frederick II., King of Prussia, 'the Great' (1712-86), typical benevolent despot, 4, 29; decay of Prussia after his reign, 5; opposed Austrian scheme of exchanging Belgium for Bavaria, 16, 17; Joseph's admiration for, 17; suggested the partition of Poland, 18; his policy, 30.
—— VI., King of Denmark (1768-1839), 32, 302, 320, 337, 347.
—— I., Duke, afterwards King, of Würtemburg (1754-1816), 225, 245, 258, 347.
—— Augustus I., Elector, afterwards King, of Saxony (1750-1827), 38, 179, 250, 259, 261, 274, 341.
—— Eugène, Duke of Würtemburg († 1797), 180.
—— William II., King of Prussia (1744-97), his character and policy 30, 31; intrigues with the Turks against Austria, 45; encourages the Belgian patriots, 48, 64; occupies Liége, 63; sends help to the Belgians, 65; makes treaty with the Poles, 85; intrigues against Austria, 85, 86; makes Convention of Reichenbach (1790), 87; won over by Leopold, 88; signs Declaration of Pilnitz with Leopold, 105; and treaty with Leopold, 109; refuses to break with Austria, 111; directed the policy of the Emperor Francis (1792), 112; orders retreat from France, 116; invades Poland and signs second partition (1793), 122; makes Haugwitz his minister, 126; driven from Warsaw (1794), 151; receives Warsaw in final partition of Poland (1795), 152; yields to the anti-Austrian party at his Court, and becomes slack in the war against France, 153; signs treaty of Basle with France (1795), 157; refuses to make alliance with France (1796), 170; signs secret supplement to the treaty of Basle, 179; death, 197.
Frederick William III., King of Prussia (1770-1840), accession (1797), 197; insists on strict neutrality, 197; attitude in 1799, 206; admires Bonaparte, but refuses to make alliance with him, 217; his territorial accessions (1803), 227; persists in his neutrality, 234, 242; inclines to war (1805), 246; utterly defeated by Napoleon at Jena, 247; signs treaty of Bartenstein with Russia, 248; spared by Napoleon on the intercession of Alexander, 250; summoned Stein and Scharnhorst to office, 290; forced to dismiss Stein, 301; obliged to sign alliance with Napoleon (1812), 304; calls out the Landwehr and declare war against Napoleon (1813), 308; desires to be revenged on France, 317; enters Paris (1814), 329; his intimacy with the Emperor Alexander, 334; present at the Congress of Vienna, 337; desires the whole of Saxony, 339, 340; gets a portion only, 341; with part of Poland, but not Warsaw, 342; and Rhenish Prussia, 344; joins the Holy Alliance, 355.
Frederick William, Duke of Brunswick-Oels (1771-1815), 293, 337.
Free Cities of the Holy Roman Empire in 1789, their College in the Diet, 34, 35; reduced to six (1803), 226; reduced to four (1815), 343.
Freisingen, bishopric of, merged in Bavaria (1803), 227.
Fréjus, Napoleon landed at, on his return from Egypt (1799) 209.
French philosophers of the 18th century contrasted with the German, 9.
Fréron, Louis Stanislas, French politician (1765-1802), 147, 155, 182.
Fribourg, canton of Switzerland, 228.
Friedland, battle of (14 June 1807), 249.
Friuli, Duke of. *See* Duroc.
Fructidor, *coup d'état* of 18th (4th Sept. 1797), 191.
Fuentes de Onor, battle of (5 May 1811), 297.
Fulda, bishopric of (1803), 227, 260.

GAETA, siege and capture by the French (1806), 256.
—— Duke of. *See* Gaudin.

# Index                                                395

Galicia, Western, obtained by Austria at third partition of Poland (1795), 152; ceded to the Grand Duchy of Warsaw (1809), 274; restored to Austria (1815), 342.

Gambier, James, Lord, English admiral (1756-1833), 277.

Gasparin, Thomas Augustin de, French politician (1750-93), 133.

Gaudin, Martin Michel Charles, Duke of Gaeta, French statesman (1756-1844), 215, 216, 240, 287.

Geisberg, battle of the (26 Dec. 1793), 140.

Geneva, its condition as an independent republic in 1789, 41; occupied by the Bernese troops (1792), 125; united to France, 228, 230; made a canton of Switzerland by the Congress of Vienna (1815), 345.

Genoa, its position in 1789, 27; formed into the Liguria Republic (1797), 192; besieged by the Austrians (1799), 203, 206, 218; annexed to Napoleon's Empire, 243, 255; capital of a French department, 283; occupied by the English (1814), 315; his proclamation at, 322; united to the kingdom of Sardinia (1815), 346.

Genola, battle of (4 Nov. 1799), 204.

Gensonné, Armand, French politician (1758-93), 106.

Gentz, Friedrich von, German statesman (1764-1832), 291, 292, 337.

George III., King of England (1738-1820), 120.

Germanic Confederation formed (1815), 442, 343.

Germany, condition of, in 1789, 33-40; spread of revolutionary ideas in, 109; resettlement of (1803), 225-227; Napoleon's rearrangement of (1806), 257-261; Stadion's attempt to rouse a national spirit in, 270, 271; reforms made in, under French influence, 288, 289; growth of a national spirit against the French in, 291-295; national rising in, 314; resettled at Congress of Vienna, 342, 345. *See* Austria, Baden, Bavaria, Hanover, Prussia, Saxony, Würtemburg.

German literary movement at Weimar, 38.

German philosophers of the 18th century compared with the French, 9.

Germinal, Riot of the 12th (1 April 1795), in Paris, 155.

Ghent, 64, 341, 552.

Girondins, French political party, in the Legislative Assembly, 106; in favour of war, 107; their sections in the Convention, 116; attacked the Mountain, 117; views on the King's trial, 119; struggle with the Mountain, 128, 129; overthrown (2 June 1793), 129; attempt to raise the provinces of France against the Convention, 131; the leaders guillotined, 128; recall of the survivors to the Convention (1795), 154; they obtain power, 155.

Giurgevo, battle of (8 July 1790), 88; armistice of (19 Sept. 1790), 88.

Glarus, 228.

Gnesen, province of, ceded to Prussia at second partition of Poland (1793), 123.

Goa, 224.

Gobel, Jean Baptiste Joseph, French bishop (1727-94), 70, 141.

Godoy, Don Manuel de, Prince of the Peace, Spanish statesman (1767-1851), 77, 126, 154, 157, 183, 255, 266, 267.

Goethe, Johann Wolfgang von, German poet (1749-1832), 9, 10, 38.

Gohier, Louis Jerome, French politician (1746-1830), 209, 211.

Goltz, Bernhard William, Baron von, Prussian statesman (1730-95), 86.

Göttingen, university of, 39.

Gouvion-Saint-Cyr, Laurent, French general (1764-1830), 275, App. iv.

Graham, Sir Thomas, Lord Lynedoch, English general (1751-1843), 314, 321.

Grand Elector, proposed by Sieyès in 1799 but rejected by Bonaparte, 213.

Grand Livre, Cambon's creation of, continued by Napoleon, 288.

Greece, 257.

Grégoire, Henri, French politician (1750-1831), 53.

Grenelle, plot to attack the camp of (1796), 181.

Grenville, Thomas, English diplomatist (1755-1846), 197.
—— William Wyndham, Lord, English statesman (1759-1834), Pitt's foreign secretary (1790-1801), 120, 166, 167, 169.
Grisons, republic of the, 41; occupied by the Archduke Charles (1799), 202; Suvórov in, 205; Macdonald invades (1800), 218, 219; formed into a canton of Switzerland by Bonaparte (1803), 228; and retained by the Congress of Vienna (1815), 344.
Grodno, Diet of (24 Sept. 1793), second partition of Poland agreed to at, 122.
Gross-Beeren, battle of (23 Aug. 1813), 312.
Gross-Görschen (Lützen), battle of (2 May 1813), 309.
Grouchy, Emmanuel, Marquis de, French general (1766-1847), 353, App. iv.
Guadeloupe, French West India island, conquered by the English, 154; restored to France by treaty of Amiens (1802), 232; reconquered by the English (1810) 276; returned to France by Sweden (1815), 347.
Guadet, Marguerite Élie, French politician (1758-94), 106, 129.
Guastalla, duchy of, granted to Pauline Bonaparte by Napoleon, 283; granted with Parma to the Empress Marie Louise (1815), 347.
Guerilla warfare against the French in Spain, 268, 297.
Guiana, 155, 191, 223, 232, 348.
Gustavus III., King of Sweden (1746-92), a benevolent despot of the 18th century, 4; his *coup d'état* of 1772 and reforms, 33; invades Russian Finland (1788), 45; makes peace with Denmark (1789), 46; overthrows the power of the nobility, 46; sympathy with Marie Antoinette, 67, 68; defeated by the Russians (1790), 95; makes treaty of Verela with the Empress Catherine (1790), 95, 96; proposes to rescue the French royal family, 109; murdered, 110.
Gustavus IV., King of Sweden (1778-1837), 110, 243, 253, 254, 279.

HAGUE, the, the Stadtholder driven from (1787), 31; congress at (1790), 93, 94; capital moved from, to Amsterdam by Louis Bonaparte, 255.
Hainault, Estates of, suppressed by the Emperor Joseph (1789), 47.
Hamburg, a free city of the Holy Roman Empire, 35; English trade removed from Amsterdam to, 184; retained its independence (1803), 226; annexed by Napoleon (1810), 282; taken by the Russians (1813), 308; recovered by Vandamme, 309; defended by Davout (1813-14), 319, 320; a free city of the Germanic Confederation (1815), 343.
Hanau granted to Dalberg, Grand Duke of Frankfort (1806), 260; battle of (30 Oct. 1813), 314.
Hanover, Electorate of, independently administered under the King of England, 38, 39; bishopric of Osnabrück merged in (1803), 227; occupied by the French under Mortier (1803), 233, 242; promised to Prussia and offered to England by Napoleon (1806), 247; part of, merged in kingdom of Westphalia, 258; and part annexed by Napoleon (1810), 282; a state of the Germanic Confederation (1815), 342.
Hanriot, François, French politician (1761-94), 129, 147.
Hardenberg, Charles Augustus, Count afterwards Prince von, Prussian statesman (1750-1822), negotiated treaty of Basle (1795), 157; opposed alliance with France (1796), 170; became Minister for Foreign Affairs (1803), 234; and State Chancellor (1807), 248; completes the work of Stein (1809), 303; accedes to the Proposals of Frankfort (1813), 316; signs Provisional Treaty of Paris (1814), 332; Prussian Plenipotentiary at the Congress of Vienna (1814-15), 337.
—— William, Count von, Hanoverian statesman (1754-1826), 337.
Harris, Sir James, Earl of Malmesbury. *See* Malmesbury.
Hassan Pasha, Turkish admiral, 45.
Hatry, Jacques Maurice, French general (1740-1802), 193.

## Index

Haugwitz, Christian Henry Charles, Count von, Prussian statesman, (1752-1832) a partisan of France and enemy of Austria, 111; appointed Foreign Minister (1792), 126; in favour of peace with the French Republic, 153; but against an alliance (1796), 170; advocated a compromise, 179; dismissed as too friendly to France (1803), 234; signs treaty of Schönbrunn (1805), 247; finally dismissed (1807), 248.
Hébert, Jacques René, French politician (1755-94), 141, 142.
Hébertists, the, 141, 142.
Heidelberg ceded to Baden, 227.
Heligoland, ceded by Denmark to England (1815), 348.
Heliopolis, battle of (20 March 1800), 224.
Helvetian Republic founded (1798), 199; replaced by the Confederation of Switzerland (1803), 228.
Henry, Prince, of Prussia (1726-1802), 111.
Hérault-Séchelles, Marie Jean, French politician (1760-94), 133.
Hercules III., Duke of Modena (1727-1803), 25, 26, 174, 175, 192, 226.
Herder, Johann Gottfried, German philosopher (1744-1803), 9, 38.
Herford, abbey of, merged in Prussia (1803), 227.
Hermann, Russian general, defeated at Bergen (1799), 205.
Hertzberg, Ewald Frederick, Count von, Prussian statesman (1725-1795), 30, 31, 85, 87, 88.
Hesse-Cassel, its condition in 1789, 38; made an electorate (1803), 225; increased in size, 227; merged in the kingdom of Westphalia, 250, 258; a state of the Germanic Confederation (1815), 342. See William IX.
Hesse-Darmstadt, increased in size (1803), 227; made a Grand Duchy (1806), 259; a state of the Confederation of the Rhine (1806), 260; of the Germanic Confederation (1815), 342. See Louis X.
Hesse-Homburg, a state of the Germanic Confederation (1815), 343.
Hildesheim, Bishop of, an ecclesiastical Prince of the Holy Roman Empire, 34.
Hildesheim, bishopric of, merged in Prussia (1803), 227; in the kingdom of Westphalia (1807), 258.
Hiller, John, Baron von, Austrian general (1754-1819), 315.
Hoche, Lazare, French general (1768-97), 140, 154, 180, 181, 185, 186, 189, 191, 193 194.
Hoensbroeck, Count Cæsar Constantine Francis de, Prince-Bishop of Liége, 39, 49, 95.
Hofer, Andrew, Tyrolese patriot (1767-1810), 273.
Hohenlinden, battle of (3 Dec. 1800), 219.
Hohenlohe-Bartenstein, Prince of, one of the chief Princes of the Empire in Alsace, 79.
Hohenlohe-Kirchberg, Prince of, Austrian general, 45.
Hohenzollern, two principalities of, states of the Germanic Confederation (1815), 343.
Holland [the United Netherlands], a member of the Triple Alliance, 13; position in 1789, 31; revolution in (1787), 31, 32; put down by Prussia, 32; designs of Dumouriez on, 119, 120; France declares war against (1793), 120; failure or Dumouriez to invade (1793), 126; conquered by Pichegru (1794-95), 149; organised as the Batavian Republic, 150; effect of its conquest on England, 184; Delacroix sent as ambassador to, 190; Hoche's scheme of invading England from, 193; its fleet destroyed at Camperdown (1797), 194; invaded by English and Russians (1799), 205; its changes of government, 254; Louis Bonaparte, King of (1806), 254, 255; colonies taken by England, 264; annexed by Napoleon (1810), 282; rises against the French (1813-14), 314. 320, 321; joined to Belgium as the kingdom of the Netherlands (1815), 344.
—— kingdom of, formed for Louis Bonaparte, 254; his administration (1806-1810), 254, 255.
Holstein, duchy of, 34, 343.
Holstein-Gottorp, Prince Peter of, Prince-Bishop of Lübeck in 1789, 39.

Holy Alliance, the, 355.
Hondschoten, battle of (7 Sept. 1793), 140.
Hood, Samuel, Lord, English admiral (1724-1816), 139.
Houchard, Jean Nicolas, French general (1740-93), 138, 140.
Howe, Richard, Earl, English admiral (1725-99), 145.
Humbert, Jean Joseph Amable, French general (1755-1823), 197.
Humboldt, William, Baron von, Prussian statesman (1767-1835), 303, 304, 323; at the Congress of Vienna (1814-15), 338.
Hundred Days, the (March-June 1815), 351-353.
Hungary, opposition to the Emperor Joseph's reforms in, 15, 16; abolition of serfdom, 16; Joseph's dying concessions to, 66; policy of the Emperor Leopold in, 90-92; looked with favour on Napoleon, 270.
Huningen, fortress to be dismantled by second treaty of Paris (1815), 354.
Hutchinson, John, Lord, afterwards Earl of Donoughmore, English general (1757-1832), 224.

IGELSTRÖM, JOSEPH, Count, Russian general († 1817), 151, 152.
Illyrian Provinces, Napoleon's, formed (1805), ruled by Marmont, 245, 256; the Ionian islands added to (1807), 256; increased (1809), 274; given to Austria (1815), 347.
Income tax imposed in France (1800), 215.
India, Bonaparte's projects on (1798), 194; the Emperor Paul's plans for invading, 220, 221.
'Infernal Columns' despatched to La Vendée, 141.
'Infernal Machine,' plot of the (1800), 231.
Inquisition, the Holy, 21, 22, 25, 297, 358.
Ionian Islands belonged to Venice in 1789, 27; ceded to France (1797), 192; taken by the Russians (1798), 207; ceded to France by the treaty of Tilsit (1807), 250; added to the Illyrian Provinces, 256; given to England (1815), 348.

Ireland, Hoche's expedition to (1796), 185; Humbert's (1798), 197.
Iron crown of Italy assumed by Napoleon (1805), 238.
Ismail, besieged by the Russians (1789), 45; stormed (1790), 96.
Istria ceded to Austria (1797), 192; annexed by Napoleon, 245.
—— Duke of. *See* Bessières.
Italian unity, idea of, in the 18th century, 22; promised by Bentinck (1813), 322; defended by Murat (1814), 344.
Italy, condition of, in 1789, 22-27; Bonaparte's arrangements in North, 192; conquered by the French (1798-99), 200; reconquered by Bonaparte (1800), 218, 219; kingdom of, Napoleon's, 238, 255; rises against Napoleon (1813-14), 314, 315; settlement of, at Vienna (1815), 345-347. *See* Genoa, Lombardy, Lucca, Modena, Naples, Parma, Rome, Sardinia, Sicily, Tuscany, Venice.

JABLONOWSKI, LADISLAS, Polish statesman (1769-1802), 87.
Jachvill, Prince, 221.
Jacobin Club, growth of its importance in France, 100, 105; debates on the war question in, 107; Hébertists expelled from (1793), 142; the headquarters of Robespierre's party, 147; closed (1794), 149.
Jaffa taken by Bonaparte (1799), 208.
Jahn, Frederick Louis, German publicist (1778-1852), 291.
Janissaries, the, dethrone the Sultan Selim III. (1807), 280; fight the new militia in Constantinople, 281.
Janssens, John William, Dutch general (1762-1835), 155.
Jassy, treaty of (9 Jan. 1792), 96.
Jaucourt, Arnail François, Marquis de, French statesman (1757-1852), 330.
Java, taken by the English (1811), 264; restored to Holland (1815), 348.
Javogues, Claude, French politician (1759-96), 139.
Jeanbon or Jean Bon (André) called Saint-André. *See* Saint André.
Jehu, companies of, ravage the south

## Index

of France in 1796, 181; in 1815, 356.
Jemmappes, battle of (6 Nov. 1792), 118.
Jena, university of, 38; battle of (14 Oct. 1806), 247.
Jerome Bonaparte, King of Westphalia (1784-1860), 258, 259.
Jervis, Sir John, Earl St. Vincent, English admiral (1734-1823), 183.
Jesuits expelled from Spain by Aranda, 21; from Portugal by Pombal, 22; from Naples by Tanucci, 23.
Jeunesse Dorée or Fréronienne, important political part played by, in Paris (1794-95), 155.
Jews, toleration to, insisted on by Napoleon, 289.
John VI., King of Portugal (1769-1826), 22, 120, 223, 252, 253.
—— Archduke, seventh son of the Emperor Leopold (1782-1863), 219, 272, 273, 274.
Jomini, Henri, Baron, French general (1779-1862), 312.
Joseph II., Emperor (1741-90), typical benevolent despot of the 18th century, 4; preferred Russia to France, 12; position in 1789, 14-17; internal policy, 15, 16; abolition of serfdom, 16; foreign policy, 16, 17; German policy, 17, 35; alliance with Russia, 17; attacks the Turks, 17; the Pope's visit to, 24; defeated by the Turks (1788), 43; prophecy in Jan. 1789, 44; policy in Belgium, 46-48; death and character, 66; why he failed, 67; comparison between, and Louis XVI., 67, 68.
Joseph Bonaparte, elder brother of Napoleon (1768-1844), King of Naples (1806), his good administration, 256; King of Spain (1808), 267; his reforms, 289, 297; driven from Madrid (1812), 306; returned, 307; finally retired from Madrid, defeated at Vittoria (1813), 315.
Joseph, Archduke, fourth son of the Emperor Leopold (1776 - 1847), 270.
Josephine, the Empress, first wife of Napoleon (1763-1814), 285, 293, 332.
Joubert, Barthélemy Catherine, French general (1769-99), 186, 200, 204.

Jourdan, Jean Baptiste, Comte, French general (1762-1833), 140, 144, 150, 172, 177, 178, 202, 315, App. iv.
Journalists, rise of their importance in Paris (1789), 61.
Jovellanos, Don Gaspar Melchior de, Spanish statesman (1744-1811), 21.
Joyeuse Entrée or Constitution of Brabant, abrogated by the Emperor Joseph (1789), 47.
Junot, Andoche, Duke of Abrantes, French general (1771-1813), 253, 265, 266, 296.

KAISERSLAUTERN, battle of (19 Aug. 1794), 144.
Kalisch, ceded to Prussia in second partition of Poland (1793), 122; treaty of (27 Feb. 1813), 308.
Kalkreuth, Frederick Adolphus, Count von, Prussian general (1737-1818), 153.
Kant, Immanuel, German philosopher (1724-1804), 9.
Katt, Lieutenant, Prussian officer, attacked Magdeburg (1809), 293.
Katzbach, battle of the (25 Aug. 1813), 312.
Kaunitz, Wenceslas, Prince von, Austrian statesman (1711-94), made the treaty of 1756 with France, 19; at the Congress of Reichenbach (1790), 87; wrote the despatch and letter which led to war with France, 108, 109; practically succeeded by Thugut (1792), 126.
Keller, Dorotheus Louis Christopher, Count, Prussian statesman (1757-1827), 65, 93.
Kellermann, François Christophe, Duke of Valmy, French general (1735-1820), 115, App. iv.
—— François Etienne, French general (1770-1835), 218.
Kempten, Abbot of, an ecclesiastical Prince of the Holy Roman Empire, 34.
Kiel, treaty of (14 Jan. 1814), 320.
Kioge, Danes defeated at, by the English (1807), 252.
Klagenfurt, Joubert joins Bonaparte at (1797), 186.
Kléber, Jean Baptiste, French general (1753-1800), 150, 172, 208, 224.

Knesebeck, Charles Frederick, Baron von, Prussian general (1768-1844), 33.
Knights of the Holy Roman Empire, 40; deprived of their sovereign rights by Napoleon, 260.
Kolichev, Nicholas, Russian diplomatist († 1813), 198, 217.
Kollontai, Hugh, Polish statesman (1752-1812), 104, 122.
Königsberg, Estates of East Prussia summoned at, by Stein (1813), 308.
Körner, Charles Theodore, German poet (1791-1813), 291.
Korsakov, Alexander Rymski, Russian general (1753-1840), 204.
Kosciuszko, Thaddeus, Polish patriot (1746-1817), defeated by Suvórov at Dubienka (1792), 122; raises standard of Polish independence at Cracow, and takes Warsaw (1794), 151; defeated by the Russians, wounded and taken prisoner at Maciejowice (1795), 152; welcomed in Paris, 206.
Kray, Paul, Baron, Austrian general (1735-1804), 202.
Kulm, capitulation of (1813), 313.
Kutuzov, Michael Larivonovitch Golenitchev, Prince, Russian general (1745-1813), 96, 281, 305; death (1813), 309.

LABRADOR, Pedro Gomez Ravelo, Count of, Spanish statesman (1775-1850), 338, 347.
Lacuée de Cessac, Gérard Jean, Comte, French administrator (1752-1841), 241.
Lafayette, Marie Jean Paul Roch Yves Gilbert Motier, Marquis de, French general (1757-1834), leads the minority of the nobility in the States-General to join the Tiers État (June 1789), 54; commandant of the National Guard of Paris, 59; brings Louis XVI. to Paris (6 Oct. 1789), 62; got Mirabeau's proposition on ministers rejected, 72; most influential man in France (1790), 73; fires on the people (17 July 1791), on the Champ de Mars, 101; placed in command of an army on the frontier (1792), 107;

offers to help the king (July 1792), 112; deserts, 114.
Lagarde, Marie Jacques Martin, French general († 1815), 356.
La Harpe, Frederick Cæsar de, Swiss statesman (1754-1838), 234.
La Marck, Auguste Marie Raymond, Comte de (1753-1833), 72, 73.
Lambesc, Charles Eugène de Lorraine, Prince de, French officer (1751-1825), 57.
Lambrechts, Charles Joseph Mathieu, Comte, French politician (1753-1823), 191.
Lameth, Alexandre Theodore Victor, Vicomte de, French politician (1760-1829), 100.
Lampredi, Giovanni Maria, Italian jurist (1732-93), 24.
Landau, siege of, relieved by Pichegru (1793), 140.
Lanjunais, Jean Denis, Comte, French politician (1753-1827), 154.
Lannes, Jean, Duke of Montebello, French general (1769-1809), 218, 269, App. iv,
Laon, battle of (9 March 1814), 328.
La Place, Pierre Simon, French astronomer (1749-1827), 216.
La Tour du Pin Gouvernet, Frédéric, Marquis de, French diplomatist (1750-1837), 338.
Lauenburg, Duchy of, a state of the Germanic Confederation, granted to the King of Denmark (1815), 347.
League of the Princes, formed by Frederick the Great, 30, 35; joined by the Archbishop-Elector of Mayence, 39.
La Bon, Ghislain Joseph François, French politician (1765-95), 139.
Le Brun, Charles François, Duke of Piacenza, French statesman (1739-1824), 214, 239, 287.
Lebrun-Tondu, Pierre Henri Hélène, French politician (1763-93), 114.
Le Chapelier, Isaac Gui René, French politician (1754-94), 52, 100.
Leclerc, Victor Emmanuel, French general (1772-1802), 223, 232.
Lecourbe, Claude Joseph, Comte, French general (1760-1815), 204.
Leeds, Francis Godolphin Osborne, Duke of, English statesman (1751-99), 28.

*Index* 401

Lefebvre, François Joseph, Duke of Dantzic, French general (1755-1820), 248, 329, App. iv.
Legations, the. *See* Bologna, Ferrara.
Leghorn, its prosperity promoted by the Grand Duke Leopold, 27; capital of a French department, 283.
Legion of Honour, the, 284.
Legislative Assembly, the, in France (1791-92), 105, 106, 108, 111, 113, 114.
—— Body, the (Corps Législatif), 214, 240, 285, 322, 326.
Legislature, the French, under the Constitution of the Year III. *See* Council of Ancients, Council of Five Hundred.
—— the French, under the Constitution of the Year VIII. *See* Legislative Body, Senate, Tribunate.
Leiningen, the Prince of, one of chief princes holding fiefs of the Empire in Alsace, 79.
Leipzig, battle of (16-19 Oct. 1813), 314.
Lenoir-Laroche, Jean Jacques, French administrator (1749-1825), 190.
Leoben, the Preliminaries of, signed 17th April 1797, 186; arrangements of, followed in the treaty of Campo-Formio, 192.
Leopold II., Emperor (1747-92), typical benevolent despot of the 18th century, 4; considered the French the enemies of Austria, 12; his administration as Grand Duke of Tuscany (1765-90), 24, 25, 83; implored by Marie Antoinette to interfere in France, 81; succeeds Joseph II. (1790), 83; his internal policy, 83, 84; position of Austria 84; appeals to England against Prussia, 86; signs Convention of Reichenbach (1790), 87, 88; makes armistice with the Turks, 88; and treaty of Sistova (1791), 89; elected and crowned Emperor, 89; letter to Louis XVI. on the rights of the Princes of the Empire in Alsace, 89, 90; his policy towards Hungary, 90-92; crowned King of Hungary, 91; reconquers Belgium (1790), 94; occupies Liége, 95; his position in 1791, 97; promises to intervene in France, 99; issues Manifesto of Padua, 102; signs Declaration of Pilnitz, 103; his letter and despatch to Louis XVI., 108, 109; makes an alliance with Prussia against France, 109; death (1 March 1792), 110.
Leopold, Archduke, fourth son of the Emperor Leopold (1774-94), 91.
Le Quesnoy, besieged by the Austrians (1793), 130.
Lessart, Antoine de Valdec de, French statesman (1742-92), 109.
Letourneur, Charles Louis François Honoré, French statesman (1751-1817), 165, 182, 188.
Letourneux, Pierre, French administrator (1761-1805), 191.
'Liberum Veto,' the, in Poland, 18; abolished by Polish Constitution of 1791, 104.
Lichtenstein, a state of the Germanic Confederation (1815), 343.
Liége, revolution in (Aug. 1789), 49; occupied by the Prussians (1790), 63; by the Austrians (1791), 94, 95; by Dumouriez (1792), 118.
Ligne, Charles Joseph, Prince de, Austrian general (1734-1814), 65.
Ligny, battle of (16 June 1815), 352.
Ligurian Republic founded by Bonaparte (1797), 192; the Doge appointed by France (1801), 220; annexed to Napoleon's Empire, 243, 283.
Lille, besieged by the Austrians (1792), 114, 118; conference at (1797), 190.
Limburg, occupied by the Austrians under Bender (1790), 93.
—— Count Augustus of, Prince-Bishop of Spires in 1789, 39.
Limon, Geoffroi, Marquis de, French *émigrés* († 1799), 113.
Lindet, Jean Baptiste Robert, French statesman (1743-1825), 132, 133, 148, 210.
Lippe, two principalities of, states of the Germanic Confederation (1815), 343.
Lisbon, occupied by the French under Junot (1807), 253.
Lithuania, conquered by Napoleon (1812), 305; absorbed in Russia, 342.

PERIOD VII.    2 C

Llanos, Don Juan Gomez, minister of the Duke of Parma, 25.
Loano, battle of (24 Nov. 1795), 151, 173.
Lobau, Napoleon in the island of (1809), 273.
Locke, John, English philosopher (1632-1704), 9.
Lodi, battle of (10 May 1796), 174.
Lombardy, belonged to Austria in 1789, its good administration, 26; conquered by Bonaparte (1796), 174; formed part of the Cisalpine Republic (1797), 192; occupied by the Austrians (1799), 206; reconquered by Bonaparte (1800), 218; formed part of the kingdom of Italy (1805), 255; restored to Austria (1815), 347.
Loménie de Brienne, Étienne Charles, Cardinal de, French statesman (1727-1794), 49, 51, 70.
Longwy, taken by the Prussians (27 Aug. 1792), 114.
Loudon, Gideon Ernest, Count, Austrian general (1716-90), 43, 45, 88.
Louis XV., King of France (1710-1774), 19.
—— XVI., King of France (1754-93), 20, 49, 54, 55, 56, 58, 59, 61, 62, 67, 68, 75, 76, 99, 100, 103, 106, 108, 111, 112, 113, 139.
—— XVII., *de jure* King of France (1785-95), 168.
—— XVIII., King of France (1755-1824), 26, 102, 166, 167, 188, 206, 217, 332, 333, 340, 341, 350, 351, 352, 353, 355, 356-358.
—— I., King of Etruria (1773-1803), 220, 232.
—— Bonaparte, King of Holland (1777-1846), 254, 255, 282, 283.
—— X., Landgrave, afterwards Grand Duke, of Hesse-Darmstadt (1753-1830), 79, 227, 259, 260, 342.
—— Philippe, Duke of Orleans, afterwards King of the French (1773-1850), 189.
—— Louis Dominique, Baron, French statesman (1755-1837), 240, 331.
Louisa, Queen of Prussia (1776-1810), 246, 304.
Louisiana, ceded by Spain to France (1801), 232; sold by Napoleon to the United States, 242.

Loustalot, Elysée, French journalist (1762-90), 61.
Louvain, 15, 48, 64.
Louverture, Joussaint (1743-1803), 232.
Louvet, Jean Baptiste, French politician (1760-97), 117, 154.
Löwenhielm, Gustavus Charles Frederick, Count von, Swedish diplomatist (1771-1856), 338.
Lübeck, a free city of the Holy Roman Empire, 35; retained its independence (1803), 226; annexed by Napoleon (1810), 302; as a free city member of the Germanic Confederation (1815), 343.
Lucca, Republic of, in 1789, 27; annexed by Napoleon (1805), 243, 255; Elisa Bonaparte, Duchess of, 283; made a Grand Duchy for the King of Etruria with reversion to Tuscany (1815), 347.
Lucchesini, Jerome, Prussian diplomatist (1752-1825), 31, 85, 87, 88, 89, 153.
Lucerne, canton of Switzerland maintained by Bonaparte (1803), 228; one of the three meeting-places of the Helvetian Diet (1815), 345.
Lückner, Nicolas, Baron, French general (1722-94), 107.
Ludovica, the Empress, third wife of the Emperor Francis II. (1772-1816), 271.
Lunéville, treaty of (9 Feb. 1801), 219, 220.
Lusatia, annexed to Saxony (1806), 259; to Prussia (1815), 341.
Lützen (Gross-Gorschen), battle of (2 May 1813), 309.
Luxembourg, the Austrians retreat to, from Belgium (1789), 64; made into a Grand Duchy (1815), 343; and given to the King of the Netherlands, 344.
Lynedoch, Sir Thomas Graham, Lord. *See* Graham.
Lyons rises in insurrection against the Convention (1793), 131; taken, 140.

MACDONALD, Jacques Étienne Joseph Alexandre, Duke of Taranto, French general (1765-1840), 203, 219, 273, 305, 306, 308, 312, 329, 331, 332.

Maciejowice, battle of (12 Oct. 1794), 152.
Mack, Charles, Baron, Austrian general (1752-1828), 200, 243, 244.
Mackintosh, Sir James, English statesman (1765-1832), 233.
Madame Royale. *See* Angoulême, Duchess of.
Madeira, occupied by the English (1801), 223, 224.
Maestricht, besieged by Miranda (1793), 126; taken by Kléber (1794), 150.
Magdeburg formed part of the kingdom of Westphalia, 258; Katt's attack on, 293; French garrison in, besieged (1814), 319.
Magnano, battle of (5 April 1799), 202.
Mahmoud II., Sultan of Turkey (1785-1839), 281.
Maida, battle of (4 July 1806), 256.
Maillard, Stanislas, French politician (1763-94), 62.
Maillebois, Yves Marie Desmarets, Comte de, French general (1715-1791), 31, 32.
Maitland, Sir Frederick Lewis, English captain (1779-1839), 353.
Malet, Claude François, French general (1754-1812), 306.
Malines, riots against Joseph's reforms at (1788), 47; abandoned to the Belgian patriots, 64.
Malmaison, château of, settled on the Empress Josephine, 293.
Malmesbury, Sir James Harris, Earl of, English diplomatist (1746-1820), 32, 184, 190.
Malta, taken by Bonaparte (1798), 195; by the English (1800), 195, 204; the Emperor Paul Grand Master of the Knights of, 207, 217; a cause of the rupture of the treaty of Amiens, 225; England refuses to surrender, 233; granted to England at the Congress of Vienna (1815), 348.
Mamelukes defeated by Bonaparte at the battle of the Pyramids (1798), 195; at the battle of Cairo (1799), 208.
Manifesto of Padua issued by the Emperor Leopold (5 July 1791),102.
Mannheim, university of, 37; taken by Pichegru (1795), 172; given to Baden (1803), 227.

Mantua, Leopold's interview with Durfort at, 99; besieged by Bonaparte (1796-97), 175, 176; part of the Cisalpine Republic, 192; besieged by Suvórov (1799), 203.
Marat, Jean Paul, French statesman (1744-93), 61, 101, 107, 117, 155.
Marceau, François Séverin Desgraviers, French general (1769-96), 172; killed at Altenkirchen (1796), 178.
Marengo, battle of (14 June 1800),218.
Maret, Hugues Bernard, Duke of Bassano, French statesman (1763-1839), 241, 316.
Maria I., Queen of Portugal (1734-1816), 22, 253.
—— Beatrice of Este, heiress of Modena, married to the Archduke Ferdinand, 25, 26.
—— Theresa, the Empress (1717-80), 19.
Marie, Grand Duchess of Saxe-Weimar, sister of the Emperor Alexander, present at the Congress of Vienna, 337.
—— Amélie, Duchess of Parma, daughter of Maria Theresa, 25.
—— Antoinette, Queen of France, daughter of Maria Theresa (1755-93), disliked in France as an Austrian, 12; opposes Necker, 55; urges Louis XVI. to oppose the Assembly, 61, 68; wishes her brother Leopold to interfere in France, 75, 80, 81; unpopularity increased by Prussian intrigues, 86; admiration of Gustavus III. of Sweden for, 95; demands Leopold's aid, 99; escapes to Varennes, 99, 100; reveals French plan of campaign to Austria, 112; ordered to be sent before the Revolutionary Tribunal for trial, 134; guillotined, 138.
—— Caroline, Queen of the Two Sicilies, daughter of Maria Theresa. *See* Caroline.
—— Louise, the Empress, Napoleon's second wife (1791-1847), 294, 330, 332, 346, 347.
—— Queen of Spain (1754-1819), 77, 267.
Marmont, Auguste Frédéric Louis Viesse de, Duke of Ragusa, French general (1774-1852), 245, 256, 306, 329, 331, App. iv.

Marseillaise, the, 113.
Marseilles opposes the Convention (1793), 151.
Marshals, Napoleon's, 239; list of, App. iv.
Martinique, French West India island, taken by the English, 154; restored to France (1802), 252; again taken by the English (1809), 276; restored to France (1815), 348.
Massa, Duke of. *See* Regnier.
—— Principality of, merged in the Duchy of Modena, 25.
Massacres in the prisons of Paris (Sept. 1792), 115.
Masséna, André, Duke of Rivoli, Prince of Essling, French general (1758-1817), 204, 218, 221, 244, 272, 296, 297, App. iv.
Matchin, battle of (9 July 1791), 96.
Maubeuge besieged by the Austrians (1793), 140.
Mauprat, M. de, reforming minister in Parma, 25.
Mauritius, the island of the, taken by the English (1809), 264, 276; ceded to England by the first Treaty of Paris (1814), 333; by the Congress of Vienna (1815), 348.
Maximilian, Archduke, third son of Maria Theresa, Elector-Archbishop of Cologne in 1789, 40.
—— Joseph, Elector, afterwards King, of Bavaria (1770-1825), his power increased by the secularisations (1803), 227; receives Swabia and the Tyrol and takes the title of king (1806), 245; receives Salzburg (1809), 257; marries a daughter to Eugène de Beauharnais, 258; member of the Confederation of the Rhine, 260; sends troops to serve under Napoleon at Wagram, 274; signs Treaty of Ried against Napoleon (8 Oct. 1813), 313, 314; attacks Napoleon and is defeated at Hanau, 314; opens the passes through the Tyrol into Italy to the Austrians, 321; agrees to support Austria and England against Russia and Prussia (1815), 341; member of the Germanic Confederation, 342; gives up the Tyrol and Salzburg to Austria, and receives Rhenish Bavaria (1815), 344.
Maximum, Law of the, in France, 128; an instrument of the Terror, 137; abolished by the Thermidorians, 149; temporarily imposed by Napoleon, 285.
Mayence, the Archbishop-Elector of, Chancellor of the Holy Roman Empire, and President of the College of Prince, 54.
—— archbishopric-electorate of, condition in 1789, 39; merged in France (1801), 193; given to Bavaria (1815), 344.
—— city of, taken by the French under Custine (1792), 118; by the Prussians after a long siege (1793), 130; besieged by Kléber in vain (1795), 172; taken by the French under Hatry (1797), 193; capital of a French department, 230; ceded to Bavaria (1815), 344.
Mecklenburg, the duchies of, their backward state in 1789, 38; made grand duchies and members of the Germanic Confederation (1815), 342.
Medellin, battle of (28 March 1809), 275.
Medina del Rio Seco, battle of (14 July 1808), 267.
Melas, Michael Baron von, Austrian general (1730-1806), 175, 204, 218.
Menou, Jacques François, Baron de, French general (1750-1810), 156, 224.
Mercy-Argenteau, Florimond Claude, Comte de, Austrian diplomatist (1722-94), 93, 94, 99.
Merlin [de Douai], Philippe Antoine, Comte, French statesman (1754-1838), 80, 137, 148, 149, 156, 159, 166, 182, 191, 209, 357.
—— [de Thionville], Antoine Christophe, French politician (1762-1833), 117.
Methuen Treaty, its effect on Portugal, 14, 21, 252.
Metternich, Clement Wenceslas Lothaire, Count, afterwards Prince, von, Austrian statesman (1773-1859), becomes State-Chancellor of Austria (1809), 275; opposes Stein's idea of rousing the national spirit of Germany against Napoleon, 310, 311; brings terms agreed on at Reichenbach to Napoleon at Dresden (1813), 311; lays down the Proposals of Frankfort, 316; in-

trigues with Murat, 322; presses terms offered at Châtillon, 324; becomes intimate with Castlereagh, 331; signs Provisional Treaty of Paris, 332; Austrian representative at the Congress of Vienna (1814-15), 338; signs treaty of alliance with England and France against Russia and Prussia (3 Jan. 1815), 340.

Middle classes in Europe in the 18th century, 7.

Milan, university of, 26; taken by Bonaparte (1796), 174; meeting of Lombard delegates at, 175; taken by Suvórov (1799), 203; by Bonaparte (1800), 218; Napoleon crowned King of Italy at (1805), 238; issues Decree of, establishing the Continental Blockade against England (1808), 251.

Milanese, the. *See* Lombardy.

Miles, William Augustus, English diplomatist (1754-1817), 78.

Millesimo, battle of (13 April 1796), 174.

Mincio, battle of the (8 Feb. 1814), 322.

Ministers of the French Directory, 166, 182, 190, 191, 210; of the Consulate, 216; of the Empire, 240, 241.

Minorca taken by the English (1798), 195, 264.

Minsk, province of, ceded to Russia at the second partition of Poland (1793), 122.

Miollis, Sextius Alexandre François, Comte, French general (1759-1829), 277.

Miot de Melito, André François, Comte, French administrator (1762-1841), 256.

Mirabeau, Honoré Gabriel Riqueti, Comte de, French statesman (1749-1791), 54, 56, 60, 61, 72, 73, 75, 76, 78, 79, 80, 98, 99.

Mirabeau, Victor Riqueti, Marquis de, French economist (1715-89), 25.

Miranda, Don Francisco, French general (1750-1816), 126, 127.

Mirandola, principality of, united with Modena in 1789, 25.

Mittau, Louis XVIII. settled at, by the Emperor Paul (1797), 206; ordered to leave (1802), 217.

Modena, duchy of, condition in 1789, 25, 26; conquered by Bonaparte (1796), 174; part of the Cisalpine Republic, 192; of the kingdom of Italy, 255; granted to Ferdinand IV., 347.

Moeskirch, battle of (5 May 1800), 218.

Moldavia, conquered by the Austrians (1789), 45; by the Russians (1810), 281; part of, ceded to Russia (1812), 281.

Möllendorf, Richard Joachim Heinrich, Count von, Prussian general (1725-1816), 153.

Moncey, Bon Adrien Jeannot de, Duke of Conegliano, French general (1754-1842), 151, 275, 356, App. iv.

Mondovi, battle of (22 April 1796), 174.

Monge, Gaspard, Comte, French mathematician (1746-1818), 114.

Montbéliard, ceded by Würtemburg to France, 227; merged in the department of the Doubs, 230; secured to France by the first treaty of Paris, 333.

Mont Blanc, Savoy organised as the French department of the, 230.

—— Cenis, 151.

Montebello, battle of (4 June 1800), 218.

—— Duke of. *See* Lannes.

Montenotte, battle of (12 April 1796), 174.

Montereau, battle of (18 Feb. 1814), 319.

Montesquieu, Charles de Secondat, Baron de, French philosopher (1689-1755), 9.

Montesquiou-Fézensac, Anne Pierre, Marquis de, French general (1739-98), 117.

—— —— François Nicolas, Abbé-Duc de, French politician (1757-1832), 330.

Monte Video, English expedition to (1806), 264.

Montgelas, Maximilian Joseph Garnerin, Comte de, Bavarian statesman (1759-1830), 209.

Montluçon, Bonaparte's treaty with the Vendéan leaders at (1800), 215.

Montmirail, battle of (11 Feb. 1814), 319.

Montmorin - Saint - Hérem, Armand Marc, Comte de, French statesman (1745-92), 78.

Mont-Terrible, department of, merged in the department of the Haut-Rhin, 230.
Moore, Sir John, English general (1761-1809), 254, 266, 269, 270.
Moreau, Jean Victor, French general (1761-1813), 168, 178, 186, 193, 194, 203, 211, 218, 219, 234, 235, 312.
Moreaux, Jean René, French general (1758-95), 144, 150.
Morkov, Arcadius Ivanovitch, Count, Russian diplomatist, († 1827), 243.
Mortier, Adolphe Edouard Casimir Joseph, Duke of Treviso, French general (1768-1835), 233, 329, App. iv.
Moscow, occupied by Napoleon (1812), 306.
Moskowa, Prince of the. *See* Ney.
Moulin, Jean François Auguste, French general (1752-1810), 209.
Mounier, Jean Joseph, French statesman (1758-1806), 51, 55.
Mountain, the French political party, germs in the Jacobin Club (1792), 107; the party in the Convention, 116, 117; attacked by the Girondins, 117; struggle with the Girondins, 128, 129; as a party ceases to exist (1795), 156.
Mount Tabor, battle of (16 April 1799), 208.
Mulhouse, Republic of, merged in the Haut-Rhin, 230; secured to France (1814), 333.
Müller, Jacques Léonard, Baron, French general (1749-1824), 140.
—— Johann von, German historian (1752-1809), 259.
Munich, taken by the French under Moreau (1800), 219.
Münster, Bishop of, an ecclesiastical Prince of the Holy Roman Empire, 34.
—— bishopric of, part of, merged in Prussia (1803), 227; in the Grand Duchy of Berg (1806), 259; part of, annexed by Napoleon (1810), 282.
—— city of, capital of a French department, 282.
—— Ernest Frederick, Count von, Hanoverian diplomatist (1766-1841), 337.
Murat, Joachim, Grand Duke of Berg, King of Naples, French general (1771-1815), 239, 259, 267, 283, 306, 322, 345, 346, App. iv.

Murbach, the Abbot of, one of the chief Princes of the Empire in Alsace, 79.
Murray, Sir John, English general († 1827), 307.
Musæus, John Charles Augustus, German author (1735-87), 38.
Mustapha IV., Sultan of Turkey (1779-1808), 280, 281.
Mysticism in the 18th century, 10.

NAMUR, riots against Joseph's reforms at (1789), 48.
Nancy, Bouillé suppresses a military mutiny at (Aug. 1790), 72, 97, 98.
Nangis, battle of (17 Feb. 1814), 319.
Nantes, Carrier's atrocities at (1793), 139, 141.
Naples, reforms of Tanucci in, 23; occupied by the French (1798), and the Parthenopean Republic founded, 200; evacuated by the French (1799), and the revenge of Ferdinand, 203; attacked by Napoleon (1804), 242; Joseph Bonaparte's rule in, 256; Murat king of, 283; Ferdinand returns to (1814), 346, 359; behaves moderately, 359.
Napoleon (1769-1821), crowned Emperor, 238; his Court, 239; his ministers, 240, 241; the camp at Boulogne, 241; organises the Grand Army, 241, 242; wins the battle of Austerlitz, 244; crushes Prussia at Jena, 247; defeats the Russians at Eylau and Friedland, 248, 249; holds interview with Alexander at Tilsit, 249, 250; the Continental Blockade against England, 251; his rearrangement of Europe, 254-257; Protector of the Confederation of the Rhine, 260; his Polish policy, 261; the Conference at Erfurt, 262; makes his brother King of Spain, 267; takes Madrid, 269; defeats the Austrians (1809), 272-274; quarrel with the Pope, 277, 278; greatest extension of his Empire (1810), 282, 283; his administration, 283-285; belief in heredity, 285, 286; aristocracy, 286, 287; reforms, 287, 288; divorces Josephine, 293; marries Marie Louise, 294; his differences with Alexander, 299-301; invades Russia (1812), 305; his retreat, 306; first

campaign of 1813 in Saxony, 309;
refuses the terms offered him by
the allies, 311; second campaign
of 1813 in Saxony, 312, 313; defeated at Leipzig, 314; first defensive campaign of 1814 in France,
319; rejects the terms offered by
the allies at Châtillon, 323, 324;
second defensive campaign of 1814
in France, 328, 329; abdicates,
331; leaves Elba and returns to
France (1815), 351; defeated at
Waterloo, 353; sent to St. Helena,
355. *See* Bonaparte.
Napoleon, King of Rome, birth of, 294;
granted succession to Parma by the
Provisional Treaty of Paris (1814),
332; but not by the Congress of
Vienna (1815), 347.
Narbonne-Lara, Comte Louis de,
French politician (1755-1813), 106,
107, 109.
Nassau, duchy of, increased in 1803,
227; merged in the Grand Duchy
of Berg (1806), 259; a state of the
Germanic Confederation (1815), 342.
Nassau-Siegen, Prince Charles Henry
Nicholas Otho of, Russian admiral
(1745-1809), 44, 95.
National Assembly. *See* Constituent
Assembly.
—— Guards formed in Paris, 57;
throughout France, 59.
Nationality, the principle of, 2, 3;
extinct in 18th-century Germany, 40;
made the French successful and the
Poles fail, 153; roused against
Napoleon in Spain, 298; in Germany, 293, 314; rejected by the
Congress of Vienna, 360.
Natural limits of France, the Rhine
and the Alps, claimed at Basle
(1795), 157; demanded by the Directory, 170; recognised secretly by
Prussia, 179; by the Preliminaries
of Leoben, 186;' by the Treaty of
Campo-Formio, 192; by the Treaty
of Lunéville, 220; abandoned by
Napoleon's annexations, 282;
offered by the allies at Dresden, 311;
at Frankfort, 316; opposed by
Castlereagh, 318, 424.
Necker, Jacques, French statesman
(1732-1804), 49, 51, 56, 58, 61, 74.
Neipperg, Albert Adam, Count (1774-
1829), 346, 347.

Nelson, Horatio, Viscount, English
admiral (1758-1805), 183, 195, 222,
242, 244, 245.
Nesselrode, Charles Robert, Count,
Russian statesman (1780-1863), 301,
332, 337.
Netherlands, Austrian. *See* Belgium.
—— The Protestant, or the United
Provinces. *See* Holland.
—— Kingdom of the, formed (1815),
344.
Neufchâtel, belonged to Prussia in
1789, 41; Berthier created Prince-Duke of, 283, 286; made a Canton
of Switzerland (1815), 345.
Neumarkt, battle of (20 March 1797),
186.
Neutral League of the North, the,
222.
Ney, Michel, Duke of Elchingen,
Prince of the Moskowa, French
general (1769-1815), 244, 296, 306,
313, 329, 332, 351, 352, 356,
App. iv.
Nice, port of, improved by Victor
Amadeus III., 26; taken by the
French (1792), 117; annexed, 118;
formally ceded to France, 174;
formed into a department, 230;
restored to Sardinia (1814), 333.
Niebuhr, Barthold George, German
historian (1776-1831), 304.
Nile, battle of the (1 Aug. 1798),
195.
Nimeguen, 149.
Nive, battle of the (9-13 Dec. 1813),
316.
Nivelle, battle of the (10 Nov. 1813),
316.
Noailles, Comte Alexis de, French
diplomatist (1783-1835), 338.
Nobility, the European, in the 18th
century, 7.
Nootka Sound, 77-9.
Nore, mutiny at the, 183, 193.
Normal School of Paris, founded by
Napoleon, 288.
Normandy, the rising in, against the
Convention, suppressed, 132, 133.
Norway, 32, 302, 320, 347.
Novi (Bosnia) taken by Loudon (1788),
43.
—— (Italy), battle of (15 Aug. 1799
204.
Noyades at Nantes, 139.

Nuremberg, a free city of the Holy Roman Empire, 35; retained its independence (1803), 226; granted to Bavaria (1806), 257.

OATH of the Tennis Court (20 June 1789), 54.
Ocana, battle of (12 Nov. 1809), 276.
Ochakov (Oczakoff), 43, 44, 96.
Oldenburg, duchy of (1815), 282, 300, 342.
Olivenza ceded by Portugal to Spain (1801), 223; left to Spain by the Congress of Vienna, 348.
Oporto, rising against the French at (1808), 265; taken by Soult, 270; recaptured by Wellesley (1809), 275.
Orange, Prince of. *See* William V., William VI.
Orleans, Louis Philippe Joseph, Duke of (1747-93), 57, 138.
Orsova besieged by the Austrians (1789), 45; taken by the Prince of Coburg (1789), 88; ceded to Austria (1791), 88.
Ortenau given to Baden (1807), 258.
Orthez, battle of (27 Feb. 1814), 321.
Osnabrück, the Duke of York bishop of, in 1789, 39; merged in Hanover (1803), 227; annexed by Napoleon (1810), 282.
Ostend taken by the Belgian patriots (1789), 64.
Otranto, Duke of. *See* Fouché.
Oudinot, Nicolas Charles, Duke of Reggio, French general (1767-1847), 312, 329, App. iv.

PACIAUDI, Paolo Maria, Italian scholar (1710-85), 25.
Pacte de Famille, the, between France and Spain, 14, 20, 77-79.
Pacy, the Norman insurgents against the Convention defeated at (13 July 1793), 131.
Paderborn, Bishop of, an ecclesiastical Prince of the Holy Roman Empire, 34.
—— bishopric of, merged in Prussia (1803), 227; in the kingdom of Westphalia (1807), 258.
Padua, Manifesto of, 102.
Pahlen, Peter, Count von der, Russian general († 1826), 221.
Palestine, conquered by Bonaparte (1799), 208.

Palm, John Philip, German bookseller († 1806), 293.
Palmella, Pedro de Sousa-Holstein, Count, afterwards Duke, of, Portuguese statesman (1786-1850), 338.
Pampeluna besieged and taken by Wellington (1813), 315, 316.
Paoli, Pascal, Corsican patriot (1726-1870), 27, 145.
Papacy the, its temporal power in the 18th century, 24.
Paris, takes part in the Revolution, 56; riot of 12 July (1789), 57; the taking of the Bastille, 57, 58; the King brought to (6 Oct. 1789), 62; keeps the King prisoner in the Tuileries, 99; massacre of 17 July (1791), 101; invades the Tuileries (20 June 1792), 112; takes the Tuileries (10 Aug. 1792), 113; massacres in (Sept. 1792), 115; people of, refuse to support Robespierre, 147; fights against the Convention, 13 Vendémiaire, 164, 165; welcomes the Empire, 238; battle of (1814), 239; occupied by the allies, 239; provisional treaty of, 331, 332; return of Louis XVIII. to, 333; first treaty of, 333, 334; return of Napoleon to (1815), 351; reoccupied by the allies, 353; second treaty of, 353, 354.
Parker, Sir Hyde, English admiral (1739-1807), 222.
Parma, city of, capital of a French department, 283.
—— Duke of. *See* Cambacérès.
—— and Piacenza, Duchess of. *See* Marie Louise.
—— ——, Duke of. *See* Ferdinand, Louis.
—— ——, duchies of, well governed in the 18th century, 25; conquered by Bonaparte (1796), 174; exchanged for kingdom of Etruria (1801), 220; annexed by Napoleon (1810), 283; granted to Marie Louise by the Provisional Treaty of Paris (1814), 332; by the Congress of Vienna (1815), 347.
Parthenopean Republic, founded (1798), 200; overthrown (1799), 203.
Passau, bishopric of, merged in Bavaria (1801), 227.

# Index 409

Paul, Emperor, of Russia (1754-1801), his accession (1796), 185; inclines to war with France, 198; declares war against France (1798), 202; receives Louis XVIII., 204; withdraws his troops from the Continent, 206; becomes Grand Master of the Knights of Malta, 207; quarrels with Austria and England, 207; makes peace with France, 207; admiration for Bonaparte, 216, 217; schemes for an invasion of India, 220, 221; forms Neutral League of the North, 221, 222; assassinated, 222.

Pavia, the university of, 26.

Peace, Prince of the. *See* Godoy.

Peltier, Jean Gabriel, French journalist (1765-1825), 133.

Peninsular War: campaign of 1808, 265, 266; of 1809, 275, 276; of 1810, 296; of 1811, 296, 297; of 1812, 306, 307; of 1813, 315.

*Père Duchesne*, 142.

Pérignon, Dominique Catherine, Comte, French general (1754-1818), 183, App. iv.

Pesth, 90, 91.

Pétiet, Claude, French administrator (1749-1805), 182, 190.

Pétion, Jérome, French politician (1753-94), 78, 86.

Pfaffenhofen, treaty of (1796), 180.

Philosophers, the eighteenth century, 4, 9, 17, 38.

Piacenza, Duchy of. *See* Parma.

—— Duke of. *See* Le Brun.

Pichegru, Charles, French general (1761-1804), 140, 144, 149, 167, 172, 188, 191, 234, 235.

Piedmont, part of the kingdom of Sardinia in 1789, 26; left to Victor Amadeus (1797), 192; occupied by the French under Joubert (1798), 200; occupied by the Austrians (1799), 206; conquered by Bonaparte (1800), 218; annexed to France (1801), 220, 230, 255.

Pigot, Sir Henry, English general (1752-1840), 195.

Pilnitz, Conference between the Emperor Leopold and King Frederick William at (1791), 102; the Declaration of, 103; its effect on France, 106.

Pisa, the university of, 24, 200.

Pitt, William, English statesman (1759-1806), 28, 45, 78, 86, 97, 120, 125, 126, 166, 167, 169, 184, 189, 190, 225, 243, 245, 264.

Pius VI., Giovanni Angelo Braschi, Pope (1717-99), 24, 66, 76, 175, 177, 200, 203, 217.

—— VII., Gregorio Barnabé Luigi Chiaramonti, Pope (1742-1834), 217, 220, 229, 230, 238, 277, 278, 347.

Plain, deputies of the Centre in the Convention called the, 117, 129, 156.

Pleswitz, armistice of (3 June 1813), 309.

Plettenberg, the Baron of, Prince-Bishop of Münster in 1789, 39.

Pléville de Peley, Georges René, French admiral (1726-1805), 190, 196.

Podolia, province of, taken by Russia at the second partition of Poland (1793), 122.

Poland, its extinction impending in 1789, 14; Catherine's policy in the first partition of, 18; Prussia's share of, and aims on, 30; treaty of Warsaw with Prussia, 85; refuses to surrender Thorn and Dantzic (1790), 87; attempts at reform, 103, 104; the Constitution of 1791, 104, 105; invaded by the Russians (1792), 121; attacked by the Prussians (1793), 122; second partition of (1793), 122; causes of the failure of the attempt at constitutional reform, 123; insurrection in (1794), 151; victory of the Russians, 151, 152; final partition and extinction of Polish independence (1795), 152; comparison between French and Polish revolutions, 152, 153; looked favourably on by the Directory, 206; Napoleon's campaign in 1807, 248, 249; Napoleon's Polish policy, 261; creation of the Grand Duchy of Warsaw, 261; serfdom abolished in, 289; the Emperor Alexander's ideas on (1814), 339; final rearrangement of (1815), 342.

Police, Ministry of General, established in France (1796), 182; abolished under the Consulate, but restored under the Empire, 241.

Polignac, Armand Jules Marie Heraclius, Comte, afterwards Duc de, French politician (1771-1847), 235.
Polish Legion formed for the service of France (1797), 206.
Pombal, Sebastian José de Carvalho-Mello, Marquis of, Portuguese statesman (1699-1782), 22.
Pomerania, Prussian, its backward state in 1789, 29.
—— Swedish, possession of, gave the King of Sweden a voice in the Diet of the Empire, 34; occupied by the French under Brune (1808), 250, 254, 279; exchanged for Norway by the treaty of Kiel (1814), 320; given to Prussia by the Congress of Vienna (1815), 347.
Pompadour, Jeanne Antoinette Poisson, Marquise de (1721-64), 19.
Poniatowski, Joseph, Prince, Polish patriot, French general (1762-1813), 121, 122, App. iv.
—— Stanislas, King of Poland (1732-98), 104, 122, 151, 152.
Ponte Corvo, principality of, belonged to the Pope in 1789, 24; Bernadotte made Prince of (1806), 277.
Pontine marshes drained by Pope Pius VI., 24.
Popes. *See* Pius VI., Pius VII.
Porentruy, district of, merged in the department of the Haut-Rhin, 230.
Portalis, Jean Etienne Marie, French statesman (1745-1807), 214, 215.
Portugal, its condition in 1789, 14, 21, 22; declares war against the French Republic (1793), 120; treaty of San Ildefonso (1796), 183; England comes to the help of, 184; attacked by Spain, and forced to cede Olivenza by the treaty of Badajoz (1801), 223; Napoleon's schemes against, 252; to be divided by treaty of Fontainebleau (1807), 252, 253; conquered by the French, 253; rises in insurrection against the French, 265; English army sent to, 265; freed from the French by the Convention of Cintra, 266; invaded by the French under Masséna (1810), 296; their repulse (1811), 297; deserted by Castlereagh at the Congress of Vienna (1815), 348.

Portuguese Legion, formed by Junot, for the service of France, 253.
Posen, province of, taken by Prussia in the second partition of Poland (1793), 122; given back to Prussia (1815), 342.
Potemkin, Gregory Alexandrovitch, Prince, Russian statesman (1736-1791), 43, 44, 45, 96.
Potocki, Stanislas Felix, Polish statesman (1745-1805), 121.
Potsdam, treaty of (3 Nov. 1805), 247.
Pozzo di Borgo, Charles Andrew, Count, Russian diplomatist (1764-1842), 301, 337.
Praga, suburb of Warsaw, stormed by Suvórov (4 Nov. 1794), 152.
Prague, congress of (1813), 311.
Prairial, the insurrection of 1st, in Paris (1795), 155, 156.
Prefectures, Bonparte's establishment of, in France, 230.
Preliminaries of Leoben signed (17 April 1797), 186.
Pressburg, treaty of (26 Dec. 1805), 245.
Prieur [of the Côte-d'Or], Claude Antoine, French statesman (1763-1832), 133, 134.
—— [of the Marne], Pierre Louis, French statesman (1760-1827), 133.
Prince-Bishops of the Holy Roman Empire, 39, 40.
*Profession de Foi du Vicaire Savoyard*, Rousseau's, 10.
Proposals of Frankfort (1813), 316, 317.
Provera, John Nicholas, Baron, Austrian general (1747-1801), 176.
Prussia, administrative decay in, 5; serfdom in, 5; a member of the Triple Alliance, 13; condition in 1789, 28-30; policy of, 30, 31; intervention in Holland (1787), 32; influence in the Diet of the Holy Roman Empire, 34; position of, in 1789, 84; anti-Austrian policy, 84-86; alliance with Austria against France (1792), 109; its share in the second partition of Poland (1793), 122; in the third partition of Poland (1795), 152; more anti-Austrian than anti-French, 152; makes treaty of Basle with the French Republic (1795), 156, 157;

becomes protector of North Germany, by the conclusion of the line of demarcation, 170, 171; its great increase in importance by the secularisations of 1803, 227; neutrality violated by the French (1805), 244; advantages obtained by its policy of neutrality, 246; desires to fight France, 246, 247; crushed at Jena, and occupied by the French, 247; deprived of its Rhenish Westphalian and Polish provinces (1807), 250; reorganisation of, under Stein and Scharnhorst, 289-291; becomes the recognised leader of the revived German national spirit, 292; Stein's reforms completed by Hardenberg, 303; foundation of the University of Berlin, 303, 304; obliged to allow Napoleon to traverse it, and to send him a contingent (1812), 304; rises against the French, 308, 309; receives part of Saxony (1815), 341; and part of Prussian Poland, 342; obtains large Rhenish province, 344; gets Swedish Pomerania, 347; as a result of the period becomes the preponderant German power, 359. *See* Frederick William II., Frederick William III.
Public Safety, Committee of. *See* Committee.
Pyramids, battle of the (21 July 1798), 195.
Pyrenees, campaigns in the, 133, 140, 144, 150, 151, 315, 316.

QUATRE BRAS, battle of (16 June 1815), 352.
Quedlinburg, abbey of, merged in Prussia (1803), 227.
Quiberon Bay, defeat of the French *émigrés* at (June 1794), 154.
Quinette, Nicolas Marie, Baron, French administrator (1762-1821), 210.

RAAB, battle of (14 June 1809), 273.
Rabaut de Saint-Étienne, Jean Paul, French politician (1743-93), 52.
Raclawice, battle of (4 April 1794), 151.
Radet, Étienne, Baron, French general (1762-1825), 278.
Ragusa, Duke of. *See* Marmont.

Ramel, Jean Pierre, French general (1768-1815), 356.
—— de Nogaret, Jacques, French politician (1760-1819), 182.
Rapinat, Jacques, French administrator (1750-1818), 199, 209.
Rasomovski, Andrew, Count, afterwards Prince, Russian diplomatist (1751-1836), 323, 337.
Rastadt, Congress at, 186, 192, 202.
Ratisbon, bishopric of, granted to the Elector of Mayence (1803), 225; to the King of Bavaria (1805), 260.
—— a free city of the Holy Roman Empire, where the Imperial Diet met, 35, 225, 257.
Reason, the Worship of, in Paris, 141; attacked by Danton and Robespierre, 142.
Receivers-general of taxes, their establishment under the Consulate, 215.
Reden, Baron, Dutch diplomatist († 1799), 87.
Regency, Portuguese, formed (1808), 266.
Reggio, duchy of, belonged to the Duke of Modena in 1789, 25; merged in the Cisalpine Republic (1797), 192.
—— Duke of. *See* Oudinot.
Regnier, Claude Ambroise, Duke of Massa, French statesman (1736-1814), 216, 239, 240, 241.
Reichenbach, conference, Congress and convention of (June 1790), 87, 88; treaty of (17 June 1813), 310.
Reichskammergericht. *See* Tribunal, Imperial.
Reichstag. *See* Diet, Imperial.
Reign of Terror in France. *See* Terror.
Reinhard, Charles Frédéric, Comte, French diplomatist (1761-1837), 210.
Renier, Paolo († 1789), Doge of Venice in 1789, 27.
Repnin, Nicholas Vassilievitch, Prince, Russian general (1734-1801), 44, 96.
Retreats, famous military: Moreau's, from Bavaria (1796), 178; Moore's, from Salamanca (1808-09), 269, 270; Napoleon's, from Moscow (1812), 306.

Reubell, Jean François, French statesman (1747-1807), 150, 156, 165, 169, 179 181, 191, 209.

Réunion, island of (Isle of Bourbon), restored to France (1815), 348.

Reuss, the principalities of, states of the Germanic Confederation (1815), 343.

Reuss, Prince Anton von (1738-96), 87.

Réveillon, Jean (1796), sack of his house at Paris (June 1789), 56.

Revellière-Lépeaux, Louis Marie de la, French statesman (1753-1824), 165, 171, 181, 182, 209.

Revolution, the reasons why it began in France, 7, 8. *See* France.

Revolutionary Propaganda, decreed by the Convention (18 Nov. 1792), 118; its effect on the character of the war, 125; the decree repealed (16 May 1793), 133; idea adopted by the Hébertists, 141; formally abandoned by the Thermidorian Committee of Public Safety, 148, 159.

—— Tribunal. *See* Tribunal.

*Révolutions de Paris*, important journal edited by Loustalot, 61.

Reynier, Jean Louis Ebenezer, Comte, French general (1771-1814), 256, 296.

Rhine, the, declared the natural boundary of France, 157; crossed by Moreau (1796), 178; by Moreau (1797), 186; by Blücher (1813), 318.

—— Confederation of the, formed by Napoleon (1806), 245; its members, 260, 261; replaced by the Germanic Confederation (1815), 342, 343.

Ricci, Scipio de, Bishop of Pistoia, Italian statesman (1741-1810), 24, 83.

Richelieu, Armand Emmanuel Sophie Septimanie du Plessis, Duc de, French statesman (1766-1822), 357.

Ried, treaty of (8 Oct. 1813), 313, 314.

Riga, besieged by the French under Macdonald (1812), 307.

Rivers, stipulations on the navigation of, 349.

Rivière, Charles François de Riffardeau, Marquis, afterwards Duc de, French *émigré* (1763-1827), 235.

Rivoli, battle of (14 Jan. 1797), 176.

—— Duke of. *See* Masséna.

Roberjot, Claude, French politician (1753-99), 202.

Robespierre, Maximilien Marie Isidore de, French statesman (1758-1794), opposes intervention of France on behalf of Spain (1790), 78; moves motion preventing election of deputies of the Constituent to the Legislative Assembly, 105; opposes war with Austria, 105; a leader in the Convention, 117; attacked by Louvet, 117; views on the King's trial, 119; his struggle with the Girondins, 129; member of the Committee of Public Safety, 133; his position and character, 134, 135; attacks the Hébertists, 142; establishes the Worship of the Supreme Being, 146; overthrown in Thermidor (1794), 146, 147; guillotined, 147.

Rochambeau, Jean Baptiste Donatien de Vimeur, Comte de, French general (1725-1807), 107.

Rödt, Baron of, Prince-Bishop of Constance in 1789, 39.

Roggenbach, Baron Joseph Sigismund of, Prince-Bishop of Basle in 1789 († 1794), 39.

Roland de la Platière, Jean Marie, French administrator (1734-93), 110, 112, 114.

—— Manon Jeanne, Madame (1754-93), her salon, 116.

Roliça, battle of (17 Aug. 1808), 265.

Romagna, the, part of the Cisalpine Republic (1797), 192.

Roman Empire, the Holy. *See* Empire.

Roman Republic, the, established (1798), 200; overthrown (1799), 203.

Rome, administration of the Popes at, 24; occupied by French troops (1798), 200; evacuated by them, 203; annexed by Napoleon (1810), 255; declared the second city of the Empire, 277, 278; capital of a French department, 283; restored to the Pope (1815), 347.

Rosas, taken by the French (3 Feb. 1795), 150, 151.

Rousseau, Jean Jacques, Genevese philosopher (1712-78), 9, 10, 41, 146.

# Index 413

Roussillon, 130, 140.
Ruffo, Alvaro, Commander, afterwards Prince, Neapolitan diplomatist (†1825), 338, 346.
Rügen, island of, belonged to Sweden in 1789, 32. *See* Pomerania, Swedish.
Rumford, Benjamin Thompson, Count, Bavarian statesman (1753-1814), 37.
Russia, condition and growth of, under Catherine, 18, 19; invaded by the Swedes (1788-90), 45, 95; obtains increase of territory by the treaty of Jassy (1792), 96; her share in the second partition of Poland (1793), 122; in the third partition (1795), 152; accession of Paul, 185, 198; her intervention in the war with France and its results, 206, 207; disapproves of war with England, 221; murder of Paul (1801), 221; trade of, 234; joins the coalition against Napoleon (1805), 242, 243; defeated at Eylau, 248; and Friedland, 249; results, 249; cessions made to, by the treaty of Tilsit, 249, 250, 261; grumbles at the Continental Blockade, 261, 300; attitude towards Austria (1809), 272; annexes Finland, 278, 299, 302; its cessions from the Turks in 1812, 281; incited by England to war with France, 301; invaded by Napoleon (1812), 305, 306; drives out the French, 306; its share in the overthrow of Napoleon, 334; its annexations from Poland (1815), 341, 342; a result of the period its taking a prominent place in European polity, 359, 360. *See* Alexander, Catherine, Paul.
Russian Armament, the (1788), 45.
Rymnik, battle of the (12 Aug. 1789), 45.

SACILIO, battle of (16 April 1809), 273.
Safety, Public, Committee of. *See* Committee.
Saint-Aignan, Paul Hippolyte de Beauvilliers, Marquis de, French diplomatist (1782-1831), 316.
Saint-André, André Jeanbon, *called*, French administrator (1749-1813), 133.
Saint-Bernard, the Great, 218.

Saint-Bernard, the Little, 151.
Saint-Claude, abbey of, in the Jura, 6.
Saint-Cloud, the Councils removed to from Paris, 210; Bonaparte's *coup d'état* of 18 Brumaire (1799) at, 211.
Saint-Cyr, Laurent Gouvion de. *See* Gouvion.
Saint-Gall, the canton of, created by Bonaparte (1803), 228; recognised by the Congress of Vienna (1815), 344.
Saint-Gothard, Suvórov's passage of the (1799), 204.
Saint-Helena, Napoleon deported to (1815), 355.
Saint-Helens, Alleyne Fitzherbert, Lord. *See* Fitzherbert.
Saint-Just, Louis Léon Antoine Florelle de, French politician (1767-94), 133, 135, 138, 140, 142, 147.
Saint-Lucia, island of, ceded to France (1783), 19; restored to England by the first treaty of Paris (1814), 333; by the Congress of Vienna (1815), 348.
Saint-Marsan, Filippo Antonio Maria Asinari, Marquis de, Italian diplomatist (1761-1828), 338.
Saint-Ouen, Declaration of (2 May 1814), 332, 333.
Saint-Petersburg, threatened by the Swedes (1790), 95.
Saint-Priest, Guillaume Emmanuel Guignard, Comte de, French *émigré*, Russian general (1776-1814), 328.
Saint-Vincent, battle of (14 Feb. 1797), 183.
Saint-Vincent, Sir John Jervis, Earl. *See* Jervis.
Salamanca, Moore's advance to (1808), 269; battle of (22 July 1812), 306.
Saliceti, Christophe, French politician (1757-1809), 256.
Salkief, circle of, in Poland, ceded to Russia (1807), 261.
Salm, petty German principalities (1789), 34; territories in Germany annexed by Napoleon (1810), 282.
—— Salm, Constantine Alexander, Prince of (1762-1828), 79.
Salomon, Gabriel René, French politician (†1792), 60.

Salzburg, the Archbishop of, alternate president of the College of Princes in 1789, 34.

Salzburg, archbishopric of, made into an electorate for the Grand Duke Ferdinand of Tuscany (1803), 225, 229; ceded to Bavaria (1809), 257, 274; restored to Austria (1815), 344.

San Domingo, Bonaparte's attempt to reconquer (1802), 232.

—— Ildefonso, treaty of (19 Aug. 1796), 183.

—— Sebastian, threatened by the French (1794), 144; taken by the French (1795), 157; stormed by Wellington (1813), 315, 316.

Saorgio, battle of (29 April 1794), 144.

Saragossa, siege of (1809), 275.

Sardinia, kingdom of, condition in 1789, 26, 27, attacked by the French (1792), 117; subsidised by England, 126; restored to Victor Emmanuel I., with the addition of Genoa, 346; got back Savoy (1815), 354. *See* Charles Emmanuel III., Victor Amadeus IV., Victor Emmanuel I., *also* Nice, Piedmont, Savoy.

Savigny, Frederick Charles von, German jurist (1779-1861), 304.

Savona, Pope Pius VII. imprisoned at, 278.

Savoy, part of the kingdom of Sardinia in 1789, 26; conquered by the French (1792), 117; annexed to France, 118; ceded by the King of Sardinia (1797), 174; made into the department of Mont Blanc, 230; left to France (1814), 333; restored to the King of Sardinia (1815), 354.

Saxe-Coburg, duchy of, a state of the Germanic Confederation (1815),342.

—— —— Saalfeld, Prince Francis Josias of. *See* Coburg, Prince of.

—— Gotha, duchy of, a state of the Germanic Confederation (1815), 343.

—— Hildburghausen, duchy of, a state of the Germanic Confederation (1815), 343.

—— Meiningen, duchy of, a state of the Germanic Confederation (1815), 343.

Saxe-Teschen, Duke Albert of, Austrian general (1738-1822), 113.

Saxe-Weimar, duchy of, 38; made a Grand Duchy and a state of the Germanic Confederation (1815),342. *See* Charles Augustus.

Saxony, electorate of, its condition in 1789, 38; receives Lower Lusatia, and made a kingdom (1806), 259; a state of the Confederation of the Rhine, 260; invaded by Schill (1809), 293; occupied by Napoleon (1813), 309; proposition to merge it in Prussia rejected (1814), 339, 340; part of, ceded to Prussia (1815), 341; a state of the Germanic Confederation (1815), 342. *See* Frederick Augustus.

Schaffhausen, Thurgau, separated from the canton of, by Bonaparte (1803), 228.

Scharnhorst, Gerard David von, Prussian general (1755-1813), reorganised the Prussian army, 290, 291, 308; mortally wounded at Lützen, 309.

Scheldt, navigation of the, declared free by the National Convention, 118.

Schérer, Barthélemy Louis Joseph, French general (1747-1804), 173, 190, 202, 203.

Schill, Friedrich, Prussian officer (1773-1809), 293.

Schiller, Johann Christoph Friedrich, German poet (1759-1805), 9, 38.

Schimmelpenninck, Roger John, Count, Dutch statesman (1761-1825), 254.

Schleiermacher, Ernst Friedrich, German philosopher (1779-1834), 304.

Schlieffen, Friedrich von, Prussian general († 1791), 63, 65, 94, 95.

Schönbrunn, treaty of (15 Feb. 1806), 247.

Schönfeld, Wilhelm Christoph von, Prussian general († 1797), 65, 93.

Schulenburg, Friedrich Wilhelm, Count von, Prussian statesman (1730-1802), 126.

—— —— Albert, Count von, Saxon diplomatist (1772-1853), 338.

Schulz, pastor of Gielsdorf, the case of, 10.

Schwartzberg, two principalities of,

recognised as states of the Germanic Confederation (1815), 343.
Schwartzenberg, Prince Charles Philip von, Austrian general (1771-1820), 294, 305, 312, 313, 318, 319, 320, 328, 329, 350, 353.
Schweitz, canton of Switzerland, maintained by Bonaparte (1803), 228.
Séance Royale, held by Louis XVI. (23 June 1789), 54.
Sebastiani, François Horace Bastien, Comte, French general (1772-1851), 275, 280.
Secularisation of the ecclesiastical states of the Empire proposed by France, 170; agreed to at Lunéville (1801), 220; its tendency, 226; carried out (1803), and its effects, 226, 227.
Security, General, Committee of. *See* Committee.
Selim III., Sultan of the Ottoman Turks (1761-1808), 44, 88, 89, 96, 280, 281.
Senate of France, established by the Constitution of the Year VIII., its functions, 214; given power to dissolve the Tribunate and Legislative Body (1803), 232; offers the title of Emperor to Napoleon (1804), 236; its position under the Empire, 240, 284; appoints a Provisional Government (1814), 330; declares Napoleon dethroned, 331.
Serfdom in Europe in the 18th century, 5, 6; abolished in Hungary by Joseph II., 16; the Russian peasant partly protected from, by his village organisation, 19; prevalent in Prussia, 29, 30; abolished in Denmark (1788), 32; abolished in Baden (1783), 37; its existence a cause of the failure of the Poles to maintain their independence, 152; disappeared from Central Europe under the influence of the French Revolution and Napoleon, 288, 289; abolished in Prussia by Stein, 290; its general abolition a permanent result of the period, 361.
Sérurier, Jean Mathieu Philibert, French general (1742-1819), App. iv.
Servan, Joseph, French general (1741-1808), 114.
Servia, conquered by the Austrians under Loudon (1789), 45; independence recognised by the Turks (1812), 281.
Shumla, 281.
Sicily, not much affected by Tanucci's reforms, 23; held by the English for Ferdinand IV., 256, 264.
Sidmouth, Henry Addington, Viscount. *See* Addington.
Sieges: Acre (1799), 208; Alessandria (1799), 203, 204; Alexandria (1801), 224; Almeida (1811), 296; Antwerp (1814), 321; Badajoz (1812), 306; Bayonne (1814), 316, 321; Bender (1789), 45; Burgos (1812), 307; Cadiz (1810-12), 296, 297; Cairo (1801), 224; Ciudad Rodrigo (1812), 306; Condé (1793), 130; Dantzic (1806-7), 248, 249; Dantzic (1813-14), 319; Dunkirk (1793), 130, 140; Gaeta (1807), 256; Genoa (1799-1800), 205, 206, 218; Giurgevo (1790), 88; Hamburg (1813-14), 319, 320; Ismail (1789-90), 45, 96; Landau (1793), 140; Le Quesnoy (1793), 130; Lille (1792), 114, 118; Lyons (1793), 131, 140; Magdeburg (1813-14), 319; Mantua (1796-97), 175, 176; Mantua (1799), 203; Maubeuge (1793), 140; Mayence (1793), 130; Mayence (1795), 172; Mayence (1797), 193; Ochakov (1788), 43, 44; Orsova (1789-90), 45, 88; Pampeluna (1813), 316; Riga (1812), 307; San Sebastian (1813), 315, 316; Saragossa (1809), 275; Stettin (1813-14), 319; Tarragona (1812), 307; Toulon (1793), 140; Valenciennes (1793), 130; Warsaw (1794), 151, 152.
Siena, 24, 283.
Sieyès, Emmanuel Joseph, Comte, French statesman (1748-1836), 53, 54, 60, 150, 156, 159, 165, 166, 182, 197, 209, 219, 211, 213, 357.
Silesia, the Prussian Army of, formed under Blücher (1813), 309; defeated the French at the Katzbach, 319; crosses the Rhine, 318: cut to pieces by Napoleon, 319.
Silistria, taken by Kutuzov (1811), 281.
Siméon, Joseph Jerome, Comte, French administrator (1749-1842), 259.
Sistova, congress of (1790-91), 88; treaty of (4 Aug. 1791), 89.
Slave trade, the Negro, condemned by the Congress of Vienna at the

demand of Castlereagh (1815), 348, 349.
Smith, Sir William Sidney, English admiral (1764-1840), 145, 208.
Smolensk, 305, 306.
Socialism opposed even by the Hébertists, 141.
Soleure, canton of Switzerland, maintained by Bonaparte (1803), 228.
Soltikov, Ivan, Count, Russian general (1736-1805), 43.
Somo Sierra, Napoleon forces the pass of the (1808), 269.
Sotin de la Coindière, Pierre, French administrator (1764-1810), Minister of Police (1797), 190.
Soult, Nicolas Jean de Dieu, Duke of Dalmatia, French general (1769-1851), 269, 270, 275, 296, 297, 315, 316, 321, 332, App. iv.
Sovereignty of the people, the doctrine of, 2.
Spain, allied to France by the Pacte de Famille, 14; its condition in 1789, 20, 21; the reforms of Aranda, 21; demands the help of France against England in the Nootka Sound affair (1790), 78; declares war against France (1793), 119; subsidised by England, 126; invades France, 130; defeated by the French (1794), 140; invaded by the French (1795), 144; weary of the war with France, 154; makes peace with France at Basle (1795), 157; makes alliance with France at San Ildefonso, and attacks England, 183; fleet defeated off Cape St. Vincent (1797), 183; Bonaparte's communications with, 223; attacks Portugal, and gets Olivenza by the treaty of Badajoz (1801), 223; cedes Louisiana to France, 232; agrees at Fontainebleau for the partition of Portugal, 252, 253; course of politics in, 266, 267; Napoleon makes Joseph Bonaparte king of (1808), 267; the Spanish people rise against the French, 267, 268; Napoleon in Spain, 268-70; the guerilla war against the French, 297; evacuated by the French (1813), 315; lost Trinidad, but kept Olivenza at the Congress of Vienna (1814-15), 348; reactionary policy of Ferdinand VII. in (1815), 358. *See*

Charles IV., Ferdinand VII., Joseph, Peninsular War.
Spanish Armament, the (1790), 78.
Spielmann, Anton, Baron von, Austrian diplomatist (†1738-1813), Austrian representative at Reichenbach (1790), 87.
Spires, Bishop of, an ecclesiastical Prince of the Holy Roman Empire, 34; and one of the Princes holding largest fiefs in Alsace, 79.
—— bishopric of, the portion on the right bank of the Rhine merged in Baden (1803), 227.
—— city of, taken by Custine (1792), 118.
Splügen pass, forced by Macdonald (1800), 219.
Stäblo, Abbot of, an ecclesiastical Prince of the Holy Roman Empire, 34.
Stackelberg, Gustavus, Count von, Russian diplomatist (†1825), 337.
Stadion, John Philip Charles Joseph, Count, Austrian statesman (1763-1824), tried to rouse Germany against Napoleon, 270, 271; succeeded by Metternich (1809), 275; inspired by Gentz, 292; Austrian plenipotentiary at Châtillon (1814), 323.
Staps, Friedrich (1792-1809), schemed to assassinate Napoleon, 293.
State, doctrine of the, 4, 292.
States of the Church. *See* Papal States.
States-General of France, summoned (1788), 43; a financial expedient, 49, 50; the elections to, 50, 51; struggle between the Orders, 52, 53; declares itself the National Assembly, 53. *See* Constituent Assembly.
Stein, Henry Frederick Charles, Freiherr vom, Prussian statesman (1757-1831), a Knight of the Empire, 40; his reforms in Prussia, 290; dismissed by Napoleon's orders, 291; pressed Alexander to war with Napoleon, 301; his work completed by Hardenberg, 303; at the Russian headquarters (1812), 304; summoned the Estates of Prussia at Königsberg, 308; his idea of rousing a German national

spirit abandoned by the allied monarchs (1813), 310; present at the Congress of Vienna, 337.
Stéphanie Tascher de la Pagerie (1789-1860) married to the Hereditary Grand Duke of Baden (1806), 258.
Stettin, French garrison left in (1813), 308; besieged (1813-14), 319.
Stewart, Hon. Sir Charles, afterwards Lord, English general and diplomatist (1778-1854), 301, 323, 337.
—— Robert, Viscount Castlereagh. See Castlereagh.
Stockach, battle of (25 March 1799), 202.
Stralsund, taken by the French (1807), 250.
Strasbourg, Archishop of, an ecclesiastical Prince of the Holy Roman Empire, 34; one of chief Princes of the Empire in Alsace, 79.
—— archbishopric of, the portion on the right bank of the Rhine ceded to Baden (1803), 227.
Stuart, Hon. Sir Charles, English general (1753-1801), 184, 195.
—— Sir John, English general (1762-1810), 256.
Stuttgart, 37, 38, 178.
Suchet, Louis Gabriel, Duke of Albufera, French general (1770-1826), 275, 297, 307, 315, App. iv.
Sudermania, Duke of. See Charles XIII., King of Sweden.
Supreme Being, Worship of the, established by Robespierre (1794), 146.
Suspects, Law of the, 137.
Suvórov, Alexander Vassilivitch, Count, afterwards Prince, Russian general (1729-1800), gallantry at the siege of Ochákov (1788), 44; defeats the Turks at Foksany and the Rymnik (1789), 45; stormed Ismail, and served at Matchin (1790-91), 96; defeated the Poles at Ziclonce and Dubienka (1792), 121, 122; defeated Kosciuszko at Maciejowice, and took Warsaw (1794), 152; defeats the French at Cassano and the Trebbia, and conquers Northern Italy (1799), 203; defeats Joubert at Novi, and crosses the Alps, 204; repulsed by the French,

PERIOD VII.

205; accuses the Austrians of causing his failure, 207.
Svenska Sound, battle of (9 July 1790), 95.
Swabia, part ceded to Bavaria, 245; part to Würtemburg, 258.
Sweden, its condition in 1789, 32, 33; at war with Russia and Denmark, 45, 46; makes peace with the Danes (1789,) 46; the *coup d'état* of Gustavus III. (1789), 46; peace with Russia, 95, 96; death of Gustavus III., 110; neutral in the war against France, 120, 124, 171; loses Pomerania and Finland, 250, 254; revolution in, and dethronement of Gustavus IV. (1809), 278, 279; Bernadotte elected Prince Royal (1810), 279; exchanges Pomerania for Norway by the treaty of Kiel (1814), 320; cession of Norway confirmed by the Congress of Vienna (1815), 347. See Bernadotte, Charles XIII., Gustavus III., Gustavus IV.
Switzerland, its condition in 1789, 41; its neutrality in the war against France, 120, 125, 171; headquarters of French diplomacy, 156; and of the *émigrés* diplomacy, 166, 167; revolution of 1798, 198, 199; invaded by the French and the Helvetian Republic formed, 199; Masséna's campaign in (1799), 204, 205; reorganised by Bonaparte as the Confederation of Switzerland (1803), 228, 229; neutrality of, violated by the allies (1814), 318; independence and neutrality guaranteed by the treaty of Paris (1814), 334; reorganised, and given a fresh constitution by the Congress of Vienna (1815), 344, 345.
Syria, Bonaparte's campaign in (1799), 208.

TAGLIAMENTO, Bonaparte forces the passage of the (16 March 1797), 185, 186.
Talavera, battle of (27 July 1809), 275.
Talleyrand-Périgord, Charles Maurice de, Bishop of Autun, afterwards Prince of Benevento, French statesman (1754-1838), consecrates the

2 D

Constitutional bishops in France (1790), 70; appointed Foreign Minister (1797), and advocated the *coup d'état* of 18 Fructidor, 190; resigned (1799), 210; advised Bonaparte to the *coup d'état* of 18 Brumaire, 210; Foreign Minister under the Consulate, 216; Grand Chamberlain of the Empire, 239; Foreign Minister under the Empire, 241; created Prince of Benevento, 277; his policy after the defeat of Napoleon in 1814, 329, 330; President of the Provisional Government of France, 330; gets the Bourbons accepted, 331; negotiates the first treaty of Paris, 333; French plenipotentiary at the Congress of Vienna (1814-15), 338; his masterly attitude, 338, 339; signs treaty with Austria and England against Russia and Prussia (3 Jan. 1815), 340; dismissed by Louis XVIII. (1815), 357.

Tallien, Jean Lambert, French politician (1769-1820), 166.

Talma, François Joseph, French actor (1763-1826), 262.

Tanucci, Bernardo, Marquis, Italian statesman (1698-1783), 4, 23.

Taranto, Duke of. *See* Macdonald.

Targovitsa, Confederation of, asks Catherine's aid to overthrow the Polish Constitution of 1791, 121.

Tarragona, English failure before (1812), 307.

Tauroggen, convention of (1812), 308.

Temeswar, the Banat of, invaded by the Turks (1788), 43.

Tennis Court, Oath of the (20 June 1789), 54.

Terror, the Reign of, weapons of, forged, 128; Robespierre deemed the author of, 135, 147; the system of, 135-138; the deputies on mission, 136, 137; revolutionary tribunal, 137, 138; the Terror in the provinces, 138, 139; excused by France because of the success of the Committee of Public Safety against the foreign foes, 141; Danton believed it too stringent, 143; rose to its height (June-July 1794), 145, 146; system abandoned, 148.
—— the White, in France (1815), 356, 357.

Tetterborn, Baron von, Russian general (†1836), 308.

Teutonic Order, the, suppressed by Hardenberg in Prussia, 303.

Texel, Dutch fleet in the, captured by French hussars (1795), 149; blockaded by the English fleet, 184, 193; defeated in the battle of Camperdown (1797), 194; captured by the English (1799), 205.

Theophilanthropy, new religion started in France, 181, 182.

Thermidor, overthrow of Robespierre on the 9th, 147.

Thermidorians, rule of the, 148, 149, 154-157; their foreign policy, 156, 157.

Thompson, Benjamin, Count Rumford. *See* Rumford.

Thorn, promised to Prussia by the Poles (1790), 85; but not surrendered (1791), 87; obtained by Prussia at the second partition of Poland (1793), 122; restored to Prussia by the Congress of Vienna (1815), 342.

Thouret, Jacques Guillaume, French politician (1746-94), 100.

Thugut, Franz Maria, Baron, Austrian statesman (1734-1818), becomes Austrian Foreign Minister, 126; his policy, 153, 154; in favour of continuing the war with France, 169; delayed the treaty of Campo-Formio as long as he could, 192; retired from office, 220.

Thurgau, canton of, formed by Bonaparte (1803), 228; recognised by the Congress of Vienna (1815), 344.

Thuriot de la Rozière, Jacques Alexis, French politician (1758-1829), 133.

Thurn and Taxis, Prince of, as Imperial Commissary, summoned the Diet of the Empire (1792), 108.

Ticino, canton of, formed by Bonaparte (1803), 228; recognised by the Congress of Vienna (1815), 344.

Tiers-État, Order of the, in the States-General, its struggle with the privileged Orders, 51, 53; declares itself the National Assembly, 53.

Tillot, Guillaume Léon du, Marquis of Felino, Italian statesman (1711-1774), 25.

## Index 419

Tilsit, the meeting of Napoleon and Alexander at, 249, 250; the treaty of (7 July 1807), 250.
Tirlemont, 48, 64.
Titles abolished in France by the Constituent Assembly, 60.
Tloczow, circle of, ceded to Russia (1807), 26.
Tobac, battle of (1789), 45.
Tobago, ceded by England to France (1783), 19; ceded to England by the treaty of Paris (1814), 333; cession recognised by the Congress of Vienna, 348.
Tolentino, treaty of (19 Feb. 1797), 177; battle of (3 May 1815), 346.
Toleration, Napoleon insists on religious, in Europe, 289.
Töplitz, treaty of (9 Sept. 1813), 313.
Torgau ceded by Saxony to Prussia (1815), 341.
Torres Vedras, Masséna repulsed from the lines of (1810), 296.
Tortona, fortress of, built by Victor Amadeus III., 27.
Toulon, 139, 140.
Toulouse, battle of (10 April 1814), 332.
Trafalgar, battle of (21 Oct. 1805), 244, 245.
Trautmannsdorf, Count Albert von, Austrian statesman (1749-1817), 47, 64.
Treaties: Amiens (1802), 225; Badajoz (1801), 223; Bartenstein (1807), 248; Basle (1795), 156, 157; Bucharest (1812), 281; Campo-Formio (1797), 192, 193; Chaumont (1814), 327, 328; Fontainebleau (1807), 252, 253; Ghent (1814), 341; Jassy (1792), 96; Kalisch (1813), 308; Kiel (1814), 320; Lunéville (1801), 219, 220; Paris, Provisional (1814), 331, 332; Paris, First (1814), 333, 334; Paris, Second (1815), 353, 354; Pfaffenhofen (1796), 180; Potsdam (1805), 247; Pressburg (1805), 245; Reichenbach (1813), 310; Ried (1813), 313, 314; San Ildefonso (1796), 183; Schönbrunn (1806), 247; of 3 Jan. 1815, secret, 341; of 1756, 11, 12, 19; Sistova (1791), 89; Tilsit (1807), 250; Tolentino (1797), 177; Töplitz (1813), 313; Verela (1790), 95, 96; Versailles (1783), 13, 19, 28; Vienna (1809), 274; Vienna (1815), 350; Warsaw (1790), 85.
Trebbia, battle of the (17-19 June 1799), 203.
Treilhard, Jean Baptiste, Comte, French statesman (1742-1810), 148, 166, 195, 209.
Trent, Macdonald joined by Brune at (1800), 219.
—— bishopric of, granted to Austria (1803), 226.
Trèves, the Archbishop of, an Elector in 1789, 34; one of the chief Princes of the Empire, with fiefs in Alsace, 79; electorate abolished (1803), 225.
—— city of, taken by the French (1795), 150; capital of a French department, 230.
—— electorate of, well governed in 1789, 40; conquered by the French under Moreaux (1795), 150; ceded to France, 193, 225; given to Prussia (1815), 344.
Treviso, Duke of. *See* Mortier.
Tribunal, the Imperial, of the Holy Roman Empire (Reichskammergericht), 35.
—— the Revolutionary, of Paris, established (March 1793), 128; its powers and effect, 137; its system of work, 138; its powers increased (June 1794), 146, 147; condemns Carrier, 149.
Tribunate, formed by the Constitution of the Year VIII., its functions, 214; reduced to fifty members (1805), 240; suppressed (1808), 284.
Trieste ceded to Napoleon (1809), 274.
Trinidad, island of, taken by the English (1797), 264; ceded to England by the Congress of Vienna (1815), 348.
Triple Alliance, the, of England, Holland, and Prussia, formed 1788, 13, 32.
Tronchet, François Denis, French jurist (1726-1806), 215.
Truguet, Laurent Jean François, Comte, French admiral (1752-1839), 166, 190.
Tudela, battle of (23 Nov. 1808), 269.

Tuileries, Palace at Paris, 62, 99, 100, 112, 113, 129, 155, 164, 165.
Turin, observatory at, built by Victor Amadeus III., 26; threatened by Bonaparte (1796), 174; occupied by Suvórov (1799), 203.
Turkey, travelling to decay, 14; Joseph declares war against, 17; campaign of 1788 against the Russians and Austrians, 43, 44; accession of Sultan Selim (1789), 44; campaign of 1789, 45; Prussia negotiates with, 45, 85; campaign of 1790 against the Austrians, 88; treaty of Sistova (1791), 89; campaign of 1790–91 against the Russians, 96; treaty of Jassy (1792), 96; looked with favour on the French Revolution, 171; defeated by Bonaparte in Syria and Egypt (1799), 208; French army in Illyria to threaten, 256; its general policy (1796-1807), 280; revolution in, and accession of Mahmoud (1807-08), 280, 281; war with Russia (1809-12), 281; treaty of Bucharest (1812), 281. *See* Abdul Hamid, Mahmoud, Mustapha, Selim.
Turreau, Louis Marie, Baron, French general (1756-1816), 141.
Tuscany, its prosperity under the Grand Duke Leopold, 24, 25; declares war against France (1793), 120; makes peace with France, 157, 171; occupied by the French (1799), 200; evacuated by them, 203; restored to the Grand Duke Ferdinand (1800), 206; made into the kingdom of Etruria (1801), 220; annexed to Napoleon's Empire (1808), 255; Elisa Bonaparte, Grand Duchess of, 283; restored to Ferdinand (1815), 347. *See* Ferdinand II., Leopold.
Two Sicilies, kingdom of the. *See* Naples.
Tyrol, the opposition to Joseph's reforms in, 15; Joseph suspends his edicts, 66; pacified by Leopold (1790), 84; invaded by Bonaparte (1797), 186; by Macdonald (1800), 219; ceded to Bavaria (1805), 245; Hofer's insurrection in (1809), 273, 274; restored to Austria by Bavaria (1815), 344.

ULM, 35, 243, 244.
United States of America, 145, 159, 160, 242, 341.
Universities: Berlin, 303, 304; Bonn, 40; Cracow, 105; Göttingen, 39; Jena, 38; Mannheim, 37; Milan, 26; Parma, 25; Pavia, 26; Pisa, 24; Siena, 24.
University of France founded by Napoleon, its constitution, 288.
Unterwalden, canton of Switzerland maintained by Bonaparte (1803), 228.
Unzmarkt, battle of (22 March 1797), 186.
Uri, a canton of Switzerland, 41, 228.

VADIER, Marc Guillaume Alexis, French politician (1736-1828), 149, 155.
Valais, the, declared an independent Republic (1803), 228; annexed by Napoleon (1810), 283; made a canton of Switzerland by the Congress of Vienna (1815), 345.
Valence, Pope Pius VI. dies at (1798), 203.
Valencia, taken by Moncey (1809), 275.
Valenciennes, taken by the English and Austrians (1793), 130.
Valmy, battle of (20 Sept. 1792), 115.
—— Duke of. *See* Kellermann.
Valsarno, battle of (26 Oct. 1813), 315.
Vancouver Island, the affair of Nootka Sound (1790), 77, 78; the Spaniards claim, 79.
Vandamme, Dominique René, Comte, French general (1770-1830), 309, 312, 313.
Van der Mersch, John Andrew, Belgian general (1734-92), 48, 64, 93.
Van der Noot, Henry Charles Nicholas, Belgian statesman (1735-1827), 48, 64, 65, 92, 93, 94.
Vandernootists or Statists, Belgian political party, 47, 48, 92, 93.
Van der Spiegel, John, Baron, Dutch statesman, Grand Pensionary of Holland, 65, 93.
Varennes, the flight of Louis XVI. and Marie Antoinette from Paris (June 1791), stopped at, 100.

## Index

Vauchamps, battle of (14 Feb. 1814), 319.
Vaud, Pays de, revolts against Berne (1798), 199; made an independent canton of Switzerland by Bonaparte (1803), 228; recognised by the Congress of Vienna (1815), 344.
Venaissin, the county of the, 76, 333, 354.
Vendée, La, the insurrection in, 128, 130, 131, 141, 143, 180, 181, 215.
Vendémiaire, the insurrection of 13th (5 Oct. 1795), in Paris, 164, 165.
Venice, condition of the Republic in 1789, 27; remained neutral in the war against the French Republic, 124; promised to Austria in exchange for Lombardy at Leoben, 186; occupied by Bonaparte (1797), 191, 192; ceded the Ionian Islands to France, 192; ceded to Austria by the Treaty of Campo-Formio (1797), 192; conclave met at (1799), 206; occupied by Brune (1800), 219; ceded to Austria by the Treaty of Lunéville (1801), 220; ceded to the kingdom of Italy by the Treaty of Pressburg (1805), 245, 255; granted to Austria by the Congress of Vienna (1815), 347.
Verdun, taken by the Prussians (1792), 114, 115.
Verela, treaty of (14 Aug. 1790), 95, 96.
Vergniaud, Pierre Victurnien, French politician (1753-93), 106, 114, 116, 129.
Verona, belonged to Venice in 1789, 27; punished by Bonaparte for the murder of French soldiers (1796), 191; Schérer attacked at, 202.
Versailles, the States-General meets at (May 1789), 51; invaded by the women of Paris (5 Oct. 1789), 62.
—— the treaty of (1783), 13, 19, 28.
Veto, the question of the, in the Constituent Assembly, 61.
Vicenza, Duke of. *See* Caulaincourt.
Victor Amadeus III., King of Sardinia (1726-96), 26, 27, 63, 117, 126, 173, 174.
—— Emmanuel I., King of Sardinia (1759-1824), 346, 354.
—— Victor Claude Perrin, *called*,

French general (1764-1841), 269, 275, 276, 297, App. iv.
Vienna, the inscription on the Emperor Joseph's statue at, 66; Bernadotte insulted at (1798), 198; the French approach (1801), 219; occupied by Napoleon (1805), 244; and (1809), 273; treaty of (1809), 274; and (1815), 350.
—— the Congress of, 336, 350, 337, 338, 340, 341, 342, 343, 344, 345, 347, 348, 349.
*Vieux Cordelier*, the, 142, 143.
Villeneuve, Pierre Charles Jean Baptiste Silvestre de, French admiral (1763-1806), 242, 244, 245.
Vimeiro, battle of (21 Aug. 1808), 265, 266.
Vins, Charles, Baron de, Austrian general († 1794), 88.
Virtue, Reign of, Robespierre's belief in a, 146.
Visconti, Ennius Quirinus, Italian antiquary (1751-1818), 24.
Vittoria, taken by the French (1795), 151; battle of (21 June 1813), 315.
Volhynia, province of, ceded to Russia at the second partition of Poland (1793), 122.
Volta, Alessandro, Italian man of science (1745-1827), 26.
Voltaire, François Marie, Arouet de, French philosopher (1694-1778), 6, 9.
Vonck, Francis, Belgian politician (1752-1797), 48, 93.
Vonckists, Belgian political party, 48, 65, 92, 93.
Vyborg, the Swedish fleet blockaded in the Gulf of (1790), 95.

WAGRAM, battle of (6 July 1809), 274.
Walcheren, the English expedition to (1809), 276.
Waldeck, principality of, a state of the Germanic Confederation (1815), 343.
—— Prince Christian Augustus of, Austrian general (1744-98), 184.
Wallachia, invaded by the Austrians (1789), 45; conquered by the Russians (1810), 281.
Warsaw, treaty made at, between the Poles and Prussia (29 March 1790), 85; occupied by Kosciuszko (1794),

151; besieged by the Prussians, 151; taken by the Russians, 152; ceded to Prussia (1795), 152; Napoleon enters (1807), 248; given to Russia by the Congress of Vienna (1815), 342.

Warsaw, Grand Duchy of, founded by Napoleon (1807), 259, 261; Western Galicia ceded to, by Austria (1809), 274; dissolved (1815), 342.

Waterloo, battle of (18 June 1815), 353.

Watteville, Nicholas Rodolphe de, Swiss statesman (1760-1832), 228.

Wattignies, battle of (16 Oct. 1793), 140.

Weimar, headquarters of the German literary movement, 38. *See* Saxe-Weimar.

Wellesley, Hon. Sir Arthur, Duke of Wellington. *See* Wellington.

—— Richard, Marquis, English statesman (1760-1842), 295.

Wellington, Arthur Wellesley, Duke of, English general (1769-1852), defeated the Danish army at Kioge (1807), 252; sent to Portugal (1808), 265; defeats the French at Roliça and Vimeiro, 265, 266; recalled, 266; again sent to Portugal (1809), 275; takes Oporto, 275; defeats the French at Talavera, 275, 276; forms the Anglo-Portuguese army, 296; campaign of 1810, 1811, 296, 297; campaign of 1812 and victory of Salamanca, 306; wins battle of Vittoria (1813), 315; invades France, and wins battles of the Nivelle and the Nive (1813), 316; wins battle of Orthez (1814), 321; his attitude towards the Duc d'Angoulême, 326, 327; defeats Soult at Toulouse, 332; succeeds Castlereagh as English plenipotentiary at the Congress of Vienna (1815), 341, 349; signs the treaty of Vienna, 350; takes command of the allied armies in Belgium, 352; defeats Napoleon at Waterloo, 353.

Werden, abbey of, merged in Prussia (1803), 227.

Wessenberg-Ampfingen, Johann Philip, Baron von, Austrian diplomatist (1773-1858), 337.

West India Islands, the French, taken by the English, 154; restored at the Peace of Amiens (1802), 232; recaptured (1809), 264; restored except Saint-Lucia and Tobago (1815), 348.

Westphalia, kingdom of, formed by Napoleon (1807), 250; its limits, 258; administration, 258, 259; member of the Confederation of the Rhine, 260.

Wetzlar, seat of the Imperial Tribunal of the Empire, 35; taken by Hoche (1796), 186; merged in the electorate of Mayence (1803), 225.

White Terror in France in 1815, 356, 357.

Wickham, William, English diplomatist (1768-1845), 166, 167, 182.

Widdin, the Pasha of, defeated at Foksany (1789), 45.

Wieland, Christoph Martin, German poet (1733-1813), 38.

William V., Prince of Orange, and Stadtholder of the United Netherlands (1748-1806), 31, 32, 149, 179, 227.

—— VI., Prince of Orange, and I. King of the Netherlands (1772-1843), 314, 320, 321, 344.

—— Prince Royal, afterwards King, of Würtemburg (1781-1864), 337.

—— IX., Landgrave, afterwards Elector and Grand Duke of Hesse-Cassel (1743-1821), 6, 38, 157, 225, 227, 250, 258, 337; made a Grand Duke and member of the Germanic Confederation (1815), 342.

—— Prince, of Prussia, afterwards German Emperor (1797-1888), 337.

Wilson, Sir Robert Thomas, English general (1777-1849), 301.

Wintzingerode, Ferdinand, Baron, Russian general (1770-1818), 319, 320, 328, 338.

Wissembourg, lines of, stormed by the Austrians (1793), 139.

Wittenberg, ceded to Prussia by Saxony (1815), 341.

Wittgenstein, Louis Adolphus Peter, Prince of Sayn-, Russian general (1769-1843), 309, 309.

Wolf, Frederick Augustus, German scholar (1759-1824), 304.

## Index

Wolkonski, Nicholas, Prince Repnin-Russian general (1778-1845), 337.
Worms, Bishop of, an ecclesiastical Prince of the Holy Roman Empire, 34; one of the chief princes in Alsace, 79.
—— city of, headquarters of Condé's army of French *émigrés*, 106; taken by Custine, 118.
Worship of Reason at Paris (1793), 411.
—— of the Supreme Being, 146.
Wrede, Charles Philip, Prince von, Bavarian general (1767-1838), 338.
Würmser, Dagobert Sigismund, Count, Austrian general (1724-97), 40, 130, 139, 140, 175, 176.
Würtemburg, duchy of, condition in 1789, 37, 38; invaded by Moreau (1796), 180; made an electorate (1803), 225; receives extension of territory, 227; invaded by Napoleon (1805), 244; made a kingdom (1806), 245; receives Austrian Swabia, 258; state of the Confederation of the Rhine, 260; of the Germanic Confederation (1815), 342. *See* Charles Eugène, Frederick, Frederick Eugène.
Würtzburg, Bishop of, an ecclesiastical Prince of the Holy Roman Empire, 35.
Würtzburg, bishopric of, merged in Bavaria (1803), 227; exchanged for Salzburg (1809), and made a Grand Duchy, 260; a state of the Confederation of the Rhine, 260.
—— city of, taken by Jourdan (1796), 177.

York, Frederick, Duke of, English general (1763-1827), 39, 127, 130, 140, 205.
—— von Wartenburg, John David Louis, Count, Prussian general (1759-1830), 308.

Zettin, taken by the Austrians (1790), 88.
Zielence, battle of (18 June 1792), 122.
Zubov, Prince Plato, Russian statesman (1767-1822), 221.
Zug, canton of Switzerland, maintained by Bonaparte (1803), 228.
Zurich, battle of (26 Sept. 1799), 204.
—— canton of Switzerland, maintained by Bonaparte (1803), 228; made one of the presiding cantons of the Helvetian Diet (1815), 345.
Zwei-brücken. *See* Deux-Ponts.

# MAPS.

Map 1. Europe in 1789.
  „  2. Europe in 1803.
  „  3. Europe in 1810.
  „  4. Europe in 1815.

---

These maps are intended to show the limits of the principal states of Europe at the beginning of 1789, after the rearrangement in 1803, at the height of Napoleon's power in 1810, and according to the settlement made by the Congress of Vienna in 1815.

The same colouring has been preserved through the series of maps in order that the boundaries of each country may be compared at these different dates.

The red line in Map 1 marks the boundary of the Holy Roman Empire.

The area in Germany left uncoloured—in all four maps—was occupied by various states too small in size to be indicated by colours.